Brontë Territories:
Cornwall and the Unexplored Maternal Legacy, 1760–1860

Penzance, 'To the Inhabitants of Penzance this Plate is Inscribed By their obedient Servant W. Penaluna,' Published May 1817.

Brontë Territories:

Cornwall and the Unexplored Maternal Legacy, 1760–1860

Melissa Hardie

EER
Edward Everett Root Publishers, 2019

EER

Edward Everett Root, Publishers, Co. Ltd.,
30 New Road, Brighton, Sussex, BN1 1BN, England.

Details of our overseas distributors and how to order our books can be seen on our website.
www.eerpublishing.com
edwardeverettroot@yahoo.co.uk

Melissa Hardie, Brontë Territories:
Cornwall and the Unexplored Maternal Legacy 1760-1860

First published in Great Britain in 2019.
© Melissa Hardie 2019.

This edition © Edward Everett Root Publishers 2019.

ISBN 978-1-911454-43-4 paperback
ISBN 978-1-911454-46-5 hardback
ISBN 978-1-911454-53-3 ebook

Melissa Hardie has asserted her right to be identified as the author of this Work in accordance with the Copyright, Designs and Patents Act 1988 and as the owner of this Work.

All rights reserved. No part of this publication may be reproduced, stored in a retrieval system or transmitted in any form or by any means, electronic, mechanical, photocopying, recording or otherwise, without the prior permission of the copyright owner.

Book production and design by Head & Heart.

For Philip,
and
two wise women,
Sarah Fermi and Patsy Stoneman

Author's Note

> Every writer has two duties; first, to receive correct impressions, and then to record them faithfully: he must try to do the first, but he is bound to do the second. It would be too much to suppose that all the impressions I have received are correct; but I have uniformly endeavoured to record them as they were received, without false colouring or exaggeration. In one respect alone have I departed from the strict letter of truth. I have used the privilege of an unknown writer in studiously disguising my own personality, only taking care that such disguise should in no respect interfere with the truth of impressions conveyed to the general reader. J. A.W.[1]

These salutary words were written by Elizabeth Catherine Thomas Carne (1817-1873), a contemporary of the famous Brontë writers and a younger cousin of their mother, Maria Branwell Brontë and of her sister Elizabeth Branwell and their siblings. Like Maria and Elizabeth Branwell (whose mother was a Carne), Elizabeth Carne was a native of West Cornwall and one of a vast network of Carnes and Branwells, two of the most prominent commercial families of Penzance.

These words appeared as an 'Author's Note' to Elizabeth Carne's first published book in 1860, *Three months' rest at Pau, in the winter and spring of 1859*. Nonetheless she had published anonymously from the 1840s in journals such as *Fraser's* and the *London Quarterly*. The Brontës may even have read her think-pieces, not realising that a cousin was the writer. She never met any one of them in person, but most certainly knew of them, their origins and their kinship, and assuredly had read their novels.[2] She may even have critiqued their fictional publications, but if so she did this anonymously. This distinguished writer was a sometime neighbour and product of the same Carne-Branwell town and neighbourhood of Penzance which had nurtured Maria and Elizabeth Branwell. Her achievement helps to shine light on the Brontës' maternal ancestry, a hinterland which has, until now, remained largely unexplored and thereby 'hidden from history'.

It is not, however, the author of the words but the message that I highlight for the purposes of this volume of papers that could also be sub-titled 'A Literary Geography of the Brontës' or even 'The imprint of the Mother'. It is my own personal attempt to expand, certainly to broaden the context or canvas of potential influences from which flowed the imaginative juices of the Brontë children. I shall adopt Elizabeth Carne's excellent principles, but shall not, like her, 'studiously disguise my own personality', since I begin from my own situation within that same geography.

Many descendants world-wide know their own connections to the 'famous Branwells' (famous mainly due to the Brontës), and visit Penzance on the trail of discovering more. Yet, strangely, many local people today, familiar with the name of Branwell, know little or nothing of connections to the Brontës. It is hoped that this study also contributes to greater knowledge of their wider family – the famous Carnes, the distinguished Battens, the artistic Cristalls, the faithful Fennells, the erratic Johnses and perhaps some others, important not for their national fame as such – though some with certainty achieved it – but for the security and confidence that they gave to Maria, Elizabeth and ultimately their combined legatees.

I have tried with this book to carry out the first duty – to receive impressions correctly – as outlined by Elizabeth Carne. I hope I have accomplished the second – to relate them responsibly and faithfully.

Melissa Hardie
Penzance, 2019

ENDNOTES

1 John Altrayd Wittitterly (1860) *Three months' rest at Pau, in the winter and spring of 1859*. Elizabeth Carne's first full-length book publication issued under this pseudonym. The book was written in the aftermath of her father's death after his long declining illness in the care of her sister Caroline and herself. See 'Elizabeth Catherine Thomas Carne, A 19th-century Hypatia' (2014) *Transactions of the Royal Geological Society of Cornwall*, vol. 23, Pt. 1, pp. 19-34.

2 Elizabeth Carne first entered the literary market anonymously and then under a pseudonym, though in her case the main reference was to a character of Dickensian creation, and her signature-initials an acronym. She did not begin to publish her writings under her birth name until after both Maria and Elizabeth Branwell's deaths, nor did she become publicly recognised as a social commentator until well after the demise of all the Brontës.

Contents

Author's Note	vii
Acknowledgements	xi
List of Plates	xiii
Abbreviations	xiii
Introduction	xv

Part I: Penwith and environs: The Land's End

1 Living at the edge	1
2 Creators of Penzance	11
3 Language, legend and literature – stories and storytellers	25
4 And then came Wesley	51
5 In the everyday	69
6 Time-line in Branwell-Carne lives	85

Part II: Origins of family lore

7 Legacies of kinship	111
8 The people called Branwell	123
9 The people called Carne	147
10 Travellers' Tales	165
11 Biographical briefs A – Z	189
12 The Document Register	209

Part III: Appendices & Index

A. A note on names and naming	231
B. Bibliographies: General and family	239
Index	265

Acknowledgements

I acknowledge with many thanks, the Brontë Society of Haworth, for the grant of the Daphne Carrick Memorial Scholarship 2013-15 to investigate the maternal ancestors and relations of the Brontë writers. The incentive this offered has driven the writing forward, as has the excellent stewardship of the late Sarah Fermi, the then Honorary Publications Officer, and Professor Patsy Stoneman, Emeritus professor of English at Hull University, both of whom became not only wise overseers but also friends. Latterly, alongside proofreading by my long-suffering husband, Philip Budden, and our friend Helen Gibson of the Dorset County Museum, this present volume would still be in progress. As all family historians know, one does get way-laid and sucked into many byways and fascinating conundrums that delay progress on primary topics. Sometimes that is valuable time spent, though not always.

The author has been assisted by a number of direct descendants locally of the Branwell group of related families, though due to marriages they no longer carry a vestige of the name. It was through the generosity of one descendant, Trewey Davy, who today ties both the Davy and the Branwell dynasties together again, that I was able to locate another, Julie Tripp, and to see the latter's scrapbooks of photographs of the Richard Branwell descent (Thomas's older brother, Maria's uncle).

None of the photographs, of course, reach back to the time of the parental families of Maria and Elizabeth, when personal cameras were as yet unknown and only vignettes painted by local talents and travelling limners were available to the rising gentry and middle classes. Penlee House Gallery & Museum[1] in Penzance, holds a large collection of Branwell family photographs of later vintage, for which there is an on-line catalogue. All of these followed the deaths of the Brontë family of writers.

On the subject of the Carne family of Penzance – the equally large family of Anne Carne, the mother of the Branwell children – several libraries and archives have been employed, and many helpers have assisted. These are the Barclays Bank Group Archives (Manchester), Cornwall Records Office, the Archives of Charterhouse School and Christ's Hospital School, the Courtney Library of the Royal Institution of Cornwall, the Morrab Subscription Library of Penzance (Lilian Oldham Archive, photographic archive), the Cornish Family History Society (Truro), the John Rylands University of Manchester (Methodist Archives), the Sedgwick Museum (Cambridge University), Shropshire Archives (Shrewsbury) and papers of the Royal Geological Society of Cornwall (RGSC) amongst others referred in the bibliography. Special thanks are due to digital archaeologist, Tom Goskar, for the discovery in the archives of the Morrab Library, an unknown (until 2016) photograph of the mineralogist Branwell cousin, Elizabeth Catherine Thomas Carne (1817-1873), which now has leapt onto the world-wide web!

The individuals who I must thank for their generosity and enthusiasm to help with this study are the following: Dr. Robin Agnew (Research, John Forbes, FRS); All Saints Parish (Administrators) Wellington, Shropshire; Andrew Ashfield (Anne Batten

Cristall); Emily and Ian Barker (Branwell house owners, Penzance); Evan Best, Australia (Cornish emigrant genealogy); Susan Broughton – Carveth (Edmunds family history); Margaret 'Meg' Brown (Penzance Ladies Reading club & Morrab Library archives), Andrew Campbell (Falmouth Packet history); David Chilcott (Carne family history, Falmouth); Skye C. Church (Kingston family, USA); Alexandra Coppock-Bunce (Branwell family descendant, Edyvean); Pery Cristall, New Zealand (Cristall & Batten families); Angela Crow (Thornton, West Yorkshire); Hector Davie, Switzerland (Carne Corin & Branwell families); Malcolm Dyer (George Dyer descendant, Cristall & Batten families); Barbara Eaton, Cornwall (Henry Martyn); Ann Erskine (of Australia & Bali, about orientalism in *Jane Eyre*); Mrs Marina Fennell and her son Dr Nicholas Fennell (John Lister Illingworth Fennell & Fennell family history) of Oxford & Winchester; the late Patrick 'Pat' French (Penzance); Bob Gamble (John Fennell & families); Sid Geake (Balwest History Society, Germoe); Helen Gibson (Cerne Abbas, Dorset); Tehmina & Tom Goskar (Penzance); Susan Griffiths & Professor Philip Hardie (Trinity College, Cambridge); Katie Herbert (Penlee House Gallery and Museum); Susan Hoyle (of Kent, & Cornwall); Alan Kent (Probus, Cornwall); Elizabeth & Tim Le Grice (Trereife, Newlyn); Sandra Marsh (Carne Collection, Sedgwick Museum, Cambridge); Methodist historians: Cedric Appleby (Cornwall), Dr John Lenton (Wellington, Shropshire & Oxford), Dr Peter Forsaith (Oxford), and Dr John Lander (Cornwall); Charlotte MacKenzie (Cornish historian, Truro); Professor Joanna Mink (Illinois); Douglas Palmer (Sedgwick Museum, Cambridge); Professor Mary Rimmer (Nova Scotia); Elisabeth Rogers (Cristall & Batten families); the late John Simmonds (Morrab Library Archivist); Mrs Marion Smith (Penzance educational history); Molly Smith (Ashton, Cornwall, family history); Andrew Symons (Researcher, Penzance); Mary Taylor (Researcher, Towcester Families website); the late Professor Charles Thomas (Truro, maternal kin); Imogen Thomas (Lyme Regis, John/s family); Phyllis Varker (Breage, Cornwall); Peter and Irene Wright (York & Todmorden, local history); Sharon Wright (London & Yorkshire) and possibly numerous others I will only recall when this book is complete and published. I value each and every contribution to this study – that which may seem small at first, often looms large in time.

Readers who helped considerably by looking at drafts and listening to papers prior to lecture delivery were Anne and Malcolm Sutton, Dr. Melinda Parrill James, Sarah 'Miki'Ashton and Alex Coppock-Bunce. I am so grateful for their conversations related to the difficulties of teasing out the fine lines between documentation, speculation, facts and truths. Many puzzles remain, and all mis-interpretations and defects are offered with my humble apologies.

Working with John and Leigh Spiers of EER and Lucy Llewellyn of Head & Heart has been a tremendous pleasure - I wish all authors had such friendly and forgiving support in drawing out the stories behind the surface."

ENDNOTES

1 A former Branwell property, built by John Richards Branwell (1822-1905), the eldest of four sons of Robert Matthews Branwell (1798-1860) well known to Maria and Elizabeth. Not discovered until 1996, the date 1864 was found to be the construction date of their home, and therefore never known by Thomas Branwell, his wife Anne and their contemporaries.

List of Plates

Plate 1 'To the Inhabitants of Penzance' W. Penaluna, May 1817.
Plate 2 *Mount's Bay*, Kershaw & Son, London, No. 994 (n.d.).
Plate 3 *Dolcoath Copper Mine, Camborne, Cornwall*, by T. Allom and J. Thomas.
Plate 4 *Wherry Mine from Newlyn*, looking to the Mount. 1818.
Plate 5 The Giant Bolster, by George Cruikshank for *Popular Romances of the West of England*
Plate 6 *Portrait of Ann Batten Cristall* (1769-1848) poet, painted by her brother Joshua Cristall, c1885. Private collection.
Plate 7 *Re-enactment by Professor Charles Thomas of John Wesley's arrival* to preach in the open air at Gwithian, Cornwall. Private collection, 2003.
Plate 8 *Market Jew Street, Penzance*, Cornwall, by T. Allom and S. Fisher, 1832.
Plate 9 *Chapel Street, Penzance*, with a view of St. Mary's, Henry Besley, Exeter, c1837.
Plate 10 *The Merry Maidens* (grid reference SW432245) Late Neolithic stone circle near St. Buryan. J. Britten, for the *Beauties of England & Wales*.
Plate 11 *The East View of St. Michael's Mount in the County of Cornwall* (n.d.)
Plate 12 The Branwell House, as it would have been, 25 Chapel Street, Penzance. Mike Dash, 2018.
Plate 13 Branwells: a family set.
Plate 14, 15, 16   Arms of the Carne family and family portraits
Plate 17 'The House of Girgius Adeeb, at Antioch' from *Syria, The Holy Land, Asia Minor*. W. H. Bartlett, William Purser, &c.

Abbreviations

BL   British Library
CB   Charlotte Brontë
COPC   Cornwall Online Parish Clerks
CRO   Cornwall Records Office
DNB   Dictionary of National Biography
ODNB   Online Dictionary of National Biography
RA   Royal Academy of Arts
RCPS   Royal Cornwall Polytechnic Society, Falmouth, Cornwall
RGSC   Royal Geological Society of Cornwall, Penzance, Cornwall
RI   Royal Institution, London
RIC   Royal Institution of Cornwall, Truro, Cornwall
RS   Royal Society, of which many were Fellows (FRS)

Introduction

In his essay 'The Maternal Relatives of the Brontës', Dr. J. Hambley Rowe[1] issued a challenge:

> While much has been written and more conjectured regarding the ancestry of the Brontës on the paternal side, their maternal forbears have been uniformly neglected. This seems the more inexplicable as it is generally considered that the distaff influences are the more important in the moulding of capabilities and temperament. In point of intrinsic interest, also, the history of the mother's family is quite as attractive as that of the father's[2]

The lives of Charlotte, Branwell, Emily and Anne Brontë seem to have been exhaustively investigated, but previous studies have left their maternal relations and networks largely unacknowledged and sometimes unnamed. This lack of identification and characterization has meant that life stories, mythical, factual and heavily laden with Cornish family freight, have not been counted into the luggage of thoughts, images and themes carried by their mother and aunt when they became emigrants to the north.

Little personal documentation of the Cornish-based families, largely carrying primary surnames Branwell and Carne, survives except for deeds and wills, and the occasional reference in newspapers or court records. No unpublished letters or diaries are left in local archives that relate to the women of the family, and it is not known where any personal correspondence sent home by the sisters in Yorkshire or sent abroad to family elsewhere would be found today.

One of the later nineteenth century Branwells[3] was a keen amateur photographer. He `used his large plate camera to capture images of Penlee House on Morrab Road, now the museum and gallery of the town of Penzance, as it was in the 1880s… extending to artistic trick photography and double exposures'; all of his visual records are well after the demise of our focal subjects and outside the period of study. This Branwell 'mansion' spoken of by some authors as evidence of family wealth was not constructed until 1864, after the deaths of the Brontës, and would not even have been a 'twinkle' in the family eyes of earlier times. This prominent building, much re-developed and important to us today, is not included in this study. It was constructed at the commission of John Richards Branwell (1822-1905), the eldest of four sons of Elizabeth and Maria's cousin, Robert Matthews Branwell (1798-1860).

Nonetheless, surprises occur such as letters made available to Fannie Ratchford through the American families of Jane Branwell Kingston in the 1950s,[4] and the 2017 find of Maria Branwell's annotated copy of the poems of Henry Kirke White (1808) put in the context of his life by the salutary work of Robert Southey and re-published in 1810 (Maria's copy). Latter-day visitors and more recent residents in West Cornwall frequently protest that they did not know of a Cornish link to the `Yorkshire writers'. This fact, however, should not obscure the very large place that Cornwall, `Cornish-ness' and Cornish contextual issues probably held in Brontë creative lives and mental imagery.

A lack of documentation has also inhibited researchers beginning from Haworth. Maria (Branwell) Brontë (1783-1821) died young in Haworth, when all of her six children were under ten years old. As for her sister, Elizabeth (Carne) Branwell (1776-1842), who stepped in to care for the children after her death, although both Ellen Nussey and Elizabeth Gaskell, and even Charlotte Brontë, have recorded information about her habits, conversation, and character, there is little direct documentation of her life or personal interests. We may find, of course, that the social and cultural traits of deference and modesty of that time make women's personal interests almost impossible to discover. But, we should look.

I am not alone in regretting this neglect. On numerous occasions, when discussing my research with others, I have heard negative comments about the dearth of general information about women's lives in particular, the lack of proof and the neglect of regard for the 'mothering' relationships in Brontë lives. The lack of acknowledgement of the older female presence in the literature has disappointed and surprised more than a few visitors to Haworth.

Virginia Woolf said of creative women that `we think back through our mothers',[5] and the purpose of this book is to show what this may have meant for the Brontë sisters – and, indeed, their brother. This is not to exclude the inspiration provided by their Irish father, the active, striving and loyal family man, but to show inexorably that he was not alone in this mission of raising the children, and possibly contributed very little initially toward their developmental education.

After all, the parish duties and Patrick's personal, literary ambitions appeared to come first, both within Maria's lifetime with him, and after her death. It is clear from almost all secondary reports, that not only his physical needs, eccentricities and home comforts were considered supreme and privileged before all else, but that his primary interest amongst the children was the son, Branwell.

By contrast, first his wife Maria and then his sister-in-law Elizabeth provided the daily cultural and domestic grind of attitude and activity for the young Brontës as children, adults and creative beings. The neglect of their stories seems more surprising when we realise that Maria was nearly thirty when she came to Yorkshire, and Elizabeth was forty-five; their knowledge and hands-on domestic experience, tastes and personalities, were formed by decades of Cornish life. They could not, however seemly it might have suited others, leave that major portion of their lives hidden or forgotten.

Also, of great importance, I suspect, though again not given their due for the most part, are the other Cornish family members who peopled their daily lives and experiences in Yorkshire, and lived not a few miles away: Aunt Jane (Branwell) Fennell, sister of their grandfather Thomas (John) Branwell, her husband, Uncle

John Fennell, and their cousin Jane Branwell (Fennell) Morgan. These people were close and intimate family, also recent emigrants from Penzance (1811-12). Acting as friends, godparents and family support at times of illness and grief in Yorkshire, they had already provided like services to the Branwell/Carne kinship circle in Cornwall.

Though the Brontë children may not have characterised un-disguisedly the Fennells and Morgans in their books, it would be surprising if they did not do so thematically or subconsciously. These people had known their mother and aunt since birth, understood their family habits and traditions and all except William Morgan had spent more than half their formative years in Cornwall as the Branwell and Carne clan expanded. Even Morgan knew other members of their Cornish family and may have visited in the county. More of this noteworthy story follows.

There is no problem establishing an immediate family background for Maria and Elizabeth: they were the daughters of Thomas (John) Branwell (c1745-1808) and his wife, Anne (Reynolds) Carne (1744-1809). My aim, however, is to create a sense of the whole milieu in which they had grown up. Once we get beyond the immediate family, however, the previous neglect of the Brontës' Cornish heritage becomes less surprising. Establishing the facts of women's histories is simply very difficult and requires concentrated contextual study of the time and place.

There is, however, no excuse for neglecting to attempt in the twentieth and twenty-first centuries, with the birth and growth of the social sciences and psycho-medical advance, to present the importance of maternal influences in the upbringing of children. Setting aside temporarily the roles of Maria and Elizabeth Branwell in parenting the Brontë children, I was more than puzzled, even astonished and then increasingly bemused to find lists such as *'The Relatives of Maria Branwell', as compiled by C W Hatfield in 1939 from Dr. J. Hambley Rowe's "The Maternal Relatives of the Brontes", corrected, and with additions from other sources*. In both of these publications only Anne Carne, the daughter of her named father and mother, is listed as a relation on the mother's side amongst eight pages of fine print about the Branwell lines. Facetiously, I must add, she was neither an only child, nor was she an orphan. Why were *her* brothers and sisters, *her* grandparents and great grandparents, *her* cousins male and female – some quite remarkable and influential people – not acknowledged as part of their immediate bloodline family?

Whereas a man's 'place' can be charted in terms of occupation, education, public records, successes and failures, these kinds of records are ignored or inaccessible for most women up until the twentieth century. A few females break through and earn our notice, usually through authorship only, special beauty, inheritance issues or misbehaviour, but they are definitely a minority and it takes serious delving to deliver them forward, i.e. they are not people of record.

Official records often did not include names of women in full, making identification impossible,[6] and even some baptismal records omit the names of mothers altogether. Family history is indeed a minefield and a black hole the further one travels into it, and if the researcher is not aware that a particular man had three wives in succession, and eight children between them, wrong turns are easily taken. A death notice which announces the demise of Mrs Johns, the wife of Mr George Johns, Esq. on Wednesday last, simply confounds all except those who knew them personally.

Establishing a genealogy, however, is only a first step in recreating the cultural milieu which nurtured Maria and Elizabeth. Traces of their reading, religious and learning activities are especially relevant because this is the only evidence of their social interface. Not least amongst those traces are the legacies of story-telling, journal reading, and direct participation in the national literary habits and obsessions of their times.

We are familiar with studies of the Brontës that include a review of the literature available to them, and a raking of Charlotte's letters to find what she might like or dislike, and who might have been her literary heroes and heroines. Fortunately, in the previous generation in Cornwall the same preoccupations of producing literature and keeping records of reading are shared and evident in the network of teachers and preachers contemporary with Maria and Elizabeth. These enlighten our searches for influence and secure our attention to their particular time in British cultural history.

The published literature of friends and relations would also have exerted influence on the social and cultural outlook of the Branwells and Carnes, being as they were amongst the town's leading citizens. There were a number of journalists, poets, storytellers, future published academics and scholars of various subjects in their political, religious and personal kinship circle. Nevertheless, there is little or no information about who the closest friends and companions of Maria and Elizabeth actually were. Genealogical connections can, with studied concentration, be found, but lines of love, affection and jealousy will probably remain hidden from view. The initial task is to identify at least a proportion of the possible and plausible connections, and this has been my leading objective.

The period under review here is that from the reign of George III to the middle years of the Victorian age, a time in the life of the British nation and the world, of momentous change and great revolutions: American, French, and not least the ongoing and home-grown 'industrial revolution' of which West Cornwall was a major centre. Contrary to received historical ideas, Cornwall was not a backwater at this period, even if it has fallen into this category from time to time. These people were the children of the so-called British Enlightenment with its large cultural legacy from France and other continental sources, and the `romantic generation [who] discovered the beauty and terror of science.'[7]

Perhaps most spectacularly, this period which enclosed the childhoods and youth of the Branwell and Carne children and their generation, also enclosed the loss of the American colonies, the whole of the Napoleonic era, its battles, its warlords, and its engagement with both white slavery raids (Barbary, Turk) and the African and West Indian slave trade and not least the entrance into a new scientific age. All of these subjects impinged upon their lives in ways that we can make visible through study.

The personal involvement of family and friends, situated as they were on a long coastal battlefront is an especially rich part of Branwell history not previously explored in terms of latent influences on the writings of the Brontës. Commonly the children's interests in battles and heroes is said to have stemmed from their father's attentive political and military interests; my guess, following this study of Cornish life and times, is that the strongest influences most probably emerged from the maternal hegemony. Military and naval exploits and crises form an exceedingly important element in Branwell history – not just in general global terms, but rooted in the family network where we find both heroes and sacrifices.

Tourists to West Cornwall frequently come to stand and stare at the balcony in the historic Union Hotel ballroom, where the death of Nelson and the victory at Trafalgar was first announced to a waiting crowd in 1805.[8] We do not know whether or not, and if so who, amongst the Branwells and Carnes may have been in that crowd, though many of the kinship circle would have been. No one wrote about it in much detail but the hotel itself has fully exploited and extended its colourful stories of Nelsonian connection into the realms of legend. The Napoleonic Collection, an archive of personal and political documents, is one of the finest that the famed Morrab Library has to offer its visitors.

It was also that period specifically in Penzance history regarded in retrospect as its 'golden age' of industrial advancement and intellectual contribution to the state of the nation. At the same time, there were intermittent recessionary periods when mines collapsed, harvests failed, and food riots, starvation, drunkenness and gambling were rife. Bankruptcy and disease were never far from the door, with little redress or potential cure.

In all of these real-life dramas, the Branwells, Carnes and their kin played more than minor roles in Cornish life, and the stories gleaned from these experiences would necessarily cast reflections and reverberations throughout their lives and conversations forevermore. Undoubtedly, their Christian faith was largely their guiding spirit and defence in dealing with the hard times that came to them all – however platitudinous that might sound in the present day.

In biographical and historical terms, this study gives as complete a cast list of participants in the lives of their constituent families as possible with current information. Without doubt, some were more important and long-lasting than others, and in any single circumstance, influence and inspiration is difficult if not impossible to measure.

The focus is on the period in which Thomas (John) Branwell, the maternal grandfather of the Brontë children and his wife Ann (Reynolds) Carne were born and brought up in a tightly circumscribed area and interdependent community in the far west of Cornwall. That period was to end with his last remaining blood-line descendants, for whom he generously, if unknowingly, provided. Little would he have suspected that money which he earned, invested and shared in family legacies would in time be used to help subsidise the publishing of poetry and the writing of wildly controversial novels. Possibly nothing would have been further from his entrepreneurial mind, but we cannot know.

The purpose of this research is to reveal possible influences derived from key figures whose childhood and youth were rooted in West Cornwall, a granite land of mine-scapes, moorlands and shorelines perched on the Celtic periphery. The stories that emerge here create a mental swell or 'rising ground' of oral tradition, experience and memory from which Maria, Aunt Elizabeth Branwell and their relations would take sustenance and meaning.

ENDNOTES

[1] J. Hambley Rowe, A paper read to the Bradford Historical and Antiquarian Society, 28th April 1911 and reprinted with additions as 'The Maternal Relatives of the Brontës' *BST* Vol 6: 33, Jan 1923, 135-146.

[2] Dr. Hambley Rowe, a medical practitioner in Yorkshire and a Cornishman, was a former chairman of the Brontë Society. He also took an active part in the Cornish language revival, and was made a Bard of the Cornish Gorsedd. He was Hon. Editor of the *Bradford Antiquary Journal*.

[3] John Branwell (1849-1929) was the photographer, eldest son of John Richards Branwell (1822-1902)a grain merchant of Penzance, who built Penlee House (now the town museum & art gallery). Three scrapbooks and a quantity of prints and glass negatives relating to the house and family living there are in the Penlee House archives. These relations are outside the time frame of this study, and do not appear in the indices of known connections. An exhibition of his photographs has featured in the 2019 programme of curated shows of work at Penlee House Museum and Art Gallery, Penzance.

[4] Fannie E. Ratchford 'The Loneliness of a Brontë Cousin, Eliza Jane Kingston's Pathetic Life-story' *BST* vol. 13, 2, Jan 1957, 100-110.

[5] Virginia Woolf (1929) *A Room of One's Own*, Edinburgh (1945 edition, complete and unabridged) Penguin Books, p. 63.*Laura Smith quotes this phrase* in her introductory essay relating to the 'Making of an exhibition led by the writings of Virginia Woolf' (2018) [in] *Virginia Woolf, an exhibition inspired by her writings*, Eds: Laura Smith, Enrico Tassi with Eloise Bennett. Smith also curated the exhibition which is made up of a breathtaking display of the arts and magnificent crafts of the women artists surrounding her in her own time and forcing our admiration in ours. She explains 'the exhibition traces many of the vital and fluid connections that can be drawn between Woolf, her contemporaries, and those who share an affinity with her work – whether such connections be tangible, anecdotal, geographical or imagined.' This exhibition not only shared my approach to the 'fluid connections' which help shape the lives of writers, but threw up an unexpected link between Woolf and the Brontës' Cornish family, which will be taken up later in this book.

[6] Though most baptismal records in Cornwall include the mother's forename alongside the father's full name, the parish of Madron did not do so in this period.

[7] The subtitle that Richard Holmes gives to his excellent collective biography of those people who participated in 'a relay race of scientific stories, and they link together to explore a larger historical narrative.' *The Age of Wonder* 'Prologue' xv

[8] A prominent legend, still sporadically fought over, relates that the announcement of Nelson's death as announced from the Union Hotel balcony was the first intimation of his demise on mainland UK. The story is that fishermen at sea received the information from passing seamen on *HMS Pickle* on its return from Trafalgar to port at Plymouth, and rushed back to the Penzance port with this shocking news, sharing it at the Union Hotel in the middle of a ball.

PART I:
PENWITH AND ENVIRONS: THE LAND'S END

Detail from Plate 1 Penzance, by W Penaluna.

Mount's Bay, Kershaw & Son, London, No. 994 (n.d.).

Chapter 1

Living at the edge:
the Penwith Hundred[1]

Perhaps the most distinctive and important fact about Cornwall is its geographical position. With outlying islands, and over three hundred miles of heavily indented coastline, its history has been largely determined by its maritime location. Located so very far from the rest of England (Cornish was spoken there until the late eighteenth century), a unique character was created amongst its people; they presented a different aspect opening onto the world by sea: a mariners' market for trade and a bulwark for defense purposes. Penwith in particular, at the very end of the Cornish peninsula, is topographically unique, and this was the environment which produced the Branwells and the Carnes, the Brontë sisters' immediate forebears.

Cornwall's Cornwall and the 'Island mentality'.

Penwith, now part of the administrative area called West Cornwall, sits on the extreme southwest promontory of Britain, where the mainland ends, extending westward only in the 'drowned landscape' of the Atlantic archipelago called the Isles of Scilly.[2] The late Gerald Priestland, a British BBC foreign and religious affairs correspondent of note, who thought of West Cornwall as the home of his heart, romantically designated it `Cornwall's Cornwall' - that part of the ancient kingdom of the Celts which lies `west of Hayle River'.[3] He suggests that Penwith itself would become an island if the sea rose about 50 feet: `Spiritually, it is one already.'

The Penwith Hundred

For almost a thousand years, until the late nineteenth century, the administrative districts of Cornwall were known as `hundreds', and Penwith was one of these. At the time covered by this history, West Cornwall was an on-shore spread of hamlets, small villages and only slightly larger towns based on the allied economies of mining (tin and copper), fishing and farming. Often a named settlement or small community was composed of no more than two or three abodes with cottage farms and grazing fields attached. Ranged all around the peninsula and still remaining today are the medieval field patterns defined by the dry stone walling that enclosed pasturage and domestic subsistence crops.

Over most of the period described here (1740s to 1840s) land transport was simple: by horse or donkey, or on foot. Wagons were few, though there were mail and passenger coaches in the eighteenth century; earlier roads were ill-defined, treacherous and muddy in inclement weather. Mule trains were used for the transport of metallic ores from the mines to the ports where they were loaded onto a variety of vessels. Traders between Cornish towns used open horse-drawn wagons, and urgent messages or money transfers could be carried by messengers on horseback.

The major way in and out of Cornwall was by sea, and cargo boats and packets could be relied upon to carry a few passengers on most routes. Transport to the north of England from Cornwall was often by sea to Liverpool or alternatively to Wales or Bristol, and then inland by stage coaches to the intended destination. Directly from Penzance and from Falmouth (the main port for Truro) a passenger could set sail for Plymouth, and board stage coaches for London. The journey from Penzance to London by stage coach took 5-6 days, with optional stops along the way.

Underpinning these main transport possibilities were the crafts and the creation of the working equipment that each occupational group required in such a peripheral position: rope-making, blacksmithing, clock and instrument-making, boatbuilding, boot and shoe-making (cordwainer), etc. In other words, independent thinking and solutions for knotty problems were of critical importance on the spot. Whatever was needed at the edge of the country, for the most part, was created locally, even if imported in raw form from elsewhere. Hence each one was, to some extent, his own 'engineer', which encouraged the independent spirit of the people and aided prosperity.

At the same time, the region with its supplies of clay (for porcelain and pottery) and mines for tin, copper, arsenic,and silver, became a major centre for raw materials rather than manufacture. And this would have important ramifications for the future, when inevitably those resources were exploited to near extinction. The shortage of fuel meant that raw materials such as coal and wood had to be imported, primarily from Wales. Wood for building purposes was sparse in this granite land, and the unfortunate wreckage of sea-going vessels along the coast was frequently used in the construction of many Georgian homes in Penzance.

The adaptability and ingenuity of the Cornish was to have some astonishing results; for example, a Cornishman, Richard Trevithick, was to take the lead role in the development of the high-pressure steam engine, leading in turn to steam locomotion and the railway.[4] Trevithick Day is celebrated each year in Camborne, Cornwall, in remembrance of its native son Richard (aka 'Captain Dick'). On another scientific front, the experimentation and discoveries of Penzance native, Humphry Davy (1778-1829), ensured that he would be universally remembered as one of the founders of modern chemistry.[5] This period, described by the historian, Asa Briggs, as 'the age of improvement, 1783-1867', was the age in which 'our' Branwells and Carnes were born and lived.

The railways were to change this isolated world, of course, but the first thrust of passenger transport by rail between Penzance and Redruth did not occur until 1852, with no throughway to Truro from Penzance until 1855. Even then, differently sized gauges meant that at least one change of train was necessary to exit east out of Cornwall. Hence West Cornwall remained an island-in-the-mind for longer than many other coastal areas. To live on the edges, meant to stay on the edges longer than most of greater Britain.

Turks and Pirates: A curious incident in 1760: Mount's Bay

An event occurred at Penzance in the year 1760, of a nature so curious as to be well-worthy of remembrance. This country was then deeply engaged in what has since been termed the seven years war[6]; and, notwithstanding the splendid successes of 1759, the nation still felt alarm from the always threatened invasion by France, and from the fear of predatory excursions, when in the night following the 29th of September the town was roused by the firing of guns, and soon after by the intelligence of a large ship of a strange appearance having run on shore on the beach towards Newlyn. Great numbers of persons crowded to the spot, where they were still more astonished and shocked by the sight of men still stranger than their vessel, each armed with a scymitar and with pistols. It was now obvious that they were Moslems; and a vague fear of Turkish ferocity, of massacre and plunder, seized the unarmed inhabitants, just awakened from their sleep in the middle of the night. A volunteer company obeyed, however, with alacrity to beat to arms, and 172 men were conducted or driven into a spacious building which then stood on the Western Green, and for some reason or other was called 'the Folly'. Eight men were found to be drowned. Before morning it was ascertained from themselves, by some who understood the *lingua Franca*, that the ship was an Algerine corsair, carrying 24 guns, from nine to six pounders, and that the Captain had steered his vessel into the Mount's Bay, and run it against the shore under a full conviction that he was safe in the Atlantic Ocean, at about the latitude of Cadiz, thus committing an error of thirteen degrees in latitude.

The instant it was known that the sailors were Algerines, a fear seized the town and neighbourhood scarcely less formidable than the other of massacre and plunder, namely of the plague. The volunteers, however, kept watch to prevent all intercourse. Intelligence was conveyed to the government, and orders are said to have been issued for troops to march from Plymouth for surrounding the whole district but most fortunately the local authorities ascertained that no cause whatever existed for such a precaution, and the orders were countermanded.

When it was found safe to visit the strangers, curiosity attracted the whole neighbourhood. Their Asiatic dress, long beards and mustachios, with turbans, the absence of all covering from their feet and legs, the dark complexion and harsh features of a piratical band, made them objects of terror and of surprise. They were on the whole treated kindly; their vessel had totally disappeared, and consequently after some delay a ship of war took all the men on board, and conveyed them to Algiers.[7]

Though the above story relates to events that occurred when Thomas Branwell and Ann Carne and their friends were in their teen years, there is little doubt that such an invasion of strangers from exotic places, lingered long in their minds and conversations. After all, the south-western coast of Devon and Cornwall had for many generations and at least two centuries lived in fear of the Barbary pirates, and their harvest in what was known as the 'white slave trade'.

"For two centuries, perhaps three, there had been an influx to Barbary states of the Mediterranean and the north coast of Africa, of almost 5,000 white slaves each year".[8] In 1625 Barbary corsairs had slipped in by night to the Mount's Bay harbour and raided the parishioners at prayer at St. Mary's Chapel. Sixty men, women and children were dragged from the pews and back to the waiting ships. From there the Islamist privateers sailed on to Looe where they struck again and took at least 200 souls back to the Mediterranean port of Algiers. From that period on, "Turkish"[9] pirates infested the coast.

It would be a Cornishman (from Penzance), also in the kinship circle of the Branwell family, who ultimately led the great squadron who tackled and smashed the evil trade which had ensnared over a million British and American people, over two centuries. This could not help but be a major line of conversation and gossip amongst the Carne-Branwells, as closely connected as they were.

In 1779, the year of Humphry Davy's birth, when Elizabeth Branwell was three years old, the Mount batteries fired on pirate ships, in what was to be the last full engagement in the Bay. But, it was not until the summer of 1816, the same year as the death of Benjamin Carne Branwell, brother of Maria and Elizabeth, when a more distant connection, Captain Sir Edward Pellew, Vice Admiral of the Mediterranean Fleet, (later the first Lord Exmouth) brought about the defeat of this scourge.[10]

Meanwhile, and certainly throughout the childhoods of Maria and Elizabeth, careful watch was kept along the battery rocks and the coastlines, for foreign raiders and enemy ships. At sea, trading vessels were also greatly at risk of being attacked and mariners taken, never to be seen again. On land, a common sight was the alms collector, who gathered funds for the attempt to buy back the unfortunate captives through exchange agencies dealing from London with Morocco.

On Chapel Street today remains The Turks Head, the oldest public house in Penzance, operational since early medieval time.[11] Now it sports as its logo a man of Asiatic mien, long beard and mustachio, with turban. Though the building has been reconfigured and extended forward to meet current eating house demands, its woods and fixings glow with the patina of age. Maria and her siblings would have passed it every time they passed up the street to the marketplace or to visit their friends.

Penzance, *Pen sans*[12]

An 1845 *Penzance Guide* claims that the town originated with a few fishermen who settled in the neighborhood of the present pier, and that their village - augmented over time - became the foundation of the town…now the 'metropolis' of West Cornwall…[13] Although Penzance is a decidedly maritime settlement, it is equally a part of the large rural parish of Madron, which stretches north from the town and includes a village of the same name. On most of the lengthy peninsula, however, and certainly in West Cornwall, a walker is no more than three miles from the sea on either side. The peninsula on any map edges the St. George and Bristol Channels to the north, and the English Channel to the south, with Land's End facing out to the Scilly Isles and the Atlantic ocean.

Penzance itself faces south-east, onto the beautiful Mount's Bay, which opens first to the Bay of Biscay and then into the wide expanse of the Atlantic Ocean. This was the last spit of land touched by the pilgrims sailing from Plymouth in old England to Plymouth Rock in the New England of the Americas. Here at the old harbor at Newlyn (now a southerly suburb of Penzance) the sailors of the Mayflower refilled their water barrels with the last fresh water they would have before reaching the far shores.[14] For the Carne-Branwells and their contemporaries this story was already legend.

The Penwith moors, lying behind and up from Penzance, stretch away to the northern coast of the peninsula in a wide belt holding stony, gorse-covered hillocks and former mine stacks from the 1800s, and part-buildings (now ruined settlements from the stone and iron ages), only six miles from coast to coast. Here, isolated and straggling farms and medieval field patterns marked with dry stone walling and hedges, share an atmospheric stage similar to that of Emily's *Wuthering Heights*.[15]

It is not uncommon to hear present-day visitors and residents, hailing originally from Yorkshire, likening the terrain of that county's moorlands to the granite-strewn moors of West Penwith, the 'Hundred' for which Penzance provides one of its fronts to the sea. Even the recent obituary of the British actor Keith Barron mentions in closing that he kept a small cottage in West Cornwall because it reminded him of his native Yorkshire homeland. One wonders whether this resemblance in reverse would later occur to Maria, Elizabeth and the Fennels who all moved north to live the remainder of their lives there.

The geographical and coastal location of the market town of Penzance had, without doubt, its upsides and downsides strongly influencing the behaviours of its citizenry. One attribute, which has survived positively to the present day, has been its noticeable lack of a rigid social class structure as expressed in its heraldic legend of 'One and All' (*onen hag oll*, in Cornish). Even Mrs. Gaskell mentions this aspect of Cornish life in her description of occupational choices of the day amongst the (mainly) male working population in Penwith.

> At that time, when our colonial possessions were very limited, our army and navy on a small scale, and there was comparatively little demand for

intellect, the younger sons of gentlemen were often of necessity brought up to some trade or mechanical art, to which no discredit, or loss of caste, as it were, was attached. The eldest son, if not allowed to remain an idle country squire, was sent to Oxford or Cambridge, preparatory to his engaging in one of the three liberal professions of divinity, law, or physic; the second son was perhaps apprenticed to a surgeon or apothecary, or a solicitor; the third to a pewterer or watchmaker; the fourth, etc…..[16]

Inevitably, fish was a staple diet, pilchard-packing sheds and wharves its workshops, and fishing boats and trading vessels its transport. The town's principal occupations were shipping and distribution, and ranged from foodstuffs (tea, coffee, grains, spices, salt in large quantity) to building materials (wood, bricks, coal, etc.) to the produce of the mines (tin, arsenic, copper, silver and gold in small quantity) which dotted the landscape. The merchants of Penzance worked with all of these commodities on a daily basis.

The ports of Penzance, Falmouth, Porthleven and Hayle clearly had strong maritime uses with watching briefs, repair yards, docking facilities and military purposes. And, yes, smuggling activity of a privateering nature also played its part in the everyday lives of (virtually all) local people. Attitudes to this kind of illegal activity, and to the evasion of customs duties slowly began to change, partly it is believed, under the influence of the Wesley brothers, their visits and crusades to improve civic responsibilities and to cut down on unlawful, drunken and rowdy behaviors. Today we are able to trace smugglers' tunnels, many metres down one side of Chapel Street from the top end in the Marketplace down as far as the harbour.

Chapel Street

In 1549, the street where the Branwell home was later constructed was known as `Our Lady Street', the name taken originally from the Chapel of St. Mary, the chapel-of-ease for the mother parish church at Madron some two miles away. This evolved in name to `Lady Street' for short, and then in the eighteenth century, at a point unknown, to become Chapel Street.

Not until well into the 19th century were houses, shops and other buildings to become part of a numbering system on Chapel Street, which altered sporadically as new buildings were inserted into gaps, or were joined on to premises next-door. It is, therefore, impossible to be sure, though some are self-identified in the literature about the town, exactly where on the street a specific family lived until the 1851 Census. Many early deeds were destroyed in fires and more recently in World War II bombing raids, creating frustrations for family researchers.[17]

"the Court end of town"[18]

When J. S. Courtney first came to Penzance from Falmouth in 1825, he commented that Chapel Street, the best street on the south had been "for many years" the most important in the town, and even when he came to Penzance it could be described as "the court end".

Most of the eighteenth century history of the place, Penzance, was played out from the Market House down Chapel Street to the quay. The social centre was the Ship and Castle Inn (earliest newspaper reference: 1747, as the house of Samuel Bennetts, innkeeper), and the homes of the wealthiest and most influential of its families. This is now the Union Hotel, because of the Act of Union (1801) between Great Britain (England and Scotland) and Ireland. Chapel Street was also the religious centre with St. Mary's Chapel near the bottom, and the commercial and professional centre with the Market House at the top. The Post Office, which now is located on Market Jew Street, was located in two separate places on Chapel Street. This was probably to be near the Ship and Castle Inn, where the post-chaise came and went, not only with post but with road passengers in later years.

Every fortnight from 1770 were special social gatherings, for conversation, card playing and promenade at the Ship and Castle (now the Union Hotel), which was the main venue for public events. With sixteen lodging rooms, five parlours, a cockfighting pit in the yard and plenty of stabling for horses and carriages, this was the natural place in 1786 for the 'elegant new theatre' to be constructed. By the following year the Theatre was open under the management of that "Father of Provincial Drama", Richard Hughes. Later in his successful career he was to be owner and manager of the Sadlers Wells Theatre, as well as theatres in Weymouth, Plymouth, Exeter, Guernsey, Devonport, Truro and Penzance. Each theatre was open for several months of the year and Mr. Hughes' company of Players moved from one theatre to the next to perform their repertoire.[19]

Here on Chapel Street were the homes of not only the Branwells and the Carnes, but also the Battens and the Johns, families with whom they married. Here also lived the schoolmaster, John Fennell, his wife Jane and their daughter, Jane Fennell. Between these families and their relations, other properties on the street and around the town were owned and controlled, either by free-hold or lease-hold.

The early streets were unpaved and muddy after rain, and used as a thrice-weekly thoroughfare for a pack train of mules that transported copper and tin to the coinage hall. Slowly over the years paving was a welcome innovation. The wearing of pattens was commonplace, and would have been habitual for the young ladies, such as Elizabeth and Maria too. That Elizabeth would continue this indoors in the much colder north of West Yorkshire is no real surprise.

Population at the edge

In terms of population Madron (inclusive of Penzance) in 1801 was the most populous parish in Cornwall overall, with the statistical record showing 4,940 residents. Nevertheless, these people were spread around in small clusters and agricultural hamlets with Penzance itself making up less than half of the total with 2,248 individuals. It was natural for the leading families to know virtually everyone (and most of their private and personal detail) and to intermarry with many local families. Here lies the source of the much later reference from W. S. Gilbert in *HMS Pinafore:* "And so do his sisters, and his cousins, and his aunts!

His sisters and his cousins, whom he reckons up by dozens, And his aunts!"
Population in 1801 - 2248 persons
Population in 1811 - 2297 persons
Population in 1821 - 2671 persons
Population in 1831 - 3293 persons
Population in 1841 - 3503 persons in the parish, and 81 persons in the Madron Union Workhouse

By 1841, when Elizabeth Branwell's life was about to come to an end, Madron Parish again headed the population statistics with 11,144 residents.[20] Nevertheless, Penzance itself had grown only by 832 people since she left the town and represented just about a third of the population of the district. At the time of her death in 1842, Elizabeth would still have known and corresponded with many relations and friends, in the area, no doubt discussing most of the families resident in the town, their progress and regress. If only she had lived another five years, she would have had the sensational news of her nieces' adventures in publishing to report. And in only fifteen, with the publication of Gaskell's *Life of Charlotte Brontë*, the fame of the Branwell-Brontës would reach the whole world.

ENDNOTES

1   Penwith was one of the ten ancient local government administrative units of Cornwall, made up in modern times by the administrative areas of Penwith and Kerrier. Until the 1760s, though the main settlement of people was in Penzance, the central civic institutions such as the gaol, the tax offices, and even the dog pound were located in the parish of Gwithian, near Hayle and across the bay from St Ives.
2   Charles Thomas *Exploration of a Drowned Landscape, Archaeology and History of the Isles of Scilly*, (London: B.T. Batsford Ltd, 1985). The working archive that Thomas employed in the writing of this modern-day classic, is part of the natural history collections of the Hypatia Trust, Penzance, Cornwall.
3   *West of Hayle River.* (with Sylvia Priestland) (1980), as *Priestlands' Cornwall* (London: Grafton, new edition 1992).
4   Richard Cavendish (2001) 'Richard Trevithick's First Steam Carriage', *History Today*, vol.51, 12 Dec issue.
5   Amongst his discoveries: sodium and potassium (1807), calcium and barium (1808) and his designs for agriculture and geology include his famous 'safety lamp' for miners' use.
6   'The Seven Years War' (1756-1763) also known as the French and Indian War (and several other names according to the country of the major protagonists) with Britain competing with France and Spain over trade routes and colonies. These were the years during which the East India Company aggressively moved from being the trading 'partner' of Bengal into being its governors and government. Such horrors as the 'Black Hole of Calcutta', the tropical climate and disease, the venal behaviour of alcoholism, gambling and brawling amongst the westerners were the stories leaked back to Britain. Hence there was constant and ongoing fear of foreign 'Turks' especially at the seaports.
7   Davies Gilbert founded on the manuscript histories of Mr. Hals and Mr. Tonkin, *The Parochial History of Cornwall* (London: J. B. Nichols and Son, 1838) vol. III: 97-8.
8   Giles Milton, *White Gold* (London: John Murray Publishers, 2015 reprint), pp. 9-10; 272-3.
9   'Turk' was the name given to any raider of North African or Moorish description and origin.
10 See further note of the Pellew connection and clear references to the fears prevalent in coastal communities of the period in Chapter 10.
11 The on-line legend: 'The Turk's Head is reputed to date from 1233 when, during the crusades, the Turks invaded Penzance, from Jerusalem. At that time the Turks were excommunicated by Pope Calixtus.'
12 *Pen sans* translates from Cornish as 'holy headland' (the noun preceding the adjective), with pen = head, top or end, and sans = holy or sacred. Pool, *History of Penzance*, p. 2.
13 J. S. Courtenay, *Penzance Guide*, 1845.

14 Tradition has it that the last port in England for the Mayflower was actually not Plymouth but Newlyn in Cornwall on the Land's End peninsula when it was found that the water picked up at Plymouth was contaminated. Scholarly works do not mention this stop, but Newlyn has a plaque to this effect on its quay. Only the year "1620" is provided, with no specific date.

15 *Wuthering Heights*, as produced by the Ilkley Players in July/August 2013, was staged at the Minack Theatre, Porthcurno, in the magnificent outdoor coastal theatre created by the famed Cornish playwright and builder, Rowena Cade.

16 Mrs Gaskell (1878 edition) *Life of Charlotte Brontë* (London: Smith Elder & Co., 1878) vol. 7, Ch. III, p. 31.

17 Esther and Kerrow Hill *The Penzance Home of Maria Branwell.* (Self-published 1996) The deeds of No. 25 were destroyed by fire in 1945 when a bomb fell on the solicitor's office where they were lodged.

18 Louise Courtney *Half a Century of Penzance 1825-1875* from notes by J. S. Courtney (Penzance: Beare & Son 1878).

19 Harvey Crane *Playbill, A history of the theatre in the West Country* (Plymouth: MacDonald & Evans, Ltd. 1980), pp. 104-06.

20 John Wallis (1789-1866) *The Cornwall Register*, Free e-book on-line. 1847. It contains collections relating to the past and present state of the county with its 209 parishes, with its archdeaconry, parliamentary divisions and poor law unions of Cornwall at the date specified.

Dolcoath Copper Mine, Camborne, Cornwall, by T. Allom and J. Thomas. Hand-coloured plate bound in to Revd. W. S. Lach-Szyrma, M.A. (1878) *A Short History of Penzance, S. Michael's Mount, S. Ives, and the Land's End District*. 'The Queen of Cornish Mines' under the stewardship of Andrew Vivian (kin).

Chapter 2

Creators of the place

> The people of that promontory of Britain called Belerion [West Cornwall] are friendly to strangers and, from their contact with foreign merchants, are civilised in their way of life. They carefully work the ground from which they extract the tin.
>
> Extracted from Diodorus Siculus, *Bibliotheke Historicke*, c44 BC[1]

Industry and trade

Halliday in his *History of Cornwall* states the case simply, writing of Cornwall centuries later in the 1700s: "Geologically the county was unique; no other region in Britain had a comparable wealth of metal below its surface, and as yet it had scarcely been worked. The next two centuries of the history of Cornwall, therefore, are essentially the history of its mining industry," its comings and its goings, and in parallel its gives and its takes.[2]

For families in Cornwall, there was no escaping the importance and the driving force of the mines, just as everyone born or living in West Cornwall has intimate relations with the sea. Studies now extant exhibit clearly the recognition in earliest recorded times of the presence of tin on the Land's End peninsula and its extraction and smelting.[3] Not only largely responsible for economic developments in the period of this study, mining and its technologies were also the drivers of its population growth through migration, and its cultural amalgam through educational and spiritual mix.

Though mining had been going on for centuries, by the mid-to-late 1600s, in order to increase output, the necessity for digging ever deeper was in progress and the processes of smelting required continual modernising and improvement. From 1663, or from the time of the great-grandparents of Maria and Elizabeth Branwell, Penzance had been designated as a Coinage town, also known as a stannary (from the word 'stannum' meaning tin) town.[4] All of the tin streamed and mined in Cornwall west of Camborne was brought – at twice-yearly sessions of at least a day each – to the Penzance Coinage Hall (at the bottom of Chapel Street near the docks) to be assayed and "coigned"(weighed and taxed). [5]

As one of the four major administrative centres for coinage purposes, in Cornwall, related smelters and mines together with the supporting businesses of rope-making, pier construction, boat and ship-building and repairing, and blacksmithing gathered around.[6] Each step in the chain required discovery, invention, innovation and application. From close observation, identification and experiment through to the understanding of maximum use and utility was the nature of the enterprise. Since tin was in greatest demand in the production of pewter, the smelter of this material into ingots ready for export was the major industry contributing to the livelihood of the town.

> ...in the early 1800s mine owners wanted to improve their output. Men with the right skills were needed as engineers to improve underground working and also experts in smelting. Germany had such people and the mine owners persuaded many to come to Cornwall. Lord de Dunstanville... brought a famous German engineer called Becher here with a team of men. New furnaces were built and the smelthouse expanded. These people were found to be Jewish and Francis Bassett had a small synagogue built for them somewhere between Camborne and Hayle.[7]

Of great import to the 'creation' of Cornwall had been from earliest times, the frequent settlement of foreigners in its towns, and especially in its coastal towns and ports – whether saintly travellers on missions to convert, specialist miners by recruitment or commercial traders with profit in their eye. Historian Keith Pearce in reporting the particular case of Jewish settlement, comments,

> It is to the credit of the indigenous population in eighteenth-century Cornwall that they recognised the Jewish newcomers could enrich the local economy. The Cornish ports at this time were especially cosmopolitan, and for their inhabitants it was a common experience to hear of the sound of many foreign tongues of the sailors, passengers and migrants who arrived on a regular basis by sea, and also by road....It was the establishment of Jewish shops in the Cornish sea-ports from the early to mid eighteenth century onwards, which marked the true beginning of Jewish communal life...[8] [in Cornwall].

Bretons were by far the largest group of émigrés, but it was not unusual for Dutch, Spanish, Portuguese migrants to make up to a third of the local populations on subsidy and tax rolls. Spanish names like 'Jose' still linger as local surnames today. Later, as more Germans arrived, coming as merchants and ships' chandlers to settle in Penzance, the Branwells in particular, were to provide leasehold homes, business premises, land for the Jewish burial ground, and the building and leasing of land for both synagogues constructed in Penzance itself (1768, 1807), though not themselves a Jewish family. The synagogue of 1807, was formed from part of the old family home on New Street, that had housed the Bramwell family of Richard Sr. and Margery (John), the parents of Maria's father, Thomas. The 'killing yard' for the family butchers (cousin Joseph 1748-1813, Branwell's business) was located directly adjacent, though ritual killing is never mentioned.

In Thomas Branwell's will of 1808, one of the wealthiest and most prominent Jewish merchants is mentioned as one of his tenants.[9] A particularly horrific event happened in 1803 when this same man's pregnant first wife died, as a result of accidentally setting herself alight with a candle while alone in an upper room in their home.[10] Her infant was delivered still-born and she died a few days later. Without doubt, and not least because the accident took place in a house owned by the Branwells, both Elizabeth and Maria would have known of this tragedy, and remained ever vigilant with open fire. In this recognition of danger, of course, they were not alone, and it was also an abiding fear in Haworth where window curtains were avoided for similar reasons.

Developing, using and serving both of these 'masters' – mining and the sea – were the merchants and grocers, brewers, lawyers and politicians, teachers, miners, farmers and fishermen. Here is where we meet the families of maternal relations – female and male – about whom we wish to know more.

The resilience and inventiveness of the Cornish mining communities is well-exhibited in the working lives of the male Branwell and Carne contemporaries and relations such as Richard Trevithick, Humphry Davy, the Harveys of Hayle, the Foxes of Falmouth, the Vivians and the Williams families of Camborne with their numerous ties to South Wales and the mines of Australia and the American states. In this study, the maternal side of the family – the Carnes – was the most heavily invested in all aspects of mining investment, management, and mineralogy, and even in specialist practice. Very little is to be gleaned about the women, but snippets appear from time to time and are included in the biographical index.

For example, Anne Carne Branwell's father, John (Calenso) Carne, was a silver and goldsmith by trade as well as a clockmaker; all of these were dependent on a local supply of precious metals. His cousin, William Carne, a partner in the Cornish Copper Company and an astute mining adventurer (investor) would become one of three merchants who established the Penzance Bank in 1795, the first one to open in the town by a decade. William Carne's father, from the early years of the eighteenth century, Joseph Carne Sr. of Gwinear, was the mining captain and bursar of the Herland mine which produced both copper and silver ores.

Joseph Carne Jr. (1782-1858), eldest son of William, grandson to Joseph Carne Sr. described above, and born the year before Maria Branwell, became the company director of the Cornish Copper Company (Hayle). He was also an outstanding mineralogist, a mining engineer and later a Fellow of the Royal Society amongst national and international roles in the spread of Methodism and missions. These achievements followed on from a childhood of collecting some 9000 Cornish minerals to form a nationally-recognised collection of specimens now in the Sedgwick Museum in Cambridge.

Joseph's daughter, Elizabeth C. T. Carne, a second cousin to the Brontë children, augmented his Cornish collection with even more specimens from abroad following his death. She also became the first woman member of the RGSC, and to publish scientific papers in their *Transactions*. She is the writer whose wise words open this book, and was an inspirational benefactor to a great number of people, perhaps including her cousins, the Brontës. Overall it would be said that the Carne family were most likely to have been amongst the foremost builders of intellectual and financial wealth in the county.

Self-sufficiency and inter-family trade were key features of domestic life, while mining, machinery, and engineering skills provided the wherewithal in fits and starts of development that promoted international trade.[11] Mining technologies were a major spur to immigration and somewhat later to emigration, which in turn impacted on the cultural tenor of the place of Penzance. Virtually everyone had family who now lived in the American states, and in the Antipodes. After the deaths of both Maria and Elizabeth in Yorkshire, the great exodus of Cornish miners and their families began in earnest, whereas there had always been a trickle who had travelled out to share their skills and hopefully to gain a fortune.

Experts and specialists came and went: it was neither a static place, nor an environment in which outside influences and interests were discouraged. Distinguished visitors of ideas and innovation included such male luminaries as Josiah Wedgwood, Gregory Watt, Christopher Hawkins, Richard Trevithick and later change-makers like Isambard Kingdom Brunel. Each of them was to leave anecdotal stories behind them which could be paraded here as possible connections – for various members of the family met with them socially and in business. However, their direct relevance to the Branwell and Carne lives are mostly unknown.

The financial implications of these developments are obvious, and the need for investors or 'adventurers' straightforward. Great wealth was to be gained (and lost) for some, while hard labour, early death and poverty were endured by many more. The Carne family were amongst those who steadily gained in wealth and influence through the mining industry. The Branwells were to thrive through provisioning, primarily in the grocery trade, in the milling and import/export of grains, and in the international trade of pilchards, aside from liberal investment in local properties.

The Mine out the back window

> If the visitor standing at Wherry Town on the south-western end of the esplanade at Penzance looks seaward he will observe at low tide at some distance from the shore a low seaweed-clothed rocky shoal, and from his now very conventional surroundings it is difficult to realize that upon this shoal, always surrounded by water, there existed many years ago a rich tin mine, unique in the boldness of its conception, romantic in the extreme in its situation and execution, and withal the effort of a poor working miner.
>
> Very fortunately in the year 1790, during the hey-day of its career, this remarkable mine was examined by a very competent observer in the person of John Hawkins (1761-1841), FRS, of Trewithen, Cornwall, and Bignor Park, Sussex, and it is to him that we owe most of the details concerning its mode of working, &c.[12]

At the edge of Penzance toward Newlyn, and directly below and to the right of St Mary's Chapel, the shaft of the Wherry Mine was sunk on a rocky reef in Mount's Bay beginning in 1778, when Elizabeth Branwell was two years old. The mouth of the mine was protected by a wooden turret operated by four men with a windlass and

Wherry Mine from Newlyn, looking to the Mount.
Transactions, vol. I, of RGSC, 1814-1818, published 1818.

ropes, as the tidal waters submerged it at every tide. Three years later, the mine was operational and extended 240 yards into the sea, with a horse and wagon bringing the tin across the sands and onto the shore.

The Wherry Town mine is specifically mentioned here because of the dramatic and astonishing presence of it, situated as it was on the shore below the back gardens of the Rotterdam buildings in which the Branwells lived through their childhood and teenage years.[13] Thomas Curtis, Sr. of Breage was the miner who finally sunk the shaft on the reef, building the aforementioned wooden turret, with a stone breakwater around its base and a platform on top with a windlass to draw up the ore.[14] When he died, his son Thomas Curtis Jr. took over, bringing in other adventurers from amongst his fellow Methodists. Carnes and Branwells would have been amongst them.

Readily visible from the back windows of their home, Wherry provided hours of viewing. One can easily imagine the young Maria Branwell believing it to have always been there, as it was before her birth until its loss when she was fifteen years old. Years later, following a storm, an American ship broke from its moorings in the Gwavas Lake,[15] smashed into the shaft head, bringing the whole structure to its end (1798). Charlotte Brontë is said to have made reference to the mine submergence in one of her stories, moving it fictionally to Ireland.[16]

The builders

It is in pier re-construction, as well as in other architectural amenities of the town (the Georgian stable theatre, the ballroom, etc.) that we find most reference to the Branwell family of masons and builders headed by Maria's grandfather, Richard Sr. The Carnes too were builders and designers. Joseph Carne FRS and his father were responsible for the construction of Regent Square, a lovely winding road of smaller Georgian residences tying Chapel Street to the foreshore a little further west. As much as they were grocers and market traders, the Branwells and the Carnes were builders, with all the applied technology and apprenticeships that this implies.

Both families were also (part) ship-owners and shipping agents working directly with their in-laws and cousins, the Battens (coal and timber), and the many tradesmen who supplied the harbour businesses working from Batten Wharf and warehouses. Thomas Branwell was part owner of the sloop *Penzance*, which transported tea and pilchards and other grocery supplies in and out, even as far as Genoa and the West Indies. The Carnes owned several merchant vessels, and for a short period Joseph Carne Sr. acted as a customs officer, a rather unpopular post. The Branwells were also part owners of the sloop *Friendship*, captained by a cousin, George Bramwell, son of Martin Bramwell, the butcher of Market Jew Street.

The sloop *Penzance* may also have been used for the frequent smuggling ventures that are known to have taken place.[17] Personal involvement is not known on the part of Thomas Branwell himself, though some other relations are recorded and suspected. Apart from any other special knowledge that may be found about individual smugglers of the area (notoriously secretive, of course, and therefore unrecorded) and the full extent of their 'traid', there is one primary and haunting question, to which we have no answer: who planned, commissioned and constructed the tunnels and *when* did that now ancient network come into being?

A local historian's note (anon) found in the Shaw Collection[18] commenting long after the fact (re: Penzance Quay 1812) that the following was composed about the supposedly sloppy contracting work of Cock and Bramble (Bramble = Branwell)[19]:

> *The quay was built with turf and straw*
> *Where Cock can't roost and Bramble grow.*

The saga of the Penzance harbour and pier is one that continues to the present day. Without recounting numerous stories of no relevance relating to it since early in the eighteenth century, the 'little smuggling town' and its 'burlesquing magistracy' have expended time, effort, money and acrimony over repeated extensions, reversals and repairs to the quay. [20]

Defending the shores

Not only was 1595 with its Spanish sacking well remembered, but the intermittent raids by pirates, smugglers and buccaneers were part of living reality. [21]

> Cornwall's defences were strengthened by the Duke of Richmond in the 1770s and 1780s as a precaution against the rise of the American Navy during the American War of Independence…
>
> …An initially sympathetic response in Britain to the French Revolution turned to alarm at the executions of French aristocrats and clergy. In 1793 the French ambassador was expelled and France declared war on Britain.

The rise of Napoleon Bonaparte during this period led to him heading an army poised to invade Britain at the end of the eighteenth century. Napoleon's invasion plans suffered a severe setback in 1805 when his fleet was defeated at the Battle of Trafalgar, and were ended in 1815 by the French defeat at Waterloo.

Preparations in Britain against a French invasion led to the strengthening and modernising of existing defences, and the building of new defences. Coastal batteries were built at Padstow, Portreath, St Ives, Whitesand Bay, Penzance, Mousehole, Mount's Bay, St Michael's Mount, Mevagissey, Charlestown and Looe.[22]

At one point Thomas Branwell was paid a fee by the Penzance Corporation for allowing the meeting of a *petit jury* to try a group of French prisoners in his home. On another occasion in 1793 he was paid his expenses for mustering the Battery guns, and arranging for a 'Watch' at the Battery. His kinsman, the town Mayor of the time, John Batten Esq., was presented with a donation, the large sum of £20, for purchasing flannel waistcoats for the British Troops in Flanders. Shortly before that he had also been paid for gunpowder. In that same year another cousin, Solomon Cock, was paid for making out the Militia Lists.[23]

Anecdotal entries in the journal of Davies Giddy (later Gilbert) reveal the 'normal' childhoods lived amongst those in the communities clustered around the Mount's Bay.

> The schoolboy entries showed that he lived a normal life of playing cards, flying kites, and shooting. Sometimes he was made to feel the pulsation of events whose significance he did not comprehend until later years. In 1779, from the cliff edge at Perranuthnoe he watched the English fleet pursued round the Lizard by the combined Franco-Spanish fleet. In the following year the American War was brought right to the Cornish coast, when the disabled troopship *The Aran* limped into St. Ives with a cargo of 1800 Hessians, and Gilbert helped his father to entertain the officers. [24]

Professor Charles Thomas in his study of `Cornish Volunteers'[25] dates the Penzance Volunteers to April, 1794, one of the earliest corps in Cornwall, under the command of John Tremenheere. In these early years 'the unit was one of a dozen serving in or around Mount's Bay in the early part of the war; these included a separate corps of Mount's Bay Volunteers and also units at Ludgvan, Marazion and Mousehole…there was much rivalry between these units…and Thomas described them as "competing for recruits from the same towns and villages, riddled with local, family and even personal jealousies."

In 1798, it was announced in the *Canterbury Journal* as notified by the War Office that Ensign Benjamin Branwell of the Mount's Bay Volunteers was being promoted to Lieutenant as of July.[26] No record of any service abroad or otherwise has come to light as yet. The following year he married his childhood sweetheart, Mary Bodinnar

Batten, from the largest house (now named The Regent) up the street.

William Carne, the younger, signed up to serve in 1803, at the age of 16, under the command of Sir Rose Price. His father, William Carne, also joined the Pioneers. They served to defend the shores with a watching brief, but could also be called upon to settle violent altercations and riots that might occur when the price of grain and fish threatened the peace as in the crop failures nationwide in the early 1800s.

Building a scientific record

Adding significantly to the bank of metallic and mineralogical knowledge in the world were the many dedicated members of the Royal Geological Society of Cornwall (RGSC) formed in Penzance in 1814. Admitted to the ranks of this newly formed body of local Members and Associates were an extraordinary number of Fellows of the Royal Society, academics, mining agents and engineers, inventors and leaders of the international industrial revolution.

Henry Boase, Dr John Ayrton Paris and Davies (Giddy) Gilbert, first formulated the concept of a geological society based in Cornwall; seven years previously the Geological Society, first of its kind in the world had been established in London. The London society was formed originally as something of a dining club, to draw together like-minded men who should know each other in their professional lives; it soon began to collect the materials – reports, minerals, rocks – to offer a centre for study and research. Amongst its thirteen founding members, was the young Cornishman, Humphry Davy. The Penzance-based society met originally in the ballroom of the Union Hotel: more about the scientific literature of this group of local gentlemen is included in the following chapter on the legend and literature of the district.[27]

As a focus for scientific observations, experimentation and publication, working later alongside the Royal Cornwall Polytechnic Society (RCPS) at Falmouth, the Penzance-based RGSC was finally in the early 21st century to help generate an academic presence in Cornwall through its development of the Camborne School of Mines (CSM).[28] The RCPS or 'Poly', the brain-child of two Quaker sisters, Anna Maria and Caroline Fox[29] of Falmouth was created in 1833 'To promote the useful and fine arts, to encourage industry, and to elicit the ingenuity of a community distinguished for its mechanical skill'. The young women recruited their fathers to establish the institution specifically to encourage education amongst the miners and fishermen. The Fox and Carne families were closely aligned in their mercantile, mining, banking and intellectual lives.

Today the RGSC continues as a scientific learned society, forming a focus for geological knowledge, covering an expanding range of disciplines in the earth sciences, but especially the role of geology in understanding the environment. Over two centuries it has also played an important role in the training and education of mining engineers, due to its original support for the establishment of the Cornwall (Camborne) School of Mines.

Of the three founding fathers of the RGSC only Henry Boase was directly related to the Branwell-Carne family by marriage, however several of the wider family were to become prominent members and to form their primary social circle from amongst its ranks. Undoubtedly, important links and connections were made through the exchange of papers and visits to both academic institutions and centres of mining activity and study.

One prominent geologist would introduce another from faraway or closer-by. This would include academics from Cambridge or Oxford, natural historians or professors from Edinburgh, or visitors from South America or Germany. A number of vicars were also keen amateurs and swelled the membership. The men who joined were of the same generation of children who grew up with Elizabeth and Maria, many of whom they would have known personally, or be introduced to by local friends.

Benjamin Carne Branwell (brother of Maria)) took up membership in the first year of RGSC formation but died, after a long illness (probably consumption) before the first published *Transactions* appeared in 1818. Cousin Joseph Carne Sr., also a founding member, was to serve as the Society's Honorary Treasurer (also a prominent banking partner with his father, William) over several decades up until two years before he died in 1858; a mineral collector since childhood, he was to contribute many notable papers and to be elected a Fellow of the Royal Society (FRS)[30] for his groundbreaking contribution on the nature of elvans.

His distinguished daughter, Elizabeth Carne[31], introduced in this volume in the Author's Note, became the first woman member of the RGSC, following her father's death, and also delivered papers to the Society. She inherited her father's mineral collection, to which she added mainly from samples gathered abroad and was an accomplished artist of landscape and environmental features. Sketchbooks of foreign and British landscapes, together with a textual and visual notebook on 'British Shells,' are lodged in local archives.

From the first, Sir Humphry Davy (knighted in 1812) was made an Honorary Fellow, and his cousin Professor Edmund Davy (later in Dublin) and his younger brother, Dr. John Davy, MD also became members of the RGSC world community, all having been born, schooled and brought up in Penzance. Both of the Davy kin were also to become Fellows of Royal Society amongst a significant number of others from the local district.

When Dr. Paris decided, in 1817, to leave Penzance to further his medical career in London, he wrote to Professor Robert Jamieson at Edinburgh University. Telling him of the continuing need for an infirmary in the mining community of West Cornwall, he asked for a physician who might have a *specialist interest in geology* while being able to sustain a general medical practice to people of all ages.

A recommendation was forthcoming for a recently qualified medical doctor, Dr. John Forbes (1787-1861), who during the Napoleonic wars had served as a naval surgeon. Returning to his native Scotland from his last appointment in the Royal Navy,[32] he had pursued studies for his Doctorate in Medicine and due to having attended geological lectures with Jamieson, was appointed to Cornwall in September that same year.

Taking over from Dr. Paris, he was to become in charge of the Penzance Public Dispensary four doors up Chapel Street from the Branwell home, and equi-distant down Chapel Street from the family home of William Carne Sr. He took over the lease of Dr. Paris's home in North Parade as well, where the Gentlemen's Reading Room had been located.

Apart from any practical medical treatments that Dr. Forbes may have given the Branwell or Carne families of the time (1817-1822), he was to have a strong and positive presence in the building up of local social and intellectual communities. He was to serve particularly as the first secretary for the newly organised Royal Geological Society, and also, with Joseph Carne FRS to establish the first Penzance Library (now known as the Morrab Library). While in Penzance, Forbes laid the foundations of his knowledge of the stethoscope, an instrument invented by Rene Laënnec in Paris in 1816. The interesting anecdotes relating to Forbes' translation into English of *De L'Auscultation Mediate* (1819) and his publication of its first edition, are re-told by Dr. Robin A. L. Agnew in his 2002 biography, *The Life of Sir John Forbes (1787-1861)* and now told in fuller detail in the new edition.

> ...There was also some speculation that his move [to Cornwall] was influenced by health reasons, as he was known to have suffered from chest symptoms in later life. Pulmonary tuberculosis was not uncommon in the Navy...He also worked in general medical practice and saw patients with a wide variety of diseases in all age groups throughout the county of Cornwall, including the Isles of Scilly. In particular, he described the stethoscopic signs of pulmonary tuberculosis in two Cornish underground miners, a group in which TB was then not uncommon. – *Life of Sir John Forbes* 2018 New edition pp. 27-28 [33]

It is quite probable that members of the Carne family became his patients, and the Branwell cousins too, as he was much liked and respected. Aunt Branwell may have consulted him in their overlap of years in Penzance, and may also have received notice of him regularly through correspondence with family, after arriving in Yorkshire. In subsequent years, he was introduced into possible correspondence with Charlotte Brontë by her friend and publisher George Smith, during the progress of Emily's final illness. When Emily left it too late, Charlotte then consulted with him in relation to Anne's illness that followed.

Though no documentation exists, to our knowledge, of the conversations between Charlotte Brontë and Sir John Forbes on her projected tour (1853), of the Bethlehem Hospital in London with him, their correspondence and exchange of books make clear a sympathetic acquaintance of each other.[34] Whether or not he shared discussion of his time spent in Cornwall and his knowledge of her mother's and her aunt's family background is not known. Perhaps she, her sisters and her father never knew that Sir John was without doubt one of the 'creators of Penzance'.

ENDNOTES

1 The earliest written record of the land we now call Cornwall, that describes the people who we now term Cornish.
2 F. E. Halliday, *A History of Cornwall* (London: Gerald Duckworth & Co. Ltd., 1959), p. 47.
3 Sir Christopher Hawkins (1758-1829), Bart, FAS 'Observations on the Trade of the Ancients in Cornwall and on the "Ictis" of Diodorus Siculus, with a view of the Mount', 1811. Hawkins was a writer-member of the Royal Geological Society of Cornwall (RGSC) from its beginning in 1814.
4 Charter received from King Charles II dated 18 August 1663, but taking some time to receive full recognition of status, due to difficulties/competition with the three-five older coinage towns who were banded together in the Stannary Parliament which administered all access to the tin trade. Miners were called 'tinners'.
5 Checking for purity, stamping and blocking in preparation for sale and transport.
6 The number of towns where coinage took place varied from time to time, with new applicants voted in or voted down by the Parliament which always had its own protectionist interests at heart.
7 Sir Francis Bassett of Tehidy, near Camborne, ancestor of the current writer.
8 Elizabeth Brock *The Jewish Community of Penzance, a brief account of their history*, 6-7, 1998. The Bassett family papers, CRO, hold this information. GB/NNAF/F84414 (Former ISAAR ref: GB/NNAF/F4527)3
9 Keith Pearce *The Jews in Cornwall, A History, Tradition and Settlement to 1913* (Wellington, Somerset: Halsgrove, 2014). The two major seaports as referred were Falmouth (for Truro) and Penzance (for Hayle and St Ives), pp. 89-91
10 Lemon Hart (Asher Lemel/Laeml ben Eliezer, 1768-1848), Trader in sugar and tea, Lemon Hart was a fellow member of the Penzance Masonic order with the Branwell men and in 1804 opened a distillery at the top of nearby Jennings Street where he produced the later famous Lemon Hart Rum.
11 *Lyson's Cornwall* (1814) In 1801, the primary exports from Cornwall were: tin, copper and fish (great pilchard fishery). Main imports were: coals, groceries, cloth & other merchandise.
12 Sir Arthur Russell, Bart. 'The Wherry mine, Penzance, its history and its mineral productions, '…a rich tin mine, unique in the boldness of its conception, romantic in the extreme in its situation and execution, and withal the effort of a poor working miner' A description in 1939, from his essay published in *The Mineralogical Magazine and Journal*, The Mineralogical Society No. 20, 5 June 1949 vol. XXVIII.
13 The name given to the terrace of three homes (now four in number as the middle one was split in two) supposedly constructed with Dutch bricks. Several stories are told as to the gathering of these bricks – from a privateer who may have taken them as prize, from scavenging amongst wrecks where they may have been used as ballast, etc. L Oldham, the Branwell historian, points out that the years 1776-1882 were those of the War of American independence, and that a Rotterdam-registered vessel may have been blown off course onto the rocky Cornish coast. *The Penzance Home of Maria Branwell*, by Esther and Kerrow Hill, 1996.
14 Pool and Laws. *History of Penzance*, 1974, p. 74
15 A smaller lake situated at the edge of Mount's Bay, formerly a 'safer harbour' for moorings.
16 Charlotte Brontë's use of the Wherry Mine disaster takes place in her short story 'An Adventure in Ireland' 1833, where it becomes a frightening aspect of a dream sequence: miners working under the sea are submerged by a massive influx of stormy waters.
17 Charlotte MacKenzie Merchants *and Smugglers in eighteenth century Cornwall* (Truro: Cornwall History, TR1 3RT, 2019).
18 Courtney Library, Royal Institution of Cornwall, (Truro: Shaw Collection).
19 R. G. Grylls. *Branwell & Bramble, a brief history* (Tring, Herts: Richard G. Grylls, 1 Longfield Road HP23 4DQ). The Cocks and the Branwells were cousins through marriages with the Carnes: all of these families were masons and carpenters by training, with each heading up his own building firm.
20 Quoted in Pool and Laws, *History of Penzance*, 1974, pp. 78-9 from the *London Magazine*, June 1751.
21 *The Autobiography of A Cornish Smuggler (Captain Harry Carter, of Prussia Cove) 1749-1809*, with introduction and notes by John B Cornish. Pages x and xi list telling references to archives such as 'The Lanisley Letters' (RIC) 1750-53 about the stationing of soldiers in the district because "the coasts here swarm with smugglers".
22 Quoted from: www.historic-cornwall.org.uk/flyingpast Cornwall County Council, Historic Environment Service.
23 Accounts of Penzance Corporation, as recorded for the years 1791-2 and 1792-3, transcribed by PAS Pool in his *History of Penzance* pp. 247-56.
24 'Davies Diary', 31 May 1779 and March 1780, as quoted by A. C. Todd in *Beyond the Blaze*: p. 16.
25 Devon and Cornwall Notes and Queries XXVIII, Pt 1 (Jan 1959) 10-13; P t 6 (Apr 1960); Pt. 7 (Jul 1960) 205.
26 *Canterbury Journal*, 7 July, 1798, British Newspaper Archive Online. Benjamin was brother to Elizabeth and Maria.
27 See J. C. Elliott, D. Freeman & M. Hardie-Budden (eds.), *Bibliography of Transactions of the Royal Geological Society of Cornwall 1814-2014*, (Penzance: RGSC, September 2016) vol. XXIII, Pt 2, ISSN: 0372-1108.

28 The combined universities of Exeter and Plymouth were to create a university college in 2000-2, the last county in Britain to form a university level presence, which has since developed into the University of Falmouth at Penryn.
29 Close friend and correspondent of Elizabeth C T Carne: *Caroline Fox, Her Journals and Letters* give us special insights into the intellectual and scientific lives of the Carne and Fox families. Both families made large fortunes in mining and were strongly committed to social welfare and public education. Both young women were serious students of theology and science, and mixed freely in the society of thinkers such as John Stuart Mill, John Sterling, Adam Sedgwick, Sir Henry de la Beche and Derwent Coleridge. These young women were distant relations of the Brontë family and exact contemporaries at birth.
30 See Carne family chapter in Section II. He was to be proposed and supported to the Royal Society by his friend since childhood, Sir Humphry Davy.
31 See Carne family bibliography. Carne's large scrapbooks (three) of views from France, Switzerland, Italy, Madeira, Britain (Devon, Cornwall, Shropshire, Derbyshire) Scillies and Newlyn (1830-1872) are located in the Estate papers of Polwhele of St Clement, CRO: PW/126, 127, 128. Titled: 'Sketches in Europe and the Scillies'. Her Sketchbook of conchology, unpublished and annotated in her own hand, is held in the Morrab Library Photographic Archive, Penzance, Cornwall.
32 He was appointed flag surgeon and secretary to Rear Admiral Philip Charles Durham of *HMS Venerable*, leaving at Portsmouth in 1816.
33 Dr. Robin A. L. Agnew *The Life of Sir John Forbes (1787-1861)*West Sussex: Shoreham-By-Sea: Bernard Durnford Publishing, 2018).
34 *Letters of Charlotte Brontë*, vol. 3, 1852-1855, 108 9n: George Smith's father and Forbes had known each other since their school days together.

The Giant Bolster, frontispiece by George Cruikshank for *Popular Romances of the West of England, or the drolls, traditions & superstitions of Old Cornwall*, by Robert Hunt FRS (1807-1887).

Chapter 3

Language, legend and literature of Cornwall

"Yes, we may surely say that Maria Brontë, as she went through the gate, tossed much of the seed" which became *Jane Eyre, Wuthering Heights, The Tenant of Wildfell Hall,* and the winged poems of Emily."[1]

1. Family Connections

With the somewhat mystifying words left by Ernest Raymond at the close of his initial chapter about Brontë lives, we open the "Gate of the Dead"[2] to our speculations about the mothering of the children and their abundant creativity. The sentiment expressed by Raymond is important, and stemmed from his assertion that the children "sought some compensation and fulfilment in imaginative writing"for the loss of their mother, which left them "incomplete and insecure".

My objective in writing this book is to examine the lives and experiences of the Carne-Branwell family as documented and explored in Cornwall, hoping to discover those imprints that the Brontë children may have received from their mother and aunt, and have carried forward into their future years and writings. It seems axiomatic that the children's early attempts at authorship illustrate a craving for drama and excitement, a craving for 'life', so to speak, and for the experiences it could offer. The histories of the Carne-Branwell families and their web of friends and relations exhibit, I believe, a similar craving, passions and enthusiasms, expressed through the same channels – stories, books and literature. This is an impression especially evident in the lives of those of their companions described in Chapter 10: Travellers' Tales, but this chapter offers a wider background to the West Country's literature.

Though we have no firm evidence, it may well have been Maria (Carne) Branwell herself who unleashed in the children the recourse to family authorship in parallel with her husband Patrick's avocations – the writing of poetry, story-making and telling, together with childish performance and re-enactment, in their own personal `playing place'.[3] Both Maria and her sister Elizabeth were brought up in a family of known story-tellers, poets and scientific writers in a legendary land of giants, bean-stalks, foundlings, changelings, spriggens and piskies, folklore, ghost stories, superstitions, riddles, miracle plays and ballad games.⁴ When Maria emigrated north, her trunk of belongings constituted not only her clothing, but, specifically mentioned, her books. What exactly remained of these former possessions – after the infamous breaking up of the shipment in a shipwreck on the Devon coast – is an ongoing puzzle, but an interesting one to pursue.

At least two of Maria and Elizabeth's contemporary male cousins – John (Cock) Carne (1789-1844, a second cousin living in the neighbourhood) and their friend and more distant relation Humphry (Millett) Davy (1778-1829) – were master performers in their youth, drawing groups of the young around them for community get-togethers. Later on they became established authors and travellers sharing their poems, philosophies and travel stories ever further. Equally well connected to literary worlds outside of Cornwall, and filled with aspirations and some success in achieving poetic notice, was the Curate, later Vicar, of Penzance, who presided over St. Mary's Anglican parish on Chapel Street. The Revd. Charles Valentine Le Grice (1773-1858), a close friend of Charles Lamb and Samuel Taylor Coleridge from his school years at Christ's Hospital, he was never slow to publish his thoughts on all and sundry, most often in verse.⁵

Though we have no detail, it is also likely that the Revd. C.V. Le Grice (CV for short) would have kept up a connection later on with his friend's son, the Revd. Derwent Coleridge, the headmaster of Helston Grammar School, since Le Grice himself was sometime headmaster of Penzance Grammar School. As Lecturer of St Mary's, he acted as headmaster of the school periodically as needed between outside appointments to the post. Derwent Coleridge and his wife Mary Pridham, the daughter of a banker in Plymouth, took on the challenging work in the 1820s of re-creating Helston school after years of deterioration, with the assistance of at least two remarkable people (probably more) important to our families.

One of these – the botanical populariser and botanist Charles Alexander Johns (1811-1874) – was a relation from a family of native creative and artistic individuals, many of whom knew and mixed with the Carne-Branwell network. Henry Incledon Johns (1776-1851), the father of Charles, later poet and professor of drawing and painting in Devonport, was born in Helston and attended Helston Grammar School.⁶ He and then his son were important and inspirational to the cultural and botanical life of West Cornwall. More about Charles's work can be found in Chapter 10: Travellers' Tales.

The Revd. Charles Johns, too, was a poet, teacher, preacher and a recorder of the natural world but his work was contemporaneous with the Brontë children's novels rather than with their parental generation. Johns was a publishing phenomenon during the lifetimes of the Brontës through his many books and booklets for the publishers of the Society for the Propagation of Christian Knowledge (S.P.C.K.), though there is no contemporary evidence that they knew of each other as authors or relations.⁷ However, there is no reason to suspect that they were completely unaware of each other in the busy professional world of Victorian printing and publishing. Johns was a lasting close friend of the novelist and social reformer, the Revd. Charles

Kingsley, who was most certainly aware of and also in touch with Charlotte Brontë in due course. Kingsley was Charles Johns' pupil at Helston Grammar School when Derwent Coleridge was Headmaster (1827-1841).

Other examples of this kind of connection with the famous names of the romantic literary generation are the wide-ranging friendships of the brothers Joseph and John (Cock) Carne, developing through sometimes unknown routes, and usually, though not always, centred in London. I give for one example the paragraph in a short biography of Jabez Bunting by the non-conformist minister James Harrison Rigg in 1909, through which I first discovered that 'old penitents' meetings were held in Penzance on Saturday evenings as a special service for Wesleyans. Rigg was recalling Bunting's early practice, first held in 1803 when he was assigned to the London circuit of the Methodist ministry:

> I may mention that at Penzance, some forty years later[i.e, c. 1844-5] I found the old penitents' meeting still kept up, with an occasional address from a minister or a senior member.
>
> That meeting at Penzance, Joseph Carne, Esq., banker and J.P., the host and friend of Robert Southey, never failed to attend, and it was a real spiritual help, although Mr. Carne himself, a reserved though kindly and genial man, seldom spoke to the company present.[8]

This was the first time I was told on paper – in a book – that Joseph (Cock) Carne was a friend of Robert Southey (1774-1843), the poet laureate of the British Isles from 1813, and the biographer (1820) of John Wesley. Presumably this was widely known. The fact has been mentioned elsewhere since then and, of course, I accept it as probably true. We know from all reports not only that Joseph Carne was a well-read man with a magnificent library of his own, but also that he was a devoted Methodist. There are, however, no letters between Carne and Southey, there are no diary entries to confirm their friendship, and naturally individuals are very circumspect about what they say of their friends, particularly on paper. This is generally true up to the present day and continually dogs the researcher and biographer.

Exactly when Joseph Carne became a friend and host to Southey is unclear, but Caroline Fox, the famed diarist of the Falmouth-based Fox family of Robert Were Fox[9] (1789-1877), pushes the possible dates back in her entry for the Christmas season of 1836, where she describes Southey's visit that year to his nephew and godson, Derwent Coleridge, at Helston. From other sources[10] we know that the Foxes of Falmouth were close friends of the Carnes of Penzance. Regularly, the Fox family breakfasted with the Carnes before attending the monthly geological lectures and the men were fellow mining captains.

> He [Southey] has been delighting them all, rather with his wit than anything poetical in his conversation. He is very tall, about sixty-five years old, and likes mealy potatoes. He gives the following recipes for turning an Englishman into a Welshman or Irishman: For the former – he must be

born in snow and ice from their own mountains, baptized in water from their own river, and suckled by one of their own goats. For an Irishman – born in a bog, baptized in whisky, and suckled by a bull. What a concatenation of absurdities![11]

Nonetheless, it could have been much earlier that the Carnes had become familiar with Southey, Coleridge and others of the circle that we now designate as active 'Romantics'. Humphry Davy had met Southey by 1800 when he was acting as chief chemist for Thomas Beddoes in Bristol and Davies Giddy Gilbert had known several of the circle from his Oxford days before that. How often Southey may have visited in Cornwall, or met with Carnes in London, is not known.

Coincidental crossings in life only become of practical interest when there is corroboration that some kind of influence arose and was recollected in 'tranquillity' or retrospective remembrance by someone who writes about it.[12] Of course, these individuals may have been mentioned in conversations in family circles, but no proofs come to hand. Nevertheless, it is fascinating to learn of the links that existed at the time, the circles within which, even indirectly, they may have moved, or, at least have been aware, and the diverse routes taken by our foremothers and fathers. Hints may, from time to time, reveal useful open doors into the past and connections that generate informed speculation and ideas.

How many of these personalities, once brought into some part of the Carne-Branwell network, were then shared, or made known to each other, cannot be known to us, as letters and diaries between them are in short supply. Nevertheless, I have often wondered, for example, how Charlotte Brontë knew where to locate Robert Southey when, in 1837 (the year after Caroline Fox's Christmas story) she wrote to him, presenting herself as a poet; and then in 1840, sending her prose work to Hartley Coleridge, Derwent Coleridge's brother. Hartley Coleridge himself wondered about this and asked Charlotte whether or not she had confused him with his father? This she denied and kept her secret.[13]

Although some of the evidence is sparse, it is nevertheless clear that the impulse to write and publish was strong in the Carne-Branwell circles across a wide choice of fields of literature, and the impulse to read widely even more so. As the period in literary terms called 'the enlightenment' moved, twisted and slid into the age of more visible emotion termed 'the Romantic', the flow of literature produced by women increased in parallel, whether acknowledged or anonymous, and the literature of social reform, spiritual enthusiasm and class revolt came into its own. The topics driving the writers of the day – whether of social reforms or scientific adventures – protest and political change were on the tongues of their family, friends and working colleagues. In Chapter 11, Biographical briefs, the reader will discover a band of individuals – some of whom are writers themselves and some about whom they write. The noise was deafening.

2 . The oral tradition & droll tellers

> Around the toys raged battles and campaigns in which Wellington and his staff fought Napoleon and his marshals according to formulas that were commonplaces of conversation in every English household…Wearying in time of battles, the children turned the Young Men to other occupations and arts suggested by their reading, changing them into make-believe publishers, authors, and antiquarians and crediting them with exploits surpassing the achievements of ancient and modern masters. (Ratchford, pp. 6-7).

The piles of stone in West Cornwall that John Wesley, working from other perspectives and tales, called 'Druid altars', in popular parlance became the resting places, the furniture, the tools and the playthings of the Giants: the source of many stories largely inhabiting our oral tradition. Those stones – not unlike a parade of wooden soldiers given by a fond father, Patrick Brontë, to his son Branwell, who shared them with his sisters – became the *idée fixe* of generations of storytellers,[14] the pulpits of preachers,[15] and then the subject of published transactions by geologists writing of the earth under our feet.[16] Fanny Ratchford, erstwhile reporter on the early writings of the Brontë children in Yorkshire describes the 'Young Men', as they called the new wooden soldiers – their own 'Parade of heroes' in the vein of Virgil's *Aeneid* – the initiators 'of an ever-lengthening series of games.'[17]

Ratchford also recounts the plausible scenario of how the children's selected characters brought themselves into being and into action, after the initial military plays of the Young Men:'Our Fellows' was the next play in the sequential development, and for this game each of the children had a large island of their own, where the people were six miles high. Here enters a stolen idea from *Aesop's Fables* [says Ratchford]. The chiefs of the play were in fact ten miles high, `except Emily's, which was only four.

William Bottrell[18] and Robert Hunt, in their separate renderings of the popular romances of the west of England, use 'the metamorphosis of the ancient giants into modern devils' as part of their collections and study of legends[19] – an ever-lengthening series of plays and stories. In the far west country, peopled with 'piskies'[20], 'knockers'[21], 'buccas'[22], subterranean 'lost lands', miners' misadventures in their underworlds and story-tellers with their peculiar words and phrases, there is a long tradition of combining the two – the pagan and the spiritual tales – and having a parade, a play or a festival to celebrate the marriage. These are the main sources for the ever-lasting series of modern-day feasts and festivals, celebrated annually as well, and all are based on the antics and activities of our fabled heroes, buccas and guardians. To live in Cornwall is to be reminded with great frequency of the legendary place that it was and is right up to the present day.

In the Christian era, the Castle on St Michael's Mount has served as a Benedictine religious house and a shrine for pilgrims, as a gaol, as the battlements to defend the bay area, and a home for some of the 'great' families of Cornwall. Buildings, both domestic and religious, hording strange and sometimes `spooking' tales have come and gone, but that which exists today dates from the fourteenth century, with additions, improvements, repairs and re-building as necessary and possible. The marvellous 'trunk of stories and fairy tales' that is St. Michael's Mount, remains in the same family as it did in the days of the Branwells and Carnes,[23] though it is now part of the chain of properties gifted to the National Trust.

A steep rocky path, leading up to the castle walls, passes the Giant's well, which in the folklore of world literature, is the well where Jack the Giant-Killer slew the giant Cormoran.

> With the true history of Jack the Giant-Killer – of him of the Bean-Stalk – and some others, we are all acquainted. We listened to those histories ere yet the dark seed of that troublesome weed – doubt – had germinated. They were poured forth from loving lips into believing ears…By this process the stories were imprinted on memory's tablets with an indelible ink, and for long years, the sponge (*sic*) and water – which is employed by the pioneers in the great March of Intellect – has been used almost in vain.[24]

Various long traditions to the present day acknowledge the healing and revealing powers of Cornish waters,[25] the waters of the Bay that cover the leavings of Lyonesse,[26] the waters drawn from springs and not least the waters of holy wells.[27] The legends that accompany the latter are listed and described in some detail also by Hunt, in his section on 'Superstitions of the Wells'. The introductory paragraphs to the Holy Well of Madron (still one of the most famous, where rags are tied to branches with prayers, and coins are thrown) Hunt takes from *Tales of the West*, by John (Cock) Carne (1789-1844), the prominent imaginative writer-member of the Carne family.[28]

Much later in the nineteenth century, when Dinah Mulock (1826-1887), the novelist (known as Mrs Craik or the author of *John Halifax, Gentleman*),[29] gave her reasons for wishing to visit the Land's End. It was its legendary qualities which drew her on:

> I had always wished to investigate Cornwall. This desire had existed ever since, at five years old, I made acquaintance with Jack the Giant-killer, and afterwards, at 15 or so, fell in love with my life's one hero, King Arthur.
>
> Between these two illustrious Cornishmen, – equally mythical, practical folk would say – there exists more similarity than at first appears. The aim of both was to uphold right and to redress wrong…Also I wished to see the Cornish land, and especially the Land's End, which I had many a time beheld in fancy, for it was a favourite landscape-dream of my rather imaginative childhood, recurring again and again, till I could almost have painted it from memory.[30]

These references to legends and their origins are meant to offer the reader a reminder of the pathways and passages that have led authors – poets, novelists, antiquarians of every kind, as well as image-makers and scientists – especially in this focal period which the modern day literary biographer Richard Holmes calls 'the age of wonder'.[31]

This was a transitional period, as literacy and increasing educational opportunity (at least for males, but also for some middle class women and girls) emerged as necessary ingredients for progress.

3. The antiquarians & the historians

> The visitor to modern Cornwall is immediately confronted with evidence that this most westerly county of Britain has a linguistic heritage all of its own. The county border is dotted with bilingual signs which read Kernow as well as 'Cornwall', while place names like Marazanvose, Ardensawah, Halabezack and Perranarworthal, sounding mysterious and sometimes unpronounceable to the outsider, stand in marked contrast to those of neighbouring Devon. Of all the counties of England, in fact, Cornwall has the unique distinction of possessing its own language which, although it died out as a spoken tongue in the late eighteenth century, is still vigorously nurtured as the single most important manifestation of Cornish identity.[32]

Virtually all of the early literature of Cornwall, riddled with its own politics, objectives and philosophies, describes a state of the 'nation' of which we now have little knowledge or understanding in practical terms. Under the auspices of religious institutions, that which emerged from the pens and scrolls of the more distant past was primarily a product of either the spiritual quest in the form of homilies or sermons, such as the work of Hucarius the Levite of St Germans (110 sermons) from before the Norman Conquest, or perhaps of John of Cornwall, writing in Latin, who travelled abroad extensively and studied at foreign universities (in Rome 1180). From such as these men, we fast forward through several notable giants of (mainly) church-based literature to the beginning of the seventeenth century, when Richard Carew of Antony steps into focus.In one gigantic leap he creates the 'playing place' for the history of Cornwall in his *Survey of Cornwall 1602*. Paul White, in his introduction to a modern reprint of this classic work, comments:

> In Cornwall we are truly fortunate that the earliest book devoted to the county is a minor masterpiece of Elizabethan prose. What is more, although an extraordinary number of titles about Cornwall have been produced in the four centuries since its publication, many people would argue that it remains the most important ever written about the county.[33]

It is noteworthy that Carew also begins his survey of his times with the legend of how Cornwall came to be the prize of a wrestling match between giants Corineus (cousin of Brute, the first conqueror of the British Isles) and the mighty Gogmagog whose neck was broken by being thrown from a cliff near Plymouth. Cornwall was the prize for the prowess of Corineus. Of course, there are other drolls available on this subject.

From that start the *Survey* is much about the naming of places, much about the tin industry, celebratory events, hurling and wrestling, delightful, if awkward, poetic thrusts at legendary people such as Merlin and Arthur, and the upper and lower crusts of the population – and many names that remain today and their families. The title implies a kind of governmental census; it is, in fact, an all-encompassing story of Cornish life in the early seventeenth century. This record is one with which most literate inhabitants of Cornwall would have been familiar. From the Civil War period (1642-1651) a new literature was to emerge building on Cornish history as laid down first by Carew. And, from that time a literary tradition comes into play, which encompasses the authors, educators and reading preferences in Branwell and Carne networks.

William Hals (1655-1737), amongst a large number of other historical contributions to books and publications of several kinds, took up the challenge of building a publishable parochial history of Cornwall, and completed the writing up of 72 parishes in folio form before – under pressure from critics – he was made to quit. The reason given for the discontinuation was that he uncovered too many unpleasant tales, reflecting poorly on county families (a la Poldark much later and in fictional form). He is said to have been perhaps too well-acquainted with the genealogy of mixed and broken families and the descent of property and its distribution, and that some or even most of this information should remain private. He was charged with too many inaccuracies (real or imagined) by the *literati* who were proud of their family names. None of his work was printed until after his death and seemed to have disappeared, piece by piece, into various archives, and was never brought together in its entirety.

Thomas Tonkin of St. Agnes took up very similar work in 1702, altogether separately from Hals, as they are not known to have met or collaborated in any way, and subsequent researchers combined Tonkin's work with vestiges of the Hals folios. When Tonkin died in 1742, no printing had been done on his further manuscripts, though by that time he had incorporated some material first written up by Hals. But people of our focal period (1740-1860) were on hand to take up the roles of historian and antiquary in increasing number as classical education was more widely valued and literacy continued to spread.

Perhaps the first of these who should be remembered in any literary review is the Cornish naturalist, antiquarian and clergyman, the Revd. William Borlase (1696-1772), the Rector of Ludgvan and the Vicar of St. Just; he was known from the childhoods of Maria's parents as the powerful cultural and social force of the district. The Borlase family of St. Just appeared everywhere, and were well-known bearers of local justice and public service, at least in their elite positions as arbiters of 'the age of reason'. William's brother, the Revd. Walter Borlase (1694-1776), served as Vicar of Madron inclusive of Penzance, as Mayor for several terms and also as a Magistrate. William exerted his mineral and mining interests as Vice Warden of the Stanneries. Possibly Walter is now most recalled as the virulent opposer of John Wesley and the invasion of West Cornwall by 'methodies'.[34]

In his own time, however, William Borlase was not only a religious leader and an amateur painter, but also an archaeologist of note. He was devoted to fields of study in geology, fossils and antiquities of Cornwall and the Scilly Isles and produced many important and personally researched publications on these subjects. In 1750 he was elected a Fellow of the Royal Society, and was known to some of Britain's literary giants – the one most mentioned being poet Alexander Pope (1688-1744) with whom he maintained friendship and correspondence in the final five years of Pope's life. When Pope moved to Twickenham and constructed a Palladian mansion, a grotto was built into the basement, and Borlase sent him crystals, ores and metallic materials for his displays (1739-44).[35]

Moving forward into the nineteenth century, yet another historian and politician, now much in the lifetimes of our families, took up the pen to complete the work (with heavy editing of unpleasant stories) of Hals and Tonkin. This was Davies (Giddy) Gilbert (1767-1839), who takes up an abiding presence in this study several times over, because of his celebrity in several fields of endeavour. He stated in his introduction (c1837) to the final issue of his *History of Cornwall* a keen interest from 'the earliest portion of my life', to see the remainder of Mr Hals' Parochial History in print, having read piecemeal some initial folios published first about 1750.

The end result of Gilbert's efforts was reviewed by critics and historians as inadequate and indifferent,[36] but nevertheless it covers the territory of Cornwall, lets us look into the issues and activities of the focal time of this study, and describes some of its more extraordinary people, as does Richard Polwhele (1760-1838).[37] Each writer surveys Cornwall almost up until the demise of Aunt Branwell, and represents a potential well of stories out of which the Brontë household could have drawn.

Gilbert's *Parochial History of Cornwall*, in four volumes, was finally to reach publication in 1838, not long before his own death and also those of John Fennell and Elizabeth Branwell in Yorkshire. Both of the latter would have been familiar with him and his prevailing influence in West Cornwall. Others of their family and Penzance connections are acknowledged by Gilbert for their assistance along the way, i.e. Dr Henry Boase, Esq. M.D. for his addition of 'An Introduction to the Geology of Cornwall' (xxv-xxxii of Volume 1), Richard Polwhele for his set of histories on all and sundry (already mentioned) and then various acquaintances notable for their published scientific contributions, since Gilbert was also the President, from 1814 until his death, of the Royal Geological Society of Cornwall and not least, following on from Humphry Davy, the President of the Royal Society.[38]

The Preface to Gilbert's *magnum opus*, as realised finally, provides a seventeen-page summary of historical publications by the giants of parochial (parish by parish) literature. It includes quick and passing reference to many of the families connected to the Branwell network though the contents are primarily related (as dictated by Hals and Tonkin) to ancient families and their estates and various entanglements amongst the landed gentry, rather than focusing on commoners or everyday concerns. That is not to say that Davies Gilbert had no everyday concerns – there were many in tow, both personal and public – and the progress of this pilgrim of Cornwall deserves rather more attention than he has so far received.

4. The Methodies

> A set of the *Methodist Magazines* from the commencement, formed part of Miss Branwell's marriage-dowry, and, doubtless, awoke Charlotte Brontë's love of the marvellous, and kindled into a flame the latent fire of her genius.[39]

Books and tracts prepared for the Christian readership of Wesleyan followers were part and parcel of the foundation and extension of Methodism as it spread through the agency of 'education for all'. In the lifetimes of the Wesley brothers more than 500 tracts, books, journal articles and musical publications flowed from their pens, with the pure objective of opening the minds and capacities of those who would listen.

> Wesley's practical enthusiasm for popular education made him a pioneer publisher of cheap literature. He did in his day what Knight and Chambers did in the next century. He filled his preachers' saddle-bags with cheap books [generally a penny a piece, and later several larger, he wrote], superseding the old chap-books…They had enormous circulation. Book-lovers may regard his abridgements – especially of Milton, Herbert, and Bunyan – as vandalism: to the practical mind of Wesley the needs of the poverty-stricken multitudes, whose intellects were awakened by the religious revival, condoned the deed. He and Dr. Coke[40] formed the first Tract Society in 1782, seventeen years before the Religious Tract Society was established, and forty years earlier thousands of copies of Words to soldiers, sailors, and smugglers were scattered broadcast."[41]

In his correspondence with preachers and in booklists, Wesley's suggestions for reading matter were made available throughout the Methodist circuits as they formed. Controlled by the annual Methodist Conference begun in 1744, in terms of price, distribution and sales, the profits from the local Book Rooms set up around the country were ploughed back to provide stipends (small though they were) and expenses for the itinerancies in which the ministers served. The purposes, of course, were to provide texts for young and old to employ in weekly classes, and to augment the interpretation and understanding of the *Holy Bible*. We know from references in local Methodist papers and reports that several members of the Carne-Branwell network were Class Leaders – William Carne, John Fennell, Anna Tyacke Branwell, etc. These resources were set up to act as back-up for voluntary class leaders, and possibly could have acted as an initial spur to the kind of writings such as we find in the single offering of a publishable tract by Maria Branwell: 'The Advantages of Poverty in Religious Concerns'.[42]

In 1748, the first educational institution at Kingswood (Bristol) was opened, under John Wesley's plan for augmenting English schooling for lay preachers and their family. The list of subjects was formidable:

...reading, writing, arithmetic; English, French, Latin, Greek, Hebrew; history, geography, chronology, rhetoric, logic, ethics, geometry, algebra; natural philosophy and metaphysics. No Roman author was to be read, who had lived later than the Augustan age, except certain sections from Juvenal, Persius and Martial. This was carrying classical Puritanism to an extreme...[43]

Working through much failure and discouragement in attempting to drive that large curriculum forward, and to make it simple enough for the children to absorb, Wesley determined to carry on:...'through God's help, I went on; wrote an English, a Latin, a Greek, a Hebrew, and a French grammar; and printed *Praelectiones Pueriles*,[44] with many other books, for the use of the school.'

Literature of this kind, of course, was didactic in style, and the content spiritual in nature. The objectives were to open resources to the previously untutored, to augment the often loveless lives of many downtrodden labourers of the working classes, and to give hope and inspiration to all who could be attracted. The negatives, as perceived by the more conservative Christian communities of the town, were identified as too emotional, too enthusiastic, and much too threatening to the social order.

The earliest Methodist journal was a monthly magazine edited by John Wesley. Founded in 1778 and originally called the *Arminian Magazine*, it later (1798) became *The Methodist Magazine,* and from 1822 renamed as *The Wesleyan Methodist Magazine.*[45] It was co-edited by Welshman Thomas Olivers, whose first assignment as a Methodist circuit preacher had been in Cornwall in 1753. For the first twelve years of its existence, Olivers' lack of formal education caused a large quantity of printing errors in every issue, finally forcing Wesley to replace him. Nonetheless he was a frequent author on political and social issues, adding articles and verses of his own into the magazines. He and Wesley remained friends, despite his dismissal in 1789, developing a father-and-son relationship – so much so, that when Olivers died, eight years after Wesley, his bodily remains were buried in Wesley's grave.

We know, of course, that the cache of books arriving with the Branwell women – Maria and/or Elizabeth – from Cornwall, included a set of *Methodist Magazines* and some *Lady's Magazines*. The *Methodist Magazines,* as referred in Charlotte's later novel *Shirley* as belonging to her deceased fictional Aunt Mary. Therein they were scornfully called 'mad magazines', reportedly full of ominous dreams, warnings and miracles. *The Oxford Companion to the Brontës* contends that these had belonged to Maria but it is doubtful that more than one set would have been kept in the Branwell family home, hence they were probably just as much Elizabeth's. The children mocked the magazine's contents in the juvenilia (for instance, Charlotte in 'Passing Events', 1836 and Branwell in 'Angria and the Angrians', 1836). Despite these throwaway remarks, it is clear that the children took excited notice, and were perhaps embarrassed by their interest, in front of parental disdain.

There is no documentation of how or why a copy of the fourth edition of *The Remains of Henry Kirke White* (1810) came into the hands of Maria Branwell, before she arrived in Yorkshire, and supposedly before she met Patrick Brontë, who had known the poet at Cambridge. But, of interest to us may also be the comment of Robert Southey before he took up the enormous and generous task of editing that which White left behind when he died at the age of 21.

> Among his letters there is a great deal of methodism: if this procures for the book, as it very likely may, a sale among the righteous over-much, I shall rejoice for the sake of his family, for whom I am very much interested. I have, however, in justice to myself, stated, in the shortest and most decorous manner, that my own views of religion differ widely from his.[46]

Barbara Heritage, in her recent essay 'The Archeology of the Book',[47] presents initially a time-line of details about the travels of the book from Cornwall by sea vessel (*Trader* by name), surviving a minor shipwreck, into the re-possession of its owner and placed in the Brontë family library collection. Though the two volume set of books of *Remains*, edited by Robert Southey were obviously obtained to be read for its content and thought by Maria, and perhaps others of her friends and family, the primary importance to the Brontë family was as a memento of their mother, and their function as a carrier of excerpts, doodles and short pieces of the children's writings – *The Lost Manuscripts* referred to in the title of the book of essays.[48] It may well have been offered for sale to local Methodist readers through the Book Room.

In Penzance, the Book Room for Methodist publications was lodged in the basement of William (Johns) Carne's home. Thereafter the collection was kept and distributed from the Wesleyan Sunday School house which the Carnes and Branwells had helped to create on Chapel Street. It is noted, in passing, that the memorial gift that was presented to Patrick Brontë on the death of Jane Branwell Fennell, Mrs Morgan, (wife of his great friend and in-law the Revd. William Morgan), was a Greek Bible. Presumably this also means that young Jane had studied the language. Since several of the class leaders were also integral members of the Carne and Branwell families, steady use of the Book Room facilities would have been an everyday matter.

5. The Scientists

> *This is the patent-age of new inventions*
> *For killing bodies, and for saving souls,*
> *All propagated with the best intentions;*
> *Sir Humphry Davy's lantern, by which coals*
> *Are safely mined for in the mode he mentions,*
> *Timbuctoo travels, voyages to the Poles,*
> *Are ways to benefit mankind, as true,*
> *Perhaps, as shooting them at Waterloo.*
> — George Gordon, Lord Byron, *Don Juan* (1819), Canto I, CXXXII, 36.

Although aware of scientific inventions, Byron[49] seemed to view them with suspicion. Humphry Davy (1778-1829) invented his safety lamp in 1803, but throughout his life was also a poet, mixing freely with other poets and writers of great variety. He met and became friends with both Byron and his final mistress, Teresa Guiccioli, through the social circle of his wife the attractive widow (Mrs.) Jane Apreece,[50] who sat at the centre of a wide international literary and artistic set. Humphry and Jane married in London in 1812, an auspicious year in which he was also knighted for his scientific prowess.

It is in many places recorded that the 'discoverer' of Humphry Davy's scientific genius was the engineer, MP, and learned antiquarian Davies Giddy,[51] who appears as Davies (Giddy) Gilbert in the section, above, on 'Antiquarians and Historians'. Giddy met Davy at Dr. John Bingham Borlase's home where he was apprenticed from the age of fourteen preparing for a career in medicine. This casual meeting – Humphry was swinging on the garden gate – brought about a more formal introduction by a mutual friend. After chatting to the boy at some length Giddy realised that his natural curiosity and keen enthusiasms for chemistry and experimentation could be encouraged in practical ways that would benefit other technical projects with which he was heavily invested. Giddy invited him to his own family library in St. Erth, said to be one of the finest in mathematics and engineering available anywhere.

Since Giddy was most interested in and engaged with engineering feats, the inventions of Richard Trevithick, Thomas Telford, Josiah Wedgwood and Jonathan Hornblower (all of whom approached him for advice and became friends) and the creation of tools and mechanisms for mining, shaping metals, and the power of steam, the equipment and books at his home were thrilling to young Humphry. From there came introductions to Giddy's friends and long-time mentors locally, such as Dr. Edwards of Riviere House, Hayle, which housed a laboratory in the basement for the technologies of smelting copper. Another friend was the Revd. Malachy Hichens, a mathematician and astronomer who had been a teacher of Giddy from youth, and who was a cousin of Henry Martyn, the missionary. Riviere House would later become the family home of Joseph (Cock) Carne, FRS, (See Chapter 9, 'The people called Carne') when he took over as managing director of the Cornish Copper Company.

The physician and chemist, Dr. Thomas Beddoes (1760-1808), at Bristol, was a close colleague and friend of Giddy, and the former chemistry don at Oxford was developing with Giddy an institution for the development of pneumatic medicine. Giddy believed that by working with Beddoes, young Davy would discover his future as an inventor and scientist, and so it came to be. From 1799 Davy supervised the laboratory testing of nitrous oxide (aka laughing gas) and remedies for tuberculosis, a field of study that Beddoes named 'pneumatic'.

Giddy provided the breakthrough for young Davy, pitching him forward to national platforms set up for advance in all fields of technology and scientific discovery. Recommendations coming from friends he trusted (such as Giddy and his friend James Watt,[52] whose son Gregory, trying to recuperate from consumption, had lodged with the Davys in Penzance) meant that his opportunities were wide open.[53] In many ways Davy can be seen as the 'poster boy' for this period in Penzance history, combining as he did a passion for learning from his earliest days, the soul and will of a storyteller and poet, and curiosity of spirit to carry him in later life to the highest reaches of scientific discovery and endeavour. How remarkable is it that a self-educated young Cornish boy, an indifferent scholar, but not a bad poet according to Coleridge, should be the inventor of a miner's safety lamp and the discoverer of Sodium, Potassium, Calcium, Magnesium, Boron, Barium and much else.

It was during his time with Beddoes that Davy came to know Samuel Taylor Coleridge, the Edgeworth family[54], and Robert Southey (1774-1843), all of whom were poets, writers, journalists, and travellers. The period from the end of the seventeenth through the eighteenth century was not only called the 'enlightenment', and the 'age of improvement',[55] but also the 'age of wonder' described so well by biographer and historian Richard Holmes.[56] With the intellectual energy exuded by an age in which rational thought was not divorced from 'wonder', Humphry Davy steps dramatically into the circle of Romantic poets, and into the consciousness of the Brontë writers. Humphry's zest for life lasted throughout his successful public life of scientific performance, and the friends that he made were inevitably shared with the wider world. Perhaps coincidently, or perhaps inevitably, these friends were also ones who appear to have had a special appeal to the Brontë writers. More about the literary giants close to Davy will be explored in the following section.

It was Davies (Giddy) Gilbert, together with Dr. Henry Boase and Dr. John Ayrton Paris who, in 1814, first formulated the concept of a Geological Society based in Cornwall; this was only the second society of its kind in Britain. The first had been established in London in 1807, with thirteen members, one of whom was Humphry Davy five years before he was knighted. Gilbert was the prime mover behind the Cornish society which

> has flourished far beyond any expectation that could have been originally formed; and the collection has been enriched by the liberality of Mr Carne, Dr Barham, Mr Henwood, and others; but, above all, by Doctor Boase, who has deposited specimens from all parts of Cornwall, collected on an actual survey extended to each individual parish. All these specimens are arranged, labelled, and numbered.[57]

Within the first year of Cornwall's Society in Penzance, the Prince Regent agreed to become patron, and the prefix 'Royal' was affixed. There were approximately a hundred founding members within the first year, and this number included Benjamin Carne Branwell, though he was not a known geologist. To some extent (not known), to belong to the RGSC was also a social attribute as well as a profession of interest.

From that time to the present it has published original research papers, essays and notes on environmental and geological subjects in its *Transactions*. Among the titles published in Volume I, 1818, are articles by brothers Dr John Davy and Humphry Davy, but also by Joseph Carne, and on the basis of his academic paper 'On Elvan Courses', Carne was elected to the Royal Society. His nomination was put forward by Davies Gilbert MP and Sir Humphry Davy along with Sir Christopher Hawkins. He is said to have authored more than 100 papers related to mineralogy of Cornwall

These men (and membership initially was all male) were the pilgrim fathers of geological intelligence locally, nationally and internationally for most of the nineteenth century. The first female to become a contributing member of the RGSC began to deliver scientific papers in 1860, two years following the death of her father, Joseph (Cock) Carne (1782-1858). He had been amongst the original founders of the Society, and its honorary treasurer for most of the years since 1814.

She was Elizabeth Catherine Thomas Carne (1817-1873), a second cousin of the Brontës, and a highly intelligent author and journalist in the fields of social reform, mineralogy and political economy. It is Elizabeth Carne who provides the epigraph to the 'Author's Note' at the beginning of this book, and further details of her writings will be found in Chapter 11, ' Biographical Briefs.

In this brief summary of the fields of literature which flowed from this corner of Cornwall there was a large place which could be allocated to scientific publications, not usually considered as a branch of the literary arts, but in this place and at that time, a most important one. Of those men contributing scientific papers to the *Transactions* of the Royal Geological Society of Cornwall during the period from 1814-1855, fifteen authors were Fellows of the Royal Society, of whom two, Sir Humphry Davy (1820-27) and Davies Gilbert (1827-30) were elected President, together holding this office for a decade.

Not all of the Cornish scientists with a claim to a place in literature were, however, quite so august. Before we leave the scientific scene, it is intriguing to note one quite surprising figure of 'irregulated character', latterly termed a well-educated rogue, who does not exactly fit any of our categories. One might even call him a droll-teller with a difference. Certainly known to the Brontë children later, and possibly known to some of the Cornish family network at the time, Rudoph Erich Raspé [58]took up residence and employment in 1782, the year before Maria Branwell's birth, in the nearby mining district of Camborne-Redruth.

By that time, already at the age of forty-five, Raspé dragged a colourful history behind him – born in Hanover, starting life as a teacher of archaeology, and keeper of a National Library – he fell from grace when it was discovered that he had stolen and sold some of the valued objects in his care. He was advertised for by the police in Hesse as "Councillor Raspé, a man with red hair, generally wearing a scarlet dress embroidered with gold, but sometimes appearing in black, blue, or grey clothes. He was arrested and imprisoned but effected his escape during the night, and made his way in safety to England."[59]

It is not known how he was located and recruited by Matthew Boulton[60] for the mining adventurers of Dolcoath Mine in Cornwall, initially as their Store-master. However, until his misdemeanours became widely known, he also had a scholarly mineralogical reputation, even with the Royal Society (Honorary FRS), and he also had good literary connections with such as Horace Walpole who loaned him money and tried to help the pitifully poor German, who could not pay his tailor's bills. The Royal Society had intended to publish some of his work on volcanic islands and petrified bodies, until they were told of his character – and whipped away his fellowship.

Nonetheless, at Dolcoath, his scientific knowledge quickly promoted him to the position of chief copper smelter to the company. The mining captain in charge of the site and all its original workings was Richard Trevithick Sr., father of Richard Trevithick, the inventor and mining engineer, friend and fellow Methodist of William (Johns) Carne, father of Joseph and John (Cock) Carne of Penzance. Trevithick Sr. had constructed the deep adit in 1765, and installed a Newcomen pumping engine in around 1775.

> At this period he [Raspé] is said to have written the original version of the *Travels of Baron Munchausen*, from which a series continued for at least a decade. Some of the old miners of Dolcoath have informed me that, as boys, 'they have watched the old conjuror working with all sorts of flames about him,' in what is now the dining room of the counting house at Dolcoath.[61]

Raspé left the mine and Cornwall in 1789, the birth year for both Charlotte Branwell and her cousin Joseph Branwell (who she would later marry) as well as John (Cock) Carne, son of William. Raspé was bound for Caithness in Scotland where he began another stream of ever-so-slightly fraudulent activities relating to mundic iron pyrites that he took with him from Cornwall to pass off as rich copper ore. Until his death in 1824, Raspe's authorship of the Munchausen narratives was unknown to his ever-growing body of fascinated readers, though probably known to a few friends and associates along the way.

In the original travel stories of the Baron, Cornwall is referred to in Chapters IX and XXIV; the latter reference relates to the white slave trade and the capturing of innocent coastal residents. One of these who did know his identity was his friend, the geologist and Cornishman John Hawkins,[62] who remains to this day a meaningful player in the literary and cultural life of Cornwall. Both he and his brother wrote numerous papers which were published in the *Transactions* of the RGSC, and were closely associated with Joseph Carne, FRS. John Hawkins was also a close friend and correspondent of Davies Gilbert, PRS who is introduced in the following section, reviewing Cornish 'literature'.

6. Romanticism – the age of revolutions and its literature

> Writers of the period were outraged by the world in which they lived, and the outrage fed directly into the culture.[63]

The final quarter of the eighteenth century, and the actors within it, seemed driven to recast the age, changing its make-up for good. The brilliant exegesis of social historian, Rachel Hewitt, in her recent study of the 1790s, mainly in Britain and France, but also in the American states, identifies the sequence of human events and their interpretations which gave us also 'a revolution of feeling.'[64] This was the period during which Elizabeth and Maria Branwell were born and finding their ways into community life, beginning to make decisions for themselves.

It was the age of revolutions, and the age of many proclamations and much political philosophy, engendered by the emotional reactions to violence, the enthusiasms of the evangelicals, the riots and revolts of the hungry, the military service requirements, the harvest failures, shortages and more.[65] Coastal towns with their harbours, docks, shipyards and busy commercial trading activities were both obvious targets by outsiders for bringing new ideas into the British Isles and important communication centres through which cultural content, military despatches and scientific findings – written material included – was transported in and out.

The long-term fascination with the fictional *Penhale Trilogy*, by Crosbie Garstin (1887-1930), and *Poldark*, by Winston Graham (1908-2003), takes our modern attention back to the time of Elizabeth and Maria Branwell, enlightening us about earlier customs, and so long as we are able to suspend our disbelief as to some of it, informing us of certain historical facts and details of recorded opinions and attitudes. They are not always very helpful, however, in determining what people read at the time.

We know that members of the Carne and Branwell families were literate and well-educated people, taking part in the political and educational activities of the town. But the details of what Elizabeth and Maria knew and read are difficult to establish. If we know little of the tales and poetry the Brontë children may have been told, or that they read in due course, proofs for the equivalent reading in the time of Elizabeth and Maria, in a quite different place, and with separate circles of potential influence, appear even more daunting. We know only of a short list of items belonging to Maria and probably also to Elizabeth, including the *Holy Bible*, the *Imitation of Christ, Methodist Magazines, The Lady's Magazine* and the copy, recently purchased by the Brontë Society, of *The Remains of Henry Kirke White*.[66]

However, the search for contemporaneous literature in the Carne-Branwell period has met with some interesting success. We can show *where* published fiction and poetry would have been available and make some educated guesses as to access and range for the Carnes and Branwells. We can also try to assess the enthusiasms and vitality of the period in which these families took an active part. Especially due to the literary work and connections of Elizabeth and Maria's cousin and friend John (Cock) Carne together with his distinguished national and international links to authors and educationalists, we have a long list of possible touchstones. With such as Davies (Giddy) Gilbert, Robert Southey, Richard Polwhele, the Batten circle of poet Ann Batten Cristall and her cousin Joseph Hallett Batten, Charles Valentine Le Grice, the Coleridges, the Quaker Fox family of Falmouth, the range of contacts and potential influence is much greater than might be expected for a small town on the periphery of Britain.

> Penzance may justly be proud of the many distinguished families and individuals connected with it: Clive, Fleming, Borlase, Tremenheere, Tonkin, Veale, John, Pellew, Batten, Carne, Davy, Boase, Colston, Giddy. It would require a volume to give even a slight history of each family and of its individual members...[67]

Though many of these families are genealogically connected to the Branwells, readers will note that the Branwells do not earn a mention – after all, they were wealthy grocers and property owners and their fame was temporal, locally political and economic rather than cultural in impact. There is no simple way of determining who and how amongst the people crowding the pages of the major histories of Cornwall, may have inspired or impressed the women – Maria and Elizabeth – without their own personal testimonies which we do not have. In Chapter 10, however, the key people closest to the Branwell family as a whole are identified occupationally, as engaged in teaching, preaching, publishing and travelling; this in itself indicates leanings which are cultural in nature, heavily laden with value-based materials of the wordy kind.

In Penzance, moreover, there was an unusually accessible general collection of reading material (and recorded in a handwritten journal kept up annually by the President), through the Ladies Book Club (1770-1912).[68] We have the list of the books that were ordered and read in the Club from 1770 through to its final choice of books in 1895. The book club, however, appeared to remain, at least in name until 1912, when it closed formally at a meeting held at Castle Horneck. There is no updated membership list accompanying the Minute Book for the Club moving through the decades to the twentieth century, but initially – before the births of Elizabeth and Maria – a number of their relations were part of the founding body of women who were readers, and some who for several terms of office (annually re-appointed) were Presidents who made the selection of books and journals.

From 1799 to 1818 there was also the Gentlemen's reading room, where newspapers and specialist journals were made available, especially through the war years. The Penzance Private Subscription Library grew out of these former 'clubs' to become the private subscription and lending library established first in 1818 at No 10 North Parade which it shared with the Royal Geological Society (founded four years previously), and then re-located in 1889 to its present location in Morrab Gardens. This magnificent set of unique collections, now entitled the Morrab Library, has just celebrated its bi-centennial year and continues in strength.[69]

Though not the first to take up the post of librarian, Joseph Carne FRS, was the librarian and general secretary and finally President of the Library from 1824 through to 1858.[70] Throughout its history it has been tightly connected to the Carne-Branwell family and others, inside and outside its local membership: researchers, authors, publishers and donors. Carne was known to purchase many of its books himself, and to encourage his relations to donate their collections to the Library. When his younger brother, John (Cock) Carne died in 1844, his fine collection of travel volumes, journals and biographies were moved from his home at the Abbey overlooking the harbour to the Penzance Library, a major donation.

Some local authors

Of the published writers of the Romantic era, perhaps the closest to the Branwells was one of their cousins by marriage (of which there were many, though not all were authors), the poet Ann Batten Cristall (1769-1848).

Maria Branwell's father, Thomas, and John Batten V (1739-1810), merchant and banker had grown up together in Penzance, in the same friendship circle and also related through marriages amongst the Tremearnes in that earlier time, both families stemming from Paul village outside of Newlyn. When Thomas Branwell died in 1808, John Batten the younger had taken over his father's legal and banking positions, and was specified by Thomas to be his executor. By this time, also, Thomas's son and Maria's brother Benjamin was already married to John the younger's sister Mary.

Portrait of Ann Batten Cristall (1769-1848) poet, painted by her brother Joshua Cristall, c1885, age about sixteen. First known publication of family miniature, presented for this family history.
Private collection.

Ann's place in the minor ranks of women's romantic poetry was to be secured with just one volume of poems published as *Poetical Sketches* in 1795, by the radical publisher Joseph Johnson.[71] Her circle of friends in London included the political philosopher Mary Wollstonecraft (1759-1797) and her sister Everina, the poet George Dyer (1755-1841), and an impressive array of other authors and well-known intelligentsia, both family and friends. The latter are presented in the subscribers' list appearing in the front of her volume. Further information about her and her interesting local family of Battens can be found in Chapter 10, 'Travellers' Tales.'

In a contribution to the *Cornish Story*,[72] Charlotte MacKenzie has uncovered a significant amount of information concerning Eliza Fenwick, a native of Penzance, a lesser-known writer of the Romantic period and an even closer friend of Mary Wollstonecraft. Of interest are the connections she reveals between Fenwick and another feminist radical novelist, Mary Hays,[73] with whom she was a close friend and correspondent for thirty years.

Due largely to her forthright self-assertion of women's rights and needs, Hays became a target for anti-feminist reviews, and was caricatured by the Cornish poet and historian Richard Polwhele in his poem, *The Unsex'd Females, a Poem* (1798). In that poem Hannah More is Christ, and Mary Wollstonecraft is taunted as Satan, while Mary Hays is lampooned as one of Mary's gang of those who over-reach their rightful place in domestic life. Hence we find, without doubt, many of the same issues of women's roles and women's education which are later found in the novels of the Brontë writers, and arise amongst the Chartists as well.

MacKenzie points to the fact that, "The earlier Cornish family origins of Ann Batten Cristall and Mrs Eliza Fenwick shared many similarities with the commercial activities and Methodism of the Branwells in Penzance. Eliza's father Peter Jaco was an itinerant Methodist preacher whose family had interests in the Newlyn pilchard fisheries and trade with southern Europe." She focuses for the first time on the impact of Fenwick's Cornish connections on her writing, and on her time as a Penzance shopkeeper in 1802-3. Her novel *Secresy or the ruin on the rock* was printed twice in 1795 by the author with an identified list of booksellers.... the gothic setting and plot of the novel both incorporated elements derived from Fenwick's knowledge of places and great landowning families in Cornwall, notably the Eliots of Port Eliot.[74]

Another local lady writer, also of distant kinship to the Branwells through the Keigwin family, was the gothic novelist, Thomasine Dennis, who published *Sophia St Clare* in 1806, also with Joseph Johnson of London. She was a self-taught farmer's daughter, mentored in the classics by the historian Davies Giddy (later Gilbert). Her novel, though said by Gilbert in print to be generally unsuccessful, was purchased by the Ladies Book Club in 1808, the year of Thomas Branwell's death. Very few novels were bought by the Presidents over the years, and hence it is likely that the two-volume horror story would have been requested and read by most of the members.

> Her superior genius displayed itself at a very early age, in reciting poetry from our best authors, and then in producing imitations of her own. 'She lisped in numbers from her mother's arms.' French was acquired with equal accuracy and facility; and then, observing that her eldest brother appeared to make an inadequate progress in Latin, occasioned by the entire want of attention on the part of the schoolmaster at Penzance, this young lady under eighteen studied a classic language for the mere purpose of helping forward her brother...the Roman author soon read, but the Greek writers followed in a rapid succession, till Aeschylus and Pindar became her familiar acquaintance.[75]

Recently, in re-reading *Sophia St Clare*, random thoughts about the structure and characters of her story, delivered in epistolary fashion, began to remind me of something. Then I started to think of Sophia taking on the role of Jane Eyre, and the pieces began to fall into a familiar order. Not exactly, mind you – there are a few differences but there are also even more similarities. Each is an orphan, being excluded from their rightful home and inheritance by selfish and unwilling relations. Both feel incarcerated – one in a convent, one in a school. Each falls in love only to be caught in moral dilemmas and forced into degrading choices. Both seek love with men seemingly out of reach socially, see frightening spectres and ghostly visions, both dream and run away to prevent loss of independence. The endings differ, and Jane's story is much the fuller, but the tropes and their depth of feeling and emotion are exceptionally close. I wonder if it is possible that Maria or Elizabeth Branwell took a copy of this novel north with them, and that it might have been slipped by candlelight into the tiny study bedroom shared by the sisters?

> Nothing of her poetry has been given to the public; nor would it now be fair to print a few trifles. Miss Dennis proved herself adequate to the occupation of any work in prose, by publishing in 1806, at Mr Johnson's in St Paul's Churchyard, 'Sophia St Clare' in name indeed a novel, but far superior in style of writing and in correctness of sentiment, to the fictions of the day. From the want of incident, however, similar to those which are characterised in the drama by producing stage effect, the work failed of becoming popular.[76]

Her poetry is part of the archival holdings in the Gilbert papers at the Cornwall Records Office. It may now be fair to look into 'a few trifles' of her work. Have we got a proto-Jane?

ENDNOTES

1 Ernest Raymond. *In the Steps of the Brontës*. Introduction. (London, Rich & Cowan 1949).
2 This refers to the gateway to the vault beneath the pavement of the church at Haworth where most of the family is buried.
3 A performance space, 'plen an gwary', employed in Cornwall in open-air theatrical rounds for entertainment and instruction in which Cornish-language miracle plays and communal games were performed. In western Cornwall (west of Truro) both the language and the playing places lingered and have modern resonance in such theatres as the Minack at Porthcurno built into the cliffs by Rowena Cade, and the open air theatre created at the rear of Penlee House Museum.
4 M A Courtney (1890) *Cornish Feasts & Folk-Lore*, Penzance: Beare & Son.
5 See Alan Kent, Ed, (2009) *Charles Valentine Le Grice: Cornwall's 'Lost' Romantic Poet: Selected Poems*, pp. 81-6: Notes and references on the publication and presentation of his named poems. Also see 'Biographical briefs', Chapter 11 for further detail on Le Grice.
6 W.H.K. Wright (1896) *West Country Poets, Their Lives and Their Works*, (London: Elliot Stock, 1896) p. 275
7 Deirdre Dare and Melissa Hardie *A Passion for Nature, 19th-Century Naturalism in the Circle of Charles Alexander Johns*, (Newmill, Penzance: Patten Press, 2008) Appendix III Publications of CAJ, pp. 214-222.
8 James Harrison Rigg, *The Life & works of Jabez Bunting*. pp.56-7: 'Early Ministry in London'.
9 Robert Were Fox the younger was a noted inventor, geologist and natural philosopher as well as a successful

Quaker merchant and shipping company magnate. His children Barclay, Caroline and Anna Maria with their parents were well travelled and intelligent observers who committed their thoughts to many social and educational actions. They were the originators of the concept and organisation of the Royal Cornwall Polytechnic Society of Falmouth which began educational reform for the miners and mariners and their families in Cornwall.

10 Also see: Robert Barclay Fox *(1979).Raymond Brett, Ed, Barclay Fox's Journal. (London:Bell and Hyman, 1979)*

11 *Journals of Caroline Fox,* Horace Pym, Ed., VI, pp. 22-3.

12 See Chapter 9 and Appendix C for a spoof story by the youthful Thackeray about his friend, Joseph (Thomas) Carne Jr.

13 M. Smith (1995) *The Letters of Charlotte Brontë 1829-1847* vol. 1, 241 and Note 25

14 James Turner (1975) *The Stone Peninsula, Scenes from the Cornish Landscape*

15 A large rock from a field near Heamoor, Penzance, was removed to a small Methodist Chapel to form the base of a pulpit. See Wesley Rock Chapel on-line. Another large granite stone at the head of the Zennor valley – also pointed out as one of the Wesley preaching places – stood as a pulpit to the open air amphitheatre lying below. Hundreds could gather to hear him speak.

16 The Royal Geological Society of Cornwall was formed in 1814, and both Joseph Carne and Benjamin Carne Branwell were founding members in the initial year. *Transactions* commenced in 1818, and publications of national importance by distinguished scientists from all over the world began to contribute and aid collaboration on mining and geological findings related to environmental sciences. Printing, publishing and binding took place locally.

17 F. E. Ratchford (1941) *The Brontës' Web of Childhood,* p. 7

18 The Bottrell family were cousins of the Branwells through the Sennen branch of both families. Mary Branwell (1776-1855) married Richard William Bottrell. William Bottrell, collector of legends and ghost stories, was born in St Levan in 1816 and was brought up by his grandparents whose stories from their childhoods began his passion for authorship and reportage.

19 William Bottrell (1870) *Traditions and Hearthside Stories of West Cornwall,*and Robert Hunt, *Popular Romances of the West of England, or The Drolls, Traditions & Superstitions of Old Cornwall.*

20 A piskie is a member of the Cornish fairy tribe, of small stature and wrinkled aged look with red hair, and wearing a pointed cap.

21 A knocker is also small in height, lives under the ground and dresses in standard miner's gear. His existence is known by the knocking sounds he makes when he is warning of impending danger in the mines, and comes from the creaking and breaking of beams before a mine collapse. Some think of him as a malevolent spirit, some as a saving grace.

22 A bucca is of the spirit folk, and may have to do with the wind and the havoc it can cause. Nineteenth-century fishermen were said to make offerings of food to the buccas, by leaving it for them on the beach. Revd. W S Lach-Szyrma interpreted Bucca as the "storm god of the old Cornish", or a devil.

23 The Mount was purchased in 1659 by the Colonel John St Aubyn; his modern descendent, Lord St Levan (also John St Aubyn) lived on the mainland until his death (2013), and has passed place and title to his nephew, James St Aubyn, who manages the public viewing with the National Trust. The Mount has been a 'place to visit' for local people and travellers making pilgrimage for many centuries.

24 A folk tale of renown world-wide, retold by every storyteller, but laced with question marks: Did Cormelian and Cormoran really build St Michael's Mount?

25 Robert Hunt *Popular Romances* 'Works of the Giants' p. 41.

26 Charles Thomas *Exploration of a Drowned Landscape, The archaeology and history of the Isles of Scilly,* 1985.

27 Quiller-Couch, Mabel and Lilian, (1894); *Ancient and Holy Wells of Cornwall.* Free download on-line.

28 John Carne (1789-1844) footnoted as *Tales of the West,* by the author of *Letters from the East.* See Biographical Briefs for further information about John's bibliography. Born in Penzance on Chapel Street, John was son of William (Johns) Carne and Anna Carne nee Cock, and younger brother of Joseph (Cock) Carne, in the same year as Charlotte (Carne) Branwell, daughter of Thomas (John)Branwell and Ann (Reynolds) Carne -Branwell, their second cousins.

29 Though Dinah Mulock, at the time of publication of *John Halifax, Gentleman,* had never been to Cornwall, it is revealed in the first chapter of the fictional novel that John Halifax was characterized as a Cornish orphan.

30 Dinah M Mulock (1884) *An Unsentimental Journey through Cornwall,* 1988 reprint with a Foreword by Professor Charles Thomas and bibliographic memoir by Melissa Hardie, pp.2-3.

31 Richard Holmes (2008) *The Age of Wonder, How the Romantic Generation Discovered the Beauty and Terror of Science,* xvi

32 Ian Soulsby (1986) 'The Cornish Language: An Tavas Kernewek', *A History of Cornwall,* IX, p. 72.

33 Paul White, (2000) 'Introduction' *Richard Carew's Survey of Cornwall 1602,* p. 5.

34 P A S Pool (1986) *William Borlase,* pp. 52-4

35 *Ibid*, pp.96-102.
36 A C Todd (1967) *Beyond the Blaze* Preface p. 7.
37 Joseph (Cock) Carne's granddaughter, Frances 'Fanny' Carne (only child of son William and his wife Fanny Cornish of Marazion) would later marry Thomas Polwhele of Polwhele, President of the Stannary Parliament of Cornwall. Curiously, in 1909, one of the executors of Thomas Polwhele's very large fortune was Edward Williams Carus-Wilson, possibly of the Carus Wilson family of Lancashire and the fictional school of Lowood in *Jane Eyre*.
38 Boase and Polwhele were in-law cousins of the Carne family.
39 T Percivel Bunting 1810-1885, The Life of Jabez Bunting: with Notices of Contemporary Persons and Events, V.I, pp.197-8
40 See Chapter 11, 'Biographical Briefs' for Dr Thomas Coke, who knew the Branwells and Carnes.
41 W J Townsend, H B Workman, & George Eayrs (1909) *A New History of Methodism*, Bk. 1 The Foundations of Methodism, vol. 1, pp. 220-223.
42 Maria Branwell (nd) as reprinted in The Shakespeare Head Brontë, edited by Wise and Symington, vol. 1, pp. 24-7.
43 Robert Southey (1820) *The Life of John Wesley* XIX, pp. .223-9.
44 *A Preservative Against Unsettled Notions in Religion* (1758) By John Wesley, M.A.
45 Oxford Centre for Methodism and Church History, Oxford Brookes University. See website for access.
46 Robert Southey to Richard Duppa (23 May 1807) Online commentary on Henry Kirke White.
47 *A Preservative Against Unsettled Notions in Religion*, By John Wesley, M.A. 14/04/2019 http://spenserians.cath.vt.edu/CommentRecord.php?action=GET&cmmtid=4842
48 B. Heritage, (2018) 'The Archaeology of the Book' in Charlotte Brontë: *The Lost Manuscripts*, pp. 22-69, Haworth: The Brontë Society.
49 Byron's unique connections with Cornwall are recorded in Chapter 11: 'Biographical Briefs'. Whether or not the Brontës knew of the Trevanion family grandparent is not known.
50 Jane Apreece was a popular hostess in both London and Edinburgh, and a family relation of Sir Walter Scott, the favoured novelist of the Brontës. In Anne Brontë's *The Tenant of Wildfell Hall* (1848) Gilbert Markham, brings the gift of an elegantly bound copy of *Marmion* to Helen Graham, the tenant, to whom he is attracted; she insists on paying for it, a gesture of independence which embarrasses their relationship for a period.
51 Until 1817 his surname was Giddy, but in that year he adopted his wife's surname of Gilbert so that they could acquire an uncle's large family estate in Sussex. From that time he was known as Davies Gilbert, though he preferred his original surname. See A C Todd (1967) *Beyond the Blaze*, Preface, p.9.
52 James Watt (1736-1819) Scottish inventor, and his son Gregory Watt (1777-1804), a geologist, became friends with Davy originally when Gregory lodged with the Davys in Penzance attempting recovery from TB. They visited Davies Giddy's home library together and became close friends. See also, Tann, Jennifer (2013) [2004]. Watt, James (1736–1819), *Oxford Dictionary of National Biography* (online ed.) Oxford University Press.
53 D.A. Stansfield, R.G. Stansfield, Dr. Thomas Beddoes and James Watt: *p*reparatory work 1794-96 for the Bristol Pneumatic Institute' *MedHist*, 1986, Jul. 30(3): 276-302 On-line article, *Cambridge Journals*.
54 Anna Maria Edgeworth, sister of the prolific novelist Maria Edgeworth (1768-1849), was the wife of Dr. Thomas Beddoes, and her father, Richard Lovell Edgeworth (1744-1817) assisted Dr Beddoes for some years in the laboratories.
55 Asa Briggs (1959) *The Age of Improvement 1783-1867 (*London: Odhams Press).
56 Richard Holmes (2008) *The Age of Wonder* (London: Harper Press)
57 Davies Gilbert (1838) *The History of Cornwall*, vol III, p. 100.
58 Robert Hunt (1885) 'Rodolph Eric Raspé, Author of *The Travels of Baron Munchausen*, Extract from *The Western Antiquary*, vol. 5, No. 4, September 1885, pp. 73-75: Paper given to the Camborne Old Cornwall Society.
59 Chisholm, Hugh, ed. (1911) "Raspé, Rudolf Erich" *Encyclopaedia Britannica* (11th ed.) (Cambridge, Cambridge University Press).
60 Of copper-producing mines, one of the largest and deepest in Devon and Cornwall: at the time of Raspé's employment there.
61 Robert Hunt (1885) *Ibid*, Note 1.
62 *Ibid*. John Hawkins, MP for Grampound, brother of Sir Christopher Hawkins, was educated at Helston School, Winchester College and Trinity College, Cambridge (1782). He was a founding member of the Royal Geological Society of Cornwall in 1814, and the Geological Society of London, in addition to his Fellowship of the Royal Society. His writings ranged from the history of art, sciences and general literature of distinction. His inheritance of the Trewithen Estate was a part of the 300-year occupation by the same family, today the home of Michael Galsworthy, a descendant, and the site of Trewithen nurseries and associated enterprises of this elegant 18th century mansion, which can be visited.

63 Duncan Wu, Editor (1999 reprint with CD-ROM) *Romanticism, An Anthology* (Oxford: Blackwell).
64 Rachel Hewitt (2017) *A Revolution of Feeling, The Decade that Forged the Modern Mind*,(London: Granta Publications, 2017).
65 See Penwith Local History Group (2000) *In and around Penzance during Napoleonic Times,* for anecdotal history in a series of essays.
66 See *Charlotte Brontë The Lost Manuscripts* (2018) and especially the contributions by Ann Dinsdale: 'Lost and Found' 10-21, and Barbara Heritage 'The Archaeology of the Book, pp. 22-69 already referenced separately..
67 Davies Gilbert (1838) *History of Cornwall,* vol III, pp. 94-5.
68 Margaret Seccombe Brown and John Simmonds (n.d., c 2000-2014) Archival register and papers, unpublished: Penzance Ladies Book Club, Initial membership (1770), Purchase list of books to 1912, List of presidents of circulating library. She points out that up until 1868, the women holding the presidency of the Book Club for a total of 98 years were Mrs John and her daughters the Misses Johns. These were all cousins of the Branwells, descendants of their grandmother's family. Also see Chapter 5: 'In the everyday'.
69 One of its strongest sub-collections is in Napoleonic studies. It was with great pride, for both organisations, that the Morrab Library trustees accepted in 2018 the donation of a landmark sub-collection, the gift of the Elizabeth Treffry Collection on Women in Cornwall and the Isles of Scilly from the Hypatia Trust.The Hypatia Trust was established first in 1996, jointly with the Special Collections Library of the University of Exeter, with the primary objective of re-discovering and replacing women's writings and achievements in the canons of literary history. Collections have since then been made available in Exeter, Cornwall, Barcelona, Bonn and other relevant venues. See www.hypatia-trust.org.uk.
70 See Penwith Local History Group (2005) *Treasures of the Morrab*, and the contribution by the late John Simmonds: 'The Morrab Library' 113-116.
71 Joseph Johnson (1738-1809) A London-based publisher and bookseller with broad and radical interests, and famous for his Tuesday night suppers to which he invited writers and campaigners; he published a wide range of political pamphlets, focusing too on the writings of dissenters. Another of his objectives was to introduce to the reading world more of the writings of women. He employed Mary Wollstonecraft as an editor.
72 The Cornish Story is an outreach project of the Institute of Cornish Studies, inviting contributions from subscribers and academics. (2019), www.exeter.ac.uk/visit/cornishstory,com.
73 Mary Hays (1759-1843) was a novelist and writer on women's lives and their educational needs. Historian Charlotte MacKenzie (April, 2019) has contributed two papers, one on Mary Hays and the other on Eliza Fenwick as Cornish connections with 1790s radical and literary circles to *The Cornish Story* (online archive).in 2019.
74 *Ibid*
75 Davies Gilbert (1838) *History of Cornwall,*vol III, pp.33-4.
76 *Ibid.*

Re-enactment by Professor A. Charles Thomas of John Wesley's arrival to preach in the open air at Gwithian, Cornwall. 300th anniversary of the birth of John Wesley, 28 June 2003. Private collection.

Chapter 4

....and then came Wesley

'I took a walk to the top of that celebrated hill, Carn Brea. Here are many monuments of remote antiquity scarce to be found in any other part of Europe: Druid altars of enormous size, being only huge rocks, suspended one upon the other; and rock-basins, hollowed on the surface of the rock, it is supposed, to contain the holy water.'

John Wesley, 1 September 1770 (*The Journal*)[1]

John Wesley, writing in the eighteenth century, here takes note of a Druidic spirit and interest which remains to this day in West Cornwall, and a community of nature worshippers and other spiritualists have long found it an accepting place for a variety of different believers and their practices. Partly, I suspect, this remains the reason for a broad tolerance of belief and disbelief in the population – and great good humour about the superstitions that abound.

Religious influences were not, however, merely indigenous. Evidence from as early as the Bronze and Iron Ages shows that between Ireland, Wales, Cornwall and Brittany there was a constant flow of traffic – an amazing exchange of people on missions of various kinds, trading and marauding through peace and war. Cornish historian Peter Pool points out that by the medieval period the maritime life of Penzance 'was no longer limited to fishing, for in 1425, 1432 and 1440, ships from Penzance were licensed to carry pilgrims to the famous shrine of St James of Campostella, in northern Spain.'[2]

Cornwall has often been described as the 'land of Saints', but not because of sacred behaviours. Many parishes, villages and towns all over the county bear the names of little known (or known about) holy men and women. Several Cornish dictionaries interpret these for those who are keen to study the legends accumulated around their names. The evidence is obscure, but it is clear that Cornish saints share some of the same characteristics memorialised in other so-called Celtic countries: Wales, Ireland, Scotland and Brittany. Hence they are usually referred to as the Celtic saints, as opposed to saints canonised within papal structures of the Holy Roman Empire.

As the saints came to Cornwall, primarily from the late 5th to the 6th centuries AD, their purposes were several: establishing chapels for contemplation, prayer and the hermit life, while also creating monastic dwellings for teaching and converting any pagans. They were missionaries, male and female, and often they arrived with broader knowledge and the ability to write and make records, symbolic or otherwise, i.e. marks confirming their presence.

Whereas one pilgrim or saint might come and remain, another would come, establish a chapel or settlement of some kind and then proceed to Brittany to repeat the performance. John Pearce[3] in his studies of early beliefs and the people that brought them, termed West Cornwall as something of a Celtic-fringe highway, circling without touching the Saxon hinterlands of Britain. Some saints' names remembered in Cornwall, in place-names given to villages and hamlets, are taken from Breton saints working in the reverse direction toward permanent residence in Ireland.

Prominent in Cornwall are such holy men and women as St Just, St Roach, St Mather (St Madern 1204 or today's Madron), St Breage, St Leven, St German, St Kea, St Austell, St Creet (*Sancti Sancreti* of 1235 or today's Sancreed), St. Sennen, St. Senara (Zennor) and how about St. Neot the Pigmy? There are many, many more, giving a special spice to the travelogue of Cornwall. When first encountering these strange and different names, a traveller often feels that he or she is treading on the soils of a 'foreign' land and should speak a different language. Some do!

In the centuries that followed, Cornwall, like the rest of Britain, saw the consolidation of Catholic Christianity which was then challenged by the Protestant Reformation. By the mid-eighteenth century, the Protestant Church of England was not only 'established' but seemed to some, at least, comfortable and complacent. This was the spiritual landscape to which John Wesley introduced Methodism, and it came very early to Cornwall, as the Methodist Archive records:

> Methodism was introduced into the neighbourhood of Penzance at the earliest possible date…for many years St. Ives was the headquarters of Methodism in the West. In 1746 England was divided into six Circuits, Cornwall being one of these. St. Ives retained the headship of a circuit until 1791 when Penzance [nine miles distant] took that position and comprised within its borders those places which now constitute nine circuits viz. Penzance, St Ives, Helston, Marazion, Hayle, Scilly Islands, St Just, St Keverne and Porthleven.[4]

John Pearce, in his very useful study of *The Wesleys in Cornwall*, pin-points the social class of families from which our protagonists emerge: the 'small gentry' in which West Cornwall abounded:

> These small gentry deserve a word to themselves. They have been compared by Charles Henderson with the *petite noblesse* of western Brittany.[5] The western parishes possessed families, in considerable number, whose names were recorded in the earliest of the parish registers. Many of them were armigerous [had the right to heraldic arms] and almost all of them connected by marriage with armigerous families. Their houses and their fortunes were modest; they had wit and morals and manners, and a refined

sense of the dignity of their family traditions. For the most part they lived peaceably in their habitations but, now and then, the odd individual would go forth into the great world and achieve distinction. Many of these families were deeply moved by the message of the Wesleys. Some of them never left the Anglican Communion, some left it for a while and returned to it again, some are still to be found in the Methodist Church. Wherever they worship today they have as a type made a great contribution to Methodism, and one which has never been acknowledged.[6]

The evangelical missions – consisting of open air preaching and emphasizing the need for personal conversion - led by John and Charles Wesley from 1743 in Cornwall were initially and roughly rebuffed, by the poor and rowdy because they were 'strangers', and by the wealthier as being traitors to their class. Perhaps this rough treatment was expressed more strongly in Penzance than in other parts of Cornwall due to dominance in public life of the Revd. Dr. Walter Borlase[7] who threatened Wesley with gaol, a charge he withdrew upon discovering Wesley was a 'Gentleman'.

As Cedric Appleby, Methodist historian, comments,[8] 'there were many reasons for the opposition to Wesley in the first instance. Despite the passage of about a century, the long memories of the English Civil War continued to cast a shadow; during that time charismatic religious groups appeared and threatened the fabric of the state. With the rise of Methodist "enthusiasm" people who already had their own line to God could well be, or were feared to be a threat to the constitution of eighteenth century government. The Jacobite uprising and invasion of 1745 proved a different cause of suspicion and accusations were made that the Wesleys were Jacobites and or Papists.' These were the conflicts fast and fiery in which the Brontë grandparents were being born and brought up.

Curiously, Wesley's missions were not unlike the forays of the early days when saints came and went. Persistence and continuity shown by the Wesley brothers and their 'saintly' preachers and a kind of 'sacred hunger' on the part of mining families, fisherfolk and small tradesmen for self-improvement, were, however, to transform the future for poor and rich alike, and not least for women. The self-confidence, community feeling and the drive to education occasioned by their influence is mentioned by virtually all commentators, even if certain of their revivalist actions were also criticised as mad and dangerous.

Most of all, the Wesleys were to bring Christian Fellowship back into the forefront of what had become a lazy and unenthusiastic body of people in the Church of England. The organizational attitude and psychological legacy of the equation has been long lasting; Pearce points out that in the first County Council set up in Cornwall (1889), no less than a third of its members were Methodists, and a large number of the two-thirds who were Anglican were also from families that had supported the civil and educational reforms introduced by the Wesleys. 'Well might Macaulay say of Wesley that his 'genius for government was not inferior to that of Richelieu'; it is not the least of the legacies he bequeathed us.'[9]

A close reading of Robert Southey's *The Life of John Wesley* clarifies not only the personalities surrounding Wesley, but summarises the means by which he sought to make converts. His review of 'lay-coadjutors', 'class meetings', 'watch nights' and 'love feasts' as well as Kingswood school and Methodism in Wales and Scotland, are clear and simple vignettes that make the time come alive.

Thus, though original reaction by the Cornish to the brothers Wesley had been rough and negative, by the time of his later visits there was a general change of heart, and, most interestingly for our purposes, a member of the Carne family was instrumental in this change. The Revd. John Horner, in his recent history of non-conformism in nineteenth century Penzance, identifies the reason:

> Amazingly, within a few years, the social standing of the Wesleyans in the borough changed completely. To be a member of a Wesleyan Society became no longer something about which to be defensive, embarrassed or apologetic. Quite the opposite. It was something that carried with it a bestowal of respect and acceptability. And this change was largely due to the life and character of one man: William Carne.[10]

Local historian Lilian Oldham records at several points in her Branwell-Carne archive that the introduction and conversion of William (John) Carne Sr. to the ways of Wesley occurred under the mentoring of Richard Andrew, a linen draper and later Freeman of the town of Helston.[11] To quote from one Cornish Methodist minister who was also a prolific religious historian, "Methodism reached down across the generations. It was in such communities of related people, humble for the most part, that Methodism became an ancestral faith. Those who were esteemed higher in the social scale of the time... were the natural leaders among them."[12] It is not known from what religious background other than the Church of England that cousin William came when convinced by Methodism, but his leadership once begun was known throughout the Duchy, and reference to him as 'father of Cornish Methodism' is often found.

The Branwell name is first mentioned in an early Methodist Society list (1767) as Jane (John) Branwell,[13] at the age of fourteen, who would later marry, and become Mrs John Fennell. However, it is clear from previous lists of members, that family members of the previous generation were already attached to the movement before this. Cousins Richard Woolcock, a shoemaker, his wife Alice (Bramble) Woolcock and their daughter, cousin Agnes Woolcock, unmarried, are also listed as members of the society. The occupational references are interesting, indicating small tradesmen, apprentices and shopkeepers amongst the men, with a preponderance of shoemakers/cordwainers, also a trade found amongst the Carnes.

The attendance at Methodist gatherings varied considerably across Cornwall, with a far greater constituency located in the western mining districts of the county. Though there are only piece-meal statistics available until the most comprehensive *Religious Census of 1851*, by that time the prevalence of non-conformism had grown to something approaching two-thirds in West Cornwall, the level in East Cornwall was nearer to one third. The patterns laid down while the parents of Maria and Elizabeth were children, and their later practices within the local congregations, would ultimately have contributed to the Branwell and Carne children's own understanding of piety and behaviours, as we can see, for instance, in Maria's letters to Patrick Brontë during their courtship, expressing her hope to be 'useful' to him in his sacred mission.

The Christian Mix – Anglican, Congregational and Quaker

Despite their serious commitment to Methodism, however, most of the families studied here were born into, and reared within the customary attendance – baptism, marriage and burial and weekly services in between – at the parish church, as they 'belonged to do'. Attending the public preaching of the Wesleys – indoors or outdoors - and later their local preachers and itinerant ministers, did not alter family patterns of Church attendance. Their open air addresses were open to all and joining an audience for these did not automatically imply conversion. Within the dissenting groups there was something of a revolving door. John and Charles Wesley, of course, died while still in the ministry of the Church of England, even though they were prescient enough to see that the split between Church and Chapel was not far away.

Careful attention was always paid to the holding of gatherings for revival and evangelizing outside of Church hours. The general routine for Sundays amongst the Methodists of the period was that recommended by Wesley, at hours that he appointed. The morning should begin at nine so as not to interfere with [Parish] Church service and to ensure that both might be attended: at nine in the morning, Wesleyan Chapel; at eleven, Church, at three in the afternoon, Church again; and in the evening once more it was time for the Chapel.[14]

The Parish Church for Penzance was at this time at Madron, but in Penzance itself there was St Mary's chapel-of-ease for local churchmen, under the auspices of the Vicar of Madron.[15] This was easier for the town's inhabitants to attend for prayers and occasional sermons, especially in wet weather when muddy roads became great mires and there was no transport, except by foot.

The seating plan of St. Mary's Chapel, in 1824, reveals probably the largest box in the building as belonging to Branwells, and a marginally smaller one to the widow of Benjamin Carne Branwell next to John Batten's family box, her brother. The perpetual curate of the time was the Revd. Charles Valentine Le Grice with whom the whole family, Branwell and Carne, Methodist or not, would have been on familiar terms.[16] They were, in other words, embedded in the established church.

The inaccessibility of the main Parish Church at Madron village also aided the spread of Methodism, since its members were willing to hold services in followers' homes and small chapels dotted about the whole landscape of Penwith, whereas attendance at Madron Church involved a long walk into the village from around the peninsula. During the lives of Maria and Elizabeth's parents, however, buildings dedicated to Methodist worship began to be erected, and the Carne family were important in this development.

From 1791 Penzance took the headship of a circuit of Methodist ministers that would later split into nine circuits as the congregations grew. Richard Treffry Sr. (See

Biographical Briefs, Chapter 11) had been one of the five ministers to be assigned in 1797 and to make an acquaintance with the Carnes, the Branwells and the Fennells which would continue through and between the two territories of Cornwall and Yorkshire. The following year Fennell was enabled with Treffry's encouragement to form a regular Sunday School for the Methodist society at Hayle. Treffry was later a future governor of Woodhouse Grove School in Yorkshire, but some years after Fennell had left the Headship to take Anglican orders.

William Carne Sr., merchant and banker, and John Fennell, schoolmaster, were two of the seven trustees to sign the indenture in 1799 allowing the 'people called Methodists' to construct and use a Preaching House or Chapel on land in the parish of Germoe, across Mount's Bay away from Penzance on the road to Helston.[17] Both of these men were known to be Anglicans of Wesleyan faith and practice. Neither wanted a breakaway from the established church; they did want discussion and renewal of commitment to God's work. One local churchman of that same strong opinion and concern, known to both William Carne and John Fennell, was John Martyn,[18] the father of the missionary Henry Martyn (1781-1812), curate to Charles Simeon at Cambridge, and supportive friend at St. John's College to Patrick Brontë.

Chapel Street Methodist Chapel, with its community centre-cum Sunday school building beside it, sits four doors away from the house where the Carne-Batten bank was established on the ground floor, the present author's next door neighbour. In the chapel buildings both William and Joseph Carne held their classes and dispensed both charity and advice. Plaques and windows bear witness to both the Branwell and Carne families, and the Brontë Society has also placed brass plates in memory of Elizabeth and Maria.

In fact, Maria would never have been in the Chapel building, nor seen it. The campaigns to raise the funds and to secure large family donations for the new Chapel had begun before the death of Thomas, but it did not become operational until 1814, when Maria was already in Haworth. Before this, the Wesleyan group of which the Branwells and Carnes were a part met in a Queen Street building that Wesley himself preached in, and which he described as 'considerably the largest and in many respects, far the best in Cornwall.' The new chapel was designed to emulate the Wesley Chapel in London. Though Maria's father and mother contributed to the purchase of the land and development of the new chapel they did not live to see it built. Nevertheless the family imprint was strongly recognised through finance provided by William Carne and his son Joseph.

Despite their Wesleyan allegiance, all of these men and their families are buried in graves and mausoleums in Anglican parish churchyards: William Carne and his kin at Gulval where they had previously lived, Joseph and family at Phillack, Hayle, where he had first worked for the Cornish Copper Company and where almost all of his children with Mary Thomas (of Wales) were born. The Branwell mausoleum sits in the parish churchyard directly behind their home. There were also clergy who were recognised within the Church of England as strongly 'Methodist' who had no intention of leaving that Church, and never did so. Amongst these were Branwells,

Carnes, Battens and many others, who in Cornwall were frequently referred to as 'methodies', due to their serious and conscientious methods of Christian practice. Though not all of these were clergy, it was not uncommon if well-educated that one or two of the sons would indeed be clerks in the Church of England, or ministers in non-conformist congregations.

The Christian Mix – the Anglican Inheritance

Before the Wesleys arrived, the Anglican Branwells and Carnes were not only parishioners but also clerics. The earliest Anglican-related ancestor known to be connected to the Branwell line is the Revd. John Tremearne, the vicar of the Royal Peculiar parish of St. Buryan at the time of the Spanish invasion and sacking of West Cornwall, in 1595. Descent from his family produced in 1674 Jane Tremearne, who married Martyn Bromwell, as his second wife, in 1705. The marriages of Jane's sisters, Dorcas into the scholarly Keigwin fold in Mousehole and Paul (St. Pol de Leon), and Susan who formed the first connection with the successful merchant family of Battens, provided a bank of antiquarians who valued traditional learning and spirituality. It is noted in Chapter 9, concerning the West Cornish strain of the Carne family that they were, from the fourteenth century, on kinship terms with the Keigwin family as well.

In the period we are interested in, however, Anglicans and non-conformists regularly appear within the same families. Benjamin Carne Branwell, Maria's only living brother, was not a Methodist in practice and his wife's family of Batten brothers and cousins included evangelical Anglicans as well as Independents/Congregationalists. Maria and Elizabeth's Cousin Joseph (Cock) Carne (1782-1856), eldest son of the William Carne, was baptised in the nonconformist chapel in Truro and educated at Keynsham Wesleyan school near Bristol. He later sent his own first son, Joseph (Thomas) Carne Jr, to Charterhouse in London, perhaps because John Wesley had received his schooling there. Joseph kept the Methodist book-room in his own house in Chapel Street during his lifetime.

The brother of Joseph, Cousin John (Cock) Carne, the author, was ordained in the Anglican Church but never took charge of a parish in any capacity. When at home from his literary travels, he often preached in local Methodist chapels. Much of his later literary work was biographical in nature and concentrated on the inspiring stories of important missionary figures. In summary, two of William Carne's sons - John, the author, and his younger brother James Carne DD - were ordained Anglican clergy, as were later nephews and cousins.

When Wesley paid his last visit to Penzance,[19] it is thought that he slept in William and Anna Carne's house in what is numbered today as 15 Chapel Street. His visit was in the year prior to John Fennell's marriage to Jane Branwell, and would have been the final time that Fennell would hear the great man preach. Such an experience of hosting Wesley would also affect William's sons, Joseph (7) and even John (5), who were ever after loyal Wesleyans and active in their missionary activities.

As well as these rather fluid connections with the Anglican Church, the Carne family was also connected to an unambiguous branch of the Anglican establishment through the Colenso family, when Eleanor Calensow [*sic*] married Henry Carne and thus became the maternal great-grandmother of Maria and Elizabeth. Two men of this family loomed large in the religious history of Cornwall: the Revd. William Colenso FRS (1811-1899) of Penzance and Napier, New Zealand (from 1834), and the Revd. John William Colenso (1814-1883), of St. Austell, much later Bishop of Natal, South Africa.

Each of these Colensos was controversial, creative, literary and outstanding in his own way. William Colenso of Penzance and New Zealand, especially, might have been followed in correspondence by Aunt Branwell, since he was a significant member of her mother's connections. Sam Colenso[20] and Mary Veale, William Colenso's parents, were both part of the circle of young people growing up contemporaneously with the Branwell family. Their eldest son, William, privately educated and apprenticed to a St. Ives printer, was selected by the Church Missionary Society (CMS) of which the Carnes were prominent members, to carry the Christian message to the Maori population of New Zealand.

The Christian Mix – Varieties of Non-Conformism

If there were many gradations of belief and practice between Anglicanism and Methodism, however, there was an equal variety both within Methodism itself, and between Methodism and other non-conformist groups. By the time of John Wesley's death, Methodism was understood as more than just a movement embracing only those that belonged to John Wesley's Societies. Whitefield, whose leadership role has often been ignored by Methodist historians, formed Calvinistic Methodist Societies, which did have considerable impact. As well as Whitefield, preachers such as Howell Harris and others in connexion with the Countess of Huntingdon were important in the Methodist movement. A chapel devoted to this connexion today of Calvinistic Methodists is located on Fore Street, St. Ives, just below the entrance to Salubrious House.

Class distinctions were also developing even within Methodism. Thomas Shaw, in his *History of Cornish Methodism*, gives us an account of a Methodist class leader (Sunday School) called

> Miss Philippa Tyack[21], a member of the Branwell family of Penzance, and a cousin of the Brontës of Haworth, who was a class leader of a different type as we may judge when we read that she regularly met two classes 'composed of the daughters of our better-to-do families, and that 'despite her taste and temperament, she was not repulsed by revival 'scenes'. She defied the custom of the time by wearing a red shawl. It is clear from these short quotations alone that two types of Methodism were developing within Wesleyan Methodism itself.[22]

Philippa Tyack, described as 'a cousin of the Brontës of Haworth', was an in-law of their parents' generation. A clue to the changing nature of Methodist practice and spiritual habits in Penzance, in the Bronte sisters' own generation, can be gleaned from a letter written by their cousin Elizabeth Carne (1817-1873) to her friend Emily Bolitho. It shows that despite Elizabeth's broad sympathies for Methodist thinking and practice, she was not one for public demonstration or of revivalist temperament:

> I have always felt the defect of my prayers to be, that they are more like passing wishes breathed to the air than real petitions offered to One who has promised to hear and answer them. I do not realize in prayer the presence of God, and that always makes them cold and lifeless. I hardly know if you will recollect what you said in your note—it seems so long ago, but you asked me if I ever felt a wish to pray with those I loved. No, I never did. To pray for them I can well understand, or even to pray with them, so far as to enjoy the same time and form of prayers when separate; but to kneel beside them and speak aloud my petitions to God—no, I do not think I ever could do this to any earthly being. Do you really mean to say you have often done this and enjoyed it? And more astonishing still that Letitia C---has done it? I am far more surprised, knowing her timid disposition, that she should ever have done it, than that she should now decline doing it. [23]

The letter gives a fascinating glimpse into the internal varieties of Methodist attitudes as they were affected by class and the passing of time.

The first non-conformists to set up as a Christian religious group in Penzance, however, were not the Methodists but the 'Congregationalists'. When the Anglican Vicar of St. Hilary was evicted from his living for his failure to comply with the *Act of Uniformity* (1662), he commissioned the building of a chapel on Market Jew Street, on the south side, not far from the butcher's shop owned by Martyn Bromwell. This was where his local followers congregated with 'the right to define and govern their own affairs' – hence the name.

Joseph Batten, the Congregationalist minister in the 1770s, is interesting in the context of this study since he was contemporary with Maria's parents, Thomas Branwell and Ann Carne, and had similar interests in both business and learning. Their wider merchant businesses worked side by side, and both were heavily active in religious and civic affairs. The Batten family home, like that of the Carnes and the Branwells, was in Chapel Street, directly adjacent to their joint banking offices, in the building now named The Regent (No. 54),[24] and some of their Batten cousins were active Congregationalists (Independents).

In addition to the Methodists and Congregationalists, at least a goodly part of their Carne cousins and close friends were Quakers. Cousin Philip Carne's family, in his marriage to Elizabeth James, daughter of Peter and Elizabeth James, were members of the Quaker Societies of both Penzance and Marazion. The Quakers, to whom their mother Ann Carne's family was largely affiliated, had their own Meeting House in Market Jew Street, and another, still standing today, in Marazion, adjacent to St. Michael's Mount. Both of these strong influences – Congregationalist and Quaker - have been overlooked until now, and thematically could bear further exploration. As the circle of Carne and Branwell relationships have come under closer scrutiny, attributes of simplicity, plain-ness of dress, and quiet independence are easily identified in their interactions.

The Baptists were another non-conformist group active in Penzance, and one interesting member of this group, a more distant but contemporary relation of the Branwell parents, was Lydia Bunster Gwennap (1772-1854), born in Falmouth, the daughter of the founders of the Emmanuel Baptist Church there. When she married John Broadley Wilson at Plymouth she became a member of the Clapham circle, a group of notable evangelical reformers centred on William Wilberforce.[25]

Another member of the Clapham Sect was Charles Simeon, who was well known to Patrick Brontë during his time at Cambridge University. Together Lydia and John Broadley were to establish their marital home at Broadlands in Clapham, in eleven acres of walled grounds adjoining those of Henry Thornton at Battersea Rise House to the north and the private road to William Wilberforce's Broomfield to the south. They were to remain modestly in nineteenth century philanthropy's shadows but to contribute heavily, as did his father Francis Wilson, to massive efforts of evangelical reform and the anti-slavery movement. Lydia Gwennap's career is another example of the fluid boundaries between non-conformist and evangelical Anglican circles.

By 1900, in Penzance, the Christian mix was rich indeed. By this time, the Methodists alone had five varieties, the Baptists one, the Quakers one and the Congregationalists another. The Salvation Army and the interdenominational Seamen's Mission completed the ten, in addition to the Churches of England and Rome and the Jewish synagogue. All of these were available by choice to something over 2,200 residents.

A large literature traces the ins and outs of this continuously splintering body of Christian believers. Though this volume will not attempt to delve into doctrinal issues raging within the wider evangelical movement, the vital part – both socially and politically - played by religion in the lives of our Cornish families, and in turn amongst the Brontës, as reflected in their writings, cannot be overlooked. In this regard (spiritually) we are finding people of independent spirit, who see their lives as part of God's purposes.

Sunday Schools[26]

Methodist Sunday schools were developed on principles of belief in the sacred scriptures, education and self-improvement. The need for believers to be able to read and to interpret those scriptures, and other publications that were to become part of the chain of Methodist book rooms, was therefore of critical import. Wesley recommended for daily use the prayers and litanies brought together by Jeremy Taylor in *The Golden Grove*, and from 1735 had published in full *The Imitation of Christ* by Thomas à Kempis for the use of his followers. The Brontë Parsonage Museum at Haworth holds the copy of this work that belonged to Maria Branwell.

For some local children the Sunday schools would provide the only 'formal' education they received. This was not the case for the children of Ann and Thomas

Branwell, nor of the Carne family and their contemporaries from the 1780s and '90s forward. Within this wider family network, however, from the earliest period were several ordained clergy amongst the Tremearns, the Battens and the Carnes, ordination being the baseline employment of many educated men. Some colleges, such as Trinity College, Cambridge, and its near neighbour, St. John's, were favoured colleges amongst the Cornish, and these required ordination for the degree to be taken or a fellowship to be conferred.

It is highly likely that both Elizabeth and Maria were assistants in the Sunday schools in the Methodist society of Penzance, just as their cousin William Carne, and Thomas Branwell's brother-in-law, John Fennell, were class leaders. Certainly, within her marriage years and with her relations and friends, Maria had on-going role models in her aunts, uncles and cousins (male and female), and their revered associates.

A Branwell daughter marries into 'methody'

In 1800, Jane Branwell, elder sister to Maria and Elizabeth, and now the eldest surviving daughter of Ann and Thomas, married a Methodist minister, Mr. John Kingston (1769-1824) who had travelled in the itinerancy and missionary fields of the West Indies and America for some eight years.[27] Arriving after a year spent preaching in Wales to join the Penzance circuit in 1799, Kingston was to become an intimate part of their Carne - Branwell circle and then some years later to bring a heavy measure of disgrace on their heads.

The ensuing scandal involved theft and sexual immorality in Shrewsbury, Shropshire, not far from Madeley, the birthplace and early home of the influential Penzance schoolteacher, John Fennell. We have no evidence of how much this influenced or was known to the local circles back in Penzance, though here is one of the tracks worth following where further study may prove fruitful to Brontë story lines.

Thomas Branwell died the year (1808) following John Kingston's expulsion by trial from the Methodist conference. That Thomas knew of his daughter Jane's plight is documented in his Will, but without personal comment. He makes clear that the money he is giving her as a legacy is ring-fenced and cannot be employed by her husband, John Kingston. Jane Branwell Kingston and her youngest infant of the five children born to her, arrived back in Penzance from America, where John had fled, soon after his dismissal from Wesleyan conference. Though the Kingstons did not divorce, they were never reconciled.

Not all of the Branwells or Carnes exhibited Methodist leanings, and certainly over time, allegiances waxed and waned. The expulsion of John Kingston from the Methodist conference and ministry and the breaking of the Kingston marriage into two separate parts, could well have influenced the family's whole attitudes toward religious practices and beliefs. But this is unlikely, as human failings are universal, to be found in most families at some unpredictable point and in any case, few details of this 'scandal' would have emerged; the Methodist Conference made no public comment and it did not hit the press in Shropshire or the West Country at the time though it is recorded (without specification of the 'immorality') in the Wesleyan Conference proceedings.

The spiritual character

A brief obituary of William Carne's wife Anna (Cock) Carne in 1822 embodies qualities that Elizabeth and Maria, who knew her from childhood, would have considered worthy of emulation:

> At Penzance, Mrs Carne, the late wife of William Carne, Esq., aged nearly seventy years. "She was a woman of sound Christian experience, uniform piety and extensive benevolence. When health and weather would permit, she wandered, with her pilgrim's staff, through the streets, lanes, and courts, seeking out the needy and the distressed, who she relieved with food or clothing, as their circumstances required. Yet she trusted not for salvation in her own works; although, while her whole dependence was on Christ, she knew that 'faith without works is dead.
>
> *Wesleyan-Methodist Magazine*, Vol. 1 of 3rd series, Vol. XLV, p. 822.

John Wesley condemned as 'damnable nonsense' the Calvinist doctrine of 'once in grace, always in grace'. Exclusivism and damnation were particular 'dislikes' of Wesley, whereas his message, he believed, was to offer joy and dedication and salvation through faith. Inevitable then was the importance in the lives of those called Methodists:

 *to be aware of the needs of the poor;
 *to be serious about both prayer and self-examination;
 *to learn so that the knowledge can be shared and employed, and
 *to be useful to one's family, friends, and those who are loved.

Evidence of how this affected the local Cornish communities in the far west, within whose confines the Branwells and Carnes lived with their extended families, is speculative in reference to individuals, but abundant in relation to the communities as a whole. Therefore, though Maria and Elizabeth and some of their siblings, along with aunts, uncles and cousins were known to be active in non-conformist circles -Wesleyan Methodism, Congregationalist and Quaker - we still do not know the nature of their personal religious practices, other than faithfully reading the Bible and other religious texts, saying their prayers and sewing for the poor. All of these characteristics are shared equally by the Brontë children, and were formative from all sides.

Maria's faith and probably Elizabeth's as well, can as easily be described as well within the broad stream of evangelical Anglican piety -a kind of Christian humanism, as explained by philosopher and theologian, James Woelfel, in relation to the spirituality of Anne Brontë.[28] This was most certainly the ambience and style amongst the so-called 'better-to-do' friends and relations amongst whom they mixed, both in Cornwall and in northern circles. And, I suspect, that this was the natural spirituality that Anne received with gratitude from her Aunt Branwell; Anne, more than the other Brontë siblings, found a mother in Elizabeth.

The family responses by the Carnes and the Branwells to their community appears to have been generosity, friendliness and piety, with a leaning, if in any one direction, toward Quakerism. Pietism was a major influence on the Wesleys, especially in the earliest years of the Methodist movement. By occupation and by marriage their lives were part of the spiritual network of the communities in which they lived at a time of unusual turbulence and upheaval. Their family instincts and actions can only be described as seeking to be useful in terms of their known philanthropy and love. Amongst Maria Branwell's books was a copy of the book which Wesley called his "great and old companion", *The Imitation of Christ*, despite his reservations as to some of the more dire messages it contained.[29]

The Brontë Connection

One of the earliest scholars to recognise the importance of the Methodist tradition in the lives and works of the Brontës was Elsie Grace Harrison in her book, *The Clue to the Brontës*, which documents her search 'for the hidden influence which had dictated the character of the Brontës'.[30] The first link in the chain of evidence which she identified was a relationship between Patrick Brontë, his Irish patron Thomas Tighe, and Wesley's travelling preachers in Ireland. Tighe's home was an inviting centre for these spiritual leaders of thought and Christian learning, and thereby a source at first hand to inspire the young Branty.

When Patrick Branty, later Brontë, travelled from his native Ireland to study at Cambridge University, he brought with him a spirit of Methodism which led naturally to a close association with evangelical Christians at Cambridge. Charles Simeon (1759-1836) was an evangelical 'bridge' between Methodism and Anglicanism known to many in their various passages in life. Simeon's Curate at Holy Trinity parish in Cambridge, Henry Martyn, was a bridge to Cornish Methodism, since his father, John Martyn, was a Cornish contemporary of William Carne and John Fennell.[31]

All of the religious influences – as enumerated in the background of Patrick Brontë – are more than matched, if not submerged, by the background of Anglican Methodism in the personal lives of the Branwells and Carnes. Direct ties between the Branwell-Carne clans, Cambridge University and the Clapham Sect, of which Simeon was a part, are especially revealed through their Batten and Venn family links. This means that when Patrick and Maria finally met in the Yorkshire school run by 'Uncle' Fennell, they recognised in each other a similar form of Wesleyan piety.

In particular, Maria adopted as her creed Wesley's insistence that a Christian life should be a useful one. In the letters that we have from Maria to Patrick during their courtship she stresses her desire to be useful to him: 'Pray much for me that I may be made a blessing and not a hindrance to you.' *[Maria Branwell to Patrick Brontë, 1812].*

Wesley's dictum that the Christian should be always active and useful is also reflected in the simple essay that Maria wrote on the positive nature of poverty. Not least are these same sentiments related by Anne Brontë, perhaps most influenced by the care of Aunt Branwell, in her novel *Agnes Grey*. The spirit that shines through the letters of Maria to her intended husband, whom she takes as a spiritual as well as a physical companion is well described by Phyllis Mack in her provocative and insightful study of Methodism and the bringing of 'heart religion' and inspiration to the tables of believers.[32]

Without a more thorough investigation of their words, actions and familiar activities, to say that Maria and Elizabeth were Methodist as opposed to other sorts of Christian pietism, means very little. However much we theorise, based on the possession of Maria's letters and her essay on the advantages of poverty, Aunt Branwell's teapot, use of snuff (a social nicety common amongst Penzance women) and possession of *Methodist Magazines* and perhaps the texts of their samplers, the truths of their spiritual practices will always remain shadowlike rather than firmly documented.

At the same time, shadows also leave imprints, and therefore have potential influence. It is without question that the Branwells and Carnes came from a progressive Wesleyan background identified as 'Arminian'. That is, they belonged to the group of Methodists who, following Arminius (1560-1609), rejected the idea of predestination and affirmed the freedom of the human will by the individual believer. There is no impression at any point in this study that the Branwell or Carne families harboured any sympathy for Calvinistic doctrines.

John Wesley was influenced significantly by the beliefs of the Moravians, perhaps especially by the missionary work of Count Nicolaus Zinzendorf, who was a Moravian Bishop of Saxony, and who preceded him to the Americas. Zinzendorf brought forward 'religion of the heart' and the community of loving spirits who had their own congregational relationship with God. Present-day readers may be puzzled to learn that Anne Brontë, in a crisis of personal faith, appealed to a Moravian minister, but in doing so she was appealing to one of the roots of her Wesleyan beliefs.[33]

To a large extent, I would share Elsie Harrison's view that a major stimulant to the characters of the Haworth Parsonage household and possibly *the most prominent one*, is the imprint, the enthusiasm and the altruistic bent to teach new standards of behaviour that Methodism introduced. The Branwells and Carnes were Church of England Methodists or so-called 'Church Methodies' who found the Wesleys to be wise and rational leaders with humane instincts and large hearts. There is no evidence as yet discovered, that puritanical, narrow, strict or moralistic characteristics are to be found in Branwell and Carne dealings or personalities, and there is, therefore, no reason to suspect much, if any, doom, gloom or opinionated outlook in religious matters emanating from the Branwell women who mothered the Brontë children.

A 'character'

'They remembered at Trewellard House, home of John Bennetts[34] in the early days, that Wesley had asked them to refrain from taking sugar in their tea. This was to be their protest against slavery. See here the genius of the man in leading an illiterate people! The symbol has never been forgotten and to this day the tradition remains that 'the Cornish do not take sugar in their tea'….The last letter he [Wesley] wrote in extreme old age was addressed to Wilberforce, asking him to play his part in removing this stain [slavery] from the national character, but already his own efforts were bearing fruit in public opinion.'

Taken to heart by Charlotte Brontë

In 1708 when John Wesley was five years old, his large family home took fire. He did not wake up when the call to evacuate sounded through the rooms. The crowd below in the yard, bolstered by neighbours, saw the small boy standing on the ledge of an upstairs window in the flaming light. Climbing a wall and some willing shoulders, a villager pulled the boy out, just before the whole house collapsed around them and burning to the ground. Safe in his mother's arms, he often referred in later life to himself as "a brand plucked from the burning," quoting Zechariah 3:2. "Is not this a brand plucked out of the fire?"[35]

Jane Eyre, describing the awesome pleas of St. John Rivers as he prayed to convince her of the Godly duties she would fulfil by agreeing to marry him and travel with him to the mission field. "He supplicated strength for the weakhearted [*sic*]; guidance for those whom the temptations of the world and the flesh were luring from the narrow path. He asked, he urged, he claimed the boon of a brand snatched from the burning." (*Jane Eyre*, Folio edition, 402)

ENDNOTES

1 Carn Brea is a hill lying between Camborne and Redruth in the mining district of West Cornwall, one of the 'high places' in the chain from Land's End where bonfires are lit, a pagan ritual employed for Midsummer Eve (St. John's Eve and for times of danger, as a warning: at Sennen, Sancreed Beacon, Carn Galver to the Tamar.
2 Pool, *History of Penzance*, p. 19 and footnote.
3 John Pearce (1964) *The Wesleys in Cornwall*, See Bibliography.
4 Extract from 'Ministers appointed to the Penzance Circuit from its Formation, 1791', RIC: Methodist Archive, Courtney Library, RIC.
5 Charles Henderson (1900-1933) Cornish historian and antiquarian, his mother was a Carus-Wilson of Westmoreland. His collection of some 16,000 ancient documents, many transcribed by him, are held by the Courtney Library, RIC.
6 John Pearce (1964) *The Wesleys in Cornwall*, Introduction, pp. 21-2.
7 William Borlase, FRS (1695-1772) Geologist, naturalist and antiquarian, Borlase was the Rector of Ludgvan (nr. Penzance) and the younger brother of the Vicar of Madron, the Rev Walter Borlase, who also twice doubled as Mayor of Penzance (1756,1765). The latter was the Magistrate who responded so vehemently to the Wesleys, thinking they were Jacobite spies. [Pool, p. 90-1 and note 17 following, pp. 77, 46] and not William (as often quoted.)
8 John Wesley's *Journal*, 2 July 1745; also J H Barr (1916) Early Methodists under Persecution, p. 154. Private communication C. Appleby, 2016 via e-mail.
9 E P Thompson (London, Gollancz, 1968, reprinted with revisions) *The Making of the English Working Classes*.
10 *Even in this Place, 19th-century Nonconformists & Life in the Borough of Penzance* (2010) Chapter 3: 'A parcel of mad, crazy-headed fellows' p. 23.
11 Standard Edition of *John Wesley's Journal*, vol. V, 144 (fn) and vol. VIII, 4 relating Helston visits when R. Andrew was his local host, who later became owner of St John's Chapel on the old road out of Helston to Penzance. Andrew was made a Freeman of the town of Helston in 1818, as was his son later. Both were leading Wesleyans.
12 Thomas Shaw (1967) *A History of Cornish Methodism*, Chapter 4 'The Great Advance' p. 64.

13 Jane Branwell (1753-1829) Jane was the sixth child and third daughter of builder Richard Branwell and his wife Margaret John. Her name is listed in the Methodist Archives list: 'The Methodist Society in Penzance 1 July 1767', at which time she would have been 14-15 years old. She is listed as Jane Branwel, unmarried, and one of a group of 32 members, of which twelve were male and eight were married. Of the twenty women listed, ten were married.

14 'Extracts from Two Small Note Books written by Mr Roberts of Gulval early in the Nineteenth Century' in Courtney, R A (1909) *"A Passell of Ould Traade"* pp. 53-4.

15 The Revd. Dr. Walter Borlase LLD (1694-1776), Magistrate, mining adventurer & official of the Stannary Parliament, and Vicar of Madron and Morvah, led the vitriolic opposition to the Wesleys in the earliest years 1743-7, the years during which both Ann Carne and Thomas Branwell were born. Later Borlase was to soften his attacks and to broaden his own outlook.

16 See Biographical Briefs. CV was a romantic poet, friend of Coleridge, Lamb, Southey, and Cambridge-educated tutor to the Nicholls family of Trereife. He married the widow Nicholls (the former Mary Usticke) in 1798, with whom he had one son, Charles Day Perry Le Grice. The Trereife estate remains in the same family today.

17 Indenture, Trustee list found and transcribed by Pauline Geake, Sid Geake and Molly Smith, with thanks: 21 May 1799, being an indenture between Joseph Sleep of Germoe and seven named Trustees.

18 Henry Martyn's father, John Martyn, was a "captain" or mine-agent at Gwennap, near Truro. It lends its name to *Gwennap Pit* where John Wesley preached eighteen times between 1762 and 1789. In the 18th and early 19th centuries Gwennap parish was the richest copper mining district in Cornwall, and was called the "richest square mile in the Old World" (Cornwall Council, 2009 Mining Heritage on-line).

19 John Wesley visited Penzance on 32 occasions, the final visit concluding on the 8th of August, 1789, when Elizabeth was thirteen years old and Maria was six. They like the Carne and Davy children would have heard him speak in the open air preaching at the Star Inn. Humphry Davy was said to have received a pat and a blessing from the saintly man.

20 Samuel May Colenso was a Master Saddler of Penzance and he and his wife Mary Veale Thomas were second cousins of the Ann Carne Branwell. Whether or not this is the same family of Veales from which a daughter, Catherine, was to produce Richard Veale (later Branwell) out of wedlock with Richard Branwell Jr, Maria's Uncle Richard, is not known.

21 Philippa Tyack of St Hilary (1777-1818) was the first wife of Robert Matthews Branwell, son of Thomas's brother Richard. She died three years before Maria Brontë and the legend is that Robert in his grief threw himself down on the lowered coffin of his wife and screamed for her return. Elizabeth Branwell would have attended that funeral. Lilian Oldham Archive, Morrab Library, Penzance.

22 *A History of Cornish Methodism*, p. 113

23 Letter 'from the top of the Faulhorn', 1844, written by Elizabeth C. T. Carne and reprinted in *Memorials of Emily Bolitho* (Penzance: Beare & Son, 21 Market Place, 1889).

24 Constructed in the early 1700s as a grand residence and family home, The Regent now houses the headquarters of the Hypatia Trust, an educational and charitable foundation (lower ground floor), legal and financial offices at street level, and residential flats on floors above.

25 Brought to my attention by art dealer David E Carter in his monograph (2013) *Lydia Gwennap, A Cornish masterpiece uncovered...*, pp. 21-5. "This man [Broadley Wilson] probably made heavier contributions and subscriptions to moral and reforming societies of the day than any other person with the possible exception of Wilberforce." Ford K Brown (1961*) Fathers of the Victorians, The Age of Wilberforce.*

26 [Author: mlb204 on-line essay] 'Parading the Cornish Subject: Methodist Sunday School Parades and Tea Treats in West Cornwall c1830-1930'

27 Details of publication in *Methodist Magazines* are found in Chapter 12, Family bibliography. A full transcription is available from the Bronte Territories Archive; a summary list of his missionary travels at the behest of Dr.Thomas Coke is included in Chapter 10, The Travellers' Tales. Trial documents are included in the Document Register, under John Kingston.

28 James Woelfel (1997) 'The Christian Humanism of Anne Brontë', pp. 8-23, 'as found in *Agnes Grey* and *The Tenant of Wildfell Hall'.*

29 Wesley and his mother agreed 'that the author of this treatise had more zeal than knowledge, and was one of those men who would unnecessarily strew the way of life with thorns.' Robert Southey relates (1820) pp 26-7 in *The Life of John Wesley.*

30 G. Elsie Harrison (1948) *The Clue to the Brontës*, Preface.

31 Max Warren (nd) *Simeon*, edited by Hugh Evan Hopkins, author of Charles Simeon of Cambridge. Copy gifted from Holy Trinity Church bookroom, with thanks.

32 Mack, Phyllis (2008) *Heart Religion in the British Enlightenment 166-7*: on 'friendship and agency'. With thanks to Dr John Lenton and Dr Peter Forsaith for their recommendations on readings about Methodism.
33 See Juliet Barker, *The Brontës* [1994] 2nd edition London: Abacus, 2010, pp. 327-8.
34 Possibly the John Bennetts married to Elizabeth Carne, sister of Ann Carne Branwell, though Bennett and Bennetts are fairly common names in West Cornwall. They were a family of mariners and shipwrights and several were related by marriage to both Branwells and Carnes.
35 Roy Hattersley *John Wesley: A Brand from the Burning* (London: Little Brown, Imprint of Time Warner, 2002), pp. 25-8.

Market Jew Street, Penzance, with a view of St. Mary's, published by Henry Besley, Exeter, c1837.

Chapter 5

In the everyday[1]

"Modern people are just like ancient ones, only more numerous"

Barbara Kingsolver (2006) *Lacuna*

The Revd. C. V. Le Grice, the perpetual curate of St Mary's, sent a letter to the *Royal Cornwall Gazette* in 1803. He had been to London and seen *John Bull*, the comedy play by dramatist George Colman the Younger, and he was feeling both defensive and bullish. Placed in Cornwall on 'Muckslush Heath', some two miles from Penzance, with access to the sea for a shipwreck, Colman writes against the ludicrously silly social class system displayed between Baronets and tradesmen of the far west.

At the centre of the play is the familiar story of the 'gentleman and the ruined maid' and the fight-back of the 'inferiors' against the newly sophisticated aristocrats, who several generations past shared their equally inferior trades, who now were 'rising' and ashamed of their forbears. Also familiar are the central mentions of mining fortunes, rapidly gained and just as rapidly lost. All of this takes place at a suitably distant location from London, where social status was defined by property and marriage and justice was dispensed (after long costly litigation) perhaps. The 'stylish way to live' says one pompous young man is bankruptcy and leaving one's bills unpaid, while escaping to the country and living off the debt-laden yokels. The way to happiness is marrying a rich heiress (preferably with country estates).

The story was not Cornish, in fact, and the sub-title gives it away: 'The Englishman's Fireside'. The use of Cornwall, and strange, rough dialect threaded with incongruous expletives, drew the Revd. Valentine Le Grice (known as CV) to comment in print:

> I know that an idea prevails, that around Penzance every wind that blows is a storm, that the few houses which are above ground are built of wrecked timber, that the underground inhabitants are the most numerous, that the above-ground gentlemen are all smugglers, and that every horse at night is a kind of will o' whisp [*sic*], and carries a lantern at his tail to decoy the coasting mariner.

> Now I beg leave to inform Mr Colman that Penzance is a very different place from the commonly received opinion. We have cards for the sedentary, books for the lounger, balls for the light-heeled, clubs for the convivial, and picnics for the gay and thoughtless. Turbot and red mullet swim almost at our doors; our fields are perfect gardens; our bay is inferior only to the Bay of Naples; and as for our climate, from the rarity of ice not a boy here can slide, and a pair of skates would be a matter of as much astonishment as an air-balloon.

What Le Grice did not mention was that Penzance also had its own theatre, which by the time he was writing had been hosting performances of classic, contemporary and comic plays for some 16 years. In 1787, when Maria was four years old and Elizabeth 11, their Uncle Richard Branwell was commissioned by Richard Hughes, the owner of an extensive theatre circuit, including the Sadler's Wells in London, to build what was called the Stable Theatre at the rear of the Ship and Castle (now the Union Hotel) on Chapel Street.

Well-known actors such as James Dawson[2] and Edmund Kean and singers such as Charles Incledon (distant kin of Branwells, through the Johns family) performed on the Stable boards. Located as it was above the horse and carriage stalls, the aromas, neighing and kicking sounds of the horses gave rise to many the derisive comment and much laughter. At least there was resonance when a player shouted 'A horse, a horse, my kingdom for a horse!' (*Richard III*, Shakespeare)

The Stable Theatre preceded the building of the Ballroom that Branwell and Hambleton also constructed four years later, commissioned by public subscription, to become an integral part of this same hotel complex. The Ballroom with its musicians' balcony would in future years become the centerpiece community room where the social and cultural events and organizations of the town were formed and rooted in the everyday. It remains a welcome site for celebratory dinners and conference events, its Georgian features delight the visitor, and this grand room continues to be the selected venue for banquets and meetings of social and scientific groups to the present day.

Well described by local historian Margaret Perry, the cultural centre situated on Chapel Street was a familiar and continuing feature of town life, from well before the births of the Branwell siblings, and even of their parents:

> During the winter months regular assemblies were held at the Ship and Castle Hotel, renamed the Union Hotel in 1801.[3] The first newspaper reference to the hotel is dated 1747 but in 1786 it was described as 'that ancient reputed and well-accustomed inn and tavern', pointing to a longer history. Sales of ships, cargoes, land and property were frequently held at the hotel, as were meetings. Above the stables was a theatre, which was used from 1787 until 1831, and there was also a cockfighting-pit at the rear of the hotel.[4]

Smuggling

Acton Castle was constructed for the use of Admiral John Stackhouse (1742-1819) as a laboratory for his studies of seaweed. It sits on the shores of Mount's Bay in the village of Perranuthnoe, and was given the surname of his wife Susanna's family (of London). When Stackhouse was not in residence the castle was tended by his tenant, a small farmer named John Carter. Possibly unknown to Stackhouse, John Carter was also the notorious smuggler called "The King of Prussia" (Prussia Cove is just by). It appears that the empty property doubled as an illicit hiding place as required.

Though circumstantial and largely unrecorded, there is little doubt, that knowledge of the Carter family of Breage and their smuggling 'supply' trade was widespread. John Cornish in his Introduction to the reprint of the diaries and autobiography of Captain Harry Carter of Prussia Cove comments:

> The accounts of the actual smuggling in the following pages are not very elaborate, but we must remember that at the time when Harry Carter was writing (1809), John Carter [the younger brother, called 'The King'] and the Cove Boys were still at it, and Prussia Cove had not ceased to be a great centre of smugglers. This would also explain the absence of any more particular reference to any of his companions...It is characteristic of the history of the smugglers everywhere that they enjoyed the support of popular sympathy. This was certainly the case in West Cornwall, where the farmers, the merchants, and, it is rumored, the local magistrates, used to find the money with which the business was carried on, investing small sums in each voyage.[5]

Ties with privateers and smuggling to the Branwell network of families were close enough to make sensible mention, though the case against them as merchants who benefitted remains circumstantial. Certainly people they considered friends and colleagues were involved from time to time, due to the shared ownership of vessels employed in the trade.

Though we have no evidence of Thomas Branwell's personal involvement in smuggling, it is unlikely that he and his fellow market town traders in tea, spices, salt and other commodities avoided these supply channels altogether. Thomas's cousin, George Bramwell, son of Martin Bromwell (butcher), and his Uncle Richard Woolcock (husband of his Aunt Alice, sister of his mother) were both mariners and privateers, with letters of marque, giving government protection for traders in war time.

Confirmation of Bramwell family involvement in customs avoidance, is found in a privately printed book about 'no ordinary Cornish family called *Our Dunkin Ancestry* by Marion Smith, a fellow researcher of the Royal Geological Society.

> In August 1791 the customs house boat on Scilly was rowed late at night close to a smuggling vessel, laden with contraband goods in Old Grimsby Harbour, near Tresco. The crew of the smuggling vessel fired repeatedly into the customs house boat so that two revenue men were killed, John

Oliver and William Millett, and another John James was seriously wounded. The inquest arrived at the verdict of willful murder. 'The smuggling vessel got off. The excise officers were well respected and left large families.' The vessel was later identified as the *Friendship* of Penzance, belonging to James Dunkin, and commanded by George Bramwell. The commissioners offered a reward of £500 for the arrest of Dunkin who fired the gun and pardons to men who assisted this and gave information about others involved in the shooting, the successful identification being rewarded with a further £200.

Charlotte MacKenzie in her very useful study of merchants and smugglers in eighteenth century Cornwall, however, cannot exonerate George Bramwell from direct involvement in these particular murderous conflicts, but cannot include him either.[7]

> In 1786-7 Bramwell was master of the Dunkins' sloop the *Liberty* and in 1788-90 he was master of one of their brigantines the *Friendship*. Bramwell was not the master of the *Liberty* in November 1789 when the revenue cutter was fired on at Prussia cove; nor was he master of the *Friendship* in August 1791 when the revenue boat was fired on at Old Grimsby. Nonetheless it is possible that George Bramwell sailed to Tresco in 1791 as Captain of the *Liberty* as the Penzance ship's register for which was out of date.[6]

Several of Thomas Branwell's relations - George Bramwell, George's brothers-in-law, Henry and Richard Ford, and Thomas's uncle, Richard Woolcock[7] spent time locked up together as prisoners of war in France.[8] Bringing it even closer to home, Thomas Love, who commissioned the building of the homes they lived in on Chapel Street, was the next door neighbour to the Branwells, and jointly owned with Thomas Branwell some of the sailing vessels used:

> It was not unusual for provincial merchants, shopkeepers, and artisans to own shares in Cornish ships. Thomas Love was a cooper who barreled and exported fish from Penzance and jointly owned ships with Cornish merchants who imported wine and spirits from southern Europe. As a shipowner Thomas Love also participated in ventures which extended Penzance's trading routes beyond the Channel and Mediterranean to America and the West Indies as well as northern Russia.[9]

Fish & fishing in the everyday

At the harbour, below the Rotterdam buildings of Chapel Street, were the fish cellars and bonded warehouses, owned by Thomas Branwell, from which he exported pilchards abroad (a strong link was forged with Genoa in Italy through pilchards), and provided them to markets and housewives around the town.[10] Here he would also receive his shipments of salt, so important in the curing of pilchards and fish of all varieties. Here he also employed jowsters, usually women, who carried the fish on their backs around the town for sale from the baskets.

Serendipitously, one of these fish-sellers may have been a young woman, Keziah Green, a devout Methodist from Newlyn and Sancreed, the mother of William Lovett (b Newlyn 1800), later a leading Chartist who departed Cornwall in 1820 for London.[11] His father, a ship's captain from Hull, Yorkshire, died before William's birth. Later Keziah married a William Carne, miller and builder of Paul, yet another branch of the Anne Carne Branwell family tree.

Jewish community and sea trading

Brock in her monograph on Penzance's Jewish community tells the story of the first merchants and ship chandlers (traders by sea of all commodities) that settled in the area of West Cornwall and how it began to grow in importance and influence as a trading port.[12] Abraham Lemael Jacob Hart, born in the eastern Rhineland on the Polish border, was amongst the earliest recorded members and set up his trade as a gold- and silversmith (not unlike John (Calenso) Carne, Anne Carne Branwell's father), and a wine and spirits merchant[13] amongst other occupations. He died in 1784, leaving several sons. One son returned to Germany as HM Consul General in Dresden, another became a chemist locally.

A grandson, who took on the name of Lemael Hart, after his grandfather, was a distiller, a dealer in sugar and tea and an astute businessman in commodities, like Thomas Branwell, with several bonded warehouses. He traded his rum under the name of Lemon Hart Rum, a famous trade name still extant today.

Lemael Hart Jr. was also the warden of the synagogue, an office he gave up at the death of his pregnant wife in 1803, killed when her nightdress caught fire from a candle.[14] Left with four young children, he married again a year later, with one Mary Solomon, a widow and a London beauty of the day in Penzance, who was known as the 'White Rose'. Their home was a fine house in Chapel Street (leased from the Branwells; Lemon Hart is by name mentioned as occupying property belonging to Thomas in the latter's will proved in 1808). In 1811 he moved to London, purchasing the freehold of land at Leskinnick (until then held on leasehold), to provide the Jewish cemetery, and also the freehold of the synagogue from the Branwell family estate, both of which he presented to the Trustees of the Jewish Community trust.[15] This is a story which was current – and strikingly poignant – during Elizabeth and Maria's time in Chapel Street.

Later when a new synagogue was needed, in the 1830s, Branwell land was again leased for these purposes at No 1 New Street (at the back of the Star Inn) which had been the original Branwell family home lived in by Martyn Bromwell and Jane Tremearne Branwell, with the attached 'killing yard'. The Cattle Market was across the road. A building fund beginning in 1836 benefited from a large Branwell family donation, though an annual ground rent of £6 was also levied. 'An archway beside the Branwell House led to a cobbled yard and stabling beside the synagogue.' (Brock, p. 9)

Sanitation and hygiene

Rapid industrialisation occurring in mining and technological terms brought on local social problems not much spoken about, but undoubtedly bothersome and dangerous to healthy living. The ratio of number of toilets to the number of houses was surprisingly low with public facilities rarely available. The result was to force workers to relieve themselves behind walls and hedges.

To make things worse, the town's wells were sometimes contaminated with sewage from overflowing communal cesspits, which were often sited uncomfortably close to people's doors. Open trenches carried effluent through the streets and down to be washed away by the sea. This was, of course, still a serious health risk for generations to come all over the country, and an issue for the Brontë family at Haworth as well, as tainted water swept downhill through graveyards. The nature of complicated dress related to costumes for the women of the day, meant that they could not avail themselves of the walls and hedges, and basically meant that they remained close to home.

At the bottom end of Coinagehall Street, nestled around the harbour, were not only the fish cellars and warehouses of the busy dockland. Here also were the squalid and tiny overcrowded homes of the poor, and the prostitutes who gave service – solace and smuggled food onboard - to the thriving sea traders or sailors away from their home bases. Inevitably this was a neighbourhood riddled with diseases of several varieties, and was a district of town avoided by the women and children of Chapel Street just above.

One can imagine that most children of the middle class, and especially young ladies of the aspiring gentry families, spent limited time away from their homes or those of their cousins nearby. Their lessons, their domestic training to become a wife and their inevitable needlework – both to create their own clothing and undergarments, but also to provide donations to the poor, were undertaken there. It is easy to understand the lingering doubts that would have assailed Aunt Branwell in her removal to the muddy, cold north of Haworth, about going out and about in an unknown town which was so different from her old home with its unique social conditions and with her siblings, friends and cousins to give direction. Nevertheless, some of the issues in home life would remain the same, and would require care routines with which she was already familiar.

Lessons in health and hygiene

Of great interest are the health hints found in a local handwritten diary that contains entries dated from the late 1780s to about 1820. The writer is anonymous, though the numbered comments are reminiscent of advice that John Wesley gave to his followers, especially in relation to strong liquors and tea.[16] The advice given, I believe, seems remarkably modern; the handwriting, though somewhat faded, is clear and easy to read.

General Remarks

1. The air we breath [sic] is of the utmost importance to our health
2. Every one that would preserve health should be as clean and sweet as possible in their houses & c
3. Nothing conduces more to health than abstinence and plain food with due labour

4. Water is the wholesomest of all drinks, quickens the appetite and strengthens the digestion
5. Strong and especially spirituous liquors are a certain though slow poison therefore the sooner they are left off the better
6. Strong liquours do not prevent the mischieves of a surfeit nor carry it off so safely as water
7. Malt liquours except clear small beer or small ale are hurtful so is strong tea
8. A due degree of exercise is necessary to health
9. Walking is the best exercise for those who are able to bear it, riding for those who are not
10. All persons should eat light suppers about seven go to bed at nine and rise at five or six in the morning
11. Costiveness [constipation] is very hurtful to health therefore care should be taken to remove it at the beginning by cool gentle purge
12. Obstructed perspiration vulgarly called catching cold is one great source of diseases
13. Water drinking alone prevents apoplexies asthmas convulsions gout hysterics madness palsies trembling & c
14. The best water to drink is rainwater caught in an earthenware pan. After it is settled draw it off clean into another vessel. It will then keep sweet a long time.
15. Cold bathing and electrifying is likewise very beneficial in all hereditary and nervous disorders and if repeated for thirty successive days will cure the bite of a mad dog.

Working women in Penzance

Paid work for women, however, was available locally in some quantity. At the mines, women were employed at the surface to select and break rock in order to extract minerals and metals on what would be described today as production lines.[17] Women often staffed the market stalls that popped up weekly to sell the produce of the farms around. Available as well were jobs mending nets, selling fish (jowsters) and packing pilchards for export abroad.

None of these occupations were taken up by members of the families studied here, though later on in the nineteenth century, spinsters of the family are known to have shared their homes as lodgings in the way of 'bed and breakfast'. To settle the debts left by her husband at his death and to bring up her children kinswoman Grace Millett Davy, set up a millinery business in Chapel Street and employed a young French woman to assist her. The latter was to be the 'first love' of little Humphry Davy, the future distinguished chemist and poet.

Mother-craft

Maria and Elizabeth were not, as often implied, isolated from family in their progress north to Yorkshire. Jane and John Fennell and their daughter Jane Fennell Morgan had been with them since their earliest memories, living beside them on Chapel Street in Penzance and standing *in locus parentis* to them. Their understanding of domestic and personal habits of the Branwell and Carne families would have been fully recognized, even if disagreed with in practice (for which there is no evidence). Elizabeth Branwell's strict ways with servants in Haworth (holding the keys to the food and drink cellars) was possibly due to untoward experiences in Cornwall. Her stated dislike of animals in the house is understandable too, given the plethora of butchers amongst the cousins and the squeals from the killing yards at the marketplace, and the cockfighting pit up the road under the theatre.

The one example that we are always given is Maria on her deathbed, wishing to be raised up to watch the servant preparing and cleaning the grate 'as it was done in Cornwall.' Without doubt much housecraft and routines of nursing, provisioning and mother-craft were automatic in their everyday lives, received through habit and tradition from their own mothers. How much these domestic activities differed from those in the north is largely unknown.

John Fennell had probably set Maria Branwell's own lessons and taught her to read. Both Elizabeth and Maria had known their Aunt Jane from birth, and possibly have nursed Jane's daughter, Jane Fennell Morgan, from her toddler days. Inevitably, all of these would believe that the patterns of home management and learning, even if faulty in modern terms, were the right ones.

The lives of the school children

The availability of educational facilities in the far west of Cornwall, appears to have been wide enough, as Richard Polwhele reports in his *History of Cornwall* (1805), though what he means by this is questionable. It was by no means education for all. The individual take-up, as elsewhere, depended mainly on social class and geographical location (in relation to a school), underscored, of course, by self-determination and family interest.

The general idea that shaped their infancy was that by the time they could walk and talk, they should begin to learn to read, and this preliminary learning was handled inside the home with the *Bible* as a textbook. This was a 'method' promoted by John Wesley from his own childhood, when he told of his mother who set aside one day in each week to concentrate with her children on *Bible* reading and 'pre-school' learning. From this format, Wesleyan support for class meetings for people of all ages developed and became a routine part of Methodist purpose to combat illiteracy and encourage devotion. A teaching mechanism to learn letters and numbers for the girls, to be completed by the age of ten, was the making of a sampler, and the working of these would take up a small part of the lessons that were part of everyday. The Branwell family samplers today are in the protective hands of the Brontë Society, as donated many years ago by relations.

At primary levels, as witnessed in the early lives of their Pellew family connections,[18] boys and girls were allowed to be schooled together until secondary classes, when they were separated by gender. How widespread the custom we do not know. At puberty most girls either dropped whatever formal education they were receiving altogether or were 'schooled' at home, by mothers, fathers and tutors brought in for special subjects.

In the youth of Elizabeth and Maria and their siblings, on a completely circumstantial basis, lessons were given at home by tutors to groups of children, and further lessons, especially in *Bible* studies, were offered in weekly Methodist classes. By the appropriate age for this split in gender amongst the Branwell children, John Fennell, with a daughter of his own to educate, was able to set lessons for any and all, being one of the town's independent school masters and as Head of his own 'Writing School'. His wife, Jane Branwell Fennell, was also known to possess a small library of books, which in future was handed on to the Brontë children for their own collection.

Richard Polwhele[19] suggests that the Branwell girls were fortunate:

> Whilst schools, for the instruction of boys, can thus be traced back for many generations; the female sex seem to have been left, almost to simple nature, untutored and uninformed, till the last half a century. [indicating 1750-1800, the period during which Elizabeth and Maria and their siblings were born and educated.] There were schools, it is true, for girls; but they professed to teach very little, and taught still less…

Clear information on educational arrangements is sparse indeed, and is only picked up in brief asides and lists extant at the time. For example, in *The Universal Directory of Great Britain for 1791* there is only one schoolmaster acknowledged in the town of Penzance, and that is John Fennell. The new school was opened (for boys only) c1789-90 and its location was at the rear of gardens adjoining the churchyards of St Mary's Chapel. The rear of the Branwell home on Chapel Street opens into that same churchyard.

In 1794, Thomas Branwell sold a tract of land (Todman's Gear, lease at CRO) behind his home to the Town Council for the construction of a school, and the impression is that this became the corporation's first primary school for children from ages six to twelve. By this date, however, Maria was already eleven years old, and Elizabeth eighteen hence their early schooling was already in hand, and they may themselves have served as assistants and instructors.

At the corner of the gardens behind the Branwell home nearest St Mary's sits the small brick building on two floors which held one of the schoolrooms for the 'Penny School' (now an outbuilding for the end house) also called a 'Dame School'. In that small building, it is believed, that the female children of the local families, received their tuition in needlework, letters, and languages. Since then, the remaining school buildings were completely destroyed by bombing in World War II, and the building materials scavenged for other buildings around the town.

Ordinarily classes were held in rooms set aside in their own homes. Elizabeth Bolitho, a modern day informant from the Bolitho clan (of Trengwainton and Chyandour) also describes the place (now dismantled) where the school for young ladies, run by the daughters of Benjamin Carne Branwell and his wife, Mary (Batten) Branwell, was located in Alverton some years later.

When Grace Lucille Boase[20] (1809-1889) described her own education in 1816, she mentions one set of the Branwell family teachers, two daughters of Mary and Benjamin Carne Branwell (*not* sisters of Maria, as identified by the writer below. She writes:

"My next school was kept by two Miss Branwells, I think they must have been sisters of Charlotte Bronte's mother [Ed. Note: No, they were first cousins, Uncle Richard's daughters], they lived in a small house on the South Parade where the Public Library was afterwards built....

> The schoolroom had a sanded floor, was half underground as the bottom of the window was level with the street, so we saw everybody that was passing, which was our only entertainment; we must have been all very small children, George used to be carried to and fro, we were arranged on low wooden forms about a foot high. Miss Mary Branwell attended to the household affairs in the kitchen which was the other side of the passage, and Miss Peggy sat in the corner of the schoolroom with a long cane by her side with which she gave gentle pats and pokings to those who were misbehaving; here we sat from 9 till 12, I forget whether we went in the afternoon, there I suppose we learnt to read or at least our letters. After my sister Maria left school she used to teach us, until Lydia went to Miss Babington's for three years, never coming home the whole time, and at 8 years old I went as a boarder to Miss Stone's.[21]

Richard Polwhele's report, quoted above, goes on from the generally poor quality of education for girls to admit that the situation was changing: 'Of late, however, seminaries for the sex, have been instituted in almost every country-town. And women have been deemed our rivals.' He then treats the reader to a polemical set of verses, penned by himself, with long florid footnotes, about the proper education for women, juxtaposing his nemesis ('satan'), Mary Wollstonecraft (1759-1797), with his ideal, Hannah More (1745-1833). The writings of both of these women would have been familiar to the Branwell, Batten and Carne families, and formed part of the circulating library of the ladies in Penzance (see following). Wollstonecraft was to become a particular friend and connection of their cousins, the (Batten) Cristalls in London, where they were known companions in the late 1780s and early '90s. The bluestocking educationalist and philosopher, Hannah More, on the other hand, supervised a boarding school in Bristol attended by Mary Phillipa Davies Giddy (1769-?), the sister of Davies Giddy Gilbert.

It adds an interesting perspective to the educational opportunities for women, if we know that to make this possible and to prepare his son Davies for entrance to Oxford, the Revd. Giddy moved his family to Bristol (1784-1787), where Davies joined the Mathematical Academy of Benjamin Donne, while Philippa finished her three years of study with More and her sisters at their school at Fishpond. School was not always essential.

Elizabeth Batten, cousin and friend of Maria's mother Anne, is reported to have been classically self-educated in Penzance, perhaps with a tutor (not specified) and to have especially fascinated by Egyptology.[22] In the generation mirroring that of the Brontës, however, it became more common for some of the wealthier families to send their daughters away to ladies' seminaries, girls' boarding schools or specialty training schools in cities such as Bath or Bristol.

As for the boys, both families produced clergy, school teachers, medical practitioners and lawyers through apprenticeships, alongside their various trades and civic appointments. By Napoleonic times, the Branwells and Carnes were very much a part of the rising middle classes, some branches and some individuals within those branches moving up the social scales faster than others, and a few falling back rather dramatically. Often this did not relate closely to educational achievement, but as ever to access to wealth and property.

By the generation of Maria and Elizabeth, however, education for boys was put on a much more formal basis. After the marriage of first cousins Charlotte Branwell and Joseph Branwell in 1812, Joseph gave up his legal clerkship and the couple opened a new academy for young men together with the Barwis family of teachers who came to Penzance from Falmouth where they had run a school for some years. The new school at the bottom of Queen Street offered both a classical education (with annual prizes) and a commercial education and continued in operation until the 1830s when the Barwis family took over its administration Mary Tyack Branwell, daughter of Robert Matthews Branwell and his first wife Phillipa, had by this time married into the Barwis family, as Mrs John Ryland Barwis.

> 1826 *Royal Cornwall Gazette (RCG)*
>
> On Wednesday evening last the respectable Inhabitants of Penzance were highly gratified by attending the Annual recitation of the young gentleman at Mr. Joseph Branwell's school. The umpires, the Revd. James Came, M.A. Dr. Boase, and Joseph Came, Esq. passed a commendation on Masters John Richards and R Branwell, (who gained the medals last year) as having ably maintained their ground on the present occasion ; and awarded the medals for this year to Master William Hosking for Latin and Greek, to Master Henry Thomas for French, and to Master William Penberthy for English ; and joining with the numerous assembly in expressions of general approbation, they praised the correctness and ability with which the classical speeches were spoken.
>
> 1826 *RCG*:   'BRANWELL's Classical. Mathematical, and Commercial Academy, Penzance'. Will re-open on Monday the 31st July. An Assistant provided for every Fifteen Scholars. Every Pupil has a separate bed. Latin and Greek taught by a Gentleman from the University of Oxford. N.B. — Mr. Branwell refers to the quantity and quality of the work done at his School, and to the consequent improvement of his pupils as the proper test of the merits of his Seminary; and as to Classical Learning, a knowledge and pronunciation

of the French Language, an acquaintance with practical Book-keeping, or any other branch of Education, there is no School whatever in the West of England, that can produce proofs of greater improvement.

Joseph (Cock) Carne FRS was one of the dignitaries who selected and presented the annual awards to outstanding pupils. At this time, he had removed with his family back into Penzance from Hayle, and taken up a partnership in the Penzance Bank with his father and the current John Batten. He was also a magistrate, the main administrator of the Library and the Treasurer of the RGSC, hence his role as influential advisor to public bodies was secure and widely respected.

The Penzance Ladies Book Club 1770-1912[23]

In 1770, a group of twenty-three ladies of the town and area around came together to take tea, and to discuss the creation of a circulating selection of books. This has been described in summary in Chapter 3, but was very much of the everyday by the time of Maria's birth and reading life. The ladies making up this group appear to have been the wives and daughters of clergy and landed gentry of the Land's End. The list of known subscribers includes only the names of initial 'founding' members; subsequently only the chosen President's name is known alongside her selected annual budget of books.

The account book which records their choices for reading, together with the rules applied to the operation of the Circle, form part of a fascinating archive at the present-day Morrab Library. Considered to be the oldest cultural society in Penzance its importance should not be underrated in establishing the general educational levels expected of the middle and upper classes of the time. It was not to be until 1818 or more than two generations later, that the Penzance Library (now the Morrab Library in Morrab Gardens) was to be established in the town, though a Gentleman's News Room was initiated in 1799.

The first rule made clear "That no gentleman be admitted as a subscriber" and this dictum was followed by twelve more, stating the sum of 6/- being the price of subscription, that suggestions should be given to the elected President for books desired, that four days were allowed for reading if locally held, and a week for readers further afield, that second reading is allowed after all applicants have had their turn, and how damages or loss were to be compensated. The books would be ordered from the bookseller by the President (between 25 and 30 annually) and were made available at his/her premises. This was not a club or discussion group, but simply a means of acquiring reading material without necessarily buying one's own copy. Once a year, the books were sold off, by 'balloting', and a new list subscribed.

Through the years no Branwell or Carne was listed as President, but several of their relations are found, with the Johns family name leading the stakes by far, as mentioned in Chapter 3. Though there is no proof that Maria or Elizabeth or their mother and her friends were subscribers, it is highly probable. One of the booksellers (with printing and binding facilities) mentioned at the end of the account book as providing the stock for reading, was Charles Fisher, Gent, the husband of Margaret

(Carne) Branwell, their second oldest sister. At the very least, both Elizabeth and Maria would have had access to the stock of his large collection and that of their cousins, Joseph and John (Cock) Carne, whose books much later were to help build and form the Morrab Library.

The books ordered by the Presidents were of wide variety – biographies, diaries, letters, poetry, fiction, drama, history and travel writings in addition to journals, parental and moral advice, philosophy and theology. The writings of Maria Edgeworth, Madame de Stael, Rousseau, Goldsmith, Anna Laetitia Barbauld, Hannah More, Mary Wolstencraft, Henry Fielding, Samuel Johnson, French texts and fairy tales are on offer alongside the *Letters of Mrs Delany*, the novels of Walter Scott and the then present-day writings of those around them. Up to three journals were also kept, including *The Lady's Magazine* which was established first in 1770, just like the reading circle itself. In the 1780s and '90s, John Fennell, the Branwell uncle, answered mathematical queries for this journal on a regular basis.

Though Elizabeth, 'Aunt Branwell' as she became known for all time, is neglected as a potential source of literary inspiration, my own suspicions are that very easily she and her sister before her would have encouraged the childhood plays and writings of the Brontë children because of their own upbringing, and to give them worthwhile pastimes. This early and somewhat latent influence would have been equally easily forgotten in terms of inspiration by the Brontë writers, and perhaps especially by Charlotte, much later on, just as credits for particular ideas are later overlooked in the reporting of them. One can surmise, though it is a speculative comment, that Elizabeth Branwell, while nurturing daily the domestic duties expected of the Brontë children as they grew, also considered herself a part of a widespread, distinguished and well-connected literary family.

Chapel Street, Penzance, with a view of St. Mary's, published by Henry Besley, Exeter, c1837.

ENDNOTES

1. Most of the material for this chapter was orally presented at the Centre for Methodist Studies, Spring seminar, Oxford, 18 April 2015. The original version is available to read at www.academia.com under the author's name, Melissa Hardie-Budden.
2 James Dawson (1865) *The Autobiography of Mr James Dawson* Truro: J. R. Netherton, *John Bull*, the play, was probably also performed in Penzance at some point, but he includes no dates in his rendering.
3 To commemorate the Act of Union between Great Britain (England and Scotland) with Ireland.
4 Margaret Perry (2000) 'The Town of Penzance', *In and around Penzance during Napoleonic Times*, p. 6.
5 John B. Cornish (1900) *The Autobiography of a Cornish Smuggler* (1749-1809), xiii-iv.
6 Charlotte MacKenzie (2019) *Merchants and Smugglers in eighteenth century Cornwall* Truro: Cornwall History,pp. 253-4.
7 In February 1795, Thomas's cousin George Bramwell of Penzance died as a prisoner of war on the Isle de Rhe, France.
8 C MacKenzie, *Merchants and Smugglers* p. 152.
9 *Ibid*. p. 150.
10 *Will of Thomas Branwell*, merchant, of Madron 1808 AP/B/5137, CRO. Reprinted in Appendices.
11 See William Lovett in Chapter 11: Biographical briefs.
12 Elizabeth Brock *The Jewish Community of Penzance*, 1998.
13 There were brewers and spirit merchants in the Branwell family too and also in the Coren clan of relations.
14 Letitia (or Letty) Michael of Swansea, Mrs Lemon Hart. Note 63, p. 230: her own name remained unidentified until 1955, when it was found in the miscellaneous papers of Cecil Roth in the Brotherton Library in Leeds. The research of Evelyn Friedlander revealed this 'personal' information. Her father-in-law, Lazarus Hart, who lived in the same house on Chapel Street, died of apoplexy a few days later, as a result. The premature delivery resulted in a dead child. Elizabeth and Maria were both, with their family, present at this tragic time.
15 Keith Pearce and Helen Fry (Editors) *The Lost Jews of Cornwall* esp. 'The Branwell Family' pp. 255-6, and numerous references throughout, related to properties and Freemasonry to which both Branwells and Harts belonged.
16 With thanks for the loan of this receipt book to Terry Chiswell, retired schoolmaster of Penzance to whom it is an inherited treasure of his late wife's Cornish family (2014). Elsewhere in the same document is the advice to engage in as much sexual activity as possible to maintain one's health!
17 These women were called 'bal maidens', *bal* being the Cornish word for 'mine'.
18 See Biographical briefs, Chapter 11, for Pellew.
19 R. Polwhele (1806) 'The Language, Literature and Literary Characters of Cornwall', *The History of Cornwall*, vol. 5, pp. 81-82.
20 The Boase family had been related to the Branwell family as cousins since the time of great-grandfather Martyn Bromwell, and had also been business partners (banking) with the Carnes from the 1790s.
21 Eva Collection, Courtney Library, Royal Institution of Cornwall (handwritten records).
22 (Ann) Elizabeth Batten (c1744-1801) married Captain Alexander Cristall, a much older widower and business colleague of her father's. They were to become the parents of watercolour artist Joshua Cristall, poet Ann Batten Cristall and the engraver-teacher Elizabeth Cristall, due solely to their mother's creative influence and education. (Their father was implacably opposed to the arts.)
23 Careful studies by the late Iris Green, the John Simmonds (Morrab Library archivist) and Margaret Seccombe Brown confirm the broad importance to this early social network of middle and upper class women who led the way in continuing education in the local community. It is noted by P.A.S. Pool (p. 119) in his *History of Penzance*, as the earliest known cultural organization of the town. See bibliography: *Treasures of the Morrab*.

Engraved by W & G Cookes from a drawing by J. Britten, for the *Beauties of England & Wales: The Merry Maidens* (grid reference SW432245) Late Neolithic stone circle near St. Buryan. 'Nineteen maidens with their fiddler turned to stone for dancing on a Sunday?' Earliest ownership found, the *Dans Maen* circle as part of the Rosmoddress (Buller) Estate, was owned amongst the estate lands by the William Carne family of West Cornwall.

Chapter 6

THE PENZANCE TIME LINE
of the Branwells and Carnes

The intention here is to annotate individuals and events amongst the Carne-Branwell families, including such of their stories that might linger in family memory. Their stories, though not always the people themselves, would crowd the minds and memories of the Branwell women – Maria and Elizabeth – and the Fennell family of John, Jane and Jane, and others in the wider network, who would, separately and for varying reasons, leave West Cornwall to live elsewhere.

Abbreviations: Cornwall On-line Parish Clerks (COPC); Cornwall Records Office (CRO);

Notable events in the lives of the related families, chronologically rendered

1710
Family: Marriage of **Jane Tremearne's sister, Susan**, to **Richard Batten.** This marriage is the original source of connection between the **Branwells** and the **Battens**, i.e. through the marriages made by sisters, subsequently mothers of dynasties of their own under the surnames of Branwell and Batten and Keigwin. The third Tremearne sister, Dorcas, married Jenkyn Keigwin of Paul (Mousehole's oldest surviving house, *Keigwin*, was their home). To the **Keigwins** were also connected the Welsh family of **Carne** of Tresillian (ancestors in the William Johns Carne lineage).

1711
Richard Bramwell Sr. (1711-1792) was the builder who with his wife Margaret **John** (belo**w),** became the maternal grandparents of the Branwell children of this study, and were known to them all. He was a mason and his entire life was lived in West Cornwall. His will, though seen in the previous century by researchers, is reportedly lost in ours. Their home, a legacy from his parents, sat at the top of New Street, at the back of the Star Inn.

c1724-26

Margaret **John** (1724-1791) was born to **Thomas John** (1686-1752), blacksmith and wheelwright, and his wife **Jane Boase (1694-1741)**. Thomas John was the uncle of a future lawyer of Penzance, **George John**, a wealthy adventurer in mining, (primarily due to inheritances from his wife, heiress of the Arundel family) whose diary at CRO reveals much about social life in Penzance from the 1780s through the 1830s.[1] George John served as Mayor of Penzance in 1812 and 1818. His brother was Samuel John, also a lawyer, but one who 'went rogue' (See 1829).

1740

The 'Battery Rocks', set up on the foreshore with canons and guns, was constructed to defend Penzance. Thomas Branwell and Anne Carne and their families were to be born and to grow up within this protective shield for Mount's Bay and the Atlantic coast of Cornwall.

1743

Birth of **Ann (Reynolds) Carne** (c1743-1809), daughter of silversmith and clockmaker, John Carne, and his wife Ann Reynolds was the wife of Thomas (John) Branwell, and mother of Maria (Carne) Branwell and her eleven siblings. Ann/e Reynolds Sr. her mother, may have come from the Newquay area of Cornwall where her father was also a known watch and clockmaker. It is surmised but not confirmed that John Carne may have apprenticed himself to John Reynolds to learn his trade and then married the master's daughter. She was baptized in 1744 (COPC) but probably born the previous year.

1744

Birth of **Richard Branwell Jr.**

Eldest son of Richard Sr. and Margaret (John) Branwell, and the father of eleven children with his wife, Honor Matthews. Richard had one base child prior to marriage with an innkeeper's daughter Catherine Veale. Both his base child (who later changed his name to Branwell and became part of the family) and his first son were christened Richard, Richard Veale Branwell and Richard Matthews Branwell, respectively (COPC).

c1745-46

Thomas Branwell born but no record of birth or baptism at Madron, the second son and second child of his parents, Richard (Tremearne) Bramwell and Margaret (Boase) John. This could mean that he was born out of county, or that he was adopted, or that his records were lost, but there is no evidence available currently of the reason for absence of documentation.

1748

Birth of Richard and Thomas Branwell's sister, **Margaret Branwell** (1748-1773) who married **Joseph Corin** in 1772, dying the following year after the birth of her son **Joseph Corin Jr. Joe Jr.** became the ward of the whole Branwell family, until his father re-married some years later. He is mentioned in his grandfather's will, and given a legacy.

1750
Birth of Thomas Branwell's sister **Elizabeth Branwell** (1750-c1802), who married John Keam (1758-1826), shopkeeper and committed Methodist.[2] No issue.
A printing press and circulating library was set up in the town around this period as mentioned in *Penzance, Past and Present*, by the local historian G. B. Millett.

1751
Penzance was almost wholly supplied with water, for a considerable period, by the rivulet from Madron well; and a reservoir was made in 1751, at a cost of £402 14s 7¼d. (CRO)

1752
Of some interest to local people of Cornwall in 1752 was the application of the *Act of March 1751* that allowed for the disappearance of 11 days of their lives (and their pay for that gap!) when Britain went over to the *Gregorian calendar*, already in use on the Continent. From the 3rd to the 13th in September dates were omitted from the year. For family historians it affects records thereafter and especially those born at the turn of the year, who otherwise would have had birthdays in the last days of the previous year.

1753
Birth of Thomas Branwell's sister, **Jane Branwell** (1753-1829), who is listed as the first annotated Methodist Society participant of the core family.[3] Later she married **John Fennell** (1762-1841), schoolmaster in Penzance and Methodist class leader and preacher. See more about John Fennell in Chapter 10 'The Travellers'.

1754
Birth of **William (John) Carne** at Gwinear, son of Joseph (Purefoy) Carne 1733-1763 and Mary (Ferris) John/s 1731-1769, who married at Phillack in 1753.

1756
Birth of Thomas Branwell's youngest sister **Alice Branwell** (1756-?), who in 1795 married **John Williams**, Gent., a purser of mines, and mining adventurer. A son of this family was John Branwell Williams who with his family visited their uncle John Fennell and the Brontë family in Yorkshire in August, 1840, drawing some contempt from Charlotte.[4] The link to the Pellew family begins here.

1760
A tsunami hit the coast of West Cornwall, caused by volcanic eruptions in Portugal, and though sustaining flooding and high winds, little permanent damage was done.

1762
Birth of **John Fennell** (1762-1841) Madeley, Shropshire. He was baptized that year

with the Revd. John Fletcher, evangelical friend of John and Charles Wesley standing as godfather.

1766
A previous marriage in 1728, was that of William Branwell to Alice Carne. Their daughter Jenifer married **Solomon 'Solly' Cock**, builder in 1766. Solly Cock partnered Richard Branwell Sr. and Jr. in ongoing construction work on the pier. 'The Old Pier' was constructed in 1766. It was then extended in 1785, in 1812 and again in 1853.
A packet delivering post, passengers and merchandise sailed from Penzance harbour, weekly, to the Scilly islands.

1767
29 April: the marriage of (Anne) **Elizabeth Batten** (1745-1801) age 22, to **Captain Alexander Chrystal/Cristall** (1722-1802) age 45. His home parish is recorded as Aldgate in the City of London. From his first marriage, he had one surviving son, Capt. John Cristall (1757-1801). With his wife Elizabeth he was to have a further five children. [5]

1768
Joshua Cristall (1768-1847 London) born in West Cornwall to Elizabeth (Batten) Cristall and her husband Capt Alexander Cristall, their first child and relation of the Branwells that are about to start arriving through the marriage of Anne Carne to Thomas Branwell.

1768
Anne Carne and **Thomas Branwell** are married at Madron Parish Church on 28th November.

1769
Anne Batten Cristall (1769-1848 Lewisham, London) born in Penzance to Elizabeth (Batten) Cristall and her husband Capt. Alexander Cristall. (COPC)
Anne Carne Branwell is baptized in April, First child and daughter of Thomas (John) Branwell and Anne (Reynolds) Carne (COPC).

1770
Second daughter of Thomas and Anne, **Margaret (Carne) Branwell** is baptized in July at Madron (COPC).
Ladies Book Club, later called the Ladies Pamphlet Club established.

1771
The third child, and first son, of Anne and Thomas Branwell born and baptized as **Thomas (Carne) Branwell** (died 23 Feb 1776 Penzance).

1772
Elizabeth Branwell I born in Penzance, the fourth child, who on the same day as

her brother Thomas above, died in February of 1776.

Jane (Carne) Branwell was born and baptized in Penzance on 29th November, the 5th child of her family. She later married and become known as **Jane Kingston**. Jane outlived all of her parents, uncles, aunts, sisters, brothers, her Bronte nieces and nephew, and at least two of her own five children. In some texts, due to a mis-reading of Elizabeth Branwell's will in 1833 at Haworth, she is referred to as **Anne**. The Anne referred to as a possible residual legatee was in fact Jane Branwell Kingston's eldest daughter Anne resident in America, showing clearly that Aunt Branwell was in contact with Jane Kingston's children after their father John Kingston's death in 1824.

1773

Birth of Joseph Corin (1773-1832), son of Joseph Corin, a merchant brewer, and Thomas's sister Margaret, née Branwell. He was baptized at Penzance on 12 January 1773 and Margaret died only a few weeks following his birth. Later, in the will of his grandfather, Richard Branwell (1792), Joseph is identified as a scrivener (a writer of legal documents and other printed material, for those who were semi-or illiterate), and had completed an apprenticeship in a law office.

1775

Birth of Thomas & Ann's sixth child: **Benjamin Carne Branwell** 25 Mar 1775 – 1818 who later became Mayor of Penzance. He was the only male child of the family to survive to adulthood. In that same year of 1775 Philip Carne, an uncle, named his son Benjamin, and Henry Carne, another uncle, also named his son Benjamin. These were first cousins to the Branwells of Chapel Street.
Benjamin Carne, son of Philip Carne born in Penzance on 30 July
Benjamin Carne, son of Henry Carne born in Penzance on 4 December

1776

Death of Elizabeth I Branwell, daughter, age 4 on 23 February (malignant fever)
Death of Thomas I Branwell, son, age 5 on 23 February (malignant fever)
The seventh child of Ann & Thomas Branwell born and baptized as **Elizabeth (Carne) Branwell II (1776- 29 Oct 1842 Haworth).**

1777

Birth year of Patrick Branty. 17 March. Ireland

1778

Joseph Hallett Batten born in Penzance, son of the Revd. Joseph Batten (Congregational Minister) and his wife Anna (Luke) Batten. (1778-1837). Kinship circle of Carnes and Branwells.
Humphry Davy born in Penzance 17 Dec 1778, the son of Robert & Grace (Millett) Davy, and (later) ward to his guardian Dr John Tonkin (kinship circle). (1778-29 May 1829 Geneva).

The eighth child of Ann & Thomas Branwell born and baptized as **Thomas (Carne) Branwell II** (1778-1779). Death at nine months.

1779

The Penzance Grammar School founded by the Corporation, and remains open until 1898.
The ninth child of Ann & Thomas Branwell born and died (as infant) named **Alice**.I

1780

The tenth child of Ann & Thomas Branwell born and baptized as **Alice II** (1780-1781).
William (Johns) Carne married **Anna (Lyne) Cock** at Helston, Cornwall.

1781

Alice II died as infant.

1782

Birth of Joseph (Cock) Carne, eldest son of William and Anna Carne née Cock, of Penzance, and is baptized at the Bethel Non-conformist Chapel at Truro. (Nonconformist Registers for Cornwall, PRO) vol. 6, baptisms & burials, transcribed by Sheila and Stephen Townsend.)

1783

The eleventh child of Ann & Thomas Branwell born and baptized as **Maria (Carne) Branwell** (15 Apr 1783-15 Sep 1821 Haworth). When Maria was born in 1783, the following siblings were alive: Anne, Margaret, Jane, Benjamin, and Elizabeth.
During this year and the year following, Richard Branwell with his building workforce of kinsman and architect Edward Hambleton and kinsman Solly Cock constructed the Rotterdam Buildings (a terrace of three Georgian houses), of which the end house closest to the Vicarage was inhabited from 1784 by the Branwell family. Though possibly not the birthplace of Maria, it was to be her home from its possession day until the death of her mother in 1809. The middle house, in later years was split into two.

John Fennell

(1762-1841) arrived in Cornwall from Shropshire as a schoolmaster.

1784

Letter to **John Fennell** in Cornwall from the Revd. John Fletcher in Madeley, concerning his faith and future.

1785

Death of the Revd. John Fletcher of Madeley, Wesley's desired successor.
Humphry Davy entered at Dr. Coryton's Latin School, Penzance; John Fennell an assistant.
Richard Branwell and Solomon Cock (masons) together with **Thomas Branwell's** investment contracted to build on a two-year contract a new quay for Penzance

harbour at a cost of £1050 to the Town Council. RB & SC were related by marriage as SC had married Jennifer Bramble.
William Wilberforce began Anti-Slavery campaign.
William Wordsworth entered St. John's College, Cambridge.

1787

William (Cock) Carne Jr was born in this year, but no birth or baptism records are found. This information is gleaned from Census records after 1841.

1789

The twelfth child of Ann and Thomas Branwell born and baptized as **Charlotte (Carne) Branwell (Nov 1789-31 Mar 1848)**
The twelfth child of Honor (Matthews) and Richard Branwell was born and baptized as **Joseph (Matthews) Branwell.** He will become the husband of Charlotte (Carne) Branwell above in 1812.
The third son of Anna (Cock) and William (Johns) Carne was born in Cornwall in June, and named **John**. His baptism if correctly found, was delayed for two years and carried out in London.
Dr Thomas Coke, friend of Wesley and head of Methodist missions abroad, invites **John Kingston** (see 1800 below) to become a Wesleyan missionary in the West Indies.
On his final mission to West Cornwall in this year, **John Wesley** stayed with the (Cock) Carne family on Chapel Street, Penzance, when son Joseph was seven years old.
Four thousand Cornish members of Methodist connections for Wesley came together on 4th August. four days before he left Cornwall for the last time, when on a rainy afternoon Wesley preached in the new preaching house, "considerably the largest and, in many respects, far the best, in Cornwall. This Preaching House was located on Queen Street (parallel to Chapel Street on its western side, sitting directly behind the home of William (Johns) Carne, where today's Salvation Army Hall stands.[6]

1790

Jane (John) Branwell (Aunt, 1753-1829), sister of Thomas & Richard, married schoolmaster, John Fennell at Madron Parish Church.
The second Penzance Grammar School was built c 1790. This was Penhale House, Queen Street and built to relieve Voundervour Lane buildings. George Coryton, Curate of St Mary's, was Master until 1802. Working with him, as well as independently, was John Fennell.
Devonport and other dockyards greatly expanded due to the growing threat from Napoleonic France.

1791
2 March 1791 John Wesley died.
The Assembly Room, the Ship & Castle Hotel (later the Union Hotel) constructed by the **Branwell** builders and paid for by private subscription.

30 May 1791 **Margaret 'Margery' John Bramwell** is buried at St. Mary's, Chapel Street. She is the mother of Thomas (John) Branwell and the grandmother of the Branwell children.

At the death of **John Wesley**, **Dr Thomas Coke** returned from America, landing in Cornwall, visiting Methodist societies on his way through Cornwall by coach. **Fennell** already knew Dr Coke from Madeley days.

The only child of Jane (John) Branwell and John Fennell is born and baptized as **Jane Branwell Fennell** in Penzance.

1792

Thursday, 19 January *Bath Chronicle and Weekly Gazette*: **Mr Fisher**, bookbinder of Penzance to **Miss Branwell,** daughter of Mr Thomas Branwell, merchant of Penzance.

15 February 1792 Death of **Richard (Tremearne) Bramwell**, with his burial two days later at St. Mary's. He was the father of Thomas (John) Branwell, and grandfather of the Branwell children.

11 May 1792 Death of **Anne Carne Branwell,** eldest child of Anne (Reynolds) & Thomas (John) Branwell, eldest sister of Maria Branwell.

Pigot's Directory of 1792, lists John Fennell with the gentry and clergy, as the 'Schoolmaster'. (Only one named in the town and district).

Richard Treffry entered the Methodist itinerancy, traveling in several Cornish circuits, whilst also attending parish church weekly for the first ten years of his ministry. Richard Treffry meets **John Fennell** first in Cornwall, and much later in Yorkshire.

1793

The war with France began.

29 November: Burial of **John (Calensoe) Carne,** father of Anne (Reynolds) Carne, the mother of the Branwell children.

1794

Fourth son of William and Anna born: the Revd. James (Cock) Carne, DD (1794-1832). More about James is included in Chapter 9, 'The People called Carne.'

1795

The marriage of Thomas's youngest sister, **Alice Branwell**, to **John Williams, Gent.** of Redruth,[7] a member of the wealthy mine-owning Williams clan. **John Williams** (1741-1823) was a foremost mining engineer and the manager of Poldice and Gwennap Mines. The Williams families of Camborne and Redruth were inventors, mining agents and mine owners. This dynastic family, included, in our target period and in our family network, the exploits and and adventures of British Naval officers, **Admiral Sir Edward Pellew** (1757-1833), first Viscount Exmouth and his younger brother **Admiral Sir Israel Pellew** (1758-1832), whose thatched cottage, Hawke's Farm, (originally their grandmother's and then parental home) still stands in Alverton. John Williams' mother had been **Grace Pellew** (deceased), Alice's mother-in-law, whom she never met. Many hours of conversation over a long war period of years was sure to have been expended on these 'heroes' and their causes.

1796

Solomon Cock, kinsman, held the rights to the fairs and markets for the year with **Richard Branwell Jr,** by licence from the Corporation, for which he pays £22.5 shillings. The Cock family is relations of the Carnes and the Branwells.

23 January – an unidentified troop ship, possibly one of Admiral Christian's West Indies convoy was wrecked within a cable length of Loe Bar (near Helston) during a "great storm" in Mount's Bay. The ship was carrying between 400 and 600 officers and men of the 26th Regiment of Dragoons; not one of the crew or passengers survived. Large quantities of wreckage were washed up including dead horses with D26 brands on their hooves. It is estimated that over 600 people died including nine people on shore.

Charles Valentine LeGrice arrived in Penzance as tutor to **William John Godolphin Nicholls**, son of Mary Nicholls née Usticke, a wealthy widow, and her late husband John William Nicholls (owner of Trereife Manor). Kinship circle of Branwells & Carnes

1797

Richard Treffry takes on the headship of Penzance Wesleyan circuit with Owen Davies.

The Penzance Bank is opened by **William Carne** (Sr), **John Batten** (Sr) and **Richard Oxnam** in Chapel Street, in the building now No. 15. Planning for it and hiring of clerks had taken place from 1795.

Tuesday, 28 February *Kentish Gazette*: **Benjamin Branwell,** Gent. To be Ensign, Vice A Scobell, who retires. There is no further evidence of his involvement with the military in future years though he may have joined the Pioneers (Penzance defense corps) in due course. An ensign is the lowest rank of commissioned officer in the British navy or coastguard.

Henry Martyn entered St. John's College, Cambridge

1798

Revival began on Christmas Day in Penzance (gaining 2000 new members in the circuit), at Redruth on New Year's Eve, and quickly spread throughout West Cornwall.

The Corporation pays **Mr Branwell** a fee for holding a *Petit Jury* in his house, for French prisoners and an Irishman, John Concerford, related to smuggling.

A ship flying a US flag moored in Gwavas Lake broke its moorings, drifted towards the Wherry Mine striking its "turret" and flooding the mine, causing it to cease trading.

2 October **Humphry Davy** left Penzance for Bristol to become Dr Beddoes' assistant at the Pneumatic Institution

1799

Margaret Branwell Fisher, second daughter of Ann & Thomas Branwell dies, the year after the Penzance death of her husband, Charles Fisher, Gent. No children.

Benjamin Carne Branwell, Gent. married **Mary Bodinnar/Bodener Batten,** both of Chapel Street, Penzance.

Humphry Davy discovers laughing gas at the Bristol Pneumatic Institution.

C V Le Grice married the widow, **Mary (Usticke) Nicholls**, and their son Charles Day Perry Le Grice, is born the following year. CV finally inherits Trereife Manor at Mary's death in 1846, becoming a wealthy man prior to his death in 1858.

In May, 1799, a 4-part series of articles began in the *Methodist Magazine* with the title being: 'Memoirs of the Life of Mr John Kingston, Preacher of the Gospel' in which he recounted his preaching missions in the West Indies and the new young states of America. At Methodist Conference in summer, **John Kingston** is appointed to the Penzance circuit in West Cornwall, and works alongside Thomas Longley, Wm Pearson Sr and **John Reynolds Jnr**. (the last, a possible relation of **Ann Carne Branwell** in the maternal line).[8]

The new Methodist chapel at Germoe is planned and built on land leased from Joseph Sleep. **John Fennell** and **William Carne Sr.** are two of the Trustees for this venture.

1800

Lydia (Tremenheere) Grenfell[9] converts to Methodism and attends meetings at Marazion, after breaking her engagement to cousin **Samuel John** (a law partner of the Branwell-Carne clan).

12 June: Jane Carne Branwell married the Wesleyan circuit preacher **John Kingston** at Madron by license. Their witnesses were Elizabeth Branwell (Aunt Branwell) and Thomas Longley (Wesleyan preacher in the circuit).

1 August: Act of Union passed in British and Irish Parliaments in March and came into effect on January 1, 1801. In Penzance, the Ship & Castle Inn on Chapel Street was re-named the Union Hotel in its honour.

William (Green) Lovett: Future Chartist. Base son of Keziah Green and her promised sea-captain of Hull (deceased before the birth), was born in the sea-port of Newlyn and brought up by his Methodist mother alone.

Richard Trevithick, Cornish pioneer in the important new field of steam engineering, builds an engine to be used to power a vehicle on the road.

1801

The first newspaper printed and published in Cornwall was the *Royal Cornwall Gazette*, first appearing in 1801, as edited by a Cornishman from Falmouth. After a stuttering start, it continued in publication until 1951. Prior to this, coverage of West Country news items was solely by the *Sherborne Mercury* of Dorset, read by merchants and people of the professional classes in the County (1737-1867).

4 Mar: The 3rd president of the US is Thomas Jefferson, following on from John Adams

Populations: Britain 10.4 million Penzance 3,382

John Kingston assigned to St Austell in Cornwall, the East Cornwall circuit, and John and Jane's first child is born: **Thomas Branwell Kingston**.

1802

Joseph (Cock) Carne was made a Partner in the Cornish Copper Company Deed of 1802, and the General Director the following year at the age of 25. **William (Johns) Carne** was already an adventurer with this company.

Humphry Davy appointed Professor of Chemistry at Royal Institution.

John Kingston assigned to Launceston in Cornwall in the Methodist circuit, and their second child, **Anne Branwell Kingston** was born.

Richard Treffry Sr. married Jane Hawkey of St Wenn, Cornwall. Upon becoming a Methodist she dressed in the plain style of a puritan Quaker, giving seven times the amount to the poor that she spent on clothes.

Cornish engineer **Richard Trevithick's** steam road vehicle is completed and used for the first time to carry passengers.

3 October 1802 **Patrick Bronte** enters as sizar at St. John's College, Cambridge.

1803

The first lifeboat in Cornwall was bought by the people of Penzance in 1803 but it was sold in 1812 due to lack of funds to keep it in operation. In 1840 Nicholas Holman of St Just opened a branch of his foundry business on the quayside. These facilities proved valuable in supporting the steamships that were calling at the harbour in increasing numbers.

The Revd. Henry Martyn, Fellow of St. John's College, became the curate to the **Revd. Charles Simeon** at Holy Trinity church, Cambridge.

Humphry Davy elected Fellow of the Royal Society (FRS).

William (Johns) Carne became a volunteer for 'Pioneers' (territorial defence army) in 1803. A William Carne became a member of the Penzance Corporation (Council) in 1833; this was possibly his son **William (Cock) Carne**, the proprietor of the Carne Grocers in Market Jew Street.

1804

John Kingston assigned to circuit in Nottinghamshire, and his third child with Jane Branwell is born. The child is named **John (Branwell) Kingston Jr.**

Dr Thomas Coke toured Cornwall campaigning for the formation of schools, and offering financial assistance to their sponsors. These could meet in chapels until separate rooms could be obtained – to teach reading, principles of religion and prayer, and to 'prepare them for heaven.'

John Fennell stands as witness for the second marriage of his brother-in-law John Keam when this Methodist stalwart and grocer marries **Mary Paynter/Painter,** spinster of Penzance. The witnesses are John Fennell and Robert Colenso (another kin from Carne family). Bride signed 'Painter'.

The Revd. Henry Martyn returns to Cornwall for a farewell tour of his friends and family, and his love blossoms for Lydia Grenfell (a second cousin with whom he played at St. Hilary where his uncle the **Revd. Malachy Hitchens** was Vicar). He asks her to come to India with him as his wife. Her family protest and she refuses. Their story is told in Barbara Eaton's biography, *Letters to Lydia*, which also chronicles

Branwell kinship and possible influence on the writing of *Jane Eyre*.

1805
John Kingston appointed to Shrewsbury, Shropshire in the Wesleyan circuit of the Birmingham district, and their fourth child, **Maria (Branwell) Kingston** is born, named in honour of Jane's sister Maria Branwell.
The Battle of Trafalgar and the death of Nelson.
George Gordon, Lord Byron enters Trinity College, Cambridge; the dormitory rooms of St. John's College overlook the Bowling Green of Trinity.
Henry Martyn sailed for India in July. He asked Lydia Grenfell to come with him as a sister, if not as a wife. Again she cannot agree, but loves him still. The Cornish missionary to India was sponsored through the formation of the Church Missionary Society (CMS) with the assistance of the Clapham sect and such friends as William and Joseph Carne, Wilberforce, Simeon and other founders of non-conformist and anti-slavery activists. He is thought to have been a partial model for St. John Rivers of Jane Eyre. He died in 1812, in the East India Company chaplaincy on his way home from Persia, hopefully to marry his Cornish sweetheart, Lydia Grenfell of Marazion.
Henry Kirke White, the poet, enters St. John's College, Cambridge, and meets Patrick Brontë who advises him on living expenses. White dies the following year in his rooms at College. The first few entries (1803-1810) on the Timeline about the life and works of the poet Henry Kirke White by Barbara Heritage in her chapter 'The Archaeology of the Book' recently found, reveal in sequence, a new perspective on the reading life of Maria Branwell before her marriage. See *Charlotte Brontë, The Lost Manuscripts* (2018), p. 24.

c1805-6
John Fennell took his wife and daughter, both Janes, and leave Cornwall to return to his home territory of Shropshire, where he took up a post of Headmaster of a boarding school in Wellington, near his old parish of Madeley.
John and Jane (Branwell) Kingston with their three children are assigned to the Birmingham Wesleyan circuit that includes Shrewsbury, Shropshire and they move from Nottingham to Shrewsbury. John Kingston is made the supervisor.
John Kingston is suspected of theft from the Methodist bookroom in Shrewsbury. Discovery of potassium by **Humphry Davy**.

1807
Abolition of the Slave Trade, though it was not until 1833 that slavery itself was abolished.
John Kingston, husband of **Jane (Carne) Branwell** comes to a trial by his peers and is ejected from the Methodist Conference, rumoured to have stolen funds from the Shrewsbury book-funds and behaved immorally with two young men.
6 November A fourth child is born to **John and Jane Kingston,** and is named for **Maria.** Her full name is **Maria Ann Kingston.**
He took his wife Jane and four children to Baltimore, Maryland where he set up a

stationery and publishing business specializing in books for Methodists. See Chapter 12, Document Register, for a copy of the Trial Notes issued by Methodist Conference.

1808
Thomas (John) Branwell, Maria's father dies, leaving legacies to all his daughters, with reversionary legacy to his son, Benjamin Carne Branwell.

Joseph Carne married Mary Thomas (1777-1835) at Haverfordwest, Wales and they made their home at Riviere House, Hayle, the Cornish Copper Company house overlooking the Hayle estuary which was at that time a busy port for import and export to Wales and Bristol.

1809
Patrick Brontë arrives in Wellington, Shropshire as a Curate and makes friends with **John Fennell** and **William Morgan**, who introduced him to **Mary Fletcher of Madeley**. He becomes a member of the Madeley circle of 'her precious young men'. This is also Patrick's first meeting with members of the Branwell clan, as Mrs. Fennell is the former **Jane (John) Branwell,** and their daughter, **Jane Branwell Fennell** has now reached the age of 18, perhaps already being courted by the curate, William Morgan. At the end of the year Brontë moved north with Fletcher's encouragement to a curacy at Dewsbury.

Benjamin Carne Branwell is chosen by the Corporation to be the Mayor of Penzance.

Ann Carne Branwell, Maria's mother dies, leaving her property on Clarence Street to her daughters, to which they move from Chapel Street in following months. Prior to her death her daughter Jane Branwell Kingston had borne five children, and her son Benjamin had fathered five of his nine children in total. Hence at her death she had at least eight surviving grandchildren.

Anne Carne Branwell died on 22 December (age 66), following the return of her eldest surviving daughter, Jane Branwell Kingston from the American states with daughter Elizabeth Jane Kingston, from Baltimore.

Lord Byron and entourage leave Falmouth by packet for a two year grand tour of Europe, at the age of 21.

In 1809 the Penzance Public Dispensary was established, for providing medical and surgical relief for any poor persons, except domestic servants, paupers, and members of friendly societies. **Dr John Forbes** appointed soon after to take charge of the Dispensary alongside establishment of his private medical practice. Dr Forbes was later written to by Charlotte over illness of Emily/Anne. See Chapter 2: 'Creators of Penzance.'

1811
Admiral Robert Carthew Reynolds and **Lt. Thomas (Matthews) Branwell** (Richard Branwell's son) went down with 2000 others in the *HMS St George* in the Baltic, due to storms on the coast of Jutland. Tom Branwell was a first cousin and companion, and Admiral Reynolds a relation of Anne Carne Branwell through her

grandmother's line of descent.

Le Grice's celebrated poem 'The Old Uninhabited House' refers to Cousin Solly Cock with a verse:

The Petition of an Old Uninhabited House in Penzance to its Master in Town'

'All is cheerless, melancholy
Save that now and then a SOLI-
TARY COCK just struts about,
Gives a peek, and then struts out.

Solomon (Soly) Cock, a mason had premises on the Terrace in Market Jew Street. He carried out building work for the Corporation, and inspected the house intermittently.

In April **William Morgan** moved from Wellington, Shropshire into a new curacy under the **Revd. John Crosse** at Bradford, a former curate of the Fletchers at Madeley. **Mary Fletcher** did not forget the faithful **John Fennell** when a new Wesleyan school was planned in the north for the children of Methodist ministers at Woodhouse Grove, Apperley Bridge, near Bradford. She encouraged him to apply and wrote a recommendation for him to the Board.

1812

Woodhouse Grove Academy opened officially on January 12, under Fennell as Headmaster, at Apperley Bridge near Bradford. It had been strongly promoted by Jabez Bunting and would educate the children of Methodist ministers. Jane Branwell Fennell was appointed jointly as the governess or matron, £100 per year for the two. From a small number of nine little boys and two staff at the beginning, it was to grow to 59 pupils by the end of the year, when both staff were giving up their tasks (for separate reasons).[10]

27 March 1812 Uncle **Richard Branwell** died, (the brother of Thomas and one executor of his family will in 1808). His will extant at CRO.

Humphry Davy knighted by Prince Regent in London (8 April) and he marries Mrs Jane Apreece, a niece of Sir Walter Scott (11 April).

Maria (Carne) Branwell departs Penzance in the spring for Yorkshire, to join the Fennells and give assistance at the Woodhouse Grove School for the sons of Methodist ministers,

16 October 1812

The death of **Henry Martyn**, M.A., Chaplain of the Hon East India Company. Born at Truro, England 18 February 1781, died at Tokat, Asia Minor, where the plague was raging, and he was en route to Constantinople and intending to travel home to be with **Lydia Grenfell** of Marazion.

29 December 1812

At Guiseley, near Apperley Bridge, the marriages are celebrated of Maria Branwell with Patrick Brontë, and Jane Branwell Fennell with William Morgan.

At Madron, near Penzance, the marriage of Charlotte Branwell, sister of Maria, to Joseph Branwell, cousin Joseph, Uncle Richard's son. Elizabeth Branwell, later 'Aunt Branwell' to the Brontës acting as Witness.

Foundation stone of the new **Wesleyan Chapel** on Chapel Street was laid by 260 local members, including **William and Joseph Carne** and those of the **Branwells** who were members.

1813

Letter One from John (Cock) Carne in Cambridge to his friend Henry Boase in Penzance.[11]

1814

The Great Revival of the Cornish Methodists began this year in Redruth and soon spread throughout the area.

The Wesleyan Methodists' chapel, built in the year 1814, is the most complete and capacious meeting house in the county. It was not until 1864 that it would be enlarged again. It would have been described in great detail to Maria by Elizabeth. There are, moreover, appropriate places of worship for the Independents, Baptists and Quakers, and a synagogue for the Jews. The new Chapel was modeled on the Central Wesleyan Chapel in London.

The **Royal Geological Society of Cornwall** was founded in the town in 1814 and about 1817 was responsible for introducing a miner's safety tamping bar that attracted the Prince Regent to become its patron.

After the extension of the pier in 1812, **John Matthews** [Branwell kin] opened a small dry dock in 1814, the first in the South West.

1815

The Battle of Waterloo

Elizabeth Branwell of Penzance arrives in Thornton, Yorkshire in the spring of 1815 to visit her aunt Jane Fennell and her sister Maria Brontë and to be present at the birth and baptism of her godchild Elizabeth Brontë, remaining until after the birth of Charlotte the following year.

John Fennell is ordained into the Anglican ministry. He is made Deacon in August, and Priest in December of this year. He writes to Mary Fletcher about this decision. Death in December of **Mary Fletcher** of Madeley, Shropshire, sponsoring patron and friend of Fennell, Brontë and Morgan.

The Corn Law was introduced to safeguard the agricultural industry of the UK by artificially keeping up prices. The effect of the Corn Law was to make the price of corn so high that the poorer classes were driven further into poverty and experienced great hardship. The main business of the Branwell family at this juncture was as grain merchants.

1816

The birth of Charlotte Brontë at Thornton, on 21 April, and named for her mother's sister Charlotte.

Lord Byron takes ship from Falmouth after spending some days in his grandmother Trevanion's home county, and never returns to England. Legend has it that he came to Penzance for an evening's entertainment with friends living at Roscadghill House (may have been either a Borlase or a Tremenheere family member at the time) in Heamoor. It would have been a notable occasion and talked about.

1817
Fennell became incumbent of Cross Stone near Todmorden, where he was to remain for the rest of his life. That same year he baptized Patrick Branwell Brontë.

1818
Emily Brontë was christened by William Morgan, August 1818. John and Jane Fennell were her god-parents.[12]
The Penzance Library established on North Parade (probably No. 10, where the Gentlemen's News Room was located; Dr. John Forbes also lived there.)
Joseph Carne elected a Fellow of the Royal Society (FRS).
27 July **Benjamin Carne Branwell** dies at age 43.

1819
Humphry Davy met up with **Lord Byron** in Lucca, Italy (though he had met him earlier in London with Lady Davy). Before returning from Italy he was also to meet Byron and his Italian mistress, **Teresa Guiccioli** at her Palazzo in Ravenna. Byron was later known to be a great favourite of the Brontë children, especially for Charlotte.

1820
Anne Brontë, named after her maternal grandmother and her aunt, Anne Carne Branwell, was born on 17th January at Thornton.
Joseph Coren, who had been bankrupted previously, was the owner of a brewery in East Street, Penzance. There were advantages in brewing at this time. The price of ale had doubled from a penny-farthing a pint to twopence-halfpenny in the inflation consequent upon the Napoleonic Wars, and he continued as a brewer until his death. (Evan Best on-line family history)
Sir Humphry Davy elected President of the Royal Society
William Lovett (Green) (1800-1877), the future Chartist, was born in Newlyn, near Penzance, the son of a master mariner of Hull who owned a small sailing vessel based at Hull, Yorkshire. His death, before William's birth and before the marriage was solemnized meant that William's mother **Keziah Green, later Carne**, a devoted Methodist, brought him up with the help of her mother. From being a housekeeper, she became a fish jowster (seller) in Newlyn and Penzance street markets. Later Keziah married **William (Colenso) Carne,** son of a Philip Carne of Penzance. His upbringing by his mother and grandmother made him fully aware and alert to the lives and struggles of women, and their needs for both education and political representation. He left Newlyn for London in 1820 to seek employment, and his own life and struggles provide a canvas of stories that Charlotte Brontë and her siblings could well have known through the national press and tract publication. See Family Bibliography in Appendix B.

1821

Elizabeth Branwell of Penzance arrived in Haworth at the beginning of May to look after Maria Brontë in her final illness.
Maria Branwell Brontë died at Haworth, Yorkshire on 15 September
Letter 3 of **John (Cock) Carne** to his sister-in-law, Mrs. James Carne (Charlotte Carne) from Marseilles, giving a long travelogue on the path he and his companion have taken from Paris.
1837 John Carne, Letters 1813-1837, https://archive.org/stream/cu31924104095504.
Letter 4 of John (Cock) Carne to his father from Grand Cairo.
1837 John Carne, Letters 1813-1837, https://archive.org/stream/cu31924104095504.
Letter 5 of John (Cock) Carne to his mother from Cairo.
1837 John Carne, Letters 1813-1837, https://archive.org/stream/cu31924104095504.
Letter 6 of John (Cock) Carne to Henry Boase from Alexandria, Egypt.
1837 John Carne, Letters 1813-1837, https://archive.org/stream/cu31924104095504

1822
Letter 7 of John (Cock) Carne to **Anna Cock Carne**, his mother from Jerusalem, in spring, recounting his travels through the Holy Land (letter partially lost).
Death of kinsman, **Charles Vivian** (born 1805 Cornwall) on 8 July 1822 in Lerica, Italy on the Bay of Spezia with **P. B. Shelley** and **E.E. Williams**. He was the boat boy working from Genoa, who had stayed behind to help with the sailing of the new vessel, the *Don Juan,* as named by **Byron** (Shelley called it *Ariel*). Charles, age 22, was the son of Andrew Vivian of Camborne (managing engineer of Dolcoath Mine from 1798), a relation by marriage of both Carnes and Branwells. (William Carne Sr.'s sister Mary was a Vivian.). Shelley's drowning in all its immediacy with the arrival at the beach of Leigh Hunt, and Lord Byron along with the wives (Mary Godwin Shelley, and Mrs. Williams) to witness the burning of the bodies is anecdotally described, pp. 150-53 of the *Letters 1813-1837*.
Letter 8 of John (Cock) Carne to his sister-in-law, **Mary Carne née Thomas,** wife of Joseph Carne, and mother of Elizabeth C. T. Carne, from Cyprus. See *Letters from the East,* vol. ii, pp. 1-180.
Death of **Anna Carne, née Cock, Mrs. William Carne**, in Penzance, Cornwall in November. See Chapters 3 and 9: `And then came Wesley' and 'People called Carne' to find extract from obituary in the *Methodist Magazine* of 1822.

1823
Letter 9 of John (Cock) Carne to his brother William Carne Jr. from Keswick, Lake District. His previous letter (now lost) refers to having been at Abbotsford in Scotland where he departed with a kind invitation from Sir Walter (Scott) to visit again. At Keswick he is staying with **John Wilson** whom he positively describes, calling him a perfect contrast visually to his friend (Carne's) **W. G. Lockhart** though both are specimens of manly beauty. From Wilson's he progresses to the home of 'the poet of the Lakes' **Wordsworth** and meets with **DeQuincy** and **Southey**. He describes Southey who he much admires for his generosity of spirit. They speak of Southey's biography of Wesley. See Document register, Appendix B for 1823.

Shortly thereafter, he spent a week or so in Edinburgh, which is recounted to his brother William in Letter 10 of the same year of 1823. In this letter, he re-tells a story first told to him by **J. Cam Hobhouse**, a close friend of **Lord Byron**, in the presence of **Walter Scott** at Abbotsford, where Carne had been visiting.

1824

19 April at Messalonghi, Greece, the death of **George Gordon, Lord Byron**, of a fever (malarial relapse or re-infection), where he had gone to fight against the Ottoman Empire.

Between 1819-24: Byron published serially his ultimately unfinished epic satire, *Don Juan* in the Italian stanza *ottava rima*.

24 April in New York City, the death of **Mr. John Kingston, publisher and stationer** at 55 years of age. At time of death he was a religious bookseller on Broadway. His condition was named as pleurisy.

The selected letters from John Carne in succeeding years (from No. 11 to his family – to his father and to his brother – to Charlotte Carne (1), William Sr. (23) and William Jr. (11) – record his various business trips related to the publications of his many books, requests for funds from his 'portion' (of his father's wealth) and newsy tales and tirades to his brother. They come from Cambridge, Switzerland, Paris, London, Blackheath and finally Ireland.

1825 The first steamer came into Penzance harbour.

The death of young Maria Brontë in Haworth, Yorkshire, 6 May 1825, age 12.

The death of young Elizabeth Brontë in Haworth, Yorkshire, 15 June 1825, age 10.

1826

Publication of *Letters from the East* by **John Carne**, and dedicated to **Sir Walter Scott** with whom he had visited at Abbotsford. "Scott was, at the time, engaged in writing *The Talisman*, and John Carne rendered him valuable assistance, in picturing to him the scenery in the neighbourhood of the Dead Sea and Engedi. Scott, however, never acknowledged in any way, except verbally, his obligation. And the mother of the present editor is perhaps the only person now living who is aware that such an obligation ever existed. She well remembers her uncle receiving a copy of *The Talisman* from Sir Walter Scott; and whilst looking through its pages here and there, he would stop, and say, 'I described this place to him whilst I was at Abbotsford.'" (Joseph Carne Ross, Introduction to *Letters 1813-1837 of John Carne*)

1827

Birth of **William John Morgan to his parents, the Revd. William Morgan and Jane (Fennell) Morgan.** His baptism carried through at Cross Stones, with the Vicar Joseph Cowell officiating. This child is the grandchild of Jane Branwell and John Fennell, their only grandchild. He is documented in the *1841 Census* as living in Bradford with his father and stepmother.

Death of **Jane Fennell Morgan** (see 1791 and 1812), at age 36; she is the wife of the Revd. William Morgan, daughter of John and Jane Fennell, and mother of the child reported above.

An amusing and anonymous satire was circulated throughout the town of Penzance concocted around the hiatus created when the Methodist 'Canorum' of Chapel Street determined that they might like to have an organ for their magnificent new building. Prime characters of this imaginative popish-musical plot entitled *The Canorum Conclave* were selected from families of **Branwell**, **Carne** and others related by marriage to them, and designated as Cardinals. The surname associated with the Branwell was 'Cardinal Scratchback' and to the Carne cousins as 'Bankum' as in 'Cardinal Bankum's son' being civil engineer, mine agent and banking partner, Joseph Carne, FRS. The author of this satire remained a mystery – though much guessed at and vilified by all the families that discovered themselves in its pages – and was finally identified as **John Harvey**, a pharmacist and chemist. (See the research paper of the Penwith History Group by Susan Hoyle in *Treasures of the Morrab*, 'The Canorum Conclave', pp. 65-72.)

1829
Death of **Jane Branwell Fennell** (See 1753) at age 76. She is buried in Cross Stone churchyard, though her gravestone shared with John Fennell and Jane Fennell Morgan is laid down beside the schoolhouse (now converted to a family home). Visited 2013 (the inscriptions are fading and covered with lichen. MH).
Death of **Sir Humphry Davy** while travelling home from Rome. He is buried in the Cimetière des Rois in Geneva, Switzerland.

1830
Another familiar building from this period is the eccentric *Egyptian House* in Chapel Street, built in 1830-38.
Gas lighting was introduced to Penzance in 1830.
John Fennell married secondly (at Halifax), Elizabeth, daughter of John Lister, merchant, Leeds, niece of Revd. Thomas Howorth, of Idel. Their children were: Mary Elizabeth, 1831, married Revd. W. G. Mayne, of Ingrow; Hannah Julia, 1834, married Dr. Edward Ilott, of Bromley; Charles John, a doctor, Royal Navy; Ellen Jane, 1838, married Mr. Salmon, barrister; Thomas Edward, 1840, of the G. E. Railway.

1831
The First Reform Bill passed enabling a wider section of the populace to vote.
The death of **Joseph (Thomas) Carne Jr.**, at age 22, of tuberculosis on the island of Madeira. He was the first son of Joseph Cock Carne FRS and elder brother of Elizabeth Catherine Thomas Carne. He was the close friend at school and Trinity College of W. M. Thackeray, and a brilliant speaker in the Cambridge Union. Aunt Branwell would have been informed of this bereavement.

1832-35
1832 The death of the **Revd. James (Cock) Carne DD** and his wife **Charlotte (Jones) Carne** in Plymouth, Devon, where they were tending cholera victims in their parishioner's homes. Both succumbed to the disease, leaving five children to be taken

in to the home of his brother Joseph Carne, FRS of Penzance. This event possibly influenced Aunt Branwell to make her own will the following year. Charlotte Brontë used this event in *Jane Eyre*.

The first of two eras of building in Penzance. 1832-35 was the building of St Mary's Church, completed in 1836. The old Market House was demolished in 1836. Its replacement, designed by W. Harris of Bristol, was completed at the top of Market Jew Street in 1838.[13]

St Mary's Church, another prominent feature of the Penzance skyline, was completed in 1836, while a Roman Catholic church was built in 1843.

1833

Penzance in 1833 had 22 public houses, and seven beer shops which were described as 'prejudicial to the morals of the town'.

Elizabeth Branwell writes her Will on the 30th of April, 1833 with executors being the Revd. Patrick Brontë, the Revd. John Fennell, the Revd. Theodore Dury, and Mr. George Taylor.

1836

The death of merchant banker **William (Johns) Carne**, 12 July 1836. He is buried at the Gulval Anglican parish churchyard in the family mausoleum, with some of his family. Twenty-four carriages followed his hearse-courtege. The shops of the town of Penzance were shut and he was much mourned. (See Todd Gray, *Cornwall: The Travellers' Tales*, pp. 119-120.)

The death of the **Revd. Charles Simeon** in November, at age 77, and is buried in King's Chapel, Cambridge.

1838

Publication of the *Parochial History of Cornwall* (Hals, Tonkin & Davies). Available on-line.

1839

Penzance Gazette first published, at what is now No. 16 Trevelyan House, Chapel Street, Penzance. This was the first and only daily newspaper ever printed in Penzance. It included the *Methodist Tidings* in the afternoon.

1841

Death of the Revd. John Fennell (buried at Cross Stone churchyard) at age 79-80.

1842

Death of **Elizabeth Branwell** at age 66. Her will proved on 12 December 1842, by the Revd. Patrick Brontë, her brother-in-law and George Taylor.

See Appendix B: Document register for a transcription of this will.

1844

Death of **John (Cock) Carne**, traveller and author, at Penzance at age 55.

1847

Publication of *Wuthering Heights*, by Ellis Bell (Emily Jane Brontë)
Publication of *Agnes Grey*, by Acton Bell (Anne Brontë)
Publication of *Jane Eyre*, by Currer Bell (Charlotte Brontë)

1848

Publication of *The Tenant of Wildfell Hall*, in June, by Acton Bell (Anne Brontë)
Death of **Patrick Branwell Brontë** at Haworth, Yorkshire 24 September, age 31.
Death of **Emily Jane Brontë** at Haworth, Yorkshire 19 December 1848, age 30.

1849

Death of **Anne Brontë**, 28 May 1849, age 29, buried at Scarborough, Yorkshire, her grave overlooking the North Sea.
Publication of *Shirley*, by Charlotte Brontë
Publication of *Villette*, by Charlotte Brontë

1854

Marriage of **Charlotte Brontë with the Revd. Arthur Bell Nicholls** at St. Michael and All Angels, Haworth, West Yorkshire.

1855

Death of **Charlotte Brontë Nicholls**, 31 March 1855, age 38, and is buried in the family tomb at Haworth.
Jane Branwell Kingston, aged 81, on 12 May, is buried in the family mausoleum in Penzance. Her daughter, Elizabeth Jane Kingston, correspondent with Charlotte Brontë, her cousin, continued to live independently until her death in 1878 (in hospital). Her story is told by Fannie Ratchford in her BST paper, 'The Loneliness of a Brontë Cousin'. See Appendix B, Bibliographie (Brontëana).

1857

Publication of *The Professor*, posthumously, by **Charlotte Brontë**

1858

Death of **Joseph (Cock) Carne** FRS, age 76.

1861

Death of **Patrick Brontë** on 7 June 1861, age 84, and buried at Haworth, Yorkshire.

The East View of St. Michael's Mount in the County of Cornwall (n.d.)

ENDNOTES

1 'Journal of George John' (1779-1833 CRO AD72/12)
2 *Universal Directory of Great Britain 1791* 'Penzance: Leading traders of the town'.
3 'The Methodist Society in Penzance', 1 July 1767, in which there were more women than men attending. List provided by the Methodist Archives, RIC, Truro (Courtney Library).
4 M. Smith, *Letters of Charlotte Brontë*, vol. 1, pp. 224-25. Letter to Ellen Nussey.
5 Three boys and two girls were born to Elizabeth and Alexander, including an artist (Joshua 1767-1847), a poet (Ann Batten 1769-1848), an engraver (Elizabeth 1771-1853), a second sea-captain (Joseph 1775-1850) and Alexander Jr (1776-1848, who ended in the workhouse with his wife, long after the death of his parents). Elizabeth's children were contemporaries with the Branwell children – they were kin and visited Penzance often, arriving by sea on the coastal ships of their father and step-brother).
6 John Horner, *Even in this Place*, p. 51.
7 A John Williams, Gent of Redruth, became the husband of Alice Branwell in 1795, youngest sister of Thomas Branwell, and aunt of Maria. However, it is not certain that this is the same John Williams, though dates seem to validate, as there are at least ten of the same name in related family branches around the mining areas of Camborne, Redruth, Gwennap, etc. The couple – John and Alice – do not appear in Cornish records thereafter and may have moved out of the county, as many wealthy Cornish gentlemen maintained homes in London. It is assumed that it was members of this family who met with the Brontë family for an afternoon visit when they were visiting John Fennell during his final illness in 1841 in Cross Stone Vicarage.
8 Note: Circuit assignments in the Methodist system are made at the Yearly Conference, which is held in mid-summer each year, when each preacher is interviewed and declared 'fit for purpose' (or not). Hence re-assignments of place occur mid-year and not by calendar year.
9 Lydia Grenfell's mother was the niece of Dr Borlase, the Magistrate and Vicar of Penzance who threatened John Wesley with gaol, and a member of the influential Tremenheere family of Penzance and Marazion. Lydia Grenfell's conversion to Methodism, her ill-fated love affair with Henry Martyn, the curate of Charles Simeon at Cambridge, together with letters from him are recounted in *Letters to Lydia*, by Barbara Eaton.
10 *The Story of Woodhouse Grove School* by F. C. Pritchard (1978), pp14-23 and Fletcher-Tooth collection at Manchester University.
11 These letters will chart the travels of John (Cock) Carne from 1813 until he retires from travelling and returns home to Penzance in the 1840s, having lost the sight in one eye and feeling the loss of his former vigour, through the onslaught of premature ageing. Carne Ross, Joseph (ed. 1885) *John Carne, Letters 1813-1837*, Privately printed, Ltd edition No 100 of 100 copies printed. Online at https://archive.org/stream/cu31924104095504 inclusive one handwritten letter from Joseph Carne Ross to his publishers 1886. The Letters will equate to the number they hold in the Table of Contents of the volume.

PART II:
ORIGINS OF FAMILY LORE

Detail from Plate 1 Penzance, by W Penaluna.

Chapter 7

Legacies of kinship, a second introduction

'Family, clan or tribe is the living unit of society; the individual, even an outstanding one, is a part of it and in part takes his colouring from it. So family history, though a somewhat neglected form, is of the first importance, as Gibbon saw; biographies, so much more popular and to the fore today...should be seen to rise properly out of the family background. It is all the more difficult to write a double family history, to illustrate the mixing of stocks, their intricate cross-connexions, their mutual fertilization, the subtleties of inheritance.'

A. L. Rowse, from the Prelude to *The Byrons and Trevanions*

The marriage of Thomas Branwell and Ann Carne in late November of 1768, in the parish church of Penzance located at nearby Madron, is the critical one for our story. These are the grandparents in the maternal line of the Brontë children. Though the children never knew them in person, much would have been known about them from Aunt Branwell and Maria in their familiar ways and means of living their lives. And, there were several other family clans of local consequence bound in by marriage to the joint family of Carne and Branwell through previous generations – John/s families, Batten families, Cock families, Vyvyan/Vivian families amongst several others. These are more briefly explored in following chapters revealing some very surprising connections, living links at the time, but not investigated by later researchers.

In dealing with the stories of Branwells and Carnes of Penzance together with their marriages into other local families, one is inevitably touching on the lives of the wider community of the Land's End peninsula. This fact is not meant as a benign generalization. Both families were unusually and distinctively civic-minded, as well as commercially engaged with the public. Their marriages linked them with many of the leading families of the town and, to a surprising degree, they were intertwined in history.

It is certainly true, as recounted by Penzance historian Peter Pool[1] that the people called Branwell or Bramble or Bremble are not known for literary output. You search for them in vain in historic publications under that surname because primarily they were commercial people trading in local and international grocery and grain markets as well as in property development. This does not mean, of course, as we shall find, that no interest or role was taken by members of the wider family in reading, writing and cultural advances in spiritual and educational terms. As Chapter 10 about 'The Travellers' will show the evidence is plentiful for creativity and learning.

Literary output was certainly not lacking, however, in the case of those called Carne and those called Batten, Keigwin, Polwhele and Kingston amongst others. Though the Carnes were also successful merchants, builders, craftsmen, grocers, clergy, and civic administrators like the Branwells, individuals from that side of the maternal descent wrote prodigiously, adding a strong storytelling, poetic, religious, scientific, academic and technological bent into the mix. Without question, the Carne literary influence on the whole of the Branwell network of families was strong and pervasive. How much their influence inspired emulation cannot be measured, though it was widely acknowledged at the time.

From the Carnes there are bibliophiles, vicars, poets, philanthropists, and travel writers who produced archaeological, antiquarian, mineralogical and geological papers as well as treatises on religion and political philosophy to fill several pages in any bibliography and the *Dictionary of National Biography*. The 'impulse to write for publication' commented on by some Brontë biographers as being a characteristic of the Revd. Patrick Brontë, was without doubt dominant and ongoing within the maternal hegemony. This period in the history of Penzance has come to be looked upon as one of 'enlightenment' spurred on by discoveries related to the industrial revolution, and the quickening influence of education brought on by the 'methodies' and their efforts in providing classes and schools.

In 1989, when the Brontë Society placed plaques on the Branwell home on Chapel Street and the Chapel in Penzance, the research undertaken by Peter Pool was aimed, as one-name studies are, at those people who carry the one patronymic, and at the business interests of the males. The wife's maiden name is given if known and perhaps her father's occupation (for the general purposes of assessing class status). This, of course, is the 'fact' of family history, though perhaps not always the 'truth', and leaves the stories of the women, their families, connections, traditions, and stories marginalised, unless the woman in question is herself a writer and puts her observations forward. Only a few of these are found.[2]

In the great-grandparental generation, the West Cornish Branwells and Carnes were mostly free men of common rather than aristocratic birth who, alongside their wives and cousins, worked their own small trades, building these into partnerships and businesses employing others. An exception to this statement is the ancient Carne dynasty stretching back in Welsh history to leading and aristocratic roles related to the Crown and to positions at court. But, at this particular point in Cornish history, as descendants of 'second sons' (junior dynasties) who did not inherit the family fortune, they were 'starter sets' for the English middle classes. It was in the nineteenth century that this status was achieved in both of the above families. Families were considered 'distinguished' if one or two of its individual males succeeded professionally and financially. Naturally, not all members met the same high standard – and women, for the most part, were ignored in these stakes except when they carried a great fortune into the family line. Otherwise they are found, if at all, continually to be falling off the page of history.

Within the two families described here, there were a few 'higher-flying' businessmen, lawyers and entrepreneurs, together with educated and practising clergy. They were the 'middle men' of the economies who spread their wings as merchants, shipping and mining agents, bankers, organisers of labour, and thereby also civic leaders and so-called 'guvners'. It was not uncommon to find the Vicar being also a mine owner or investor, and to have been a lawyer at some point (and often a Magistrate). Most of the men in this study did more than one thing in their occupational lives.[3]

Most of the women in this study appear to have led closed and domestic lives, whether married or single, because little of anything refers to them. They kept the homes going, usually with one or two servants – the Battens at one point approaching a staff of twelve at home – providing the meals, seeing to the domestic detail of clothing, house linen, washing, cleaning and marketing, as well as nursing the many babies that arrived to families and friends. The spinster women remained in their family homes, supporting the local churches, attending the sick and helping to bury the dead. Only a small minority had documented occupations or avocations that have been publicly noticed, but many assisted in the family businesses and were engaged in teaching their children. The multi-tasking quality of their working lives alongside the cultural ideas about 'what was respectable behaviour' for women successfully shrouded their personalities for the most part as well as their `out of home activity'. By the time that the Brontës were writing their novels in Haworth, changes in attitudes and challenges to that *status quo* were well afoot.

Amongst the female kin about whom we have found some detail are Anna Carne née Cock of Helston (1753-1822), the wife of William (Johns) Carne (1754-1836), merchant banker, and mother of Joseph Carne, FRS (1782-1858). (See 'People called Carne); Grace (Millett) Davy (1750-1826), the mother of the future Sir Humphry Davy (1778-1829) and his brother Dr John Davy (1790-1868); Thomasine Dennis (1770-1809), self-taught linguist, novelist and poet of St. Levan nearby; Anne Batten Cristall (1769-1848), first cousin of Mary Batten Branwell (1777-1851), wife of brother Benjamin (1775-1818), and published poet (1795); Keziah (Davey) Green (1780-18??) and Faith Green, mother and grandmother (n.d.) of William Lovett (1800-1877), the future outstanding Chartist, and one or two more who feature in small anecdotes. Brief references concerning these and more characters of the time will be found in Chapter 11. In most cases, it is the famous sons of these women who reveal their gratitude and devotion to their mothers. These are women who Maria and Elizabeth would meet regularly, and with whom they would find friendship, solace and discussion (gossip too), and with whom they would celebrate their triumphs, large and small.

Kinship, of course, does not necessarily imply friendship or camaraderie. This was as true then as it is now. Some stories of disaffection and dislike surface from time to time in the narratives of the day, and provide extra fields for further study. It is also salutary to remind ourselves that it is now possible, due to extensive records and greater expertise in research methods, to trace family roots and origins in greater detail than ever before. This means that we can make connections between families that they may not have known about, and with greater accuracy than their own memories could recount even if they did know. Though it is the purpose of this report to expose possible paths of influence on literary themes taken up by the Brontës, much can only be considered ground for speculation, and may always remain unconfirmed.

Families often took in the nephews, nieces, and cousins, left motherless or fatherless by disease or disaster, and this is true for both of the main families of the circle studied here. The general theme of the 'orphaned' child,[4] and reliance upon the good will and beneficence of distant family members is constant and common, as was the slowly-growing need for women to learn and to be part of the recognised working world. Another thread which haunts the fabric of the community as well as the future novels of the Brontë children, was 'legacy' and the holding of money until certain tasks are undertaken, promises fulfilled, or specific ages achieved.

It is in the generation of the Brontë children's parents that a noticeable rise in social class status can be found, when the industry, invention and market developments that the seniors had nurtured within the agrarian, marine and mining communities, began to pay off for their children. In the generation of Thomas Branwell and his siblings, individual men's names appear in reference lists sometimes (though not invariably) as 'gentry', and in the following generation still, some are listed as Esquire, as in Benjamin Carne Branwell, Esq., the brother of Elizabeth and Maria. At that time Esq. or Esquire intimated that this person was independently and financially secure, and lived primarily on their properties, inheritance and interest. Of course, this would include some layabouts and gamblers, as well as some hardworking, energetic farmers and builders.

Genealogy and kinship: people of Penzance

In the eighteenth century Branwells and Carnes 'set up their carriages'[5] in which the later ones travelled throughout the following century. A strong argument can be constructed to show that of the earlier Branwells, it was Thomas Branwell, father of Maria and Elizabeth, whose hard work engineered the family fortunes that followed, based on the entrepreneurial instincts of Richard Sr. (Thomas's father), and the merchant and farming inheritance of his mother's (Margaret John) family.

Equally, cousin William (Johns) Carne's (1754-1836) industry, influence and perspicacious investments provided the platform for the general welfare and wealth of his clan, while other members of the family enabled a literary, theological and scientific tradition to unfold. Father Thomas Branwell's musical talents have also been noted – he played the violin and the flute – and there was a piano in the parlour.[6] Cousin Joseph (Cock) Carne FRS, appearing in the next generation, was talented on the fiddle. Into the mid-twentieth century from the 1820s, the Branwells provided the musical accompaniment to Methodist services on the organ at the Chapel Street Methodist Chapel. A concert hall or musical room also existed for the community at the rear of the historic inn, the Turk's Head, a few houses away from their homes on Chapel Street. Here were often gathered various players and singers of the community on chosen nights of the week. Whether or not women were included is not known.

Unfortunately, two of Thomas Branwell's three sons died early,[7] and his brother Richard's sons all thrived, primarily with finance and starter businesses passed on to them by Thomas through various investments and partnerships with his brother and others. In fact, the following generations of Branwell children of both Thomas and Richard, owed their designations as merchants and gentlemen, and perhaps even their inclination to public service, to the example set by Thomas. And, yet, curiously I think, at his death there was no mention in any newspaper or journal that I have located, and no known family outcry of any kind. For a person who accomplished so much (it seems) it is surprising to find no records of his birth, baptism, and only a public record of his burial with no obituary. His will remains, otherwise I would wonder who he really was?

Thomas's older brother, Richard, who had begun as a builder, in later years leased the Golden Lion Inn from Thomas and became an innkeeper; the rents he paid contributed to the family legacies to the Branwell daughters as well as his own spinster daughters.[8] Certain properties belonging to Thomas were part-shared by Richard, but whereas Thomas took a role in Penzance civic life and was noted as 'gentry' the same was not true of Richard, nor their older half-brother, Martin, who owned his own butchery and butcher's shop. The sons of Richard and Martin would gain that status through emulating the shrewdness and acumen of their uncle Thomas.

Families did specialise and there are several shoemakers (cordwainers) in the Carne kinship circle, and numerous grocers, butchers and grain merchants amongst the Branwells. Both sides of the combined families harboured clock and watch-makers, both had builders and architects (masons, carpenters) and both had clergymen of several varieties. Both men and women could serve as Methodist class leaders and both Branwells and Carnes served in this way. It is not true, however, as stated by John Sutherland in his compendium of Victorian fiction, that Patrick Bronte had married a daughter of a Cornish parson in 1812.[9] The closest he came to such a position, was as a member of the Methodist Society and perhaps (unknown) as a class leader, as were his contemporaries William Carne, John Fennell and Anna Tyacke Branwell.

Cohorts

Cohort I. Earliest connections, to 1768

The following list documents those family surnames which Ann Carne and Thomas Branwell brought into their marriage in 1768, those that were part of their own separate family histories. In so doing they become related by marriage, and therefore 'kin'. In this early period, most of the marriages were amongst local families who were known to each other, often sharing occupations such as boot and shoemaking (cordwainers), fishing (mariners, seamen and dockyard workers/owners), miners/mining captains and agents/adventurers (investors), merchants and shopkeepers of various kinds.

A few were to be particularly successful, such as William (Johns) Carne, John Hallett Batten, George (Williams) John and somewhat later the Bolitho family, in the sense of amassing large fortunes, through marriage, mining, shipping, banking and property owning. One or two were to marry into those Cornish families described as the 'Great Families of Cornwall', the landed gentry and patricians who traced their histories back to the Norman Conquest. A number, of course, would lose their fortunes, squander their opportunities and legacies, or die early before their Biblical allotment. Then, as now, it was mostly about 'getting and spending'.[10]

Primarily, however, our subjects were resilient, hardworking, self-made and self-educated people of Breton, Cornish, Irish and Welsh descent, who contributed most strongly to the building of the British empire abroad through trading links and scientific invention, as well as being at the 'top table' or forefront of the Industrial Revolution of the nineteenth century. Little is known about the women in these clans, often silent and discreet by tradition, if one is 'a lady'. Otherwise a woman would be exposed by name if of ill-repute or 'hanged' for murder, etc. To a large extent, the coming of the Wesleyan traditions related to learning and independence for all individuals (including women) made a large impact on social attitudes and transformed many social attitudes.

The following are surnames found in the family kinship records and trees. The date following the surname is the year that a member of that family 'married in' to 1) *The Branwell clan* and took up that name or some one of its derivations, and 2) *The Carne clan* and carried that name thereafter. **Those highlighted appear in both families – Carne and Branwell at this early period.** Though not an exhaustive list, family researchers bearing the following surnames may be able to trace connection to Brontë lives.

BRANWELL +

Anbarne 1656
Base 1704;
Bastard of Crowan 1766;
Batten 1710;
Boase 1690
Carne 1728, 1768;
Carpenter 1754;
Champion 1740;
Cock 1766;
Ford 1766;
Freethy 1738;
Horskin/Hosken 1671;
John/Johns 1742;
Keigwin 1705;
Lamerton 1708;
Leah 1746/7;
Lawry 1704;
Lobb 1711;
Man/Mann 1731;

Matthews 1757;
Middleton 1758;
Morrice 1753;
Nowell 1714;
Rawling 1717;
Redolph 1730
Richards 1725;
Roberts 1719/20
Sampson 1730;
Slogget of Lanteglos 1753;
Sutherland 1763;
Tanner 1711;
Thomas 1702, 1757;
Tonkin 1720;
Tremearn/e 1705;
Warn/Warren 1703;
Wedge 1763;
Woolcock 1737

JOHN/JOHNS +

Within their kinship circle Margaret (Boase) John (1723-1791) of Paul and Sancreed married Richard(Tremearne) Branwell in 1742 at Madron. These were the great grandparents-to-be of the Brontë children. Through this marriage to Margaret John, daughter of Thomas John, blacksmith, and his wife Maria (Boase) John, the yeoman Branwells begin to connect to and associate with families of greater fortune and education than previously, which undoubtedly had influence on succeeding generations. Following are the surnames of people Margaret John came from and knew, and was *bringing into* the Branwell orbit. These are also families which produced contemporaries and cousins of Thomas and Ann Branwell, with whom they mixed and befriended. **Highlighted are those that were already connected to the Branwell family circle**; the others are new relations. It has not proved possible to research all of the marriage dates of these families.

Arundel 1610, 1761;
Bennett/Bennetts c1650;
Boase 1742;
Boone of the Lizard;
Branwell 1742;
Eathorn/Ethoren;
Faby 1716;
Grose/Grosse of Cury
Harris (of Kennegy Manor, Gulval);
Heame/Heyme 1663;
Hitchens;
Humphrey 1600;
Incledon of the Lizard;
Jenkyn;
John/Johns of Madron;
John/Johns of Truro & Phillack;

John/Johns of Helston & Wendron
Pascoe;
Passingham;
Pearce 1670;
Pellew 1702
Pendarves/Stackhouse (of Truro);
Penrose (of Falmouth);
Plomer of St Keverne;
Scadden;
Tonkin 1742;
Tyack/e
Trevelyan;
Vage/Page 1745;
Warren of Wendron 1697;
Williams of Helston & Wendron 1734;

CARNE +

In the maternal line, when John Calenso Carne (1715-1793), silversmith and clockmaker, of Penzance married Anne (?Roberts) Reynolds at Madron Parish Church in 1740, he was 25 years old, and a son of cordwainer Henry Carne and his wife Eleanor Calenso, both of longstanding West Cornwall families. He brought yet another group of families, the Reynolds, and some of the same, into the kinship circle. Highlighted are those families who joined in with both Branwell and Carne lines of descent.

Ackford;
Batten;
Bloomfield;
Branwell;
Calenso/Colensoe/Colensow 1703;
Chellew;
Clark;
Cock;
Coke;
Cornish;
Davy;
Downing;
Faull;
Giles;
Grose;
Hammett;
Harvey;

James x 2 1814;
John of Gwithian;
Johns;
Johnston of Edinburgh;
Lane;
Line/Lyne;
Reynolds;
Richards;
Sampson;
Smith;
Thomas of Kidwelly, Wales;
Trewhella/wheela;
Tyack/e;
Vivian/Vyvyan of Trelowarren;
Vivian of Camborne;
Williams

Cohort 2. 1768-1812
The families bearing the following names, through marriage with Branwells and Carnes, were the contemporaries of Maria and her siblings, and were most likely to know of their kinship with each other and to call each other cousin, aunt, uncle, etc. as appropriate. These are people with whom they attended church, celebrated their weddings and baptisms and attended their funerals. They also had nicknames for those with the same forenames and surnames, only some of which are known.

Andrew 1801;
Argall 1797;
Batten 1799;
Bottrell 1797;
Branwell 1812;
Bromley 1784;
Brontë 1812;
Bosence 1833;
Carter of Nth Shields 1809;
Cristall of Rotherhithe
Cock 1794 (2nd);
Corin/Coren 1772;
Cunnack 1782;
Dennis of St. Levan;
Duncan 1799;
Edmonds 1794;
Edwards 1801;

Fennell 1790;
Fisher, Gent 1792;
Ford 1766;
Freethy 1797 (2nd);
Fudge 1794;
George 1810;
Keam 1788;
Kingston of Towcestor 1800;
Lawrey 1753 (2nd);
Linthwaite (of Leics Militia), 1781;
McDonald (6th Reg) 1772;
Matthews 1771, 1772(2nd, 3rd);
Morgan 1812;
Oates of St Just 1785;
Odgers 1806;
Osborne of Sancreed 1802;
Paddy, Gent 1805;

Pascoe 1794;
Paul 1780;
Permewan 1801;
Richards 1807 (2nd);
Rodda 1808;
Russell 1799;
Sampson 1817 (2nd);
Selby 1797;
Semmens 1812;

Stevens 1800;
Thomas 1793 (2nd);
Tyack 1797;
Vosper 1799;
Williams, Gent 1795;
Williams 1803;
Williams, Mariner 1787;
Wilson 1811

Cohort 3. 1813-1861

The rationale for including this cohort of marriages with the Branwell & Carne families, is that these are kin about whom Maria and Elizabeth might have known before leaving Cornwall, but would only hear further about through correspondence with siblings and cousins at home. It might only be in subsequent years that some of them would 'claim kin' due to the notoriety of the famous Brontë sisters of Yorkshire, who can be said to be 'belonging to we' in common Cornish parlance.

Barwis 1831;
Batten;
Branwell 1819
Guscott 1839;
Harris 1836;
Hawes 1834;
Hawke 1814;
Honey, mariner, 1843;
Hosking 1844;
Jones 1852
Kingston: Sargent, Bergstrasser (USA),
Ladner 1840;
Moore 1847
Oats/Oates 1830;
Paul 1838;

Polwhele;
Richards 1815, 1819, 1823;
Roberts 1846; Shutte 1815;
Ross;
Stanbury 1824;
Tonkin 1827;
Treadwell 1854
Tregarthen 1824;
Tuke Treleaven 1841;
Tyack 1849;
Vingoe 1822;
Vivian 1820, 1824;
Williams 1833;
Wilson 1814;

ENDNOTES

1 Peter Pool (1989) 'The Branwells of Penzance' Paper delivered at Penlee House, limited distribution, unpublished in 1990. Also 'The Branwell Connection' by P.A.S. Pool, M.A., F.S.A. in *Brontë Society Transactions,* vol. 18 No. 3, 1989, pp. 217-21.

2 See 'Some Remarks on Mr G B Millett's Madron Registers' Paper read at the Annual Meeting (Nov 18, 1904) of the Penzance Natural History and Antiquarian Society. See also *"A Passel of Ould Traade"* by R. A. Courtney (1909) in which Courtney remarks "I need hardly say this list seems to refer to sons alone, daughters being evidently of no account, as you would find…where the women in the Marriage Register are as a rule entered with a Christian name only." In Madron Baptismal records (unlike other Cornish parishes) only the father's name is given when baptising his child.

3 Students of family trees can be easily confused about the occupational lives of various members of a family, sharing the same forename, but practicing different trades and professions. Sometimes there may in fact be only one person in question, who may have had several occupations in their lifetime: sometimes several people with the same name are found as contemporaries, because cousins followed the same 'family forenames' and in everyday life were known by nicknames for differentiation.

4 A thematic trope employed by Charlotte Brontë with regularity.

5 Expression employed by John (Cock) Carne, son of William, Banker, cousin & author, to describe the good fortune of their kinsman, George (Williams) John, solicitor, (1830) in his old age, in a letter to his brother William. *John Carne Letters 1813-1837* Letter 33.

6 A flute book and miscellaneous notes were found in Branwell material (Oldham archive, Morrab Library).

7 The one son who reached his majority, Benjamin Carne Branwell, served as Mayor of Penzance in 1809, the year his mother died. His suggested occupation is that of merchant (clockmaker and miller) following receipt of his father's estate; otherwise he is listed here and there as a Gent. outliving his parents by ten years only.

8 See 'Will of Thomas Branwell' in Document Register, Appendix B.

9 John Sutherland (1990 paper edition) *The Longman Companion to Victorian Fiction* p. 84-5.

10 In relation to benevolence, however, the Carne family through several generations were known especially for their gifts and works for charitable causes, and for their simplicity of behaviour and dress.

The Branwell House, as it would have been when first built c1783. 25 Chapel Street, Penzance.
Drawn and hand-coloured by Mike Dash, Architect. © 2018.

Chapter 8

People called Branwell

'The trees in the streets are old trees
used to living with people,
Family-trees that remember your grandfather's name'
Stephen Vincent Benét

Lilian Oldham[1] during her recent twentieth-century tenure, converted Number 25, as it became when numbering was introduced in the nineteenth century, into a small museum dedicated to Brontë and Branwell memories. She began her description with the following:

> On opening the front door with its high latch and lower iron knob, the eye travels along a white walled passage to an archway framing a small hall, from which ascends a short flight of stairs. These stairs turn to a tall deep set window, through which sunlight and moonlight pour down into the hall below. A second short passage at floor level, paved with grey slate slabs leads to a door opening into the south facing walled garden, a veritable suntrap.
>
> Ten rooms in the house had fireplaces, with blue slate hearths, all well used. All the hearths remain and three bedrooms retain their original fire places. There were three bedrooms with a small dressing room and a linen room; above these are both a large attic and a small attic...Candlepower, lamps fuelled by fish oil and firelight were the sources of illumination after daylight had faded.
>
> Beyond the old kitchen was a back kitchen, the floor of which was an extension of the garden path, [made] of old bricks, granite slabs, odd slates and cobblestones....There was no house drainage or sanitation, as we know it, and the earth closet was at the bottom of the garden, combined with a midden or ash pit emptied by soil-cart when full and sold to the farmers as fertiliser.

About the Branwells of West Cornwall

Families of Paul, Sancreed and Penzance, also St Just in Penwith[2]

Branwells, under several and variously spelled derivations, were present in West Cornwall engaged in farming, fishing and mining – for an indeterminate period extending to as much as 200-300 years. These families reach back into an illiterate past, since they were not part of 'the great families of Cornwall' about whom there is a large literature.[3]

Due to the size of the families involved, it has not been possible to trace each individual in great detail nor would it be relevant, though undoubtedly there is always the possibility by neglecting to do this, that relationships that were very important in their own time are missed out altogether. With families being the building blocks from which communities are born, however, a preliminary survey of the marriages made within the given time period of Elizabeth and Maria (Carne) Branwell, reveals potential fields of enquiry.

Much more is known about the extended and extensive Branwell family in genealogical terms than about the Carne clan, due to the extensive research of Richard G. Grylls who published *Branwell & Bramble, a brief history of a West Cornwall Clan* in 2006.[4] Without that excellent preparatory work, which substantially builds up on past reviews,[5] it is doubtful that this follow-up study could be completed within the given time. Attempting to trace family lines of descent takes hours and hours of frustrating and even bewildering work, as family historians know.

With all the uncertainties and unknowns that are recognized by Grylls as inherent with broken and often faulty and sometimes indecipherable documents, he has accomplished an amazing feat of detective work, with the help of several collaborators and archival institutions. From the 1600s through to the end of the 1900s, with some overlap at both ends, he has laid out twelve detailed trees of the 'greater Branwell families', much of which centers on West Cornwall and the Isles of Scilly. There is no intention herein to replicate this work nor would it be relevant, though a few small gaps have been filled through the current study, and some additions made to the general record. His work has always proved trustworthy as I have journeyed through many of the same documents and over similar fields of enquiry. The Branwell-Carne Archive, gathered under the auspices of the Hypatia Trust, holds a wide spread of printed material related to the many individuals of these families, and will be available for further study after the publication of this book.

The Branwell family descent to the Brontë children of Haworth, Yorkshire

BRANWELL Table 1: Eight generations of the family
Direct descendancy to Brontë

Male line ↓   The partners

Male line ↓	The partners
1. John Bremble c1590 + Nine children, one of whom is ↓:	Sibell (surname unknown= SU), d1656 5x-grandparents
2. Martayn Brymmel/Bromo//Bremble + c1610 Four known children, one of whom is ↓:	Moade (SU) 4x-grandparents
3. John Bromo/ Bromewell+ c1635 Six known children, one of whom is ↓:	Constance (SU) 3 x-grandparents
4. Martyn Bromwell 1674-1719 + Seven children, one of whom, with Jane, is ↓:	1) Margery Bennetts / 3 children 2) **Jane Tremearne** /4 children G-G-grandparents
5. Richard Bramwell 1711-1792 + Eight children, one of whom is ↓:	Margaret John 1711-1791 Great grandparents to Brontës
6. Thomas Branwell c1745-1808 + Twelve children, one of whom is ↓:	Ann Carne 1743-1809 Grandparents to Brontës
7. Maria Branwell 1783-1821 + Six children, all born in Yorkshire	Patrick Brontë Parents
Notes on these 1-6 families follow	**8. Six children Brontë**

BRANWELL Table 2: The Richard Bramwell Senior family:
Richard (Tremearne) Bramwell + Margaret (Boase) John and eight children

1	2	3	4	5	6
Richard + Honor Matthews	Thomas + Ann Carne	Margaret + Joseph Corin	Elizabeth + John Keam	Jane + John Fennell	Alice + John Williams
12 children	12 children	1 child	No issue	1 child	5 children

Notes:
1. Richard John Bramwell Jr (1744-1812) + Honor Matthews (1745-1811) [12 children] builder, innkeeper.
2. Thomas Branwell (1745-1808) + Ann Carne (c1744-1809) [12 children] Merchant, grocer
3. Margaret Branwell (1748-1773) + Joseph Coren (1745-1821) 1 child Joseph, scrivener and brewer. Margaret died following the birth of her son Joseph Coren Jr. and the child was cared for by Thomas and Ann Branwell, until Joseph Sr. remarried.
4. Elizabeth Branwell (1750-1802) + John Keam (c1757-1825) No issue Shopkeeper; at least one son in J. Keam's second marriage to Mary Painter/Paynter (1804).
5. Jane Bramwell (1753-1829) + John Fennell (1762-1841) 1 child Jane Branwell Fennell Schoolmaster;
6. Alice Bramwell (1756- unkn.) + John Williams (dates unknn) 5 known children, perhaps more, mining agent & purser, gentleman. Williams name too common to trace with confidence.
Descendants of this family visited Yorkshire from their London and Brighton homes.
7. & 8. The two siblings who died in infancy and childhood were both named Martin.
Note: *The spelling of the surname is, as explained, variable. Sometimes in records it is written as Branwell and alternatively Bramwell, even within the same family unit and generation.*

The Great, great grandparents: the beginnings of the Brontë legacy
See Branwell Tables 1 and 2 above
The first marriage of Martyn Bromwell (Baptized 1674- 1719) and Margery Bennetts (Unknown -1603) in c1694 (no records).
Martyn Bromwell's first marriage to Margery (Bennetts) produced three children and she died following the birth and death of the third child, also named Margery.[6] Their eldest child, Martyn Branwell Jr (1696-1763), from an early age, followed his father's occupation becoming a butcher's boy, tending the cattle farm at Paul and selling produce from the family business located at the foot of Market Jew Street on the seaward side. From his father he inherited that business and carried it on into his own descending line of Branwells. The meat trade as a whole was an important element of Branwell family commerce for several generations, and familiarity with it, so close to home, may have had some effect on Aunt Branwell's seeming aversion to animals in the home. This is only speculation, and it should be remembered that her opinions on this, even if true, were not enforced in the family.

Martyn's second child with Margery was a daughter, who received the name Maudlin or Maudlyn (c1698-1743). She married John Tonkin, a shipwright, in 1720. Bennetts was also the family name of the owner of the Ship and Castle Inn on Chapel Street, which was to become the Union Hotel in 1801 at the passing of the Act of Union between England and Ireland. This relationship may also have determined the choice of builders (Richard Branwell Sr. and Jr.) invited to build the ballroom, community gathering rooms and the Stable theatre at the Ship and Castle in the final decades of the eighteenth century.

Martyn Jr. married and produced nine children with his wife Elizabeth (unknown surname), only one of whom, George Bramwell (aka Bramble) (1741-1795), appears to have married and produced four known offspring. Not only was George Bramwell born within the same cohort as Thomas Branwell (Maria's father), but their children's births and names were intermixed in the same years as well. This meant, for example, that there were two Elizabeth Branwells born in the same year, 1776, one (to be Aunt Branwell) to Thomas and Anne Branwell, and one to George and his wife Maudlyn (Cunnack) Branwell.

Perhaps the most interesting character of Martyn Jr.'s family was this mariner son George who captained sailing vessels that carried a range of goods, some of which was merchandise for cousin Thomas (John) Branwell, or salt with which the pilchards were cured, also for Thomas. With this connection comes the possible link of the Branwell family to several communal practices related to smuggling.[7] Though not damning, certainly suspicions may be raised by the 1778 refusal of Thomas Branwell to allow customs officers to search his home for smuggled goods.[8] George Bramwell was a sea captain on a coastal trader, and Thomas (John) Branwell was a part owner in more than one sailing vessel on which he worked. George Bramwell also earns a section to himself in Charlotte MacKenzie's new book (2019) on merchants and smugglers in eighteenth century Cornwall:

> When George Bramwell sailed on the *Swallow* with Captain Henry Carter in 1777 the crew of ten included three of his relations: his cousin Richard Woolcock[9] and two of his brothers-in-law Henry and Richard Ford; they were imprisoned in France together…In the 1780s Captain George Bramwell appears to have prospered. Captain George Bramwell lived in one of the new houses built by John Hampton at Penzance quayside; in 1787 his daughter Margaret Bramwell (1769-?) married the mariner John Williams. In 1786-7 Bramwell was master of the Dunkins' sloop the *Liberty* and in 1788-90 he was master of one of their brigantines, the *Friendship*."

Though MacKenzie is careful not to indict George Bramwell as a smuggler, he was certainly a privateer, and had many opportunities in wartime to provide the necessary transport of goods between ports engaged in various secretive ventures and engagement with the networks supporting these. MacKenzie also reports his death as a prisoner of war on the Isle de Rhe, France in 1795, unknown until recently.

The second marriage of Martyn Bromwell (1674-1719) 2 July 1705
In 1705, Martyn Bromwell married for the second time, Jane Tremearne (c1674-1754) being the spinster daughter of John and Katherine Tremearne (née Stevens) of Paul village.[10] The Tremearnes were a farming and clergy family whose roots had been in Paul parish at least since the Spanish raid of 1595; the Revd. John Tremearne (a g-great grandfather) was the Vicar of Paul during that earlier period, when his church and its records were destroyed by fire and destruction. He served the parish as Vicar and Perpetual Vicar of the Royal Peculiar from 1581-1624

under the patronage of Queen Elizabeth I. Martyn's leased land for grazing his cattle was local to Paul.

From Martyn's second marriage to Jane Tremearne there were four children. Two were daughters – Margery and Alice – and two were sons – Richard and Joseph. All of these four names are carried forward in the naming pattern of the Branwell family. The two daughters seemingly died before their widowed mother, and the two sons, Richard Sr. (1711-1792) and Joseph (1715-1758) were to produce the further Bramwell/Branwells of the Penzance families, alongside their older half-brother Martyn (c1696-1763).

Dorcas Tremearne, Jane's older sister, married Jenkin Keigwin, Gentleman of Paul, a descendant of the principal inhabitant and family of Mousehole, who was killed by a Spaniard's cannon ball in 1595. His house remained standing alone and preserved in the devastation of the village and surrounds. The Keigwin families were distinguished soldiers and scholars, and lived in the mansion of Mousehole still standing, called the Keigwin Arms. She was Aunt Dorcas Keigwin to Richard Bramwell Sr. The Keigwin family was also connected to the Carne family as related in the following chapter.

Jane's younger sister, Susan Tremearne, married Richard Batten of Penzance in 1710, making the first Branwell family connection with that future leading civic and merchant family of Penwith.[11] Richard Batten's brother, John Batten, related by marriage to the children of the Branwell line, and the string of John Battens into which he fitted (at least seven in quantity, and most overlapping), feature largely in both the lives of the Branwells through marriage, and the Carnes through business and marriage, in future years, and were a prominent part of the political structures governing the town. Benjamin Carne Branwell provided a second major link by marriage when he married Mary (Bodinnar) Batten in 1799.

When these couples married, they were part of the final Celtic-speaking generation, though they may not have been native-speakers of Cornish. There is no evidence that they spoke anything other than the King's English of the time, though they may have understood and employed both Cornish and English terms. The Keigwin and Tonkin relations of Jane Tremearne, however, were already distinguished as 'Cornish scholars and antiquarians', demonstrating that the decline of Cornish-speaking was not only well underway (or finished), and required translation. A brother-in-law, John Keigwin, had mastered the French, Latin, Greek and Hebrew languages in addition to Cornish and English. He was a nephew of William Scawen, also a major scholar of the Cornish language, since Scawen's sister Elizabeth had married his father Martin Keigwin.[12]

Hence it is in this marriage of Jane Tremearne with Martyn Bramble that we begin to gather the names and trace the social and commercial lives of the Branwell line of descent in Cornwall to the Brontës in Yorkshire. From this marriage, also, the name of *Jane* reverberates through repetition in every branch of the family lines through to the young Brontës – including a respectful nod in the novel of *Jane Eyre*.

Martyn Sr. was relatively successful, as when he died his will[13] reveals that he left his business, leased farmland for livestock (from the Carveth family, also kin) at Paul village, horse with saddle, together with slaughter premises in Penance to his eldest son, Martyn Jr, of his first marriage, and two freehold houses to his wife Jane, the one they had lived in (the house at the top of New Street at the rear of the Star Inn, as previously described) and another that they leased out, together with his goods and chattels.

Martin's four children by his second marriage with Jane Tremearne were all minors at the time of his death, though all survived to adulthood and marriage. The two sons – Richard (1711-1792) and Joseph (1715-1758)[14] – received inheritances from their mother Jane in her will thirty years later, as did her daughter Alice's widower Richard Woolcock. The other daughter, received no notice in the will and presumably had died previously. Jane did not re-marry and continued to live on New Street, around the corner from Chapel Street, until her death in 1754. It is possible, though not known, that her son Richard and his wife 'Margery' (John), as she was known, began their married life with her in the family home.

Paternal grandparents:

Richard (Tremearne) Bramwell Sr. (1711-1792)
+ Margaret 'Margery' (Boase) John (1711-1791). See Branwell Table 2.
The eldest son of Martyn/Martyn and Jane (Tremearne) Branwell, Richard Bramwell married Margery John, the daughter of Jane née Boase (1694-1741), and Thomas John (1694-1752), a blacksmith of Penzance. The couple married at the Penzance Chapel of Madron Parish on 28 November 1742, and produced eight children over the following seventeen years, all of whom were born in Madron Parish. These are the paternal grandparents of Maria, Elizabeth and their siblings, and would have known all of their Branwell grandchildren, except for those of their daughter Alice born after their demise – at least 25 in total – from birth. Richard Sr. is variously listed as a builder, a mason, and a contractor with his own established firm of architects and tradesmen.

In her own mother's line of descent, Margery was a member of the distinguished literary family of Boase from which in future came the banker and author Henry Boase (1763-1827), his son Dr. Henry Samuel Boase FRS (1799-1883) amongst several others, and the historian and author George Clement Boase (1829-1897), the bibliographer and antiquarian.[15] At least some of this family Maria and Elizabeth would have known, and most certainly their parents did. Members of the Boase family were close friends and business colleagues of the William Carne Sr. family of bankers and authors.

Margery's father's lineage was more mixed in outcome though equally well known and well-connected to both Branwells and Carnes down the generations.[16] Thomas John, a blacksmith, was the brother of William John (5xMayor in earlier years) and thereby became uncle of the John brothers, George and Samuel John, whose family home and legal offices were later situated in Chapel Street, a few doors down from the Penzance Bank of Batten, Carne and Oxenham. Margery's brother Peter John (c1723- c1792) worked with his father in the blacksmithing firm and both were active in local politics as part of the corporation.

In the year that his sister Margery died, Peter John remained in the court of assistants in which Thomas Branwell also served. Socially designated as a Gentleman, it is thought that he was married to Phillis Williams, a cousin in his grandmother's maternal line. Solicitor George John (1759-1847) was Mayor in the year Maria Branwell left Penzance for the north (1812) and again a few years later; he was married to a wealthy heiress, Jane Arundell Harris, who for many years presided over the Ladies Reading Circle (See Chapter 5: 'In the everyday'). He also served as Town Clerk, working with various members of the extended Branwell family (administrators and town officials throughout the nineteenth century) for many years until his death.

The relationship circle of Margery John included also a large family of creative artists and writers who spread their descendants from West Cornwall (Helston and Gwinear nearby) to Devon, London, Hampshire, Ireland and internationally to Australia and New Zealand. The story of the John family, some of whom became the Johns family after migrating to Devon, is explored in *A Passion for Nature, 19th-century Naturalism in the Circle of Charles Alexander Johns,* published in 2008. Though no documentation of close family ties has emerged as yet, the links between the immediate networks of the John/Johns/Branwell and Carne families are numerous and include the Derwent Coleridge family, the Fox family of Falmouth, the Stackhouse family of Trehane, the Emily Trevenen family of Helston, the Charles Kingsley family, and the Vivian family of Camborne and Trelowarren amongst others.

Originally a young nature lover, just as Joseph Carne was a youthful mineral collector, Henry Incledon, after attendance at Helston Grammar School like his father before him, was placed in a banking position at the Dock Bank in Plymouth. This became a partnership opportunity which failed when his elder partner died leaving non-disclosed debts which the younger partner could not cover. In the general bank downturn of 1825, Henry changed course to his first loves which were poetry, art and trekking in nature– becoming the Professor of Drawing and Painting at the new Plymouth Grammar School, and offering private tuition. His life and the lives of the children born to Maria and Henry, are exemplary of the dictum quoted at the head of Chapter 10: 'The Travellers: 'Tis education forms the common mind; Just as the twig is bent the tree's inclined.' The perceptive reader will readily see from Table 3, the many familiar forenames of the children of the Carne-Branwell network.

BRANWELL Table 3: The John/Johns family and Margery (John) Branwell

Henry Incledon John and his wife Maria Incledon John (b. 1786) – cousins who married
Third cousins of Helston and the Lizard, later of Plymouth
Henry Jr. (1804) Teacher and journalist;
Maria (1806) author of children's books, and editor of *The Ladies Almanack;*
Elizabeth (1808) died young;

Sophia (1809) died young;
Charles (1811) world-famous botanist, author of *Flowers of the Field*, vicar and headmaster of both Helston Grammar School and Winton House School, Winchester;
Emily (1814) poet and artist, Mrs. Henry Carrington (daughter was Edith Carrington, children's writer);
Julia (1816) Teacher and illustrator;
Bennett (1819) infant death;
Bennett George (1820) Vicar, Administrator of the London School for the blind, novelist;
Jane (1822) Artist and governess, then school proprietor with sisters Emily and Anne;
Anne (1827) Artist and governess;
John Jacob (1829) Bank clerk, railway cashier and journalist, USA

The parental generation of Maria Branwell, her siblings and her cousins
Tables 4 and 5

Richard (John) Branwell (1744-1812), aka Richard Jr.
Uncle Richard Branwell was approximately two years older than his brother Thomas, and later survived him by four. Richard Jr, like his father, Richard Sr, was a mason by trade and they worked together in their own firm of builders and contractors. Most records of their work are invoices and receipts and refer to commissions to rebuild coastal amenities such as the docks and slipways at the wharves. With others, mostly cousins it seems, they also took on civic commissions such as the Assembly Rooms of the Union Hotel, financed by public subscription in 1791-2, following the Stable Theatre in 1787, the town's theatre at the hotel.. Relations such as Solomon Cock (cousin of Anna Cock Carne, the wife of William John Carne, Banker, and Edward Hambleton, architect worked with the firm on all manner of construction projects, into which Thomas Branwell also invested. A family business office was maintained, headed by Samuel Paddy, as shipping clerk and office manager.

Richard Jr.'s first child, to which he gave his fore name, was born out of wedlock in 1765, with Catherine Veale at Penzance. Nothing is known about the relationship as such except that some years later a bond was posted for child support, and witnessed by the family business manager, Samuel Paddy, who later married Richard Jr.'s daughter, Julia. Richard Veale followed his father into the innkeeping business latterly and in 1799 married Ann Russell and changed his name to Branwell. His wedding was witnessed by two of his half-brothers. In 1771 Richard Jr. married Honour Matthews (1745-1811), the daughter of Christopher and Elizabeth Matthews of Paul. The couple had eleven children together.

BRANWELL Table 4: The eldest son Richard John Branwell 1744-1812, and his family with Honor (Hammond/Hamen) Matthews 1745-1811

Richard Veale/later Branwell 1765 – 1845	1st son of Richard Branwell, base child with Catherine Veale of St. Just. R Veale in 1799 m Ann Russell of Sithney, wedding witnessed by two Branwell half-brothers. He changed his name to Branwell later in life. He became a brewer of Penzance, in business with his father who ran the Golden Lion Inn.
Richard Matthews Branwell 1772 – 1815	1st son of Richard Branwell with his wife Honour Matthews. Like his father before him, was served with a Bastardy bond in 1804: father of base son with Elizabeth Lian of Helston. A Freemason, he left Penzance to become a bank clerk in Somerset. Died unmarried in Bridgewater, Somerset, age 43.
Honor M I	Born 1773 and died as infant.
Robert Matthews Branwell 1775 – 1833	1) Married Phillipa Tyack 25 July 1797 at St Hilary. She died in 1818 one month after the death of Benjamin Carne Branwell, her cousin by marriage. 2) Married Jane Vivian, Jan, 1820 at Camborne where the Vivian family lived at Reskadinnick House. The family there is recounted in *The Vivians, A Family in Victorian Cornwall* by Molly Vivian Hughes. The Vivians are also married with the Carnes, Thomas and John families.
Catherine M Branwell 1776 – 1841	1794 m John Edmunds/Edmonds, Gent. of Redruth, Cornwall Five children identified; C W Hatfield (compiler) lists their noteworthy grandchildren in his review (1939)
Honor M Branwell 1777- ?	1797 she married Richard Silby/Selby at St Andrew, Plymouth. At Madron in 1809 she married Matthew Chraster of North Shields as her second husband.
Thomas M Branwell 1779-1811	*St George* went down at Jutland in the winter of 1811 taking Lts Branwell of Penzance, Tippett of St Erth & Rogers of Penrose with it as well as Rear Admiral Robert Carthew Reynolds. (Kin)
Thomasine M Branwell 1780 – 1853	Married William Argall (1776-1801) in 1797. One son: Philip Argall (1798-1840) Fell overboard during a storm (see info at argallfamilyworldwide.com – First cousin 1xremoved)
Julia M Branwell 1782 – 1835	Married Samuel Paddy, yeoman in 1805. Samuel Paddy is listed as co-bondsman for the 1804 Bastardy bond issued to Richard M Branwell by the Court. He was the business manager of the Branwell joint companies.
Margaret M Branwell Eliza (M) Branwell	Spinsters – Both of these childhood friends of Maria and Elizabeth. 1782-1816 – Margaret died before Elizabeth left Penzance 1786-1835-
Joseph (Matthews) Branwell 1789 – 1857	1812 married 1st cousin Charlotte Branwell, youngest daughter of Thomas and Ann, at Madron. Grylls lists his occupations as clerk, schoolmaster, agent, accountant, banker, gentleman, i.e. a rising 'light' and the father to professional children who went on to make their careers in London..

The second son: Thomas (John) Branwell (c1745-1808) and his family with Ann/e (Reynolds) Carne (1744-1809)

For unknown reasons, birth or baptismal records are missing for Thomas Branwell, Maria's father. His projected birth year is c1746. This may mean that he was not born in Cornwall, or that he was adopted, but there is no evidence of either alternative. Thomas, from the beginning, appears to have been entrepreneurial and to have a wide variety of interests. His first business was in groceries and into this he brought the help of his nephews, who then branched out into food and drink-based businesses as brewers and grain merchants, grocers, millers, and property owners.

In 1768, at the age of 23, he married Ann Carne (1744-1809), the 24 year-old daughter of a Penzance silversmith and clockmaker. In later years one of Thomas's nephews, Robert Matthews Bramwell (1775-1833), a handsome Byronic figure, began his occupational career as a watchmaker also— and he may have apprenticed himself to John (Calenso) Carne (Anne's father) whose working space was located in one section of the ever-expanding grocery premises in the marketplace.

Of the twelve Carne-Branwell children, seven lived to their majority, but aside from Maria and Elizabeth, are largely unknown. Even if mentioned they have consistently been mis-counted, in virtually all records. Maria was, in fact, the eighth daughter of nine girls born to the Branwells, and the fourth of the seven children who reached their majority. The lives and deaths of all of these would have had impact on those remaining longer within the family walls and occupations, actually and metaphorically, and especially on Aunt Branwell, Charlotte Branwell, and Jane Kingston – the latter outlasting all of the siblings of that generation.[17]

Table 5: Thomas Branwell 1745-1808 + Ann Carne 1744-1809

1. Ann Carne Branwell
b 19 April 1769 Penzance, Cornwall
d 11 May 1792 Penzance
(23 at time of death) No issue.

2. Margaret (Carne) Branwell
b 15 July 1770 Penzance
m Charles Fisher, Gent at Madron 1792
d 1799 Penzance, Cornwall, following her husband's death the previous year.
(28 at time of death) No issue.

3. Thomas Branwell I	4. Elizabeth Branwell I
b 11 August 1771 Penzance	b 8 September 1772 Penzance
d 22 February 1776 Penzance (4 ½ at time of death)	d 23 Feb 1776 Penzance (3 ½ at time of death)

5. Jane (Carne) Branwell [See 'The Kingstons']
b 29 Nov 1773 Penzance
d 1855 Penzance, Cornwall, Five children
m John Kingston (1769-1924), Methodist preacher at Madron Parish Church on 12 May 1800.

6. Benjamin Carne Branwell [See 'The Benjamin Carne Branwells']
b 25 March 1775
m Mary Batten (c1777 – 29 Nov 1851) at Madron Parish Church in 1799
d 27 July 1818, Nine children

7. Elizabeth (Carne) Branwell II [See 'The Brontës']
b 2 Dec 1776 Penzance, Cornwall
d 29 Oct 1842 Haworth, Yorkshire

8. Thomas Branwell II	9. Alice Branwell I	10. Alice Branwell II
b 24 March 1778	b 1779-80	b 5 December 1780
d 19 Jan 1779	d 8 May 1779 'infant'	d 25 October 1781

11. Maria (Carne) Branwell
b 15 April 1783
m Patrick Bronte 29 December 1812 Clergyman
d 15 September 1821 Haworth, Yorkshire, Six children

12. Charlotte (Carne) Branwell [See 'The Joseph Branwells']
b 10 Nov 1789 Pz
m Joseph Branwell (1st cousin) 29 December 1812
d 31 March 1848 Launceston, Cornwall, 11 children

Ten months after the early deaths of a brother, Thomas (4 ½), and a sister, Elizabeth (3 ½) brought on by contagious fevers in February of the same year, Elizabeth Carne Branwell was born in December of 1776. She received the name Elizabeth 'to keep alive the memory' of the recently departed one, and to honour Aunt Elizabeth, her father's second sister. Greeting her as siblings in the family were her older sisters, Anne (age 7), Margaret (age 6), Jane (age 3) and her sole brother Benjamin (age 1).

When Maria Branwell was born in the April of 1783, seven year old Elizabeth was the only addition to that number and her mother Ann was nearing the end of her childbearing years. This was a good age to take the new little one under her wing, helping her with learning her numbers and alphabet, and the basics of bathing, dressing, eating and sewing (the latter including a range of needlecraft techniques such as sewing, knitting, embroidery, even lace-making). This was just as Elizabeth's older sisters Anne, Margaret and Jane would have done for her. Hence, for Maria, these were probably indulged years, the youngest to four older sisters and one brother, and the cousin to dozens of others.

The 1790s were a pivotal time for the Branwell siblings, in that even those children who had survived to adulthood began to leave the family for one reason or another. In 1792 the eldest daughter, Anne who remained living at home, succumbed to either a fever or consumption (not known) just as she was about to take up employment with one of her cousins (possibly Colensoe) owner of a drapery shop in Penzance.[18]

In 1799, the year following the death of her husband, Charles Fisher, the second daughter of the Branwells, Margaret Branwell Fisher, also passed away in March. The Fishers had been married since 1792, and lived separately in a house on North Parade nearby where Charles had maintained a bookbindery.[19] Because of the early interest shown by the Brontë children in the making and binding of small books at Haworth, it seems possible that both Maria and Elizabeth may have experienced bookbinding techniques – of the stitching and decorative cover variety – in their youth and shared this knowledge with them. With the marriage of Benjamin in 1799, only daughters remained at home in Chapel Street.

Margaret (John) Branwell (1748-1773), the eldest daughter

Margaret married brewer Joseph Corin at Madron in 1773. She died shortly after the birth of her only son, Joseph Corin, at the age of 28. The baby 'Joe' was contemporary with his cousins, the older children of his Uncle Thomas and Aunt Ann Branwell's family, and he was taken in by them as one of their own. When Joseph Corin Sr. married again to Elizabeth Rawlings of Wales, Joe Jr. joined his father again and acquired more brothers and sisters, but he never forgot the kindness of the Branwell family. When later he married, his first son though christened Philip Burne Corin was always known as 'Branwell Corin'.

Margaret Corin's death left her surviving sisters as the paternal aunts to the Branwell children of Thomas and Ann and to Richard and Honour. Of the remaining three sisters – Elizabeth (John), Jane (John) and Alice (John) Bramwell – Aunt Jane, who married John Fennell in 1790, was the great favourite amongst the nieces and nephews, and took a strong hand in their upbringing.

Elizabeth (John) Branwell (1750-c1802), sister of Richard and Thomas

Relatively little is known about Elizabeth except that she grew up to marry John Keam in 1788, a local shopkeeper and fellow Methodist. She probably assisted in the shop as they had no children. After her death, John married again in 1804 at Madron, and his new wife was Mary Painter/Paynter of the Boskenna estate near Paul village, with whom he had a son. One of the witnesses to Keam's second marriage was John Fennell showing closeness within the family to their brother-in-law and Uncle Keam of Maria and her siblings.

Jane (John) Branwell (1753-1829) sister of Richard and Thomas

Perhaps first in importance of those named Jane, who would be known personally to the Brontë children, was Thomas Branwell's younger sister, Jane (John) Branwell who became Mrs. John Fennell. Jane was named in memory of her grandmother, Jane Tremearne Branwell, who died the year following her birth. She is the first Branwell to be listed by name in Methodist records, as mentioned previously. At the age of 37, Jane married the Methodist class leader and schoolteacher, John Fennell. With this marriage another important trail into the future lives of the Brontë writers was secured for all time. Jane's life with John Fennell in Penzance, and the birth of their daughter, also Jane, is covered in more detail in Chapter 10, 'The Travellers', as they were to be the reason for Maria's invitation to Yorkshire.

Alice (John) Branwell

Alice was the final daughter to survive to adulthood, to marry and to have children. The problem faced in tracing this line is the all-too-common name of Williams in Cornwall, and the probability that they moved away from the central family focus and spent greater time in London and elsewhere in Cornwall. John Williams of Camborne-Redruth and St. Agnes, whom she married, is one of about twenty so-named, all alive simultaneously. Her son John Branwell Williams with his wife and daughter, were the 'unwelcome' visitors (according to Charlotte Brontë) to the Brontë family on their holiday in the north visiting John Fennell – in the year before the latter's death.

Remaining Branwells in Thomas's line:

a) Benjamin Carne Branwell
b) Joseph (Matthews) Branwell with Charlotte (Carne) Branwell

- a) Benjamin (1775-1818), though not the eldest son of Thomas and Ann Branwell, was the only male child to survive to his majority and therefore the only brother of Elizabeth and Maria. In various lists he is noted as 'Gent', and in the first year's Membership list of the Royal Geological Society of Cornwall (RGSC), as 'Esq'. His name is found in the membership lists of Freemasons and Knights Templar thereof, but no occupation is listed for him at any point, except for the brief service he gave in the Territorial Army during the Napoleonic wars.

BRANWELL Table 6:

The nine children of Benjamin and Mary Batten Batten Branwell

1800	Thomas	Born & died	11-Mar	
1801	Thomas Batten	Died in London	1836	Attorney
1803	Mary (Batten)	Died in Penzance	1874	School mistress
1804	Emma (Batten)	Died in Penzance	1891	School mistress
1806	Benjamin (Batten)	Mental incompetent	1893	Lodger
1810	Lydia (Batten)	Died in Penzance	1878	Lived at home
1811	Adolphus	Born & died	12-Jun	
1814	John Batten	Died in London	1853	Warehouse clerk
1815	Amelia Josepha	Died in Penzance	1892	School mistress

In January of 1799 Benjamin married Mary (Bodinnar/Bodener) Batten (1777-1851), sister of merchant banker John (Bodinnar) Batten and childhood friend in the kinship circle. In the year following his father's death 'Ben' was elected Mayor by his fellow town councillors, though for one year only.[20] Perhaps his long-term decline leading to his death began at this time, as it was customary for popular Mayors to be re-elected frequently. He signed up for membership in the RGSC in 1814, though no papers or mention of him followed, before or after his death. Mary and Benjamin were not Methodists. As regular attendees at St. Mary's Chapel, and following Benjamin's death, Mary Batten Branwell retained her gallery box, in between her brother, the (frequent) Mayor and Merchant John Batten, Esq., and the Revd. W. Tremenheere.[21]

Benjamin died in 1818 aged 43 years, leaving large debts to his friend and brother-in-law, John Batten (a banking partner in the Penzance Bank which his father established with William Carne and Richard Oxnam). John Jr. the younger Batten was also the executor of Thomas Branwell's Will, as previously mentioned. However, the story of Benjamin Carne Branwell, Esq. is only half-told. When he died in 1818 after 'a lingering illness' (probably consumption), he had 'mortgaged' almost the whole of the legacy he had received, by borrowing against the properties passed to him by Thomas in his will. His wife, Mary Branwell (née Batten) and the family of children were left considerably embarrassed. Henceforward, the family fortune was dissipated in Thomas's line.

Benjamin's eldest son, Thomas Batten Branwell (1801-1836) left Cornwall, where he had been apprenticed to his cousin George John, to set up law offices in London but did not live long or practice successfully (undischarged bankrupt). Three of the four remaining daughters began their own 'Dame School' for young girls. All of these were first cousins to the Brontë children and nieces and nephews of Elizabeth and Maria. In a letter to Patrick sent from Woodhouse Grove where she was staying with her Aunt and Uncle before her marriage, it is noted that Maria does not mention her brother.

One younger son of Benjamin and Mary Branwell, Benjamin Batten Branwell, was mentally defective, and had to be cared for during his long life. He can be followed as a lodger with various families around the town, through the Census returns, after his mother's death in 1851. He became the longest surviving child of that Batten-Branwell branch.

Legal opinions were sought, over Benjamin's debts and the ownership of rents that were mortgaged to the Batten family by Mary, though final judgment is not found to date. The payments of the legacies to the remaining daughters – Jane Kingston, Elizabeth Branwell, Maria Brontë and Charlotte Branwell were not affected because the obligation to continue those payments was incumbent upon John Batten, Esq. [Mayor], executor to Thomas's Will, who lent the money to his brother-in-law and took over the properties and their incomes from his sister Mary when she inherited.[22]

Meantime, Benjamin had employed some of the family money to construct legal offices on Chapel Street for his eldest son, Thomas Branwell, re-naming a lane leading to Queen Street as 'Chancery Lane'. This investment does not, however, seem to have paid off for father or son in setting up a legal career for Thomas. He remained in the Cornish district until about 1826, and was listed as a member of the Freemasons in St Ives, Redruth and Camborne. In London, he took up residence at the Queen's Arms Hotel in Cheapside, but made an inauspicious start as his name appears only as an Insolvent Debtor. By 16 October 1828 he is found applying for discharge from bankruptcy in *Perry's Bankrupt Gazette*. The listing is for Thomas Branwell, Gentleman, of Penzance, attorney and solicitor[23]

The fact that in his will, Thomas (John) Branwell had left one house (Clarence Street, behind Causewayhead) without encumbrance to his wife Ann Carne, which in turn was passed to her daughters, meant that the Branwell daughters' inheritances were secure. This is the rent money written about by Charlotte Brontë to Eliza Jane Kingston, which she acknowledges on behalf of Patrick.[24] Mary was forced to pass over to her brother the properties inherited from Thomas, and which paid the annual annuities to Thomas's daughters, in return for an annuity for herself and the remaining children (nine in all).

There is no doubt that Aunt Branwell was informed of this situation concerning her brother's poor financial dealings, and may even have been an intimation that she was probably better off where she was, than returning to a dissipated family scenario at home in Penzance. This is probably also the time that Elizabeth would have switched her financial accounts from the 'family' bank of Batten, Carne & Carne, over to the Bolitho Bank of Chyandour, as mentioned in her will. That she was still in close contact with her older sister, Jane Kingston, is also clear due to the mention in her will (of 1833) that she had forwarded contributions (related to an intended legacy to Jane and her daughter Eliza Jane) to her previously.

Charlotte (1789-1848) and Joseph Branwell (1789- of Gulval, West Cornwall

These two first cousins were born in 1789 within weeks of each other, and knew each other all their lives. Joseph was the youngest child of Richard John Bramwell, and Charlotte was the youngest child of his brother, Thomas. We know nothing of their love story, but family-centred and romantic they must have been.

Their Cornish wedding at Madron Parish Church on the 29th December of 1812, was planned and developed to take place at the same hour on the same day that the same ceremony was being held in Guiseley, Yorkshire, for Charlotte's sister Maria and

Patrick Brontë and for their mutual cousin, Jane Branwell Fennell who was marrying The Revd. William Morgan, Patrick's good friend. These three young women had grown up together in Penzance, and those around them all as witnesses and friends were almost all close family members.

Witnesses for Joseph at Madron were two of his brothers, and for Charlotte were her sister Elizabeth Branwell (later aunt Branwell) and Charlotte's close friend, Grace Thomas (also probably kin). In Yorkshire, Aunt Jane Branwell Fennell and Uncle John Fennell, now concluding their first (and final) year in charge of Woodhouse Grove School nearby, represented the Branwell family as none of the parents of the Branwell family were alive to witness these betrothals. The Fennells, of course, on that day became the father-in-law and mother-in-law of William Morgan.

At home in Penzance where they initially settled after their marriage, Maria's sister Charlotte and her cousin Joseph were to have their first child at Christmas of 1813, a son named for his father. The second son was christened as a namesake for Richard Bramwell Sr. who had died the year before. Some four months later Maria Brontë was to bring her own first-born child, Maria, into the world of Yorkshire, giving her the gift of her own name. At this stage, Elizabeth Branwell was still resident in Penzance, living possibly with Jane Kingston and her young daughter, Eliza Jane Kingston, in the house left to them by their mother in Clarence Street near the marketplace.

Joseph Branwell's occupations were several over his lifetime, recorded as Clerk, Schoolmaster, Agent, Accountant, Banker, gentleman (*1851 Census*) and the general impression of him was positive and good-humoured. The family was firmly dedicated to Wesleyan Methodism, and their baptisms and most of their burials are recorded in Nonconformist Registers for Cornwall (PRO).

For several years Joseph and his wife, sister Charlotte, ran a classical and commercial school at the bottom of Queen Street (see Chapter 5), and newspaper cuttings show a full programme of languages and mathematics with annual awarding of prizes by independent judges. After some years as a schoolmaster, Joseph took up banking and the family removed to Launceston. Charlotte died in 1848, just as the Brontë daughters were becoming known in the pantheon of authorship. Soon after Joseph remarried to an old friend, Eliza Cornish and returned to live in Penzance until his death in 1857.

BRANWELL Table 7:

Eleven children of Charlotte (Carne) 1789-1848 and Joseph (Matthews) Branwell 1789-1857, of Penzance, Liskeard and Launceston

Joseph Branwell
b 26 Dec 1813 Penzance
d 21 June 1819 Penzance

Richard Branwell
b 18 Feb 1816
m Susan Tuke Treleaven 1841 Falmouth
Occupation: Solicitor
d 1865 Islington, London

Thomas Brontë Branwell
b 20 April 1817 Penzance
Attended Eton College
m Sarah Hannah Jones 1852 Tynemouth
Civil servant- War Office
d 1897 Peckham, London

Maria Branwell
b 5 March 1820 Liskeard
d 1875 Penzance

Joseph Branwell
b 29 October 1821 Liskeard
d Buried at sea 1846

William Branwell
b 23 June 1824
m Elizabeth Hannah Treadwell (nd) Croydon, London
Occupation: Clerk, General Post Office
d 1876, Battersea, London

Charlotte Branwell
b 26 July 1827
d 1896 Penzance

George Taylor Branwell
b 13 Dec 1828 Launceston
d 1831 Launceston (bur Wesleyan)

Charles Henry Branwell
b 13 May 1830 Launceston
Occupation: Midshipman RN
d 1851 (bur Dockacre Cemetery) Launceston

Elizabeth Anne Branwell
b & d, 1832, Launceston

John Bedford Branwell
b April 1834 Launceston
d 1838 Launceston (bur Wesleyan)

Two of Joseph's sons, Arthur and Auckland founded a firm of merchants in London, Arthur Branwell and Company, in 1904. Most of the Branwell descendants who still bear the Branwell name come from this branch of the family. Charlotte, Joseph's daughter, who never married, kept a boarding house in Trewithen Road, Penzance, which she named 'Shirley' after Charlotte's novel of the name, so there was definitely pride and recognition in the lines of descent. The name of Branwell, as applied to various lanes, buildings and estate agents' details when family homes (that were) are marketed now, remains a source of curiosity and interest to local people and to many visitors not familiar with the family chronology and connection.

Thus, when the spinster Aunt Branwell travelled north to take charge of the Brontë tribe, the fact that she was not, then or later, a mother herself, did not mean by any stretch of the imagination, that she had no experience with children. She had not only her siblings to learn from, but also at least 18-20 young cousins to mix with, perhaps to care for, and even to mourn, as she grew older. This was also true for her sisters Jane Kingston and Charlotte Branwell who remained in Cornwall. She had also observed the grief that naturally followed many deaths within the family clans surrounding them. Here were many loved ones to follow, and many with which to communicate by letter. We do not know the extent of her correspondence, nor is there information about what happened to her letters and papers following her death in Haworth.

The Branwell family – From top left: Jane Branwell Kingston, Anne & Thomas, parents; Elizabeth (later Aunt Branwell) Maria Branwell Brontë, Charlotte, young & older Brother Benjamin Carne Branwell not present

ENDNOTES

1 E & K Hill (nd) *The Penzance Home of Maria Branwell, Mother of the Brontës*, Penzance: self-published; E & K Hill is a pseudonym for Lilian Oldham.
2 For possible origins of the clan and the surname, see the discussions of Richard G Grylls (2006) in his extensive researches for *Branwell and Bramble*.
3 See Crispen Gill (1995) *Great Cornish Families, A History of the People and Their Houses*. Of note is Gill's opening sentence in which he states: 'Cornwall is rich in landed gentry but short on titled aristocrats.' His choice of families, arbitrary as he admits, nevertheless covers a few of individuals mentioned in this study, such as 'Foxes of Falmouth', 'The Gallant Grenvilles', 'St Aubyns of St Michael's Mount', 'The Romantic Trevanions [Lord Byron]; the Vivians (relations of both the Branwells and the Carnes), the Vyvyans of Trelowarren and 'The Mining Williams' (Branwell-Carne connections).
4 Richard G Grylls (2006) *Branwell & Bramble* 64 pp including 12 family trees. He was also aided considerably by Hilary Cook, one of the author's correspondents, and a member of the Cornish Family History Society, being a Branwell descendant also.
5 C W Hatfield's review of 'The Relatives of Maria Branwell' of 1939 (BST) corrected and added to J H Rowe's 'The Maternal Relatives of the Brontës' of 1911. These early articles attempting to provide genealogical information, while admirable for a time when historical records could not be easily accessed, online or otherwise, have often been based on faulty and very patchy biographical data provided by G C Boase in his massive work *Collectanea Cornubiensia*. Information provided by Grylls and the present study has been checked and verified by parish records of the county of Cornwall through Cornwall On-line Parish Clerks (COPC), a reliable and excellent resource. Nevertheless, some gaps remain, and there may be more to find.
6 *Ibid.*
7 R G Grylls (2006) George Bramwell who married Margaret Ford: C. MacKenzie, (2019) *Merchants and Smugglers*, pp. 151,219. .
8 Brought to my attention by Sharon Wright, author of her recently published biography of the love story of Maria Branwell and Thomas Brontë, as found in the National Customs House records of that year.
9 Richard Woolcock's first wife was Alice Bramwell, daughter of Martin Bromwell and first wife Margery Bennetts, i.e. a half-sister of Thomas Branwell whose mother was Jane Tremearne, his second wife.
10 G M Trelease (2006) *The History of the Church in Paul Parish*; also listed as a 'Royal Peculiar' outside the jurisdiction of the Bishop of Exeter.www.theclergydatabase.org.uk, based at Lambeth Palace.
11 See Chapter 10: Travellers Tales
12 See DNB: entries for John Keigwin, scholar, and Richard Keigwin of the East India Company.
13 AP/B/3003 Will of Martin Bramwell, butcher of Penzance 1719. Abstracted in App B.
14 Joseph Bramble (1715-1758) was the final child born to Martyn and Jane, and was Richard Sr.'s younger brother, and later to be uncle of Richard Jr. and Thomas Branwell. According to Grylls, he may have been a blacksmith and possibly worked with Thomas and Peter John. He married Jane Freethy at Perranuthnoe in 1738/9 with whom he had eight children. His son and namesake, Joseph Branwell (1748-1813) married Temperance Matthews (linked with Honor Matthews, wife of Richard Jr.) and became the main butcher in Penzance.
15 G C Boase is the dedicated bibliographer of the same family line who much later co-authored the *Bibliotheca Cornubiensis* (1874-1882), and then tackled the impressive further reference book, *Collectania Cornubiensia* (1890). The Boase cousin known to the Branwells and Carnes in the early 19th century, was Henry Boase, banker and journalist. See Biographical Briefs, Chapter 11.
16 The links of the Carne networks with the Johns and John family are perhaps more numerous than with the Branwells, but not as fundamental as a grandparent in the female line, as Margery John was. See Chapter 9, People called Carne following.
17 Aunt Jane Branwell Kingston died in Penzance in 1855, three months after the death of Charlotte Brontë in Haworth. She was the only daughter of the core family of Branwells to remain alive to know of the literary recognition earned by her younger sister's children. Some of Benjamin C Branwell's family (Mary Batten and her schoolmistress-daughters) also knew of it. Joseph Carne FRS, who died in 1858, and his daughter Elizabeth Carne remained alive to learn of it, but we have found no local comment that circulated.
18 L. Oldham papers, Morrab Library, family notes with no documentary evidence.
19 He also maintained a large private library which was left to his wife and the Branwell family at his death. Probably his collection joined the contributions made by the Carne family, during the tenure of Joseph (Cock) Carne as the administrative secretary of the Penzance Library established in 1818.
20 Battens served twelve terms between two carriers of the name John Batten (father and son) within the period

of this study. See Pool's *History of Penzance* for the conventions surrounding the election of Mayors, which were self-governing and internally rather than democratically elected, resulting in a sort of 'buggin's turn' cycle. This remains so to the present day. Some were able, others not so, as to be expected. It is presumed that B C Branwell was one of those relatively unsuccessful, because very few Mayors served only one term.

21 The seating plan of St Mary's Chapel 1824. West Penwith Resources, *Penzance, Past and Present* extract.

22 Benjamin Carne Branwell was the sole residual heir after annuities to Thomas's wife and daughters, as was Joseph Carne, FRS, when his father William died in 1836. However, whereas Benjamin Branwell was possibly profligate or ill (or both), Joseph Carne was astute and healthy. See Document register, Chapter 12, for a copy of the legal application for High Court opinion (1835).

23 On-line British Newspapers Archive, 31 October 1828; *Perry's Bankrupt Gazette*.

24 Smith, M. *The Letters of Charlotte Bronte*, 8 May 1846, vol. 1, p. 472.

CARNE

The Arms of the Carne family of Tresillian, Cornwall

Portrait of Joseph (Cock) Carne, FRS
Geologist, mining engineer, banker

Photograph of Elizabeth Catherine Thomas Carne
Geologist, benefactor, author, banker

Miss [Maria] Branwell belonged to the Methodist family of the Carnes, of Penzance; the latest representative of which, Joseph Carne, FRS, was distinguished yet more by his steady piety and uniform attachment to the Church in which he was trained, than by his attainments in science, and by his high general position in his native county.

John Carne, his brother, a man of accomplished mind, a very elegant writer, and a devoted Wesleyan, became well known to the world of literature...[1]

Chapter 9

People called Carne

Carne families had been settled in Cornwall for at least three centuries, and comprised several branches, around Truro, Falmouth, Gwennap and Gwinear and industrial Hayle, reaching back to Welsh Carnes. They continued regular contact with Wales, especially with Glamorgan, and particularly within the tin and copper trading families that contributed so strongly to the industrial revolution as it developed in the coming generations. It was in exactly this generation of the 1780s-forward that their fortunes were accumulated and their intellects and hard work appreciated and even celebrated.

Hals, Tonkin and Gilbert in their joint *Parochial History of Cornwall*, already described in Chapter 3, point with due respect to the pedigree line that was brought to Cornwall at least by the mid-1500s, by one Richard Carne the younger (of Camborne). The family arms, as described therein, are found applied to some documents in local Carne records. It also appears on the title page of John Carne's privately printed *Letters 1813-1837*.

> …Richard Carne gave for his arms (as appears by his seal) a pelican in her nest, with wings displayed, feeding her young ones, which coat is still to be seen in Trevannence seats, and in the roof of St. Agnes' church. He was descended from the Carnes of Glamorganshire, in Wales, who derive their pedigree from Ithal, King of Gwent, whose direct ancestor was Belimaur, the father of Cassibelan; which Carne settled in Cornwall, as we have it by tradition, upon his ancestor's marriage with the heiress of Tresilian, in the parish of Newlyn. [Newlyn East, nr. Newquay][2]

Branches of the family of Carne are known to have settled in West Cornwall in the fourteenth century and were connected by marriage at the time with the Keigwin of Mousehole and Borlase families (also linked to the Branwells). Habitations of related branches can also be found at Kenwyn near Truro, Roscolla near St Austell and prominently in Falmouth where a whole family of related Carnes lived (with similar forenames). In West Cornwall relations are found residing in Ludgvan, Gulval (where family graves are also found in the churchyards), Wendron and Gwennap aside from Penzance.

Two distinct branches of the family – meaning that they stem from two brothers/sons of the same line - form part of the Carne network in West Cornwall, and therefore would have had frequent roles to play in the lives of the Branwell people. A distinguishing mark is the same cadence of forenames, even though this cannot be considered definitive in all cases.

Great care has to be taken to avoid both confusion and conflation amongst the several William Carnes, the many John Carnes, and even the multiple Joseph Carnes that appear and overlap in the same period within the Carne-Branwell dynasty established in Cornwall.[3] In fact, it may prove impossible at this distance to avoid mistakes in degree of relationship, due to breaks in county records, and misconnections made in biographical history books and largely in modern-day genealogical records such as Ancestry.com and others, where documentary evidence is not found, but connections are contributed by ad hoc subscribers who copy from one another, without checking public records, or understanding the local geographical territory, thereby making frequent faulty connections. To illustrate the size of this problem, a brief summary of the entries in parish records for the three male Carnes mentioned is listed for the focal years of 1740-1840. Even these statistics are not definitive for this family, because Joseph (Cock) Carne was not married in Cornwall and neither was his brother John (Cock) Carne.

CARNE TABLE 1: BMD: COMMON NAMES OF THE CARNE FAMILY 1740-1840

Name	Births/baptisms	Marriages	Burials
William Carne	560	16	116
Joseph Carne	105	17	25
John Carne	727	155	139

The *Bibliotheca Cornubiensis* and the *Collectanea* records have incomplete documentation also and many misprints. Tables revealing what can be documented so far can be found in tables following. They were collated, of course, without the assistance of computers and internet technology of any kind, hence they are remarkable and noteworthy in any case.

Genealogy in the Carne family is altogether a more onerous exercise than for the Branwells, because the Carne families in this period blossomed with sons and few daughters, who then married in the Carne name and produced children, i.e. more cousins and contemporary cousins than for the Branwells, with a constant and consistent sharing of the same forenames. Hence, in this Carne narrative, the concentration is more on selected individuals whose dates correspond with and were known for certain by the Branwell family; these would have been acknowledged by them to be in a position of potential influence and interest.

The two lines of Carne interest in this study are those of a) John (Calensoe) Carne with his wife Anne Carne née Reynolds, parents of Maria Branwell's mother, Anne (Reynolds) Carne, and b) William (John/Johns) Carne with his wife Anna Carne née Cock, second cousins of the Branwells.

a) Grandfather John (Calensoe)[4] Carne 1715-1793
[father of Ann Reynolds Carne]

CARNE TABLE 2: SIX GENERATIONS OF THE FAMILY: DIRECT DESCENDANCY TO BRONTË

1. **Henry Carne** + No records found, born about 1650 Six children, the third of whom was:	**Elizabeth Chellew**, born 1650 at Ludgvan, daughter of John & Joan Chellew. Elizabeth married Henry 1674 G-G-G - Grandparents
2. **Henry Carne** 1683-1740 + Occupation: Cordwainer Eight known children, one of whom was:	**Eleanor (Ellenr) Calenso/Colenso** 1678-1767-8 G-Great Grandparents to the Brontës
3. **John (Calenso) Carne** 1715-1793 + Occupation: silversmith & clockmaker Nine children, one of whom was:	1) **Anne Reynolds** 1724-1766 2) Alice Symons (no issue) Great grandparents to the Brontës
4. **Anne (Reynolds) Carne** 1744-1809 + Twelve children, two of whom were:	**Thomas Branwell** c1745-1808 Occupation: Merchant Grandparents to the Brontës
5. **Maria Branwell** 1783-1821 + &**Elizabeth Branwell** 1776-1842 sister	**Patrick Brontë** Parents of the Brontës
	6. **Six children Brontë**

John Calensoe Carne was a silversmith and later also known to be a clock repairer and watchmaker. His relation, Joseph (Ferris) Carne, Esq. 1733-1762, father of William (Johns) Carne 1754-1836 of Chapel Street, Penzance, had been a mining captain engaged with silver mining in the area of Perranarworthal and Gwinear so this may have been a familiar interest and natural choice of occupation for his kin.[5]

John (Calenso) Carne's father Henry (1683-1740), a boot and shoemaker, lived with his wife Eleanor née Colenso and eight known children in Ludgvan, a village near Penzance. John's mother lived for another 28 years following Henry's death and died in the same year as her granddaughter Anne Reynolds John Carne married Thomas Branwell (1768). Thus the Carne-Branwell family begins its life from the mother's bloodline.

It was not for another twelve years, in the early 1780s, that second cousin William and Anna Cock Carne made their home in Penzance, shortly after their marriage. Whether or not having relatives already living in the town was a reason for this coming together as a clan, is not known, but the Gulval and Ludgvan districts appear to have been the seat for a cluster of Carnes throughout the years. William Carne Sr. is buried in Gulval churchyard within a large family mausoleum.

The Calenso/Colenso family from which grandmother Eleanor came has quite a distinguished and interesting history, much of which can be followed on the internet, and unfolding after her own lifetime, but concurrent with and exceeding the life-spans of the Branwell and Carne cousins. Colensos, a surname with many variations in spelling – Calensow, Calensoe, Colenso, and even Collensow - remained constant in the population of Penzance, and the Branwells and Carnes would have known them as kin. See Chapter 11, Biographical briefs for more information about the Colensos and their connections.

It is probable, though unknown, that the silver watches and items belonging to Aunt Branwell, that she itemizes in her will and distributes amongst the Brontë children, would have been made by her grandfather, John (Calenso) Carne, and given to her and her siblings on ceremonial days. Perhaps some of these would also have been in Maria's possessions in her lifetime. No mention is made – insofar as yet known – of the distribution of Maria's letters (except to Patrick during their courtship), papers or clothing and possessions following her death. The common or traditional habit was to burn personal letters and papers at the death of a family member to preserve privacy and ensure that the more 'embarrassing' events were smoothed over. In that Aunt Branwell and the Fennells were in attendance at Maria's demise, her personal belongings other than letters to her husband, were probably shared within the women-folk of her core family in Haworth and Cornwall.

CARNE TABLE 3: THE FAMILY LINE OF ANNE REYNOLDS CARNE, MRS. BRANWELL, 1744-1809

Mother of Elizabeth (Carne) and Maria (Carne) Branwell

Parents:
Anne Reynolds 1724-1766, spinster of Madron at marriage
m John (Calenso) Carne by licence, 11 October 1740
Occupation: Silversmith & clock maker

Children (Siblings of Anne):

Benjamin Reynolds Carne 1741-1773

ANNE REYNOLDS CARNE 1744-1809
m. Thomas (John) Branwell 1768

Eleonora Carne 1747-1747

John (Reynolds) Carne 1748-1749

Grace (Reynolds) Carne 1751-1752

Elizabeth (Reynolds) Carne 1755-unknown
m John Bennetts of Gwennap

John (Reynolds) Carne 1756- unknown

Thomas (Reynolds) Carne 1759-unknown

Eleanor (Reynolds) Carne 1760-1824
m James Downing (1766-1847)
Schoolmaster at Paul, 7 children

Henry (Reynolds) Carne 1761-1800
m Anne (surname not known)

SECOND MARRIAGE OF JOHN (CALENSO) CARNE
To Alice Symons on 17 October 1775
Witnesses: Thomas (John) Branwell and John Morgan

Note: John Carne is included in the Penzance list collated by H Miles Brown in his book, *Cornish Clocks and Clockmakers* (1961 and 1970 editions). One of Richard Branwell's sons, Robert Matthews Branwell is also listed. (See Bibliography, Chapter 12)

b) The second cousins

There is much more known about this line of second cousins, who lived near the Branwells on Chapel Street, than there is about the parental generation of Maria's mother. This is probably due to their public leadership qualities, their tireless civic service, their active Methodist mission and their much respected financial acumen. The comments placed at the head of this chapter, as taken from the biography of Jabez Bunting, show without doubt that the relationship between Maria Branwell and her noted kinsman, Joseph Carne FRS, was a well-known fact.

CARNE TABLE 4: 'The second cousins' [highlighted are focal family line]

Jeronimo Carne, Gent., 1676-1744 of St Ives
1st wife: Avis Purefoy c1673-1749 whose children were:
Jeronimo Jr; Elizabeth; Jane; **Joseph**;
John; Robert; Francis; Margaret.

Son: **Joseph (Purefoy) Carne 1733-1763**
m Mary (Ferris) Johns 1731-1769
Occupation: Bursar & mining captain
Herland Mine, Gwinear Mining district
[Wills & admon. Of Gwinear, 21 Sept, 1762-64]

1. William (Johns) Carne 1754-1836 who married Anna (Lyne) Cock of Helston (4 children) settled on Chapel Street, Penzance, Cornwall, c. 1780.
Children: Joseph C, John C, William C and James C

2. Joseph (Johns) Carne of Truro 1757-1832 who married Jane Stevens of Truro (7 children)
Children: Mary S, Jane S, Susanna S, Joseph S, Nanny S, William, Francis*
(* mistakenly assigned to Wm Johns Carne in 2014. See note 3.)

3. Mary (Johns) Carne 1759-1813 who married John Vivian of Roskear (10+ children); Note: All of Mary's children, carried the Vivian surname.
Children: Phillipa (Johns) V, Joseph J V, Mary J V, Ann J V, John J V, Elizabeth J V, Anne Carne J V, Matthew J V, William J V

Note: Historian Peter Pool has stated that these two Penzance families- the Carnes and the Branwells - are second cousins, but includes no further information as in which generation the link is found. In tracing lines of descent no connecting link springs to light through the name of Carne, though there is ample trace through John and Johns (through the mothers of Thomas Branwell and William Carne. Without a family Bible however, there is little solid or even indicative evidence, except in the limited pool of names. There is the possibility that the relationship is sealed through maternal lines as the families intermingle at several points in and through marriages in the Cock, Boase, Batten, John/s and Vivian kinship circles. They were also working colleagues, often fellow 'methodies', and neighbours. Biographical briefs at Chapter 11 may lead some readers to make useful links.

William (John/s) Carne, Joseph Carne's father, was born, as the eldest son, into a mining family of Carnes in Gwinear, Cornwall, on the eastern side of Hayle from Penzance, near Helston. William named his eldest son for his own father, Joseph (Purefoy) Carne (1733-1763). His mother Mary (Ferris) Johns [6] (1730-1769), was a daughter of the Johns family of Phillack, near Hayle, where her family owned land. There were also large families of Johns and John relations in the Helston and Gwinear (including Breage) area where William would begin his working career, and meet his future wife, before they married and moved to Penzance.

It is projected, though currently not proved definitively, that the Johns contingent is the same John/Johns family represented in the Branwell bloodline, by Margaret John, mother of Richard Branwell Jr., and a member of the George John family of Chapel Street. Margaret John's father is noted as an uncle of George and Samuel John, descendants of Nicholas John of Wendron and the Lizard,[7] making Margaret and George first cousins; other family names such as Williams and Vivian are shared in Carne, Branwell, John/s and Batten families. In looking through snippets of family trees as found (in no way exhaustive) there are many duplicate connections leading to shared ancestry which would take years to follow up, and would actually prove little to our understanding of the interrelations and mingling of family lines.

Unfortunately for our study, the surnames Carne and John/s (singular and multiple) were almost as common as Williams (all being Welsh names as common as Smith and Jones), and the repetitive sequence of forenames do not define the individuals from each other. Hence, though there is certainty in their connections with each other (often through their business connections if in no other way), there is also a measure of speculation in exact relationship terms. Another source of some confusion is the fact that when members of the John family of Wendron moved to live in Plymouth, where Bennett John worked as a surveyor and architect in the drawing offices of the Royal Engineers during the Napoleonic era, their surname of 'John' was changed to Johns by their own choice.

Selected Carnes, known by the Branwells in daily life

William (Johns) Carne (1754-1836) Mining adventurer, merchant, banker, the `Father of Cornish Methodism'

William, a Methodist converted and energised by John Wesley's missions to Cornwall, arrived to settle further west of Gwinear where he had been born and brought up to the age of eight. Orphaned by the death of his father Joseph Carne in 1763, his mother Mary Johns Carne moved into St. Ives, with her three children (William

9, Joseph 6 and Mary 4). Five years later the widow Mary Carne married Thomas Davey, Esq.[8] of Camborne, a merchant with a thriving furnishing and draper's company. Davey is said to have been very kind to William, and helped him to gain a place in the joinery trade.

At the age of 25, William J. Carne married Anna (Lyne) Cock (1753-1822)[9] at Helston, where he worked as a carpenter in her brother's building firm; her father Francis Cock Sr., also a building contractor, had died the year Anna was born. She had been brought up with her older brother, also Francis, by their mother Grace and her Lyne family. Later the whole of the Cock family re-settled in Penzance, and brother Francis was active in local government and the grocery trade. The name of Cock is found severally in town-sponsored activity such as building works, market management in the town centre, and also on the town's council as an assistant, the same office that Thomas Branwell fulfilled over some years.

CARNE TABLE 5: THE WILLIAM (JOHN) CARNE FAMILY OF CHAPEL STREET, PENZANCE

William (John) Carne of Gwinear (1754-1836)
married **Anna (Lyne) Cock** (1753- 1822) at Helston, 1780
↕
Children of William Carne & Anna Cock:
Joseph (Cock) Carne (1782-1858) FRS of Penzance m **Mary Thomas** of Pembroke in 1808 (Table 6 following) 8 children
Revd. John (Cock) Carne (1789-1844) author, m **Ellen Lane** (1801-1868)
Adopted the child of her brother Theodore Lane:
Emma Jane (Lane) Carne 1826-?

Revd. James (Cock) Carne DD (1794-1832)
m **Charlotte Smith** (d. 1832)
(5 children)
Edward Turner Carne Esq (1820-1851); Francis Frederic Carne (1821-1841); Catherine Charlotte Carne (1825-1913); Anna Maria Molesworth Carne (1825-1913) m Rev Henry Batten; Charles Thicknesse Carne (1826-1852, died in Hull, Yorkshire)

William (Cock) Carne (1797-1861) m **Eliza Johanna James** (1793-1860)
(2 children)
Rev John (James) Carne (1824-1860) m **Isabella Emily Holland**;
Eliza Carne (1829-unknown)

Note: When James and Charlotte Carne died in 1832, ministering to his parishioners in Plymouth during the cholera epidemic of that year, all of their children were taken into the home of their Uncle Joseph Carne on Chapel Street, Penzance, to be looked after by the family. Their grandfather William was alive until 1836 and he and Joseph provided homes and legacies for them.

According to Davies Gilbert in his *History of Cornwall* (VIII, p. 95),

> Mr. William Carne came to Penzance about sixty years ago, where, by active and intelligent industry, he has acquired an ample fortune. Of his son, Mr. Joseph Carne, it would not be an easy task to speak in terms sufficiently laudatory: I therefore refer to his communications in the *Transactions* of the Geological Society of Cornwall, to his most ample and valuable collection of natural history and to his patronage of every institution established for the diffusion of knowledge.

William became an `adventurer' (investor in copper and other metals) and a self-made merchant king in the county. Though the Carnes were younger than Anne and Thomas Branwell and had been married only shortly before moving to Penzance, their children were probably schooled together with the Branwells in their earliest formal lessons. These children were contemporaries of the younger Branwell daughters, Elizabeth, Maria and Charlotte.

Without doubt, Maria and Elizabeth, as well as their Uncle Fennell and Aunt Jane, held in their collective memories the personal goodness and the liberality of their kinsman, William Carne in Penzance. Sliding over his great wealth and his numerous responsibilities in banking and trade, they would remember his wanderings with his wife and with 'pilgrim's staff' through streets, lanes, and courts, seeking out the needy and distressed, giving food and clothing.' Most of all, perhaps, he gave respect to people at every level of the social class 'system' of the time, especially those in dire straits due to disabilities and illness.

In terms of local regard, William Carne Sr. stood high. A Wesleyan preacher and writer, Richard Treffry (1771-1842), president of the Methodist conference of 1833, wrote of him during William's illness of the time, "Nothing can exceed his cheerfulness and kindness. I find it a great privilege to be under his conduct as a leader...there is that sort of influence connected with himself that no one, I think, can come into cordial contact with him without being better."[10]

William served for many years as the Treasurer for Missions of the Cornwall Auxiliary Society. With Thomas Branwell he also provided the accommodation for the itinerant Methodist preachers that were assigned to the Penzance circuit on yearly appointments. Following Thomas Branwell's death in 1808, the combined family tradition of assisting the Wesleyan ministers in every possible way, was carried out by the Carnes, Boase and Branwell support through acquiring new leases and seeing to the amenities of daily living for those in the itinerancy.[11]

His Christian character and commitment was evidenced in his deeds. He was a wealthy banker and was known for his generosity. In fact it was estimated during his life he had given over £10,000 – a colossal amount in those days. His involvement in the Wesleyan cause was known so widely that he was called the 'father of Cornish Methodism.' Upon Carne's death, 24 carriages followed his coffin to the family vault in Gulval churchyard, while shops in the town closed during the obsequies.[12]

Joseph (Cock) Carne 1782-1858, Eldest son of William (John) Carne and Anna Cock

Joseph (Cock), the eldest son of William and Anna was born the year before Maria Branwell, and named for his deceased grandfather Joseph (Ferris) Carne of Gwinear. The family had worked in various capacities in the mining of metals – tin, copper and silver – for several generations, as mining agents, pursers, adventurers and traders. From Joseph's childhood, he was known as a mineral collector, walking many miles to various mines and paying a few pence for a sample piece for his growing collection. After initial schooling in Penzance (possibly at some point with 'Cousin John Fennell') Joseph went away to study at the age of thirteen to the Methodist school at Keynsham, Bristol. He returned to their native Wales to find his own wife, Mary Thomas, about whom nothing is known, except that her father was a medical doctor in Haverfordwest, and his family line originated as Thomas of Kidwelly.

CARNE TABLE 6: THE JOSEPH (COCK) CARNE FAMILY OF RIVIERE HOUSE, PHILLACK, HAYLE, AND CHAPEL STREET, PENZANCE

Joseph (Cock) Carne (1782-1858) FRS of Penzance

married **Mary Thomas** of Haverfordwest, Pembroke, 23 March 1808 in Wales

(8 children)

1. Joseph Thomas Carne (1809-1831) of Phillack d Madeira
2. Mary Carne (1811-1890) m Dr Archibald Colquhoun Ross of Lanark (8 children)
3. Anna Carne (1813-1887) m Dr David Johnston of Edinburgh & Bath (no issue)
4. Elizabeth Carne I (1814-1818) of Phillack
5. Caroline Carne (1815-1900) of Phillack & Penzance
6. William Thomas Carne (1816-1852) of Phillack m Frances Cornish (1 child)*

    *Frances (Fanny) m Thomas Polwhele of Polwhele
7. Elizabeth Catherine Thomas Carne (1817-1873) of Phillack & Penzance
8. George Thomas Carne (1821-1822) of Penzance

\+ the five children of Joseph's youngest brother, the Revd. James (Cock) Carne, and his wife Charlotte (Jones) Carne, who died in Plymouth in the cholera outbreak of 1831. (Children listed in **Carne Table 5**.)

Joseph became one of the finest intellectuals that Penzance was to produce, a pre-eminent son, a geologist and mining engineer and in 1818 a Fellow of the Royal Society. Impressions are that he was quite a quiet and private person, dedicated to his work and perhaps respected more than he was liked. For many years he was also the President of the Morrab Library and its erstwhile manager for many of these, and a sometime President of the Penzance Natural History and Antiquarian Society. For the Royal Cornwall Polytechnic Society (RCPS) he was a founder member with his Quaker friends, the Foxes of Falmouth, and their children Caroline, Anna Maria, and Robert Were Fox – it was a family project to provide education and creative industry for miners and mariners. In later years Joseph was one of its Vice Presidents.

Joseph had amassed a large mineral collection, which his youngest and most brilliant daughter, Elizabeth Catherine Thomas Carne, received upon his death in 1858. Later the Collection would become the subject of some rancour and disappointment when it was offered to the Cornish Geological Society by Elizabeth who wished also to donate a room under Joseph's name to house it. For whatever political reasons – probably due to a large dollop of jealousy (minuted to some degree in the closed files of the RGSC) -her offer was refused and then withdrawn.

Elizabeth and her sister Caroline proceeded to build a mineral museum to house it at the bottom of Queen's Street, equipping and cataloguing it to the highest standards. The building remains today but with other uses. The Collection was sold to the Sedgwick Museum at Cambridge University, in the 1890s, when the Carne Bank finally failed, under the mis-management of Joseph's grandson, Charles Campbell Ross, MP. Ross had taken over the Penzance Bank and its shares at the death of Elizabeth Carne in 1873, at which time its reputation was solid and reputable. The mineral collection was only saved due to hard work of fundraising by members of the Cambridge University faculty. [See Document Register, Chapter 12, for the year 1898.] Joseph had been an Honorary Member of the Cambridge Philosophical Society for many years, and namesake son who pre-deceased him had been a student of Trinity College, Cambridge in natural sciences.

1824 Joseph Carne became secretary to Penzance Library until 1832 and for all practical purposes manager over many years. He attracted many gifts from colleagues with large collections, and he also purchased many of the books himself to fill its shelves.

1831 Joseph (Thomas) Carne Jr., eldest son of Joseph Carne FRS, died of tuberculosis in Madeira. See Chapter 12: 'Document Register' for a brief record of his youthful friendship with W. M. Thackeray.

1832 Death of Joseph's youngest brother, the Revd. James Carne DD and his wife Charlotte in the cholera outbreak at Plymouth. See Carne Table 5.
On his walking tour of this year, John Stuart Mill spent two of his days amongst the

woods and the moors of West Cornwall, with Joseph Carne and his 'remarkable' (JSM description in his diary) daughter Elizabeth to guide him. [J S Mill, 'Walking Tour Diary', 1832] quoted from 'A 19th-century Hypatia: Elizabeth Catherine Thomas Carne' in RGSC *Transactions,* XXIII, Pt. 1: pp. 16-39.

1835 Mary (Thomas) Carne, wife of Joseph, died in Penzance, at their home in Chapel Street. This was four years following her eldest son's death. Two of her spinster daughters Caroline and Elizabeth were left to take over the household, and to take on the five additional cousins that arrived to join the immediate family after the deaths of their parents Revd. James and Charlotte Carne at Plymouth.

1836 The funeral of William Carne Sr., Joseph's father

'An Unidentified Young Woman': She had travelled from Bristol by boat with her father and this appears to have been her first visit to West Cornwall. They stayed at Poltair, just outside Penzance. [Vessel arrived at Hayle after 37 hours voyage].[12]

1837 The year following his father's death, Joseph Carne was nominated as High Sheriff of Cornwall but he declined to serve. His career is a reminder that under the system of Trusts, begun by the Wesleys and modified by Conference, service was expected of (and given freely by) Methodists regardless of standing in everyday life.

John (Cock) Carne (Author) 1789-1844

Born in the same year as the youngest child of the Branwell family, Charlotte, his childhood studies would have been spent, like those of his older brothers being taught by their mother and tutors, the same as the Branwell children. Young Jane Fennell would have been in this group as well, and they may all have been taught by the schoolmaster, John Fennell in their earliest years. Joseph Carne, John's oldest brother, had been sent to boarding school at Keynsham Methodist School (Headmaster: Thomas McGeary, M.A.) near Bristol, and it is believed that all the sons were prepared there at about that age.

Much flows from a stream of letters written by John (Cock) Carne, author and traveler, addressed to his family and friends at home in Penzance, Cornwall.[13] It is through these missives written from many European destinations, Middle Eastern and African states that it has proved possible to confirm the identity and relationship of some family members in the shadowy genealogy of the William Carne family, the search for which has been a major time-consuming feature of past months and years. Through the Carne family there comes a vastly extended social and literary network revealed for connection to the wider Branwell-Carne families and their associates.

'A character of John Carne' rendered by William Jerdan 1782-1869 (*The Autobiography of William Jerdan,* Vol. 4, p. 213.) Published 1752-53.

> Another of the cherished intimacies which grew out of
> this date, and which was fruitful of years of after enjoy-
> ments, was with John Carne, the amiable and much

esteemed author of "Letters from the East," and other very interesting and justly popular works. When in London our habits led to almost daily familiar intercourse, and when my friends (for I gladly include the congenial wife, sister of Mr. Lane, the admired artist), retired to their country home, my excursions to Cornwall, with its charms of scenery, attractions of mines and museums, and circles of social hospitalities, furnished recreations such as only slaves of the pen can fully appreciate. Cornwall seems to me to be the most interesting county in the island, though Derbyshire possesses many striking features ; and at Penzance and Falmouth the well-known scientific mineral and natural collections of Mr. Joseph Carne and Mr. Fox, as well as the superior intelligence of their owners (worthy compatriots of Davies Gilbert and Sir Humphry Davy) supplied very gratifying additional sources of pleasure and instruction.

'Mr. Carne's younger brother, John, died at Penzance on April 18. Christopher North (pseudonym for *Blackwood's* John Wilson, the great favourite of the Brontës, not least Branwell and Aunt Branwell) described John Carne as ' the most wonderful story-teller I ever listened to. The publication of *Letters from the East*, and his talent for society (story-telling) brought him into familiar intercourse with many distinguished men of letters, amongst them were Scott, Southey, Wordsworth, Carlisle, Campbell and Lockhart. He departed this life at Penzance in his 55th year, and he was buried in Gulval churchyard in the family vault. He never had an enemy, and was beloved by his friends; his social habits rendered him a general favourite.'

It is likely that Aunt Branwell, in her purchases of magazines for the Brontë household, was greatly led by her interest in the progress of John Carne's literary career.

The letters John wrote are lively, full of travels and enquiries about the welfare of those back home. One can only wish that they were extended in reach at both ends of the time-scale: they begin just after Maria has departed Penzance for the north (hence her parents are dead) and they conclude seven years before the death of Elizabeth Branwell (when John himself was also in decline from conditions related to premature ageing and withdrawn from authorship). Though they do not specifically mention members of the Branwell family, there is some minor reference to joint family connections such as Boase, Batten, Johns and perhaps one or two others. References often (as commonly found in literature of the time) are quite formal in tone even when referring to family, but nevertheless explanatory to what is happening 'back home'.

It is not implied here that the family letters that John (Cock) Carne wrote home to his family would have reached the Branwells themselves, but nonetheless, the issues and events he raises related to local people, make the indigenous scene vivid and much clearer. When taken alongside the books and papers based on exotic adventuring in parallel – which were available locally and found liberally advertised in national newspapers and journals – there was a large range of material from which not only the Branwells but also the Brontës in due course could gain much of interest, enjoyment – and even inspiration.

James (Cock) Carne DD (1794-1832) and his wife Charlotte Carne née Jones

James was the fourth and final son of William and Anna Carne, and the youngest brother of Joseph Carne FRS. James and Charlotte had been living and serving the Church of England in Devon since 1827, when William Carne had presented him to the Diocesan of the City of Plymouth.

The Probate of the Will of James (Cock) Carne DD, the Vicar of Charles, Plymouth, Devon was proved on January 5th, 1833. In that same year Elizabeth (Carne) Branwell decided in Haworth that it was the right time to make her own will. Whether these two events had something to do with each other is unknown, but the reverberations of this sad demise of her youngest cousin in William Carne's Chapel Street family, whom she had known since birth, echoed through the circle of relations.

James and his wife Charlotte died within four days of each other while nursing parishioners in their own homes during the cholera outbreak in Plymouth in 1832. There is an anecdotal passage, only slightly changed from this family story, used by Charlotte Brontë in *Jane Eyre* to explain the lonely background of St. John Rivers and his sisters.

James took his early lessons at the grammar school in Penzance, probably for some time with John Fennell before being sent to Westminster School in London prior to attending and achieving his degree from Oriel College, Oxford B.A. (1817), M.A. (1821), B.D. (1827), D.D. (1830). In August of 1818, he married Charlotte Jones, sister of his best friend at Westminster School, the Revd. Anselm Jones, who also joined James in the Anglican priesthood, serving as the Vicar of Stockton on the Forest, Yorkshire (a village near York) until 1838, when he also died young (age 43). This connection may have been known by Aunt Branwell. Thematically there could be further links to the story of Jane Eyre's fictional family history as well.

Charlotte and James Carne were to leave behind three sons and two daughters, who were taken into the home of Joseph (Cock) Carne and cared for and educated by the family until they reached legal age. All of these five children joined the cadre of family members who became 'orphans', and their futures would have been of major concern to the family as a whole, not least their grandfather William Carne. The latter, both the 'rock' and the ladder that his family relied on, was able to ensure through the arrangement of his properties and his Will, that portions were available to all of his sons as needed and to his grandchildren, following his demise.

The children of Charlotte and James Carne were the following:
Edward Turner Carne Esq. 1820-1851, 12 years old at death of parents
Francis Frederic Carne 1821-1841

Catherine Charlotte Carne 1823-1846
Anna Maria Carne 1825-1913 who married the Revd. Henry Batten of Penzance
Charles Thicknesse Carne 1826-1852, mariner who died in Hull, Yorkshire

Elizabeth Catherine Thomas Carne 1817-1873
Daughter of Mary (Thomas) and Joseph (Cock) Carne, FRS

Elizabeth and her sister Caroline took over the household management following the death of their mother in 1835. They lived in the large family home (now a luxurious hotel) directly adjacent to St. Mary's Parish Church on Chapel Street and this was run by an establishment of servants for the stable and the heavy duties of the large household, which now included the orphaned nephews and nieces of brother James and his wife Charlotte. Elizabeth was her father's intellectual companion from her youth and dedicated as he was to the establishment of educational causes such as the RCPS in Falmouth, and a full range of social welfare and spiritual improvements. An example of the practical social opinions voiced by Elizabeth Carne in one of her campaigning roles was remembered in her obituary (1873) in the *Cornish Telegraph*, long before Eliza Jane Kingston's death in the workhouse hospital ward:

> With all her dislike to pauperism, one scheme which some people say to induce it, was a favourite with Miss Elizabeth Carne. That lady would have had the memorial of Sir Humphry Davy [ed. note: erected in 1872 in front of Market House, Penzance] take the form of almshouses for the decayed or drooping inhabitants of the great for whom it is a native town, and she offered land and £1000 towards the benevolent project.

The proposed building of almshouses is a project worthy of inclusion in the long list of social welfare gifts for which Elizabeth Carne in her day was widely known and celebrated. Her own bibliography is impressive, especially so for being representative of the movements gathering toward the enfranchisement and freedom of women to take up their places in spheres traditionally occupied by men.

Beginning to publish openly under her own name following her father's death, she had already contributed much journalistic work anonymously since the 1840s. Remarked upon from childhood, by such as John Stuart Mill and John Sterling, and the closest of friends and correspondents with the famed diarist Caroline Fox, her accomplishments in private study – said to include all of the classical languages and some of the modern such as German and French – were only a part of her wide range of achievements.

Elizabeth Carne (1817-1873) and her older sister Caroline (1815-1900), due to their large legacies after Joseph (Cock) Carne's death, were able also to continue the family tradition of patronage to the town and surrounding areas. They promoted the construction of schools for the poor (at least three) and the distribution of food, books and clothing to the sailors and indigent – roles set for them by their Cornish mothers. [14]

Though the following must be considered speculative, it is at least plausible and likely that it was Caroline Carne who undertook to pay for the admission of Eliza

Jane Kingston, her kinswoman, to the hospital wards (as a paying patient) of the Madron Poor House where she died in 1878. This was after the death of Elizabeth Carne herself, but prior to the death of Caroline Carne, the longest lived of them all. However, despite her many local relations, Eliza Jane was buried in a pauper's grave. This would seem to challenge the idea of a sympathetic and kindly family circle, but we do not know the prevailing circumstances nor do we know the familial relationships. Elizabeth Jane Kingston had lived for 54 years after her father's death, and 23 years since her mother's death.[15]

ENDNOTES

1 Quoted from Thomas Percival Bunting (1859) *The Life of Jabez Bunting, D.D.*, vol. 1, pp. 197-8. Available on-line through the Hathi Trust website.
2 D. Gilbert, *Parochial History of Cornwall* vol. I, pp. 9-10. Also repeated in Gay, S. E. (1903) *Old Falmouth*, relating to William Naylor Carne (1840-1906), a second cousin x 4 removed. The coat of arms can be viewed on-line in various images on heraldry sites.
3 In a recently published article (April 2014)of mine in the *Transactions* of the RGSC about Elizabeth C. T. Carne, I made two clear genealogical mistakes which I have now noted as picked up and used in both Ancestry.com and in further research papers of others. These are corrected in this volume. See Carne Table 5: William (Johns) Carne family, in this chapter for a corrected version to date.
4 Calenso is another name the spelling for which is unstable in early records, and can be found as Calensow, Calensoe, Colenso, and even Collensow – related to Collings, Collins and Cawlins.
5 'Silver and copper mines and related industries were going strong in the 18th and 19th centuries, Rosewarne and Herland mines produced silver, and this is where the Carnes gathered. In those days, the parish was a thriving mining community and one of the first steam engines ever to be built was installed at the Herland mine in 1758.' Abstract: Genuki, UK for Gwinear, Gwennap, Hayle. It is not a surprise that John Carne (Ann's father) was a silversmith.
6 COPC Database The John/Johns of Phillack is one branch of an equally widespread family, also of Welsh connection, who like the Branwells and Carnes had 'dozens of cousins.' The John/Johns alliances are strong on both sides of the Branwell-Carne marriage of 1768.
7 Another source of some connection is the Gwinear and Helston family of Charles Alexander Johns, author of *Flowers of the Field*. His father and mother, distant cousins to each other, moved to Plymouth from Cornwall on marriage and proceeded to have a large family with the following forenames: Henry, Maria, Elizabeth, Sophia, Charles, Emily, Julia, Bennet, Jane, Anne and John. See bibliographies in Appendices. Their family story, emerging from Cornish natural history is told by this author with Deirdre Dare co-author, in the 2008 biography of Charles A. Johns, entitled *A Passion for Nature*.
8 COPC Database Record of Marriages: 13 June 1767 at Gwithian. She is listed of Gwinear, a widow, and he is listed from out of the parish (otp). Thomas John and William Davey are listed as witnesses.
9 COPC Database Record of Marriages: 20 August 1780 at Helston. Witnesses: her brother, Francis Cock, and friend, John Jago/Jaco.
10 Quoted in John Horner (2010) *Even in this Place,19th-century Nonconformists & Life in the Borough of Penzance*, p. 23. Richard Treffry (1771-1842) was a Wesleyan preacher and writer. Treffry was for five years the chairman of the Cornwall Wesleyan District and twice assigned for two-year periods to Penzance in its preaching circuit. In 1833 he was president of the national Wesleyan Conference, and would have known the Branwell family well.
11 BRA833 Cornwall Deeds, Estate papers and Mining papers, Turner Collection/CRO: 4 June 1814 Lease property at Regent Terrace, Penzance: new house for Richard Treffry, Methodist preacher. Term 99 years or 3 lives. The protecting three lives were: John Freethy, age 13 (son of R M Branwell, grocer); William, age 13, (son of John Boase), merchant, and Joseph, age 5 (son of Joseph (Cock) Carne, merchant of Riviere).
12 Todd Gray (2000) *Cornwall-The Travellers' Tales* vol. I: 'An Unidentified Young Woman, 1836' pp. 115-120. The editor of this compilation found an essay at the Bodleian Library, Ms Don. C166, folios 245-8, from a young woman's diary, reporting on the impressive funeral given to William Carne on 12 July. She comments 'originally nothing more than a common carpenter & has probably died the richest man in the County.'
13 These may be read on-line (John Carne, *Letters 1813-1837)* and considerably extend our knowledge of this family

of Carnes, and John's troubles and successes as a journalist and author. See family bibliography. See John Carne (1789-1844) in *DNB*.

14 All three sons of Joseph (Cock) and Mary (Thomas) Carne, had died before the death of their father, and the remaining four daughters, two married women and two singletons, inherited the family fortune, which was large indeed.

15 See Chapter 11:'Biographical briefs' for Eliza Jane Kingston, the youngest child of Jane Branwell and John Kingston. Fannie Ratchford asked who might have done this for her, in her Brontë Society paper 'The Loneliness of a Brontë Cousin' *BST* vol 13: 2, Jan 1957, 100-110.

'The House of Girgius Adeeb, at Antioch' from *Syria, The Holy Land, Asia Minor* by John Carne, Esq., author of *Letters from the East*. Illustrated by W. H. Bartlett, William Purser, &c.

Chapter 10

Travellers' Tales

'Tis education forms the common mind: Just as the twig is bent the tree's incline.[1]

'Let the twig follow its bent' – was the phrase used by a later cousin Francis 'Frank' Johns[2], Head Master of Winton House School for young gentlemen established by his father, Charles Alexander Johns, in Winchester, Hampshire. Shortly before Frank's death in 1948, he published his memories of the novelist and Victorian 'best seller' Charles Kingsley. The latter, a close family friend, had been schooled first in Helston, Cornwall, at the Grammar School led by Derwent Coleridge, where his father was initially assistant, and then after Coleridge as Headmaster. Kingsley and Johns had been firm friends since 1833 in Cornwall, and the dictum travelled with them throughout their lives and into the lives of their children. The entire quotation is another form of Alexander Pope's poetic phrase recorded above.

The phrase is relevant here on at least two accounts. Firstly, it can be said to characterize the Carne-Branwell family as a whole in their pushing forward in curiosity and independence, and in the liberality of their approaches to communal life. Secondly, it recognizes movement, choice and inclination toward common goals of learning for the future. In Chapter 6, a time-line of family events has been provided, but this cannot be descriptive of personal activities in any detail without attempting to produce a modern day dictionary and source book. This is being done concurrently in the so-named Carne-Branwell Family Archive of the Hypatia Trust. It remains a work-in-progress, however, and can, in future, be consulted under the auspices of the Elizabeth Treffry Collection, an archive with 'a room of its own' in the Morrab Library, Penzance, Cornwall. Only some of these 'spirits' or ghosts of times past, if we may call them this, would grow from Cornish roots into Brontë lives. In the past chapters, the immediate Branwell and Carne families have been listed or 'tabled', but it is difficult if not impossible to visualize character from just a name and a position in the family.

In this chapter, the intention is to focus on the key figures who have led us – as they led Maria and Elizabeth, and thence the Brontë children - into potentially new territories, both imaginary and real. No one individual can be pointed to and said to be 'the guide' who tutored the minds of the Brontë writers. But a great number undoubtedly played a part. To follow up with greater detail on published facts (dates, etc.), the reader will find each of the following family groups, related in some form to the Branwells and Carnes in Cornwall, represented in brief notes in Chapter 11, A – Z. First, there are the main travellers in our stories about whom we need to know more. Coming as they did from the peripheries of the British Isles, how did they come together in the West Riding of Yorkshire? This is the most constant question that I am asked: "Why are 'you' studying Cornwall when the Brontës came from Yorkshire?" My answers to this question do not, of course, lie only in geographical place, though necessarily territories and landscapes are part of the soup. The further additions of people, their ideas and the expression of those ideas, make up the rich ingredients.

29 December 1812

At St. Oswald's Parish Church, Guiseley, Yorkshire, the Revd. William Morgan married Jane Branwell Fennell, the only daughter of Jane Branwell and Mr. John Fennell, Governor of Woodhouse Grove Methodist School, Apperley Bridge, nr. Bradford. In the same ceremony the Revd. Patrick Brontë married Maria (Carne) Branwell. Morgan and Brontë presided over the marriages, each of the other; John Fennell, acting as patriarch, gave the two ladies away to their grooms with Jane (Branwell) Fennell, mother, in attendance.

At the same hour, on the same day, at faraway Madron Parish Church in the Land's End district of Cornwall, Charlotte (Carne) Branwell, sister to Maria, and cousin to Jane Fennell, married Joseph (Matthews) Branwell, her first cousin, son of Honor (Matthews) and Richard Branwell.[3] Witnesses for that wedding were named as Robert (Matthews) Branwell and Richard (Matthews) Branwell, both of whom were brothers of Joseph, the groom. Her sister, Elizabeth Branwell (Aunt Branwell-to-be) and Grace Thomas, a Quaker friend, were witnesses for the bride. None of the parents of Charlotte and Joseph were in attendance, as no one of them remained alive; the late Uncle Richard (John) Branwell, father of Joseph, groom, had died only a few months before his son's marriage to his niece.

The person of John Fennell

An abiding mystery hangs over the arrival of John Fennell in West Cornwall, a young man of 21 years, hailing from Madeley in Shropshire, in the year of Maria Branwell's birth (1783). We can find no definitive reason for his choice. Nor do we have a photographic image of him as yet, despite attempts to discover one through descendants in the present day.

John Fennell was born in Madeley, Shropshire in June of 1762, the second son of collier Thomas Fennell and his wife Mary Hotchkiss (also found as Hodgkiss).[4] His baptism was held in the Anglican parish church of St. Michael's with the incumbent priest standing as his godfather. This former Swiss national, now English parish priest, the Revd. John Fletcher (1729-1785) was the major interpreter and theologian of Wesleyan Methodism of the time.[5] He was also the personally-preferred successor to Wesley (1703-1791), though he steadfastly refused the position and finally pre-deceased in 1785, his much-admired friend and co-worker.

At Madeley, there is every reason to suppose young Fennell would have heard and perhaps met the Wesley brothers several times throughout his childhood because of his close association with the Fletchers. As shown in numerous letters and sermons, in both of these associations – the Fletchers and the Wesleys – John Fennell was most fortunate, and he believed himself 'blessed' by their friendship.

With the intelligent guidance of John Fletcher, young Fennell undertook a full schedule of classical study, including French, Greek, Latin, Hebrew and Biblical studies, which carried him through his early years. Taking his lessons with Fletcher, John kept to a schedule which his mentor checked up on each week.

At fourteen on the death of his mother, John was apprenticed to a 'grocer'.[6] But, it seems his choice at the end of his seven-year apprenticeship, leaned to teaching; the likelihood is that he was first employed as an assistant master in the local grammar school in Penzance, Cornwall (established 1779), well before setting up his own 'Writing School' (a preparatory school for young men interested in commerce and trade) in the late 1780s.[7]

John's religious life in Cornwall was busy, with a regular slot on the Methodist preaching rota for West Cornwall, and in weekly classes as a Class Leader. Like his godfather and mentor, Fletcher of Madeley, he remained in the Anglican fold,[8] but dedicated himself with evangelical zeal to re-invigorating, in Wesleyan fashion (often preaching in the open air), a doctrine of love and forgiveness.

He published memorials for spiritual living and lives for the *Methodist Magazine*, answered mathematical queries for *The Lady's Magazine*, and issued periodic newsletters for the local Methodist chapels. He has a brief entry in the large *Bibliotheca Cornubiensis* of Boase and Courtney (Vol. 1, p. 147) and initiated the Sunday school and classes at Hayle, Cornwall in the heart of the mining industry. He was also made a Trustee for a new Methodist chapel at Breage nearby, alongside his cousin by marriage, William Carne Sr. as mentioned in the previous chapter.

Just before Christmas in 1790, Fennell married Jane (John) Branwell, nine years his senior, the younger sister of Thomas (John) Branwell, Maria's father. Jane Branwell Fennell, their daughter, was born the following year, the only child that Fennell and his first wife were to have. Thus John was to become in future years the longest-standing central figure in the lives of the Branwell siblings Elizabeth and Maria, one they seem to have turned to as to a parent or as to a much loved brother. In fact, Maria knew him and her Aunt Jane for longer, in terms of time, than she knew her own mother and father.

Aunt Branwell named him as one of the executors of her will in the 1830s, having known him for 58 years of her life, and was to help his second wife to nurse him in his final illness a decade later, according to Charlotte's letters.[9] Both John Fennell and Elizabeth Branwell died in West Yorkshire within a year and within a few miles of each other. Probably, also, Elizabeth's willingness to remain in Yorkshire was made more likely due to the presence of her Aunt Jane who died in 1829, her young cousin Jane Morgan who preceded her mother in death in 1827, and John Fennell himself, in addition to the needs of her sister Maria's children. These provided her with an alternative central family, even though it seems that Yorkshire was never to outshine the gaiety and centrality of her home and family circle in Cornwall.

Though no exact date is known, it is believed that the 'Writing School' as it was known, the new school established by John Fennell in Penzance, was opened c1792. Prior to this he had been an assistant schoolmaster situated on land sold to the local council by Thomas Branwell at the back of three houses known as 'the Rotterdam Buildings' where the Branwell home was located. The buildings are no longer there, though the girls' small schoolroom remains overlooking the entrance to St. Mary's Church who were in overall supervisory charge at the time.

Fennell opened the private Writing School in his own home (leased from the Veale family of Rosemorran, Gulval) further up Chapel Street, though the exact location has not been identified. Strangely enough, it could even be the home that I occupy with my family today. His pupils included young men preparing themselves for further education or business interests elsewhere, but who needed the basic elements of reading, writing and arithmetic. Fennell's own strength as mentioned, was in mathematics, but he was well-grounded classically and generally due to his lessons with John Fletcher.

Leaving Penzance in 1806 for a new beginning, the Fennell family travelled to John's home county of Shopshire. John already knew Madeley and the Wellington district well because of his birth, family, church and schooling there. Fennell was offered the headship of a boarding school and at the same time took up a regular preaching role at the Wesleyan chapel in Wellington, of which the Revd. John Eyton, was a Trustee, while also being the Vicar of Wellington. They became friends and John Fennell also met, for the first time, the Revd. William Morgan, Eyton's curate, who had arrived in Wellington in 1805 from Wales. When the Revd. Patrick Brontë arrived in Wellington as an additional curate in 1809, the men came together who would be friends and relations for life, and mentors to the future Brontë children.

John Eyton was a good friend and admirer of Mary Fletcher too, the (now) widow of the much-loved John Fletcher, and part of her circle of evangelical friends and allies. Morgan soon introduced Patrick to his friends in Shropshire and Patrick became re-acquainted with an old college friend, the Revd. John Nunn, now curate of St. Chad's in nearby Shrewsbury. Samuel Walter, John Fennell, Charles Hulbert, John Eyton and Joshua Gilpin (Vicar of Wrockwardine) along with William Morgan and John Nunn were frequent visitors to Mary Fletcher's home at Madeley.

Fennell's daughter Jane seems to have been an attractive young lady, and not least to the young curate, William Morgan, who later in Guiseley, Yorkshire, married her. Claire Harman in her recent life of Charlotte Brontë, points out a personally-annotated volume of Patrick Brontë's *Cottage Poems* located in the Berg Collection of the New York Public Library. Published first in 1811, after Brontë had left Wellington for Yorkshire, it is inscribed: 'To Miss Fennell, By the Author, as a Token of his purest Friendship, and Christian Love'. Whether or not this was a courtship ploy as Harman tentatively suggests it might have been, it is clear that Patrick was close enough to the Fennell family to know of their Cornish background even before meeting Maria in Yorkshire.

After Fletcher's death Mary Fletcher played a pivotal role in the friendships forged between John Fennell and several key figures in the Branwell - Brontë circle, and a guide to their spiritual lives and careers. Correspondence in the Fletcher-Tooth Collection at Manchester University shows clearly the importance of her long term friendship and guidance to John Fennell, to William Morgan in his turn, and also to Patrick Brontë during his brief sojourn in Wellington in 1809. Mary was also an old friend of the Revd. John Crosse in Bradford, who had previously taken an interim ministry at Madeley, and to whom John Fennell, once he entered Holy Orders, would serve as curate. Hence she was well placed and instrumental in the career moves of three of 'her precious young men' from Wellington to Yorkshire.

All of these were part of the group of younger men who took support, affection and inspiration from Mary Fletcher in the so-called 'Madeley Circle'. Whether or not John Kingston (following section) was even informally a part of this circle is not known, but it is clear that Mary Fletcher had heard of him and to some extent had connections with him. John Kingston references both John and Mary Fletcher in later books (1814) which he wrote and published in America, acknowledging that he had been in their home in Madeley in previous years (c 1806-07). In the Foreword of his life of Fletcher, Kingston refers to time spent in the great preacher's study amongst his books.[10] Much later in the century, an oblique reference to Kingston's long-ago misdemeanours is linked with a story about Mrs. Fletcher's conversations with her husband in her dreams.[11]

The first to move on to the next stage in his life as a parish priest was Patrick Brontë in 1809, with Mary Fletcher's help. He remained just a little under a year at Wellington before, he was appointed to a curacy at All Saints, Dewsbury and thenceforward to Hartshead. Secondly, William Morgan was invited to a curacy under the aforementioned Revd. John Crosse, the vicar of Bradford, where he would also serve as vicar of Bierley (a private living). That northern place was a kind of mecca, made more historically glowing by the prestige in evangelical circles of the Revd. William Grimshaw formerly of Haworth. In much earlier years Mary herself had converted to Methodism under the influence of John Wesley, and is widely credited for convincing him that women should be able to preach God's mercy in public places, and to take on leadership roles as needed. That she succeeded is of vast importance to the history and agency of women in the ministry today.

Fennell was the third of the friends to arrive in Yorkshire in 1811 with the backing of Mary Fletcher, who supported his application to become the first House Master of the new school being organised for the sons of Methodist ministers at Woodhouse Grove. The new institution opened in early January of 1812 with nine pupils only, but was to expand at what was proved to be an unmanageable rate throughout the following months. Jane Fennell, now 59 years old, was on a joint wage (£100 per annum) with her husband, acting as housekeeper for the establishment.

> Woodhouse Grove School resulted from two matters of growing concern in Methodism: the need for a second school in the North similar to what Kingswood had by then become in the South as a school for the sons of Methodist ministers; and the need for a trained and educated ministry. The two problems were not entirely separate.[12]

The very best and lucid summary of the events leading up to the introduction of Fennell's friend Patrick Brontë to his future wife Maria, up until the present day, has been rendered by Frank Pritchard in his 1978 history of Woodhouse Grove School at Apperley Bridge, Bradford. For more up-to-date developments and many images of its buildings (including Brontë House) an excellent history is provided by Nigel Watson in *Xa!Pete Woodhouse Grove: The First 200 Years*.[13]

Though reports of teaching and theological inspiration were good, early complaints were made of lack of beds and bedding, and the quality of the food. Much of this was outside the control of the Fennells who applied for additional funds as the numbers of pupils grew, though the necessary support was not always forthcoming or efficiently delivered. From reports in the histories of Woodhouse Grove, there appeared to be chaotic administration, but this may well have been a function of the minimal staff being only Fennell as the Commercial tutor and the Revd. William Burgess, the Classics master, with Mrs Fennell acting as House governess together with some assistance in the kitchen.

Hence Mrs Fennell did the necessary and asked her niece, Maria, now aged 29, to come up to Yorkshire and assist her with the household management. Maria was pleased about this, mainly because she needed occupation, her parents were both dead and going to her close family was a safe and satisfactory option. She and sister Elizabeth would now have to make their own lives and chances, even though there were numerous family relations in and around West Penwith.

Lock and Dixon describe Fennell's future thus:

> But John Fennell's tenure of office was to be brief. For a year he would bestride two worlds-that of the old Evangelical school of Methodism and that of the new, more militant kind that no longer wanted men like himself, Crosse, Morgan and the others. The Methodists now intended to fend for themselves, to recruit from the sons of their own ministers, and they no longer looked to the bosom of the Church to supply their needs. Chapels, schools and ministry quite separate from the C of E had sprung up everywhere with mushroom growth. Fennell would have to make his decision; and he was to choose the Established Church.[14]

It is through this set of opportune circumstances that Maria Branwell of Penzance met the Revd. Patrick Bronte. Their courtship was relatively brief – they admitted to falling in love at first sight - and in December of the same year, in a double wedding ceremony with her cousin Jane Fennell and William Morgan, Maria and Patrick were married. On that same day and at the same time, as carefully arranged by post and with sister Elizabeth's help, Maria's younger sister Charlotte Branwell married her first cousin Joseph Branwell at Madron Parish Church in West Cornwall. Thus a triple wedding was carried out in this close-knit family in which all of the women were Cornish-born and with the same parentage.

Fennell put in his notice of leaving Woodhouse Grove school to the Methodists and informed them that he was to seek Anglican ordination. After a brief few months as a curate at Keighley near Haworth, he then succeeded his friend and now son-in-law William Morgan as curate to John Crosse of Bradford Parish Church. Later that same year he also baptized Elizabeth Brontë.

TABLE 10.1: CLERICAL RECORD OF THE REVD. JOHN FENNELL OF CROSS STONE, TODMORDEN

Deacon	6 August 1815	
Priest	17 December 1815	
Curate	Keighley, Yorkshire	6 August 1815
Curate	Bradford St. Peter	17 December 1815
Perpetual Curate	Cross Stone	24 April 1819

In 1819[15] Fennell became the incumbent of Cross Stone near Todmorden, where he was to remain for the rest of his life. That same year he baptized Patrick Branwell Brontë and later acted as godfather to Emily Brontë.

The Revd. William Morgan 1782-1858

> Of William Morgan Vicar of Christ Church, Bradford, much has been written in scattered form, but we yet await the full story of the useful life of this strenuous worker in the cause of religion and temperance. He was of a choleric and irascible temperament, and it was reported of him that on one occasion he sent his cook to jail for making thin sauce!
>
> J. Hambley Rowe, 'The Maternal Relations of the Brontës'

William Morgan was born in Crickadarn, Brecknockshire, Wales, son of David Morgan of Pentremoel (yeoman) and Elizabeth Morgan née Davies. He was probably educated in Builth Wells (about 5 miles away). At the age of 22, he was ordained Deacon in the Anglican faith by the Bishop of St. David's and appointed to a curacy of St. Cynog's Church, Boughrood, Radnorshire. His ordination to the priesthood took place at Abergwilly, again by Bishop Thomas Burgess of St. David's.

From Wales he moved over the border in 1805, to Wellington, Shropshire where he was to take up a curacy with the Revd. John Eyton, who proved to be like-minded and Wesleyan in outlook. The following year John Fennell and his family returned to Shropshire from Cornwall and picked up his long friendship with the area.

Michael Walker confirms that "One of the joys of William's curacy at Wellington was that it is very close to Madeley, where lived Mary Fletcher, the widow of John Wesley's nominated successor, John Fletcher. Here, at Fletcher's home, William and his clerical friends would often meet to listen as Mary spoke of her late husband and his evangelical work."[16] Another joy it appears was to cement a strong friendship with the schoolmaster, John Fennell, and to meet his bright and attractive daughter Jane Branwell Fennell, who would, when she became of age (in 1812), also become his wife.

Early in January of 1809 Patrick Bronte arrived as a new curate, from Wethersfield in Essex, and he was very much in tune with his new vicar, John Eyton. They had both studied at St John's College, Cambridge. He and William Morgan became close friends quickly. William introduced Patrick to his friends in Shropshire and Patrick became re-acquainted with an old college friend, the Revd. John Nunn, now curate of St Chad's nearby Shrewsbury. These three along with Samuel Walter, John Fennell, Charles Hulbert, John Eyton and Joshua Gilpin (Vicar of Wrockwardine) were frequent visitors to Mary Fletcher's home.'

In 1815 Christ Church Bradford was consecrated on October 12th, where Morgan was to remain Priest- in-charge until 1851. William Morgan began a new publishing venture by editing and circulating *The Pastoral Visitor*, in monthly issues. Amongst the contributors were both Patrick Brontë, and his wife Jane Fennell Morgan who penned several articles. This may, in fact, have been the organ to which Maria Branwell was intending to submit her brief article on the advantages of poverty, which Patrick kept with her letters posthumously and gave to Charlotte. The small journal was to last for two full years, finally finishing in December, 1816.

Children of the family

1816 William Morgan is the officiate at the baptism of Charlotte Branwell Brontë.
1818 20 August: Officiates at the baptism of Emily Jane Branwell Brontë, Godparents: Jane Morgan and the Fennells.
1820 25 March: Officiates at the baptism of Anne Branwell Brontë.
1821- 22 September: Officiated at the funeral and burial of Maria Branwell Brontë.
1825 Officiated at funerals of Maria (aged 12) and Elizabeth (aged 10) Brontë

Records are non-existent covering the sad years of 1827 to 1829, when first came the death of the much-loved daughter of Jane Branwell and John Fennell, probably caused by the after-effects of childbirth. Her son, and the Fennells' grandson was born on 16 July 1827 and given the name of William John Morgan; he was baptized by the Revd. Joseph Cowell, Rector, at Cross Stone church. Jane Morgan then died in the final week of September 1827. William John was to be the only surviving son of William Morgan, though William Sr. did marry again some years later, and then again in his old age. Morgan's biographer Michael Walker writes that Patrick attended Jane's funeral, and a few days later received the keepsake gift of Jane's Greek Prayer

Book from William Morgan.[17] There is no mention of Aunt Branwell, Jane's cousin with whom she grew up in Penzance.

A little known fact, that has strangely been overlooked, is that some three months before she died, Jane and William Morgan produced a son who was named William John Morgan. Though no medical detail is known, Jane probably died from complications of childbirth such as puerperal fever. Lock and Dixon erroneously assign this child to Morgan's second marriage to Mary Alice Gibson of Bradford, but since he did not remarry until nine years later, this is clearly false since the career of their son is traced through until at least 1902 (M Hardie-Budden and Bob Gamble, unpublished research).

24 September 1827

> …there came news to grieve Patrick. For years it had been his dear old friend William Morgan who had served him as minister in all his family needs. He had married Patrick, christened four of his children and recently buried his wife and two little girls. Now it was Patrick's turn to console Morgan – on the loss of his young wife Jane. She died on 24th September 1827, aged 36. There being no burial ground at Christ Church [Bradford] the funeral was at her father's [the Revd. John Fennell's] chapel on the 27th, conducted by the Revd. Joseph Cowell, minister of Todmorden. Jane Morgan was buried in the east churchyard of Cross Stone Chapel.'[18]

16 July 1827:   A son for Jane (Branwell Fennell) and William Morgan
West Yorkshire, England, Births and Baptisms, 1813-1910: The birth of William John Morgan, son of the Revd. William Morgan, incumbent of Christ Church, Bradford and his wife Jane Fennell Morgan was baptized by the Revd. Joseph Cowell, Rector of Cross Stones, Todmorden, West Yorkshire. John Fennell, minister of the parish and grandfather of the child did not officiate at the baptism. Godparents were not listed. Baptismal entry: No. 1175, Cross Stones in Halifax.

The now elderly Jane Fennell Morgan, aged 76, known in the family as the 'Duchess', died two years later. She was, of course, not only Fennell's wife but also William Morgan's mother-in-law, the aunt of Elizabeth Aunt Branwell, and now the grandmother of the two year old William John Morgan. It is exceedingly strange to my mind that no one has noticed this last child of the core Branwell lineage, i.e. the grand- nephew of Thomas Branwell and Ann Carne. Books belonging to Aunt Jane Fennell are known to have been in Branwell family hands since before the births of Elizabeth and Maria, unless the 'Duchess' had abandoned her own books in Cornwall, and these she left with the Brontës. Walker also mentions that Jane Morgan wrote a number of short pieces that were published in William Morgan's newsletter, *The Pastoral Visitor* that he published regularly for two years. But, all in all, we know very little about her

Three months later the Brontë children, presumably accompanied by Aunt Branwell, arrived at Cross Stone to visit Uncle John. On this occasion, at the request of her aunt, Charlotte Brontë penned her first known letter to her father to let him know when they will be returning home and what they have been doing.[19] In December of the same year John took in four boys as boarders for tuition in languages, so his teaching bent was not at end.

An afterword -

Nowhere in Brontë biographical literature is there mention of Fennell's grandson, William Morgan's son and the last of the Branwells in that bloodline. Further research by this writer and Brontë scholar Bob Gamble has followed this Branwell-Fennell-Morgan connection up to the present day, and it is very intriguing to discover that William John Morgan became an East India merchant, based in Calcutta, and in London, and that one child of his, William John Fennell Morgan attended Rugby School for a year in 1863-64.

Even more interesting, from a Cornish perspective, is the fact that William John Fennell Morgan, approximately 95 years after his namesake great grandfather arrived in Cornwall to begin his working career in teaching, the young man married a daughter of a Falmouth merchant. From there the couple moved via Plymouth to his grandfather's (Revd. William Morgan's) home territory of Wales. Initially he was a shipping agent and commercial traveller and finally in 1901 as a widower, he became a foreign correspondent. This is yet another traveller's tale, but well outside our Brontë focus.

June 10, 1833—To Miss Arthur's half-year's account for Mr. Morgan's little boy …8 12 9. A note about this was found in account papers some years later which misled researchers into thinking he was contributing to the welfare of a charity child as mentioned by Michael Walker in footnote 25 in his informative article on William Morgan.[20]

In *Pigot's Directory of 1834*: Revd. William Morgan, Head, Gentlemen's Boarding School, Darley Street, Bradford, Yorkshire. Once again, within the family, tutoring, mentoring and the setting up of teaching institutions arises. This would probably encompass the teaching of his own son, William Jr. In 1836 Miss Mary Alice Gibson of Bradford, became the second wife of Morgan, solemnized by the Revd. Samuel Redhead at Calverley Church.

Two years later (1838-39) Branwell Bronte moved to live near his Uncle Morgan at Brunswick Place, Bradford, and must have known William John Morgan, his cousin, who by this time was eleven years old, and living at home. The **Census of** 1841 lists the Revd. William Morgan, his wife, his son: William John Morgan (b. 1827 at Bradford, son of Jane Branwell Fennell Morgan), together with one servant, living in Bradford. In 1848, Morgan officiated at the funeral of Branwell Brontë.

Morgan exchanged livings with the Rector of Hulcott, Buckinghamshire in 1851. Soon after the move the second Mrs. Morgan died and her husband's last written work was entitled *Simplicity and Godly Sincerity exemplified in the Life and Death of Mrs. Morgan of Hulcott, Buckinghamshire and late of Bradford, Yorkshire.*

In October, 1854 in Aylesbury, Buckinghamshire, William Morgan, at the age of 73, married Mary Howell (1800-1869), the daughter of Benjamin and Elizabeth Howell of Bristol. As far as is known they remained together until William's death in March of 1858, when they were living or staying in Bath, Somerset. Charlotte Brontë included him at the head of her invitation list to her wedding to the Revd. Arthur Nicholls, though he and his wife could not attend.

TABLE 10.2 THE WILLIAM MORGAN FAMILY OF BRADFORD, YORKSHIRE

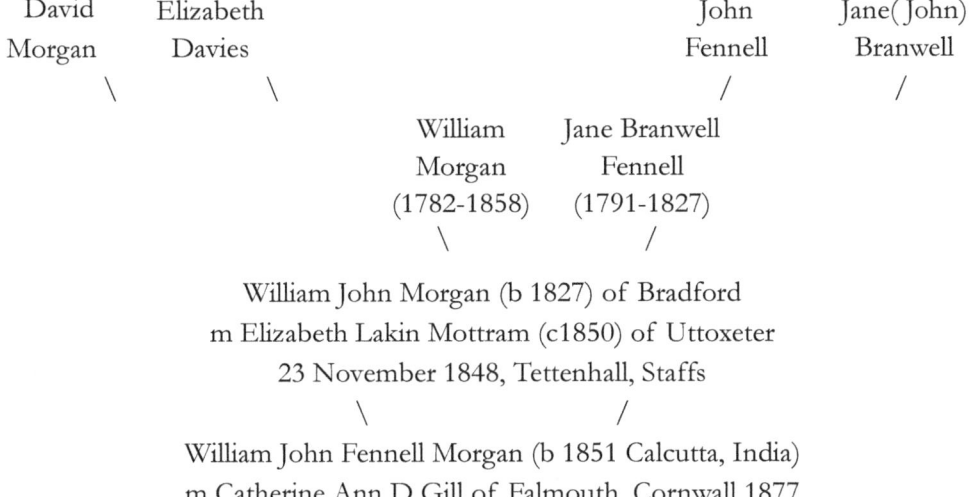

Amongst the Branwells
The first brother-in-law: Charles Fisher 1769-1798

On January 7, 1792, Margaret (Carne) Branwell became the first child of Ann and Thomas Branwell to marry. She was just 21 years old and her spouse a young man of 22. Having lived her entire life in West Cornwall, it is noteworthy that her chosen husband came from the other end of the county, a village not far from Launceston with the very Cornish name of Egloskerry (Church of Keri). How they met is not known, and it may be as simple as his intention to seek his fortune elsewhere since he was the third son of at least five with three sisters as well.

Though styled as a 'Gentleman' in the parish records of their marriage he is elsewhere found in family and archive records as a bookbinder. Clergymen also appear in every generation of his family so far explored, including Charles's father, the Revd. William Fisher, son of the Revd. John Fisher of Bodmin, and a brother the Revd. Thomas Fisher, sometime curate of St. Germans and Mawgan (near Helston). The latter is noticed for his published sermons, and not least for his published poetry in the literary review of the *Bibliotheca Cornubiensis*. There is, in fact, little trace of Charles himself, except in a note that recognises his generosity in making available his large book collection to the Penzance Library (now the Morrab Library collection) upon his demise.

Unfortunately their marriage was short-lived. Margaret's elder sister, Anne Carne Branwell, the first born of Thomas (John) and Anne (Carne) Branwell, one of the witnesses to the Fisher wedding at Madron, died four months later at the age of 22 (reason unknown) and is buried in the family mausoleum in St Mary's churchyard. Charles Fisher followed her five years later, and Margaret died in 1798, at the age of 28, both suffering for some time with consumption. From her own birth, and with the exception of sister Anne's before her, Margaret had inhabited a home of eleven other siblings of whom only five would then survive to adulthood: Jane, Benjamin, Elizabeth, Maria and Charlotte.

The second brother-in-law: John Kingston 1769-1824

Born in Towcester, Northamptonshire, John Kingston 'in the sixteenth year of my age', by way of Methodist preaching, came under the compelling spell of John Wesley and decided to give his life to the Lord and His missions. His parents were against this diversion in his life and plans which were perhaps to follow his successful staymaker father into the commercial world of manufacturing. Instead John left for London and was taken in to a worthy family who offered residence and keep to Methodist missionaries. In the final two years of his life, John Wesley became his mentor and guiding light, preaching and teaching in prisons and work houses in the East End of London.

In 1791, in attendance at that summer's Methodist conference he met with Dr. Thomas Coke and the latter's new commission to provide travelling preachers in international missions. By the following year he had set sail from Falmouth to the West Indies and was in Barbados (1792). Then forward he travelled to Nevis (1793) and Grenada, where he fell ill (1794) and migrated to America to recuperate (Boston, Baltimore and Philadelphia, and New York during periods of plague and fever). In 1796 he returned to Dominica and for two stints to Grenada, before finally in 1799 was brought back home to enter the domestic Wesleyan circuit. Along the way many of his fellow ministers had succumbed to illnesses of various kinds and lost their lives.

After a one-year assignment in Wales, John Kingston arrived in the West Cornwall circuit in 1799, as heralded in the *Methodist Magazines* of the time.[21] His memoirs make fascinating reading and convince the reader of his emotionally driven nature and his heartfelt beliefs. Though we know nothing of the courtship, Maria's eldest surviving sister, Jane Branwell married the handsome young Methodist preacher the following year.

He was to become an intimate part of their Carne and Branwell circle and then some years later to bring a measure of disgrace and shame into their lives. How much the ensuing scandal, involving theft and sexual immorality in Shrewsbury, Shropshire influenced or was known to the local circles back in Penzance is nowhere revealed, though here is one of the tracks to follow where further study may prove fruitful to Brontë story lines.

No record of the relationship of the two Johns, Fennell and Kingston, positive or negative - has been found, but it is clear that John Fennell, having known young Jane (Carne) Branwell (1773-1855) since the girl was about eleven (the fifth child of Thomas and Ann), he would not have been a disinterested observer of the marriage that subsequently occurred.

After their marriage in 1800 at Madron, Jane Branwell and John Kingston moved on in the itinerancy to St Austell and Launceston in Cornwall, then Nottingham and finally in the summer of 1805 to Shrewsbury, Shropshire. A child was born in each place, culminating in Shrewsbury when their fourth child, a daughter Maria, was born.

Arriving from Nottingham after 1805 Methodist Conference Kingston was assigned to Shrewsbury until 1806-7, designated as supervisor. His wife Jane Kingston was about to produce their fourth child in this period and no documents have been found of a personal kind such as place of residence or other information.

The Kingstons were, of course, already known to John and Jane Fennell from Cornwall, who were about to arrive in nearby Wellington to take up a new teaching post. It is possible also that the Fennell family returned to John's native county in order to be of assistance to Jane and her children. By hearsay, it is also probable that much may have been known of successive events to the curate of St. Chad's, Shrewsbury, the Revd. John Nunn (a former room-mate of Patrick Brontë at St. John's College, Cambridge), as Kingston was a Methodist colleague in Nunn's Anglican parish. Possibly it was a 'godsend' to Jane Kingston to have her own Uncle and Aunt Fennell and niece Jane Fennell within visiting distance at Wellington (13 miles away). Arriving from Nottingham after Conference in 1804, Kingston had been assigned to Shrewsbury until 1806-7.

Due to alleged misdemeanours, fiscal and moral, arousing suspicions from 1805, during his Shrewsbury assignment, Kingston was brought to Wesleyan trial and formally ejected from the Methodist fold at Conference in 1807. The couple lodged there until he was evicted from Conference on the transgressions of theft and immorality. The trial documents may be viewed in the Document Register, Chapter 12. Bibliographic information attesting to Kingston's voluminous writings are found in Appendix B: Family Bibliography.

There is no way that the Fennells would not have known about this situation, as would the Carnes, and any itinerants who attended Methodist conference on a regular basis. Did Aunt Jane Fennell, Jane Kingston's namesake, help the family pack up to leave for the American states? The family did depart, emigrating via Liverpool to live first in Baltimore, Maryland where Kingston set up his own publishing and stationery business.

His fifth child, daughter Elizabeth Jane, was later to say that though he was an emotionally sensitive and enthusiastic person, he was not a good business man. In 1809, the couple separated, ten months after Elizabeth Jane was born in Baltimore; Jane's legacy from her father at his death in 1808 allowed the beleaguered young mother to have sufficient funds to return to Britain with her youngest child. It was said that Jane could not live in the heat of American summers and was frightened of the numerous fevers that afflicted the populations on a regular basis. Perhaps there was a plan for them to reunite when John had earned enough to bring the other children back to England, but in fact they were never to reconcile.

What the Brontë children may have learned about this family 'scandal' is unknown, but the fact that Aunt Branwell played her part by standing by her sister over many years is clear. From her will, formulated in 1833, (See Document register, Appendix B, for 1842) we discover three things: i. that she had given her sister Kingston (Jane) an advance on the legacy that she intended to give her upon her death, ii. that her financial estate was to be split four ways, one portion to go to Jane's youngest child, Elizabeth Jane, together with one each to Charlotte, Emily Jane and Anne Bronte, and thirdly, iii. if all of her intended legatees died before reaching the age of 21, that the money in its entirety would go first to her niece Anne Kingston (this is Jane Kingston's eldest daughter, Anne Branwell Kingston, born in Launceston, who married Joseph Bergstresser in New York City in 1830). The final backstop that Aunt Branwell specified was that the children of her (late) brother and sisters would receive the residue. All in all, this will reveals a continuing contact with her sister Jane and knowledge of Jane's children by correspondence in the USA.

It is unlikely, however, except in passing, that Kingston's misdemeanors would remain a topic of conversation or that the connection to the Branwells would necessarily be known by the time Patrick Brontë arrived in Wellington in 1809. There is little doubt, however, that he would know about it in the long term, whether or not Maria, Elizabeth or John Fennell would be the carrier and discussant of the episode. Not only his former roommate at Cambridge, John Nunn, was a local curate where the Kingstons were assigned, but John Fennell and William Morgan, had also been present in Wellington when the Kingston trial occurred and was reported.

Knowing that this scandal would have been kept as secret as possible for numerous reasons, it would be of detrimental effect on both the Fennell family, the Branwell family at home in Cornwall and the cause of Methodism within Anglican circles. Jane Kingston was a niece of Jane Fennell's, just as Elizabeth and Maria were, but nothing is known about their relationship at the particular time – only that they lived close-by for long months while the scandal was brewing, and until the Kingstons left Britain for the American states.

TABLE 10.3: THE FAMILY OF JOHN (OSBORNE) KINGSTON (1769-1824) AND JANE (CARNE) BRANWELL (1773-1855).

Name	Died	Born
<u>Thomas Branwell Kingston</u>	1801-1875 St Austell, Cwll	Somerset (Hotwells)

A pen maker's clerk once returned to Britain after his father's death
Married Sarah Sargant, Three sons and two daughters

<u>Anne Branwell Kingston</u>	1803-1835 Launceston, Cwll	Milwaukee Wisconsin

A dressmaker
Married Joseph Bergstrasser/Burgster, a successful businessman. One daughter (dec) and one son (a Presbyterian minister educated at Princeton University.

<u>John Branwell Kingston</u>	1804-1880 Nottingham, Notts	New York

A gardener in Saratoga, New York state
Married Nancy Smith, One daughter: Susan

<u>Maria Ann Kingston</u>	1807-1819 Shrewsbury, Shrop	New York

Died of influenza

<u>Elizabeth Jane Kingston</u>	1808-1878 Baltimore, USA	Penzance

Lodging house keeper, bookseller
Died, in Madron, Cornwall hospital ward for mazed patients
Buried in an unmarked pauper's grave in St. Mary's Churchyard

Their fifth child was born in the USA, and soon after, the couple separated. Thomas Branwell, her father, had died meantime (5 April 1808), leaving Jane enough money to return to Penzance, bringing her ten-month old infant daughter Elizabeth Jane, with her. This she achieved the following year, in time to be with her mother Ann before the latter died in December of 1809. The Kingstons were never to reconcile.

Depending greatly on how much of this dramatic turn of events the Brontë children learned over the years from their parents and relations, about the Kingston family and their various histories, their imaginative powers may have found a major source on which to build years later. There is a plot, of some appeal, which could be said to resemble that of Anne Brontë's *Tenant of Wildfell Hall*. All of this family story would have been known to Elizabeth Branwell, Maria and the Fennells. Both of them were in Penzance to witness and assist with Jane Kingston's return. That Aunt Branwell did not forget the Kingston family is clear, and evidenced in her will. See Chapter 12: Document register for a full transcription.

That Thomas knew of his daughter Jane's plight as an unhappy wife is documented in his will, but without personal comment. See Will of Thomas Branwell in the

Document Register. He makes clear that the money he is giving her as a legacy is ring-fenced and cannot be employed by her husband, John Kingston.

The shutters appear to have been drawn down on this whole debacle, and records concerning it are not known about in Cornwall today. However, the documentation of the missionary travels of John Kingston primarily in the West Indies, was available in four parts in the *Methodist Magazine,* as was his engraved portrait some years following the articles. If these were available to the Brontë children, and they were to realise that John Kingston was their Uncle, there is something of a potential new world of reference there which at a minimum would have thematically affected the story of *Jane Eyre*. A whole book can be written about this volcanic passage in the lives of the Branwells and Carnes.

The Batten-Branwell connection

Batten, Anne Elizabeth (c1745 -1801) who grew up as Elizabeth Batten, was a cousin and friend to Ann Carne Branwell and eldest daughter of John and Ann (Nicholls) Batten. Due to her private passion for the classics and Egyptology in youth she was the force behind the arts education given to her children Joshua Cristall, the watercolourist, and Anne Batten Cristall, the poet. Elizabeth Batten's husband, the widower Captain Alexander Cristall of Rotherhithe, a highly regarded sea captain who was twice her age when they married, was against such wasteful pastimes as art or literature, finding the sea to offer the only worthwhile career.

Alexander **Cristall**, mariner and shipyard owner (of Rotherhithe, Penzance and Fowey) was a business colleague of young Elizabeth's father John Batten IV (1709-1792), a lawyer and shipping merchant. Elizabeth's mother (Ann Nicholls) had been dead for five years when Elizabeth married the Captain in 1777. This may have been symptomatic of her romantic desire for adventure, or even because she was pregnant with their first child (Joseph, thereafter called Joshua) but this is speculative and based on rumoured bashfulness about his birth, also in 1777, when later biographers began to enquire.[22] Ultimately it was an unhappy and stormy marriage, through which their children also suffered a rough childhood, sympathetically helped along considerably by their supportive grandfather in Cornwall, who provided a separate income for their mother. This money she used to support the children's creative instincts and artistry.

Thankfully, he already had one son from his first marriage who followed in his footsteps, becoming a sea captain in his own right which mitigated some of the focus he might have given his off-spring with Elizabeth. Five children were born to this marriage, the older son being the watercolour artist Joshua Cristall (1767-1847), born in Camborne, Cornwall, and the older daughter being the poet Anne Batten Cristall (1769-1848), born in Penzance, the author of *Poetical Sketches*. Both brother and sister were friends and sometime correspondents of Mary Wollstonecraft in London.[23] For most of their young lives, their home was on the southeast coast of Kent in Blackheath, and harmonious only when their father was at sea (which appears to have been frequently in accordance with his record of extensive voyages).

The Rev Joseph Hallett Batten DD, FRS (1778-1837)
Here enters another cousin.

Hallett Batten, as he was known, was the son of the Congregational minister of Penzance, the Revd. Joseph Batten (1749-1823). His mother was Joseph's first wife Anna Luke (d 1781), sister of Dr. Stephen Luke, the well-known physician to the Royal Court of George IV. Hallett was born two years after Elizabeth Branwell, and the year before his later friend and relation John (Cock) Carne, author. After early schooling in Penzance, possibly with John Fennell and then Truro, he attended St. Paul's, London before entering Trinity, Cambridge, at age sixteen in 1794. There he was to become 'Third wrangler' leading to a Fellowship in 1799. At home in that same year his first cousin Mary (Bodinnar) Batten married Benjamin Carne Branwell, a childhood friend and neighbour.

In 1809 the East India College at Haileybury opened with Hallett Batten, an outstanding classical scholar, and Robert Malthus, the most distinguished political economist of the day on its teaching staff; Batten had married Catherine Maxwell of Scots descent in 1807. Malthus, twelve years senior to Batten, had already published his first and most famous book in 1798 (anonymously), *An Essay on the Principle of Population*. Their respective families became great friends.[24] Later Batten was to become Principal of the College.

…Professors Batten and Malthus, were close friends with much in common. Both were Cambridge men, clergymen, and Fellows of the Royal Society, with a wide variety of interests; both had charming wives and delighted in hospitality; both were original appointments to the College and spent the chief part of their lives in its service. " Dr. Batten, who held office [by] far the longest, was much admired for his social charm and brilliant conversational powers. His family came in for admiration too, especially his daughter, Priscilla, whose name, carved by a love-lorn student, could be read for a hundred years on a tree by the Terrace."[25]

He was elected to the Royal Society in 1816, and of the ten sponsors who claimed personal knowledge of him and proposing his fellowship, his childhood friend, Sir Humphry Davy, was one.

John Hallett Batten FRGS, MRAS (1811-1886). Born at Haileybury in 1811, John Hallett was the son of Catherine Batten ne Maxwell and Joseph Hallett Batten (above) and was educated at the East India College, first by resident 'aunts', Ann and Elizabeth Batten Cristall. More about the poet Ann Batten Cristall from Penzance and her circle of literary friends, is found in Chapter 3: 'Language, legend and literature'. The parents of these ladies had died in 1801-02, and their cousin Joseph Hallett was able to offer them rooms in the College in part recompense for acting as governesses to his children. This included regular holidays in Cornwall as part of a large, close, and wealthy local family. Life in the college environment gave him easy entry to an international and global career. Later, John married Mary Sarah Beckitt in Bengal, and finally died in retirement at Heavitree, Exeter, Devon. He joined the Bengal Civil Service, and wrote up geographical notes and journeys in the 1830s and 40s. See family bibliography in Appendix B.

The Revd. Samuel Ellis Batten (1792-1830)

The half-brother of Joseph Hallett Batten, Sam Batten was born in Penzance, to the Congregational minister of Penzance, the Revd. Joseph Batten and his second wife Elizabeth Ellis. Born three years following the youngest Carne-Branwell child, Charlotte, he also grew up on Chapel Street, taking his elementary education at the Grammar School and probably with John Fennell. At the age of seventeen he matriculated at Trinity College, Cambridge though later migrated to Pembroke where he took his degree.

Following the death of his first wife, Emma Jeffreys of Little Parndon, Essex in 1819, he married secondly Caroline Venn of Clapham, Surrey (1799-1870), the daughter of the Revd. John Venn (1759-1813) and his wife Katherine King. The Revd. John Venn was the son of the Revd. Henry Venn of Hull, Yorkshire and his wife Eling Bishop. Henry Venn had died in 1797 in Clapham, founder of the Clapham Sect group of social reformers and evangelicals and father of John. Though Sam Batten would not have personally known Caroline's parents or grandparents, he could easily have met Charles Simeon at Cambridge and William Wilberforce in social and political circles. He became an Assistant Master at Harrow School, but died at the early age of 38.

Perhaps the most surprising link coming forward from Sam's marriage to Caroline Venn, is one which still resonates strongly in the present day. Caroline Venn was the younger sister of Jane Catherine Venn (1793-1875), both born like their sister Maria in Clapham, Greater London, and growing up amongst the anti-slavery campaigners, called the 'saints', of the circle around them.

In 1822, two years following Sam's marriage to Caroline, her sister Jane married James Stephen (1789-1859) of Cambridge, becoming over time the parents of six Stephen children (one child, who did not survive for long, was given the middle name of Wilberforce). One of these children, though born after Samuel Ellis Batten's death, was the future Sir Leslie Stephen (1832-1904), the first editor of the *Dictionary of National Biography*, and the father with his wife Harriet Thackeray of Adeline Virginia Stephen (1882-1941), who as Virginia Woolf, of course, was the iconic author of the future 'Bloomsbury group' of artists and writers. Hence, the literary network widens and lengthens, embracing new territories for connection to the imaginative family of Haworth. Interesting too are the further connections with Thackeray. Pursuing these threads is a never-ending carpet, of course, and well beyond our focus period. Just as one regrets the demise of Maria and Elizabeth Branwell, before their children blossomed into print, it is fascinating to see 'what runs' through certain family groups.

The Pellew connection

Issues arising from Cornwall's position on the Barbary coast and its marine location in general, were not insignificant at the time we are exploring. The Pellew, Batten and Branwell families were each deeply involved in daily confrontation with the sea – though in mixed and separate ways. Whereas the Battens and Branwells were primarily focussed on local import and export trade with shipping, ship repairs, fisheries and food supplies, together with the piratical attacks and smuggling that attended these, the Pellews engaged themselves as sea captains, naval defence, and general military support in national conflicts.

After their Cornish sea captain's father died in Dover in 1764, the Pellew family of three boys and two girls returned to Cornwall where their grandfather Humphrey Pellew was a merchant in Falmouth. From there they moved to Penzance to be brought up by their mother and grandmother at Hawkes Farm, Alverton, Penzance. This thatched house still stands today, with its blue historical plaque, on the western reaches of Penzance. Constantia Langford Pellew, their mother, remarried in 1768 to a local gentleman gardener, Samuel Woodis, and began a second family of half-sisters and brother to the Pellews. Thomas Branwell and Ann Carne married four months later that same year, also at Madron. Hence the Pellew-Woodis and Branwell children, would grow up in Penzance together, during their early years.

After primary schooling in Penzance, Edward, Israel and John attended as weekly boarders at Truro School, each leaving as soon as possible to join the armed services. Edward, for example, left Truro School one day in 1770 at the age of 14, to avoid a beating – and joined the first frigate he could find at the Falmouth docks. Israel followed him as soon as he could a few years later. Both were successful in making their ways to the top of the admiralty. The youngest son, John Pellew, joined the British Infantry at the age of seventeen, and was killed the same year in the American Revolutionary battle at Saratoga, New York (1777). This was the year following Elizabeth Branwell's birth (Aunt Branwell to the Brontës) and would have been a source of horror to the small town of Penzance.

In 1795, Thomas Branwell's youngest sister, Alice (John) Branwell (1756-unkn), married John (Pellew) Williams, Esq. of Redruth (1741-1823). John, noted on their marriage certificate as a Gentleman, was the son of Grace Pellew (1701-1761) of Penzance, and Stephen Williams (1715-1755) both of whom had been long dead before the marriage occurred. His mother was Grace Pellew, whose close kinship circle (of first and second cousins), based in Penzance included such highly-regarded naval commanders as the brothers Edward Pellew and Israel Pellew.[26] This Williams family was amongst the wealthiest landowning and mining clans in Cornwall, and John (Pellew) Williams' relied on copper interests (as an adventurer) and properties, as a member of the landed gentry. They made their home in Gwennap parish at St Agnes, where the Wheal Rose mine with its 'Williams shaft' was operating. Alice and John's son, John Thomas Branwell Williams was baptised in Penzance in 1797, with her sister Jane and brother-in-law John Fennell acting as godparents.

Though it is easily understood, that the Pellew children went their separate ways prior to the births of the younger of the Branwell children, the exploits and achievements of these brothers, (second or third cousins) would without doubt, be a main topic of gossip and story-telling in the family and also for the whole of the community.

John T. B. Williams married Caroline Matilda Anne Corder and the couple had two daughters, Caroline Williams (1816-1884) and Eliza Williams (1820-unkwn). It was this family – the parents and their second daughter Eliza – who visited Yorkshire in 1841 to pay a lengthy visit to John Fennell and his second wife Elizabeth Lister Fennell. On one afternoon they called in to see Aunt Branwell and meet the Brontë family for the first time. The Revd. Fennell died later that same year, and Aunt Branwell the year following.[27]

Edward Pellew participated with valour in both the American revolutionary and Napoleonic wars, and is most closely associated with *HMS Indefatigable*. He supported Wellington's land battles, by sea, during the Peninsular War, and was highly respected as a frigate captain by the Duke (Charlotte Brontë's prime hero) who valued his personal friendship.

Perhaps of special significance in the banks of memories of the Branwell women and also the Fennells, was the final feat of liberation which Admiral Edward Pellew achieved: the ultimate smashing of the white slave trade carried on by the Barbary pirates over as many as ten generations. European and British coastal communities had been living in terror, frustration and loss from the 1600s to their present day and little but strong words and hostage payments (sometimes) had been rendered by the governments of countries under this ongoing siege.

Having been forceful in backing the abolition of the black slave trade (1807, 1811 forward), Lord Castlereagh was stung into action by charges of lack of care for our own people, in relation to white slavery issues. He determined to send a formidable fleet of ships to the Mediterranean in 1816, to force the Barbary sultans to quit raiding, seizing and trading human captives, who more often than not, died of starvation, gruesome and cruel punishments, apart from rampant disease, never to return to their various homelands.

There was never any doubt as to who would command this great squadron. In public life he was known as Lord Exmouth, the Vice Admiral of the Mediterranean fleet. But among his friends and family in his native Cornwall he was more familiar as Sir Edward Pellew....the right man to tackle the slave traders of Barbary....[he] wanted nothing less than the total capitulation of every corsair and slave trader in North Africa.[28]

An early Pellew, Thomas, aged only 11, and curiously of a branch in the same family of Penryn, had fallen captive with his uncle, Captain John Pellow.[29] Three ships had been taken by the corsairs on the same day, the *Southwark*, whose Captain Richard Ferris had attempted rescue of the *Francis*,[30] and the *George*, returning to England.

> One of the newly captured men – Captain John Pellow of the *Francis* – had been forewarned of the perils of his trading voyage to the Mediterranean. Yet he had shunned the danger with characteristic bravado, sailing from Cornwall to Genoa [with pilchard barrels] in the summer of 1715. His six-strong crew included his nephew, Thomas Pellow....It would be many years [23 years prior to his escape] before his parents would receive news of their unfortunate son.'[31]

Admiral Pellew's target, a century later, was the port of Algiers, and the attack that he led from the deck of the *Queen Charlotte*, was both devastating in its destruction of Algiers and finally, despite obstinate resistance, also victorious. More than 1600 maltreated, skeletal slaves emerged from their imprisonment in caves along the cliffs, the captives were released, and the heavy work of repatriation was begun. Pellew could return with the message that Tunis, Tripoli and Morocco were closing their slave camps, setting the males, females and child- slaves free, while closing in perpetuity. When Pellew finally returned home to his native Cornwall, he was given a hero's welcome. For the first time in centuries the local fishermen and traders could put to sea without risk of being captured and held as slaves.[32]

The stories of young Thomas Pellow and his Uncle John Pellow who died in captivity from his sufferings, were known by the Pellew family down the generations and the merchants and ship owners of the Cornish coastal communities, not least in West Cornwall. The Honours then heaped on Edward Pellew for his crushing defeat of the white slave trade were world-wide, many titles bestowed by other European governments, whose captives he had also relieved. Soon after he was to become the first Viscount Exmouth. All of this occurred in the year 1816, and would have been a matter of great pride and interest to the Branwell - Williams family, and to the wider circle of relations as well. These are, of course, the relations from the south, that Charlotte Brontë describes with some hauteur to Ellen Nussey in her letter of August 1840: 'To my eyes there seemed to be an attempt to play the great Mogul down in Yorkshire —'[33]

One might wonder about the choice of 'Mogul' in this context, but it illustrates its own logic. For Charlotte, too, would have been told the family stories and be fully aware of the family connections to the famed Pellew clan as well as the havoc and fears that the Barbary slave trade had introduced into southern British ports and trade. Equally, the thrilling stories shared by their cousin John (Cock) Carne of Penzance, the writer, in his journal publications (1820s) of the chapters of *Tales of the East*, alongside their readings in the stories of the *Arabian Nights*, would bring the seraglio to life in Charlotte's mind.

All of these may add to discussion of the sources for Charlotte's frequent uses of 'oriental' vocabulary relating more to white than black slavery in *Jane Eyre*.[34] This topic has been explored recently in the work of Australian researcher Dr. Ann Erskine on 'orientalism' as a thematic trope in Charlotte Brontë's novel. Erskine's perceptive delving opens some new perspectives on the inner life of the novelist.

ENDNOTES

1 Alexander Pope (1732) *Epistles to several persons*, Epistle 1, on-line page 14.
2 See Chapter 11: The Johns family (kin of Carne-Branwell) in Biographical Briefs. Edward Francis Johns (1861-1948), aka Frank.
3 Pallot's Marriage Index for England 1780-1837, Madron Parish records (COPC)
4 Marriage of Mary Hodgkiss to Thomas Fennell (IGI Individual Record), at Madeley, Shropshire, England, 26 May 1760,
5 See Document Register, Chapter 12 for further references to the Revd. John Fletcher and his wife, Mary Bosanquet Fletcher. Both were instrumental people in the lives of John Fennell and William Morgan (at different stages) and to a lesser extent to Patrick Brontë. Both were highly influential in Methodist activity and educative power.

6 Formal registered apprenticeship was undertaken by Fennell from the age of fourteen with John Guest, Grocer, Chandler and Baker of Broseley.
7 There was no Methodist school in Penzance at the time; in 1779 a Grammar School founded by the Corporation was established, which closed formally in 1898.
8 John Fennell never left the Church of England. He was not a Methodist minister, though he would have been welcomed as such, as listed in the *Cornubiensia* and the *Bibliotheca Cornubiensis*.
9 M. Smith, *Letters of Charlotte Brontë 1829-1847*, vol. 1: To Ellen Nussey (? 3 July 1841), p. 259.
10 Fletcher, John, 1729-1785: *Fletcher's appeal to matter of fact & common sense : or a rational demonstration of man's corrupt and lost estate, with the address to earnest seeks for salvation and an appendix, to which is now added the life of the venerable author, compiled for this work from the most authentic source /* (Baltimore : J. Kingston, 1814), also by John Kingston (page images at HathiTrust).
11 'Mrs Fletcher's Dreams', the first section in 'From My Note Book' by Revd. J B Dyson in *The Methodist Recorder*, Winter Number 1895, p. 96. Mrs Fletcher was known for recording her post-death conversations with her late husband, in which she was obliquely informed that the superintendent (John Kingston) 'at Shrewsbury *is* a bad man' much to her surprise at the time, though he decamped soon after.
12 F. C. Pritchard The *Story of Woodhouse Grove School* (Apperley Bridge, Bradford: Woodhouse Grove School, 1978) pp. 2, 14-22.
13 With thanks to the School for presenting a copy of this book to our Brontë Territories Archive on our visit in 2016. It was a pleasure to tour the central buildings and rooms from which the School grew.
14 J. Lock and W. T. Dixon, *A Man of Sorrow, The Life, Letters and Times of the Revd. Patrick Brontë,* (London: Thos. Nelson, 1965), p. 119.
15 Church of England: www.theclergydatabase.org.uk Accessed 20/8/2013
16 M. Walker, 'William Morgan, B.D.', *BS*, pp.214-16.
17 Michael Walker, 'William Morgan, B.D. 1782-1858', *Brontë Studies*, vol 30, November 2005, p. 223.
18 Lock and Dixon, *A Man of Sorrow*, p. 269.
19 M. Smith (ed.), *Letters of Charlotte Brontë*: To the Revd. Patrick Brontë, 23 September 1829, vol 1, p. 105.
20 Walker, Michael, 'William Morgan, B.D. 1782-1858' *Bronte Studies*, vol 30, November 2005, p. 225. This son is mentioned in the *1841 Census*, and was perhaps mistakenly identified by Lock and Dixon as the son of Mary Alice. In the article about William Morgan B.D. in *Bronte Studies*, it specifically lists an account to be paid for the care of 'Mr Morgan's little boy', which at least two other sources suggest was a charitable act on his part. I am confident in asserting that this was the child care payments that he was making for the early care of his own son.
21 Memoirs of the Life of Mr John Kingston, Preacher of the Gospel' *Methodist Magazine*, 22 (May, 1799), pp. 209-13; (June, 1799), pp. 261-5; (July, 1799), pp. 313-7; (August, 1799), pp. 365-7.
22 John Tisdall (1996) *Joshua Cristall (1768-1847) In Search of Arcadia*, p. 24 Joshua was to become a leading and influential painter in watercolours, and President of the Society of Watercolour Painters in 1816.
23 Both have full entries in the *Dictionary of National Biography* (see bibliography). Joshua's biography is told in *Joshua Cristall, In Search of Arcadia*, and Anne's work, *Poetical Sketches* was published in 1795. They were both friends with Mary Wollstonecraft and her sister Verena, and also George Dyer, who brought together the Dyer Collection of 18th and 19th century watercolours.
24 J M Pullen, Entry for Thomas Robert Malthus, *ODNB* (on-line).
25 C M Matthews, *Haileybury since Roman Times*, pp. 150-153.
26 Edward Pellew (1757-1833), lst Viscount Exmouth: Lieutenant in 1778, 1st Lieut & post-Captain in 1780 and Knight of the realm 1793 in capturing the French frigate, *Cleopatra*, made Baronet 1802, Admiral of the Blue in 1814 and Viscount Exmouth in 1816. Admiral Sir Israel Pellew, K C B (1758-1832) Among other triumphs, he commanded the Conqueror, 4th ship in weather line at the Battle of Trafalgar 1805.
27 Charlotte's letter to Ellen Nussey ?14 August 1840.
28 Milton, *White Gold* pp. 274-7.
29 The orthography of the name Pellew, similar to the changes in Branwell, changed over the years to such as Pellowe, Pellow, Polieow, etc. and can be found interchangeably in public records.
30 Brown & Pellow (1740 repr) *The History of the Long Captivity and Adventures of Thomas Pellow*. The owner of the *Francis* was Valentine Enys, a then merchant of Penryn. The on-line Enys family archive, also records this story.
31 (*Ibid.*, p. 2-3)
32 Milton, White Gold, p.278
33 M. Smith (ed.) *Letters of Charlotte Brontë*, vol. 1, p. 224.
34 Ann Erskine "Fevered with Delusive Bliss": Charlotte Brontë's Jane Eyre and the Ambiguous Pleasures of The Turk", *Australasian Journal of Victorian Studies*, 2018, vol. 22.

Chapter 11

Biographical briefs

A TO Z

All of the following people are part of the network in which both Branwells and Carnes lived and moved. Some they would have known well – whether through family relationship and hearsay, or through their occupational and spiritual connections. Others they would know as acquaintances or as subjects of discussion. The purpose of this final chapter is to share with readers, some of the possibly many territories of experience and relationship that may have been available and accessible to the Brontë family through their Cornish background. There is little, as with most family histories, that can be 'proved' with documents and confirmations, but much that is within the bounds of the probable and possible, given the keen and eager thrusts of the 'age of revolutions'. Where there are important studies of these people, a brief reference list is also given.

Batten family

The Batten Connections

> The family of Batten have been for some time the leading merchants of Penzance. They have recently lost Mr. John Batten 1709-1792, distinguished by the intelligence and liberality incident to gentlemen in that profession [the law]; but he has left a family more than promising to support his reputation and the credit of his ample fortune; and this family has the honour of possessing the Revd. Joseph Hallett Batten, D.D. Principal of the East India College.[1]

The interconnections of the Batten, Carne and Branwell families are strong but successfully hidden from general view due to the patronymic system of naming. Starting with John Batten II and Alice Nicholls, we have the parents of three sons, one of whom is: Richard Batten who married Susan Tremearne, sister of *Jane Tremearne*, the grandmother of Thomas (John) Branwell. This is the point at which the Battens became first cousins to the senior Branwells. Secondly, we find the parents of Mary Bodener Batten and her brother John Batten VI, working colleagues of both Carnes and Branwells, a cousin who became the daughter-in-law of the Branwells by marrying Benjamin Carne Branwell (1775-1818), Maria Branwell's only surviving brother. This young couple produced nine first cousins for Maria and Elizabeth, of which eight survived to adulthood; this latter family is listed in 'Chapter 8, the People called Branwell', Tables 5 and 6.

John Batten V (1742-1810) the son of John Batten IV and Ann (Nicholls) Batten, was a friend, cousin and working colleague of Thomas Branwell, and the original owner and shipping merchant of Batten's Wharf, Penzance. This was the main dock of Penzance and located where the Jubilee Pool Lido is today. Like the Branwells and Carnes the Battens were successful merchants in their own right in wide-ranging commodities and as shipping agents and repairers. The main Batten family home is today's Regent House, 54 Chapel Street, Penzance, a Palladian mansion and one of Penzance's oldest family homes.

John Batten V was also the banking partner of William Carne and Richard Oxnam in setting up the Penzance Bank in 1795. His solicitor son, John Batten VI (called Batten Jr. in his father's lifetime) was the Trustee and Executor of Thomas Branwell's will (1808), and Branwell's son-in-law: Benjamin Carne Branwell married Mary Bodener/Bodinnar Batten at Madron Parish Church in 1799.

Knowledge of these personal connections would have been realised by the Brontës through Elizabeth Branwell and also furthered by Patrick Brontë and his links with the Cambridge evangelical scene. Not least are the network of connections between all of these with the East India Company and its outreach. Merchant shipping, of course, was a major and lucrative concern of the time with its handling of a wide range of commodities, those of the mining industry but also the fishing trade, i.e. salt for preservation and 'pilchards for Genoa', tea and spices, beverages, etc.

TABLE 11.1 THE BATTEN CONNECTIONS

John Batten I   Unknown dates + Maud (no identification)
John Batten II   1652-1692 + Alice Nicholls (kinship circle)
John Batten III   1679-1769 + Mary Hallett
John Batten IV   1709-1792 + Anne Nicholls (kinship circle)
 John Batten V   1739-1810 + Alice Bodener/Bodinnar
    Thomas Bodener Batten 1762-1832 + Anne Rowe
    John (Bodener) Batten VI 1769-1834 + Mary Ann Pidwell (5 children)
    The Revd. Henry (Pidwell) Batten 1809-1863+ Anna Maria Molesworth Carne
    Mary (Bodener) Batten 1777-1851 + Benjamin Carne Branwell
    (Anne) Elizabeth Batten   1745-1801 + Alexander Cristall
    Joshua Cristall, Artist-painter
    Ann Batten Cristall, Poet and teacher
    Elizabeth Cristall, Engraver and teacher
    Joseph Batten 1749-1823 + Anna Luke, Elizabeth Ellis
    The Revd. Joseph Hallet Batten, DD, FRS 1778-1837
    The Revd. Samuel Ellis Batten 1792-1830

Foremost of these was probably the Revd. Professor Joseph Hallett Batten (1778-1837), Principal of the East India Training College at Haileybury and close friend of the controversial economist Thomas Malthus, already described in Chapter 10. His half-brother the Revd. Samuel Ellis Batten (1792-1830), also born in Penzance, and like his brother a Trinity man at Cambridge, died in post as an Assistant schoolmaster at Harrow School.

Sam Batten was married to Caroline Venn, the daughter of the Revd. John Venn, a member of the Clapham Sect, and a founder of the Church Missionary Society. Cousin Joseph (Cock) Carne FRS, also a member of the Royal Society with Humphry Davy and a stream of other Cornish relations like John Hallett, were also active in the Church Missionary Society. More about this part of the Carne-Branwell clan can be found in Chapter 10: Travellers' Tales.

The Boase Connections

Henry Boase of Penzance 1763-1827
Banker, financial journalist, one of the prime movers of the Royal Geological Society of Cornwall
1788 Ransom, Morland & Hammersley Bank, London
1810 Batten, Carne & Boase, Penzance Bank
1821 Fellow of the Royal Society of Literature
1823 Partner in the Penzance Union Bank

A letter to Henry Boase from John (Cock) Carne (Cambridge, 1813). A sideways view of Cambridge life is available to us from a younger Carne son, John (Cock) Carne, the traveller and soon-to-be journalist. It was found by descendants, not even knowing that John had been a student at Cambridge, in the British Museum, when his letters were being collated for a published edition in 1885. This document would not have been available to anyone at any time outside the family circle, except its recipient, Henry Boase, a kinsman of both Carnes and Branwells. The letter is, in fact, a fascinating tirade about university life of the period and useful for evaluating the social conditions of a student experience. Whether or not its observations were shared in passing or in gossip within the family and circle of friends is unknown.

Jane Boase 1694-1741 Great grandmother to Elizabeth and Maria and their siblings, initiating the kinship, but not known to them personally. She was married to Thomas John, blacksmith, and father to Thomas Branwell's mother, Margaret 'Margery' John.

Bunting, Jabez 1779-1858 Thomas Bunting in his father's biography[2] lists the principal leaders of the national party strongly opposed to separation from the Church of England and amongst these he names William (John) Carne and Henry Martyn's father, John Martyn[3] both of Cornwall.

In the same long footnote Bunting Jr. also attacks Mrs Gaskell's anachronistic taste in labelling John Fennell, Maria Branwell's uncle, as tarred with "the fanaticism of a Whitefield"[4] and makes the following comment: 'Everybody is tired of correcting the mistakes and indiscretions of the daughter's [Charlotte Brontë] clever but random biographer.' [Mrs Gaskell]

Byron, George Gordon, Lord (1788-19 April 1824) 'a fallen child of light'.
Humphry Davy wrote a long poem, on hearing of the death of Lord Byron, that he entitled 'On the death of Lord Byron composed at Westhill [? Aberdeen] in the great storm, 1824.' It began,

> 'Gone is the bard, who, like a powerfull spirit
> A beautiful and fallen child of light'

The friendship of Davy and Byron had spanned more than a decade, since meeting through Davy's wife, Jane Apreece, whose circle of friends and frequent get-togethers for elegant suppers ensured that Davy met a wide-ranging group of literary greats, about whom he wrote to his mother and brother. For example, this would also include the meeting of the famed French woman of letters, Madame de Staël, and not least her own famous kin and family favourite.

> On the evening of June 20, Byron was invited to Lady Jersey's to meet Mme de Staël, the great literary lady of the continent who had just arrived in London. And the next day he dined with her at Lady Davy's along with Sheridan and others, and was amazed by the talents of this extraordinary woman who talked the men into silence..."certainly the cleverest, though not the most agreeable woman he had ever known." Vol. 1 Chapter XI: 1813, p 393, *Byron, A Biography*, by Leslie Marchand

Humphry Davy and Lord Byron had met in London as early as 1813, soon after the marriage of Davy and the young widow and *bas bleu*, Jane Apreece. She was the youthful cousin of Walter Scott, and had travelled with him in the Hebrides following the death of her first husband. Byron was much taken by Jane, and later when Davy visited in Rome, Byron introduced him to his final mistress, Teresa Guiccioli, who Davy liked equally. He was to keep in touch with Guiccioli even after Byron had died.

Carne, Elizabeth Catherine Thomas (1817-1873) Second cousin
Maria would perhaps have been astonished, if she had lived so long, to find her kinswoman, Elizabeth C. T. Carne, born in Hayle in the same spell of years as her own children, acting as Head and Chief Partner in the Carne Bank of the 1860s, and a contributing geologist member to the Royal Geological Society of Cornwall in which her own brother, Benjamin Carne, had been also a founding member.[5] Elizabeth was the eighth child of nine children born to Joseph (Cock) Carne FRS and his wife Mary Thomas, and the final birth to take place at Riviere House, Hayle. See Chapter 9, `The People called Carne' Table 6. Her home for a brief time had been the large mansion constructed for the director of the Cornish Copper Company (CCC) and his family, which boasted of laboratories in the basement: in these experimental rooms, the

youthful Humphry Davy had learned about the qualities and uses of copper amongst other revelations (before the residency of the Carne family).

Elizabeth and her sister Caroline were also to continue the family tradition of patronage to the town and surrounding area in the construction of schools for the poor, the sewing for the poor, and the distribution of food, books and clothing to the sailors and indigent – roles set for them by their Cornish mothers. Though the following must be considered speculative, it is at least plausible and possible that it was Caroline Carne who undertook to pay for the admission of Eliza Jane Kingston, her kinswoman, to the hospital wards (paying patient) of the Madron Poor House where she died in 1878.[6]

The Revd. John (Cock) Carne 1789-1844. In John Carne is found the consummate creative writer of the family, until we reach the Brontë children themselves. Whether or not they knew much of their cousin is unknown as yet, though certainly Aunt Branwell and their mother had known him well. He was born on Chapel Street, in the same year as their sister, Charlotte Branwell and their cousin Joseph Branwell, who would later marry each other in 1812.

George Clement Boase, who wrote the entry for John Carne in the *Dictionary of National Biography* (DNB) in his *Reminiscences of Penzance*, waxed rather lyrical about him and his original talent.

> He passed his youth and early manhood at Penzance, occupied in the cultivation of elegant literature. His first fruit was a volume of poems entitled *The Indian and Lazarus*, published in 1820. Removed by circumstances [his father's wealth] he rose above the necessity of choosing a profession and possessed of great natural sensibility… The publication of *Letters from the East*, and his talent for society (story-telling) brought him into familiar intercourse with many distinguished men of letters, amongst them were Scott, Southey, Campbell and Lockhart. He departed this life at Penzance, 19th April, 1844, in his 55th year, and he was buried in Gulval churchyard in the family vault. He never had an enemy, and was beloved by his friends; his social habits rendered him a general favourite.[7]
>
> 'By a native'

The Cock family of Penzance and Helston
Cock was a common name in Cornwall, and still remains to this day. When editing *The Visitations of Cornwall of 1530, 1573 and 1620* for the purposes of census-taking and taxation, Lt. Colonel J. L. Vivian wrote in 1887, that "the name of Cock is so prevalent that the editor has not been able to obtain any clue to the descent of this family." Hence in the history of Penzance, it is not that surprising to discover in our searches that both the Branwells and the Carnes have marriages with Cock families.

In 1766, Jenifer Bramble (c1740-1779) married Solomon Cock, builder of Gulval parish nr. Penzance. She was a daughter of William Bramwell, cordwainer, and his wife Alice Carne (1702-1767) of Paul. They had six children in all, four boys who survived long enough to be mentioned in the 1790 Will of their grandfather William Bramwell. 'Solly', of similar age to Richard Branwell, was also a builder with his father, Richard Sr., and it appears that they often worked on jobs together, and in constructing the fine buildings of Chapel Street.

In 1780 Anna Cock of Helston also married into the Carne family, then represented by William (Johns) Carne (1754-1836) of Truro, who is believed to have been a carpenter at that stage in his life, perhaps in the employ of Anna's family firm of builders in Helston; his family led by Francis Cock Jr. was later to move to Penzance, and to work alongside the Branwell family as grocers and builders as well. At the time of their marriage William (Johns) Carne is on record as resident in Truro, and certainly their eldest son, Joseph (Cock) Carne was baptised there in the Nonconformist Bethesda Chapel in 1782. Later, of course, it is this William (Johns) Carne who became the 'father of Cornish Methodism' and wealthy banker-father of an illustrious family.

Coke, Dr. Thomas 1747-1814
The so-called 'Father of foreign missions' in the Wesleyan connection, the Revd. Dr Thomas Coke was the son of a wealthy apothecary in Wales who took degrees in jurisprudence at Oxford. Though allied to the Methodist cause from student days, he did not meet Wesley until 1776, thereby becoming one of his closest allies. He also visited Cornwall with frequency, and set sail from Falmouth to his mission in the West Indies. It was Thomas Coke who invited John Kingston (before John Kingston had been in Cornwall) to accept missionary work in the West Indies. See Chapter 10: Travellers' Tales.

Colenso Family (variations include Calenso, Calensow, Calensoe, Collenso) The direct connection with the Carne-Branwell family was through Anne Reynolds Carne, whose grandmother was Eleanor Colenso (1678-1767), the mother of Anne's father. Though Anne Carne would have known her, perhaps quite well, being her grandmother, Eleanor died the year before Anne married Thomas Branwell.

There is an excellent one-name study available through the auspices of Australian researcher Ann Collins, and an active Colenso Society and Research Project in New Zealand, to which the current researcher is a founder/correspondent. To understand the tenor of the project, here are some words from their website:

> 'Printer of some of the most significant documents in New Zealand history, missionary, explorer and botanist, a free wheeling politician and controversialist William Colenso was a maverick.'

The person being honoured by the Colenso Society is the Revd. William Colenso, FLS, FRS, born in Penzance in 1811, and a contemporary of the Brontë children. His cousin was John William Colenso, born in St. Austell, Cornwall in 1814, second wrangler at St. John's College, Cambridge, and later a Fellow there in the 1830s. He was to become the first Anglican Bishop of Natal, South Africa in the 1860s and died in Durban in 1883.

William was the eldest child of Samuel May Colenso, a saddler and town councillor of Penzance, and his wife, Mary Veale Thomas, the daughter of a solicitor. The

Branwells and Carnes would have known the family well as local traders and in the Town Council as well as being kin.

William was first apprenticed to a printer in St Ives, and in 1834 travelled to New Zealand as an (un-ordained) Cornish Christian missionary. He was responsible for the printing of the Māori language translation of the New Testament. A keen botanist and illustrator of plants, he became a frequent correspondent and provider of specimens to Kew Gardens of unrecorded New Zealand flora. He became the first New Zealander to be elected as a Fellow of the Royal Society (1866).[8]

Davy, Humphry (later Sir) If Davy's youthful abilities were not obvious to his schoolmasters, they seemed to have been happily recognised by his companions, as reported by all the biographers who have looked at his life closely. Evidently they asked his help with lessons and familiarly begged his romantic and expressive instincts and skills to write their valentines and letters. His lively imagination, strong dramatic power, and retentive memory combined to make him a good story-teller, and many evenings were spent by his crowd of friends beneath the balcony of the Star Inn, in Market Jew Street. His tales of wonder and spooks intrigued them all, scraped whole then embellished from the *Arabian Nights* or from his grandmother Davy. From her and his much loved mother he appears to have inherited and developed much of his character and instinctive curiosity.

Davy was attracted to the study of the sciences nurtured first perhaps by his 1795 apprenticeship to the apothecary and surgeon John Bingham Borlase. He was barely sixteen when beginning his medical training. The family had moved into town from the farm at Varfell on the death of his father (1794). Left with debts Grace Davy initiated a millinery business of her own, hired a young French émigré to help her, and took in a lodger to support her family with the help of their long-term family friend Dr John Tonkin. Dr John Davy FRS (1790-1868) a chemist, later his biographer, and his cousin Professor Edmund Davy FRS (1785-1857), all from Penzance, were also drawn into the scientific stream, and were to follow him into the Royal Society in their turn. Both of these Davy kin assisted Humphry at the Royal Institution, working in his laboratories and participating actively in the excitements and joys of discovery. Each contributed greatly to the science of chemistry, Edmund especially in his posts in Ireland (Cork and Dublin).

Humphry Davy (knighted in 1812) was made an Honorary Fellow immediately upon the establishment of the Geological Society in Penzance, and his cousin Professor Edmund Davy (later in Ireland) and his younger brother, Dr John Davy, MD also became members of the RGSC world community, all having been born, schooled and brought up in Penzance. All of the Davy kin were also to become Fellows of Royal Society amongst a number of others from the local district.

In his earliest days in Penzance Humphry attended both the Grammar School (now bearing his name) and the Writing School, under the tutelage of local schoolmaster John Fennell, alongside the slightly older Branwell son, Benjamin. Humphry was also the apprentice apothecary who delivered the medicaments that Dr Tonkin[9] prescribed for his patients.

His first experiments into chemical substances and reactions were made in the small laboratory above the pharmacy in the same small lane shared by the Branwell family home at the top of New Street. He was the lad who wrote long poems and stories and 'acted out', spouting in the great tradition of Celtic story-telling from the balcony of the Star Inn across the street from the Branwell and Carne Grocers.

Maria Branwell departed Penzance in 1812. She and her remaining siblings would have been closely aware of Davy's knighthood (also 1812) and his continuing celebrity throughout his lifetime. For a small town in the farthest corner of England, Sir Humphry was a great deal of which to boast, and it is difficult for the modern reader to understand the world-wide fame that he enjoyed in his time, not only as a scientist and inventor, but also as a literary figure. That he came from Penzance, and was a relation, would have been a great source of pride to the émigrés to Yorkshire.

Thomasine Dennis 1771-1809

Sophia St Clare (1806), the novel lightly reviewed in Chapter 3, as a predecessor of *Jane Eyre*, was published by the same publisher, J. Johnson, St Pauls Church Yard, as was Ann Batten Cristall for *Poetical Sketches* (1795). Joseph Johnson (Publisher) was well known as a radical publisher, a religious dissenter, and a supporter of women's literary efforts. He was also the publisher of Thomas Malthus, Mary Wollstonecraft, George Dyer, etc. It is likely that Davies Gilbert would have suggested to Miss Dennis that JJ would be a likely conduit for her gothic-style novel, the underlying theme of which was the future of women's freedom from society's narrow strictures. And it could have been Joseph Johnson, through his efficiency in hiring Mary Wolstencraft who was the central figure in that literary circle which united a number of the Carne-Branwell clan. Davies Gilbert wrote,

"the only object worthy of attention in St Levan church is a plain monument to Miss Thomasin Dennis, with the following inscription: [10]

>Thomasin Dennis,
>De Trembath,
>Ingenio, suavitate, virtute
>Insignia,
>Doctrina insignissima.
>Nata xxix die Septembris, 1771,
>Vai!
>Lenta sed premature morte
>Erepta
>Obit xxx die Augusti 1809,
>Anno aetatis xxxviii.

Fox family of Falmouth

In social connection, the Joseph (Cock) Carne family of Chapel Street was on the friendliest terms with the prominent Quaker family of Foxes of Falmouth: the parents were friends, and their children were active correspondents and companions

when the distances could be overcome, or when they met in London. Each of these families was known for their intellectual interests and great philanthropy.
Anna Maria and Caroline Fox have been credited with the idea and promotion of the organization developed as the Royal Polytechnic of Cornwall in their home town of Falmouth.

> The Cornwall Polytechnic Society was founded as early as 1833 in Falmouth, the first polytechnic in the country and the brainchild of the 17-year old Anna Maria Fox of Penjerrick. Her family, Quaker industrialists and exemplary employers, were part owners of the Perran Foundry near Falmouth. She knew that there were many intelligent men among her father's workforce because she saw the numerous inventions and models that they brought to him, and realized 'what an advantage it would be to those men if there could be some fitting arena provided for all this inventive talent…'[11]

Published diaries by both Caroline Fox and her brother Barclay Fox are listed in the Cornish bibliography, and contain references and correspondence with Elizabeth C T Carne, the contemporary and cousin of the Brontës. The Fox family were related to the Fry and Barclay families in spiritual orientation and in mercantile activities; Elizabeth Fry (1780-1845), the social reformer and educational campaigner, was known to visit Cornwall to stay with her cousins, the Fox family, and to distribute small book collections to the mariners – sailors and fishermen – to support literacy and the valuable use of their time while aboard ship. Amongst their network of contacts and associates were many of the great names in the arts and sciences of the period, including such people as John Sterling, John Stuart Mill, Derwent and Mary Coleridge and brother Hartley, the Revd. Andrew Sedgwick, the Carlyles, and many others who they visited in London and elsewhere, and often hosted in Cornwall.

Fox, Robert Were FRS (1789-1877) the younger, was a close friend of Joseph Carne FRS.
An outstanding resource for Cornish historians is the Quaker woman diarist and letter writer, Caroline Fox (1819-1871), one of his brilliant daughters. Her diary entries report steady familiarity with and anecdotes about national figures also known to the Carnes, Branwells and Brontës by correspondence or by repute, such as Humphry Davy, Henry Martyn, William Wordsworth, Elizabeth Fry, F. D. Maurice, the Coleridges, John Sterling, the Carlyles, John Stuart Mill, Charles Kingsley, Charles Alexander Johns amongst others, and whose letters are written from Falmouth to her friend in Penzance, the moral philosopher, philanthropist, banker and mineralogist Elizabeth Catherine Thomas Carne. Both of these correspondents and authors were contemporaries of the Brontë children, but not personally known to them so far as I am aware. Equally the brother of Caroline and Anna Maria Fox, Barclay Fox (1817-1855) kept a diary and was abreast of technical and literary events within the circle of Quaker industrialists and believers so prominent at the time.

Gilbert, Davies (Giddy) PRS 1767-1839
1791 Fellow of the Royal Society, and MP, author and engineer
1792 High Sheriff of Cornwall
1804-1806 MP for Helston, Cornwall
1806-1832 MP for Bodmin, Cornwall
1808 Married Mary Ann Gilbert of Eastbourne
1814 First President of the Royal Geological Society of Cornwall, Penzance
1827-1830 President of the Royal Society

Davies was the son of the Vicar of St Erth, and a well-connected and educated mining engineer, politician (MP), and author. Stemming from five years at Oxford, spent between Christ Church and Pembroke, his lively intellect pushed forward from childhood by his ambitious father and the nearby Vicar of St Hilary, Malachy Hitchens, his pool of relationships widened exponentially. His best friend from Oxford was the brilliant chemist Thomas Beddoes, to whom later he was to direct the talents of Humphry Davy in Bristol. In 1808 he married Mary Ann Gilbert, who wrote and published on agricultural subjects, a curiosity at the time for a woman. In 1817 he adopted her surname to ensure an inheritance through her uncle, and this secured a large estate in Sussex (the Manor House at Eastbourne), which was to become their primary residence thereafter, while also serving as an MP for Cornwall, and returning there with great frequency.

Though not his only contribution to Cornish history and publishing – Gilbert sustained a constant antiquarian interest in the collection of Christmas carols as they were formerly sung in the West of England, and published books about them.[12] Though negatively criticized for its uneven treatment of local issues of community interest, such as education for the masses which he vocally opposed in parliament as detrimental to the social class system which he upheld, the *Parochial History* was his major work.

Gilbert was not responsible for any specific scientific advances or inventions himself, but he was a believer in the practical outcomes of such study and methods. He was willing to stand up in parliament and support the expense and importance of these endeavours – i.e. a promoter of future directions in emergent technologies, and the 'giants of science' thereof. As a President of the Royal Society, he was respected for his administrative abilities. Without doubt, he sat at the centre of a large network of friends, relations and associates and was singularly important to the life of Penzance.

A long-time Member of Parliament, first for Helston, and after for Bodmin, he was one of the founding three who established the Royal Geological Society of Cornwall in 1814, serving as its first President until his death. In 1820 he was elected to the Society of Antiquaries, and in 1832 an Honorary Member of the American Academy of Arts and Sciences. Gilbert was to go forward from membership (1791) of the Royal Society, and then to its Presidency following Sir Humphry Davy in office from 1827-1830.

West Briton, 3 January 1840 "Death of Davies Gilbert Esq." Quotation:"His preliminary education was conducted at home; and at a very early age he contracted an intimacy, which continued until death, with the Revd. Malachy Hitchens, vicar of St. Hilary, a gentleman of high and well-deserved celebrity as a mathematician and astronomer, and as editor of the Nautical almanack."

Johns, George and Samuel

To study these two brothers is virtually to set off a Catherine-wheel, with ribs taking off into the wild blue yonder. Two brothers, George and Samuel John, became the premier lawyers of Penzance, maintaining their family home and later their offices on Chapel Street. They were the sons of William John and Catherine née Williams of Helston, nephews of Thomas John (Margery John Branwell's father), second cousins of Margaret John Branwell (grandmother of the Branwell children) and kin of Thomas Branwell.

George (1759-1847) married Jane Arundell Harris of Kenegie Manor, gaining great fortune and estates through her family's mining inheritance. They lived at Rosemorran, Gulval (a large estate) and the family home on Chapel Street (next door above the Chapel Street Methodist Chapel), where Samuel also lived prior to building his own home in Alverton (The Orchard, which is now the YMCA). George and Jane John had at least eight children; the daughters were educated privately, and George Dennis, his tall and handsome son was to be a pupil of John Fennell prior to his further education.[13] George Dennis in the future was to have four marriages (through deaths of his wives), and pre-deceased his father by one month.

George John, Esq. (1759-1847) was attorney to the Penzance Corporation and partner to and brother of Samuel John. George was sent to present the Penzance Harbour Bill of 1817 to Parliament. He served as Town Clerk and Mayor in 1812 and 1818.

Samuel John, Esq. (1773-before 1845) was the legal partner of his brother from 1812, coinciding with his brother's first term of Mayoral service. Until 1800, Samuel had been the fiancé of Lydia Grenfell of Marazion; she broke her engagement to Samuel, and suffered depression and anxiety for many years, believing that she was the cause of many of his future problems. He married unhappily a young woman of the Helston Grylls family but within the year they were then divorced (See Barbara Eaton's book, *Letters to Lydia, Beloved Persis* for further detail worthy of *Wuthering Heights* for sure, and much that would have been closely followed by Elizabeth and Maria and the whole family).

Samuel and his brother George grew up as cousins in the same family circle as Elizabeth and Maria, their family home also on Chapel Street (derelict 2017). Possibly the children would have been schooled together. George John in one of his mayoral years (@1800 records in his diary that he is sending his son, George Jr, to Mr Fennell (John Fennell of the Writing School) to begin his education. Benjamin Carne Branwell's son, Thomas Batten Branwell, was apprenticed to the law practice of George and Samuel John in later years.

In the *'Examiner',* dated 13th September 1829, there is a mention in the Police report from Bow Street, London, which refers to Samuel John:-

NEWS FLASH 'FORGERY. - Thursday, the Revd. J.G. Wrench informed the Magistrates that forgeries, to the extent of between 30,000*l.* and 40,000*l.* had been committed by Mr Samuel John, a solicitor of Penzance, who, it was believed, had absconded to France. A letter was produced by Mr Wrench, from which it appeared that the culprit had committed forgeries on the country banks, had defrauded a Mr Stephens of 10,000*l.* and had been carrying on his knavish system for these 10 years. "He had always (said the Revd. Mr Tonkin, writer of the letter) such an appearance of open frankness, of honest, upright conduct, with an affability and cheerfulness of manners that rendered him a delightful companion everywhere, that his delinquency is astonishing, and at the same time shocking and deplorable."

Sir R. BIRNIE told Mr Wrench that he was ready to afford every assistance that might lead to the detection of so daring a depradator. He then requested him to give a description of the person of the accused. Mr Wrench stated that Samuel John was rather a low-sized man, but most gentlemanly and insinuating in his manners. He had acted as clerk and steward to the writer of the letter, and had been the confidential agent to several gentlemen of large properties in the neighbourhood of Penzance. Having written a detailed description of the person of the accused, Mr W. took his leave'

A rough estimate of this sum of £30-40,000 today is calculated to be at least £2-3 million. Had the charges been proven the punishment for this forgery would almost certainly have been execution. This was the gentleman who had been engaged to marry Lydia Grenfell of Marazion until she converted to Methodism and fell in love with the Revd. Henry Martyn.

Elizabeth Jane Kingston 1808-1878 [14]– the fifth child of Jane Branwell and John Kingston

A few members of the Branwell and Carne families, one being Elizabeth Jane Kingston (born 1807-8 in Baltimore, Maryland, America) with a childhood memory of Maria and Elizabeth, and they of her, remained alive to see this remarkable rise in affluence and social status of those named Branwell. Nonetheless, personally, Elizabeth Jane did not benefit from it. For some unknown reason or reasons, there was little sign of a helping hand from the wealthier cousins when Elizabeth Jane was in dire financial straits following her mother Jane's (Branwell-Kingston) death.

The only financial support that Elizabeth Jane received was from her mother's estate in 1855, from shares that had been purchased in Cornish mines and railways at the advice of uncles and cousins. Both of these were notoriously difficult and unreliable investments for her to manage alone. After her mother's death she took lodgers into her small house, and then later she is found in census records as a tea seller and a bookseller. She is also said to have written a novel, but there is nothing found to substantiate this claim. Also by this time in Elizabeth Jane's life, most of the relations who might have advised or helped her, having known her since childhood, were dead. Her investments were based on her mother Jane's life annuity of an annual sum of £50 from grandfather Thomas, and the kindly legacy from Aunt Branwell in Yorkshire in 1842. Aunt Branwell, as mentioned, included Elizabeth Jane in the division of her estate between her Brontë nieces and the youngest daughter of her older sister.[15]

When Elizabeth Jane herself died, she was a resident in the paying section of the Madron Union Workhouse, which also served as the hospital. At this point she was penniless, not through profligacy as some reviewers have implied, but due to the downturn of mining in Cornwall which ruined many at the time. Her place in the hospital would certainly have been underwritten by her wealthy cousins, Carne or Branwell, as a matter of family honour, but no records of this are known.

It is interesting to note that her philanthropic Carne cousin, Elizabeth C. T. Carne argued at separate times that money raised to build the majestic statue of Humphry Davy in the centre of town, would be more wisely spent in building almshouses for looking after the shelter of 'drooping elderly local residents' left uncared for and virtually homeless. She may well have taken her failing Branwell cousin under her wing and paid for her hospitalization. Her elder, also spinster, sister Caroline spent much of her large remaining fortune upon help to poor mariners and their families suffering in the dockyards.[16]

Le Grice, Charles Valentine

A contemporary of the Branwell family in the Anglican fold was the Revd. Charles Valentine Le Grice (1773-1858) who became the Curate of St Mary's chapelry, Penzance, in 1806, and remained in post until 1831. Born, unlike most locals, outside of Cornwall, Le Grice had attended Christ's Hospital where he was a classmate of Samuel Coleridge, and a close friend of Charles Lamb, whose home he visited often on school holidays.

A son of the vicarage in Bury St. Edmunds, he entered Trinity College, Cambridge in 1792, receiving his B.A. in 1795 and his M.A. in 1805. His coming to Cornwall was due to accepting the post of Tutor to William John Godolphin Nicholls of Trereife (estate in Newlyn, near Penzance). In 1799 he married Mary Ustick Nicholls, the widow of his pupil's father. That same year he was ordained deacon and became a priest the following year. Five years later he became the Perpetual Curate of Madron and the Lecturer of St Mary's, Penzance. When Mary Le Grice died in 1821, CV inherited the whole of the property, becoming a wealthy man.

Le Grice, like Richard Polwhele of previous mention, was a prolific writer of poetry and prose. Just as Polwhele had attacked Methodism in 1799, so Le Grice made a similar attack, identifying the whole movement with excessive revivalist fervour. The revival which he took particular exception to affected Penzance in 1814. The attack was in a published sermon delivered at St. Mary's Chapel, Penzance, on Sunday 24 April 1814 on the fruits of the Spirit.[17] The excesses of the revival are described by him: 'manifestations of a charismatic nature not unknown today'. Apparently there had been jumping and falling on the floor as well as crying out and groaning. He believed that such revivals were artificially arranged and that damage was done to religion and peace. Le Grice also took strong exception to the Methodist emphasis on conversion, assurance and the work of the Holy Spirit.

Richard Treffry refuted these charges in a published letter to Le Grice pointing out that Methodism was a great and widespread movement.[18] Le Grice was judging and condemning "thousands of respectable men in the county of Cornwall" in various situations in life. Methodism was not an obscure fanatical sect. He went on to say that the doctrines that Le Grice took exception to were held by the Church of England and enshrined in the Homilies. Treffry viewed Le Grice as deficient in the teachings of his own Church as well as in his grammar and the clarity of his writing.

Lovett, William 1800-1877, Chartist and author, working man and prisoner

In one sense we see Cornwall as being in the forefront of industrial society at that time, with its mining tradition and all that entailed. But many of the mineworkers were 'tributers' or 'tut workers', direct contract workers, some of whom varied their work with pilchard fishing and farming. The big recent influence in their lives at that time is likely to have been Methodism.

In his autobiography Lovett tells the story of Honor Hichens, a woman of some 30 – 40 years, who, with her father, was cleaning fish in a small stream when a press-gang landed. She was deaf and her father was seized before she realised it and was being borne off. She snatched up one of the dog-fish she was opening and repeatedly hit her father's captor across the face with the rough skinned fish; holding him at bay until other women and girls came to her assistance. Lovett writes that fishermen were seized from their boats at sea and often never heard of again. [*William Lovett of Newlyn*, J.J. Beckerlegge]

A surprising but interesting twist of fate was the coming together of Keziah Green, the mother of William Lovett, the famous Chartist, with another man of West Cornwall location, also named 'William Carne', found later to be the son of a Philip Carne (of which there were several locally). This William Carne was a fisherman, later described as a miner, and from the time of the birth of their first son, John Carne in 1809, she was known as Keziah Carne, though their marriage was not solemnized until 1817 at Paul.

A second son, baptised as Thomas Carne, was born in 1818 and the family was living in Newlyn. Thomas Carne apprenticed himself to a builder in Penzance, and later worked in the building trades on his own account. Meantime, and throughout William Lovett's youth in Newlyn and Penzance, Keziah worked as a fish jowster to support her son and mother. There is even a possibility that Keziah worked locally in the market on behalf of the Branwells whose pilchard works were located at the harbour. It was a strong Methodist family and he attended classes at Chapel. William was taught to read and to study hard in a variety of subjects by his educated grandmother (his mother's mother), with whom he lived most of his young life. He departed Cornwall in 1821, gaining passage to London via his joinery skills. His biography is told in many reviews and papers, and was possibly recognised by the Brontë household as a fellow to be read and followed. Whether or not they knew of Lovett's personal background is more problematic. From his autobiography we know that he returned twice to Cornwall before he died, once in 1840 to recuperate from his imprisonment in Warwick Gaol, where he began with a fellow prisoner to write the Charter, and secondly in 1852 to see his mother before she died.

> *"In the plan of the NATIONAL ASSOCIATION, we have provided for the admission of female members on the same conditions as males; and as some prejudices exist on the subject of female education, and especially against their obtaining any knowledge of politics, it may be necessary to give a few reasons in support of our proposition . . . . there has seldom been a great or noble character who had not a wise or virtuous mother . . . . As our perceptions are awakened and faculties matured, her wise or foolish conduct towards us leaves lasting impressions of good or evil; her habits, conversation, and example are readily imitated, and form the foundation of our future character.'* From . . . Plan of the National Association — Chartism (1840).

> *". . . women are the chief instructors of our children, whose virtues or vices will depend more on the education given them by their mothers than on that off any other teacher we can employ to instruct them. If a mother is deficient in knowledge and depraved in morals, the effects will be seen in all her domestic arrangements; and her prejudices, habits, and conduct will make the most lasting impression on her children, and often render nugatory all the efforts of the schoolmaster. If, on the contrary, she is so well informed as to appreciate and second his exertions, and strives to fix in the minds of her children habits of cleanliness, order, refinement of conduct, and purity of morals, the results will be evident in her wise and well-regulated household. But if, in addition to these qualities, she be richly stored with intellectual and moral treasures, and makes it her chief delight to impart them to her offspring, they will, by their lives and conduct, reflect her intelligence and virtues."* From Chartism (1840)

Masonic Lodges, West Penwith Resources, On-line

Druid's Lodge No 176 "Love and Liberality", Redruth, Cornwall. This organisation was a substantial affair and, though it is some distance outside of West Penwith, had many members from there, especially after the lodges in Penzance and St. Ives disbanded. Founded before 1777, it had members from all of Cornwall and some as far afield as London, Wales, the north of England and Norway(!) including seven French prisoners of war in 1791. Recorded amongst the members from West Penwith are Richard Mathews Branwell 161. Richard BRANWELL (4 Oct 1808, merchant of Penzance aged 36, eldest son of Innkeeper and builder Richard Johns Branwell) and 172. Samuel COLENSO (3 Dec 1809, saddler of Penzance, kin of the Carnes).

A chapter of Royal Arch Masons (No. 79 "Love and Liberality" Redruth) was opened on 15 Jul 1791 and included in their number were 100 members. Richard EDMONDS (28 Apr 1819, attorney at law of Penzance aged 44, kin), and Thomas Batten BRANWELL (16 Aug 1826, attorney at law of Penzance aged 25, son of the late Benjamin Carne Branwell).

There was also a conclave of the Knights Templar of St John of Jerusalem as a sub group of this lodge. It was founded on 19 Jun 1792 with John KNIGHT as

Master and disbanded on his death in 1829. Amongst the knights was Thomas Batten BRANWELL (14 Aug 1827, solicitor of Penzance aged 26).

Henry Martyn, Anglican Missionary 1781-1812: Born at Truro, England, February 18, 1781 and died at Tokat, October 16, 1812. Henry grew up in Truro and attended Truro Grammar School from 1788. His father John Martyn, was originally a working miner but one who became a mining captain at Gwennap and his family was at this time reasonably prosperous. William Carne Sr. and John Martin collaborated on Wesleyan affairs and attended Methodist conference together.

His mother died of tuberculosis (the family weakness) when he was two, leaving two sisters and a half-brother from his father's first marriage. He departed Cornwall in 1797 for St. John's College, Cambridge and his academic successes were many. He took his degree in the first class division of the Mathematical Tripos, as 'Senior Wrangler', and shortly thereafter, the first Smith's Prize man. Invited to a Fellowship in 1802, his quick facility with languages came to the fore and he won the first Members' Prize for Latin prose. Meantime, his father died suddenly in 1800, and Henry had in family fashion turned to religion, which up until then he had mostly ignored. Martyn was also the person, who wrote to William Wilberforce on behalf of Patrick Brontë to secure scholarship monies for his continued study at St. John's.

At Cambridge he came into firm involvement with evangelicals grouped around the lecture circuits and preaching of the Revd. Charles Simeon (Fellow of King's College, Dean of Divinity from 1789 and Vicar of Holy Trinity Parish Church, Cambridge since 1782). Inspired by the zeal of William Carey, Baptist Minister (Indian missionary) and the work of David Brainerd amongst North American Indians, he received an appointment to the chaplaincy of the East India Company. En route to going abroad, he visited Cornwall to say his goodbyes to family and friends

> ...He dined with Wilberforce in the evening and went with him to the House of Commons where he was surprised and charmed by Pitt's eloquence. He next broke the journey at Stoke, Plymouth Dock, Devon, where he stayed for three days with a cousin, the Reverend Thomas Hitchins, and his 'amicable' wife, Emma, whose younger sister was called Lydia Grenfell. Henry was about to fall in love.
>
> Barbara Eaton, *Letters to Lydia*[19]

Unfortunately Martyn was unable to convince Lydia Grenfell to marry him and travel with him to India. This story, known by Maria and Elizabeth, may have become the character, in the form of the fictional Revd. St. John Rivers, who lives in the world of *Jane Eyre*, as imagined by Charlotte Bronte. Amongst his published works are his many translations and sermons, such as *The New Testament* which he translated into the Hindoostanee language, from the original (Greek), and a *Compendium of the Book of Common Prayer*, similarly rendered from the English.

Southey, Robert 1774-1843
In 1795. Southey married Edith Fricker, a friend from childhood in Bristol and one

of three sisters, another of whom became the wife of Coleridge the following year. Setting aside the relations between the future three families, well documented in general and personal biographies and literary works, it is of interest to note that in 1799, Humphry Davy, Coleridge and Southey joined together on Davy's experiments in Bristol on the possible uses of nitrous oxide (laughing gas). In 1803, Davy visited Greta Hall, Keswick, the home of Coleridge and his family, where he was to become a responsible parental figure to both families, for the remainder of his life. Both Joseph (Cock) Carne FRS and his brother John, the author, were known as friends of Southey, as were many in the kinship and friendship circle of the Carne-Branwells.

Thackeray, William Makepeace 1811-1863

We must not assume in the next generation that because Joseph (Cock) Carne's eldest son, Joseph Jr, was at Charterhouse School with William Thackeray, and that they were good friends, going up together to Trinity College, Cambridge to the same professor, that this was known or even of any importance to the remainder of the Cornish relations. Neither was famous at the time, nor would either of those young gentlemen work through to a degree. Thackeray only remained a year before tiring of the experience, and Joseph Jr died the following year in Madeira of consumption, presumably contracted at Trinity. Nonetheless, a lampooning letter found in the archives of Charterhouse Library between Thackeray and another friend about young Joseph and his Cornish family life shows Thackeray's satirical nature even in his schoolboy days.

A signed letter from W M Thackeray to one of his schoolmates at Charterhouse – undated, but sometime between 1824-28, when all were day boys in London at term time, but at home over the holidays. The following is extracted from a holiday letter:

> *Have you heard anything of Carne? In return for your news about Smith's bishopric, I must inform you that his father's bank failed, and he, that is his father, tied himself up with a rope, his wife came to cut him down but she recieved [sic] so violent [a] kick from him in the stomach that it killed her. Carne and his eldest sister died of grief, the rest of the family are in a very dangerous state....Write soon....*

very faithfully yours
W M Thackeray

Treffry, Richard Sr. and Jr.

In June, 1829, Richard Treffry Jr. married Eliza Baron, daughter of Mr Baron of Hull, Yorkshire. He became terminally ill with T.B. and was made a supernumery. His father writes:- "My son was then in the prime of life, not quite twenty-six years of age; he had an amiable wife, and an infant child; such a talent for usefulness; and it cannot be a matter of surprise that he was desirous of life, and was willing to use all the means which at all calculated that end." Accordingly, on November the 10th, accompanied by his wife, he set out from Leeds, with the intention of travelling to Cornwall. They arrived at Helston on the 27th November.

In that same year Richard Treffry Sr. took up the post of Chairman of the Local Management Committee (1829-1832) of the Woodhouse Grove School near Bradford. Here was another 'old friend', known to the Branwells, Fennells, Kingstons and the Carnes, steeped in Cornish ways, who turned up in northern evangelical circles.

ENDNOTES

1 Davies Gilbert, *Parochial History of Cornwall*, vol. III, p. 95.
2 Thomas Percival Bunting (1859) *The Life of Jabez Bunting DD* p. 197 note.
3 The missionary Henry Martyn assisted Patrick Brontë to obtain financial support at St John's College, Cambridge, where he held a fellowship. See his entry in this list for more detail of his Cornish life. His father, John Martyn, was a "captain" or mine-agent at Gwennap. It lends its name to Gwennap Pit where John Wesley preached eighteen times between 1762 and 1789. In the 18th and early 19th centuries Gwennap parish was the richest copper mining district in Cornwall, and was called the "richest square mile in the Old World" (Cornwall Council, 2009 Mining Heritage).
4 The Rev George Whitefield, a student with the Wesleys at Oxford, though Chairman of the first Methodist Conference, relinquished that post afterwards, was unable to locate an Anglican parish in which to work, and took to the open fields to preach Calvinism. Whitefield and Wesley were theologically opposed though remained friends. Whitefield ploughed the mission fields of America and died there in 1770; Wesley preached his funeral oration.
5 Elizabeth Catherine Thomas Carne (1817-1873) a prominent woman of science in 19th century Cornwall, author of scientific papers, and social commentaries relating to the 'state of England' and its moral decline. She and her father, Joseph Carne, FRS were key figures in the Wesleyan Methodist community, as Joseph's father William (note 23) had been before them. Elizabeth Carne is the subject of a *Transaction* for the RGSC in their bi-centennial year of 2014, as mentioned previously.
6 See entry for EJK, the youngest child of Jane Branwell and John Kingston. Fannie Ratchford asked who might have done this for her, in her Brontë Society paper 'The Loneliness of a Brontë Cousin' *BST* vol. 13: 2, Jan 1957, pp. 100-110.
7 A collection of articles written for the county newspapers under the pseudonym of 'A Native', later brought together and edited by P.A.S. Pool in 1976 and printed in pamphlet form. Available at the Cornish Studies Library, Redruth.
8 See online entries for both Colenso Society and Te Ara and for a detailed life of cousin William, *The On-line Encyclopedia for New Zealand*.
9 Dr. Tonkin's brother James painted some of the miniature portraits of the Branwell family now in the Bronte Parsonage Museum, by gift of the Penzance family.
10 Gilbert & Tonkin, *Parochial History of Cornwall* vol. III, pp. 33-4.
11 A. Round, 'The Royal Cornwall Polytechnic Society (Falmouth)', in M. Hardie (ed.) *Artists in Newlyn and West Cornwall 1880-1940, Dictionary and source-book* (Bristol, Art Dictionaries Ltd., 2009).
12 Davies Gilbert *Some ancient Christmas Carols, with the Tunes to which they were formerly sung in the West of England*, London: J Nichols and Son (1822, 1823).
13 The diary of George John records sending his son George at age seven to John Fennell's of Penzance to learn to write. Here the fees were 16 guineas per annum with ten shillings and sixpence entrance. Later he went on to Truro School, so this was a local preparatory school CRO AD72/12 Diary of George John.
14 Elizabeth Jane Kingston (1808-1878) The most complete story of Eliza Jane Kingston is related by Fannie E Ratchford 'The Loneliness of a Brontë Cousin' *BST* vol. 13: 2 Jan 1957, pp. 100-110.
15 The Will of Aunt Branwell was written in 1833, and named the Rev John Fennell, her Uncle, as an Executor. By the time she died, he had pre-deceased her in the nearby parish of Todmorden, West Yorkshire. See Document Register, Chapter 12 for a transcription.
16 Caroline Carne is complimented on her charitable works in Flynn, J. S. (1917) *Cornwall Forty Years After* London: Truslove and Hanson Ltd., Chapter XII: 'Women of Cornwall'.
17 Le Grice 1814*The Proofs of the Spirit, or Considerations on Revivalism*. A SERMON preached at St. Mary's Chapel,

Biographical briefs

Penzance on Sunday April 24th 1814 by C V Le Grice MA. Perpetual Curate of Penzance.

18 Treffry R 1814 *A Letter to the Rev C Val Le Grice, occasioned by his Sermon entitled* "Proofs of the Spirit or considerations on revivalism." Published at Helston

19 Barbara Eaton *Letters to Lydia: 'beloved Persis'* (Penzance: Hypatia Publications, 2005) relates the facts and fictions of the 19th-century love affair between Henry Martyn, a chaplain of the East India Company and his 'beloved Persis' in Cornwall, Lydia Grenfell, Based on their letters and diaries. Part Three of this volume considers the Brontë Connection in a chapter entitled 'Reader, I married him', pp. 337-42.

Chapter 12

Documentary Register

Note: Chronological, highlighted names indicate members of the kinship circle and/or an ancestor in the direct lineage.

General
'List of mayors of Penzance': Wikipedia.org/wiki/List: based on P A S Pool's *History of the Borough of Penzance*, and Penzance Town Council information.

1679
Will of **JANE STEVENS**, widow, of Gwithian written: 4 March 1679, proved: 8 March 1679 [L is the sign for £]
daughter: KATHERINE TREMEARNE 4L
son-in-law: JOHN TREMEARNE 1 sh.
granddaughter: DORCUS TREMEARNE 3L
granddaughter: **JANE TREMEARNE 3L**
Jane Tremearne became the wife of Martin Bromwell, as his second wife, and the grandmother of Thomas Branwell. In the family naming pattern she and her mother are the first Janes, from whom the others appear to take their names.

1719
Martyn/Martin Bramwell/Bromwell
Martin BROMWELL of Penzance, Butcher
Dated 22 Apr 1719
To sons **Richard** and Joseph, and daughters Maudlyn, Margery and Alice, 1s each
To son Martin, 66 foot of land rented from Mr John CARVETH, and 1 bay mare with saddle and bridle
To wife Jane [Tremearne], house and garden where I now dwell, [New Street, now attached to the Star Inn] house where Edward Betty TAYLOR lives in Penzance [one slip from Market Jew Street down from New Street slip], and executor
Sign of Martyn Bromwell

Witnesses: William TONKYN, Henry MICHELL, Richard CANNACKE
Proved 1719 (Ref. Vol 4, p 356 – LDS Film No. 0090187)

1752
THOMAS JOHN, Blacksmith, of Penzance
written: 24 Jan 1750/1
proved: 30 Apr 1752
son: PETER JOHN of Penzance, Blacksmith 50L in trust for the use of my daughter:
MARGARET w/o **RICHARD BRANWELL** of Penzance, mason; apart from her husband, and he shall not intermeddle in it; it is not to be used for his debts; if MARGARETT die then the 50L is to the use of her children if she have any.
daughter: ELIZABETH 60L, bed & bedding & furniture where she now dwell
son: PETER all the rest & executor.
witnesses: SAMUEL DEY, STEPHEN RAWLING, NICHOLAS JESPER
Vol. 3, p. 506 Will book

1768
Will of Eleanor Colenso Carne
Eleanor Carn, Penzance relict and administratrix of husband Henry Carn, cordwainer
written: 16-Sep 1758 , proved: 4-May 1768, pages: 359/360
sons - Henry, **JOHN**, William
grandson – Philip [who later emigrates to Australia]

1783
Will of Francis Cock, Penzance grocer
   written - 4-Aug 1783, proved - 6-Oct 1783, pages - 504/506
   wife – Jane; mother - Grace Cock, sister - Grace (unmarried)
   daughter - Jane Cock, son - Francis
   sister - **Anna, wife of William Carne** [later Banker]
   wife's brother - John Cunnack
   brother-in-law - **William Carne**
   witnesses - Cha: Jacka, Henry Rogers, **Eliza Branwell***
[* This is Thomas Branwell's sister, Elizabeth Branwell, who later became the wife of John Keam, shopkeeper. The importance of this Will is to show the close family relationships between the Carnes, the Cocks and the Branwells through cross-marriages.]

1784
Letter to John Fennell in Cornwall from the Revd. John Fletcher in Madeley, Shropshire, his godfather and former teacher/mentor.
Copy of a Letter from Revd. John Fletcher, published by J. Fennell, dated Penzance, *Methodist Magazine* 23 July 1800 , xxiv, 91-93 (1801)

Madeley, Nov. 28, 1784.

Dear John, — I rejoice to hear that you think of a better world, and of the better part, which Mary [Fletcher] and your late mother, another Mary, chose before you. May all her prayers, but, above all, may the dew of heaven, come down upon your soul in solemn thoughts, heavenly desires, and strong resolutions to be the Lord's, cost what it will. Let the language of your heart and lips be, at any rate, "I will be a follower of Christ; yea, a member of his, a child of God, and an inheritor of the kingdom of heaven." A noble promise this! and of which I have so peculiar a right to put you in mind. But, in order to be this happy and holy soul, you must not forget that your Christian name, your Christian vows, and ten thousand reasons besides, bind you to turn your back upon the world, the flesh, and the devil; and to set yourself steadfastly to look to the Father, Son, and Holy Ghost, to your Creator, Redeemer, and Sanctifier.

My dear John, you have no time to lose. We have calls here to the young without end: they die fast. I lately buried two brothers and sisters in the same grave. Be you also ready. I was some nights ago praying for you on my bed, fill my sleepless hours; and I asked for you the faith of righteous Abel, the chastity of Joseph, the early piety of Samuel, the right choice of young Solomon, the self- denial and abstinence of Daniel, together with the zeal and undaunted courage of his three friends. But, above all, I asked that you might follow John the Baptist, and John the Apostle, as they followed our Lord. Back earnestly, constantly, back my prayer. So shall you be faithful, diligent, and godly; a blessing to all around you; and a comfort to your affectionate old friend and minister, J. Fletcher

1791 Universal Directory
Following is a select list of principal inhabitants of Penzance:
(known cousins or kin *)
Corporation
***John Batten**, Esq. *Justice*
***Thomas John** Esq. (Margaret John's father, Great-grandfather to Branwells)
Common Council
***Peter John**, Gent (F) (Margaret John's brother, Uncle to Branwells)
***John (Bodenar) Batten** Jr (Benjamin Carne Branwell's future brother in-law)
***Thomas Branwill** [*sic*] (Margaret John's son, grandfather of the Brontës)
Clergy
***Rev Joseph Batten** (Dissenting minister, Congregational, kin)
Law
***George John**, Attorney (cousin)
***Samuel John**, Attorney (cousin)
Traders, etc.
***Richard Bramwell**, Innkeeper (older brother of Thomas, Uncle to Maria)
***Joseph Bramwell**, Butcher (nephew of Thomas, married to *Temperance Matthews, sister of ***Honor Matthews** Branwell, Aunt)
***William Caine/Carne** Jr. [*sic*] Grocer (cousin)
***John Fennil** [*sic*], Schoolmaster (in-law of Branwells, Uncle)

*****Edward Hambleton**, Architect (cousin)
*****John Keam**, Shopkeeper (in-law of Branwells, Uncle)

1792
Bath Chronicle and Weekly Gazette, Thursday, 19 January 1792, p. 2
The marriage is announced between **Miss [Margaret] Branwell**, daughter of Thomas Branwell, Merchant of Penzance, to Charles Fisher, bookbinder.

1795-97 to 1890s
A brief history of the **Penzance Bank,** the first bank established in Penzance, and the people involved:
Founders: **John Batten***, **William Carne*** and Richard Oxnam, merchants.
John Batten d 1810; Henry Boase* (Alverton) became a partner Sept. 1810; Richard Oxnam retired 1810 and d1844. Renamed BATTEN, CARNE AND BOASE 1810-1823; Henry Boase retired 1823; John Batten junior* entered firm 1823; Joseph Carne* (son of W Carne) became a partner 1823. Renamed BATTEN, CARNE AND CARNE 1833; John Batten junior d 1834; William Carne d 1836; John Batten the third*, also merchant of Penzance became partner 1834. Philip Marrack (Newlyn) employed by bank since 1810 left his position as manager, became a partner 1844; John Batten the third, retired 31 Oct. 1849 and d 1875; Joseph Carne, FRS d. 1858 and his daughter Elizabeth Catherine Thomas Carne* became partner 12th Oct 1858; Thomas Hacker Bodilly, merchant, Penzance joined the firm 1859; John Josias Arthur Boase became a partner in 1859 and retired 30 June 1859; A new banking house was built in the Penzance Market, and opened 1864; Nicholas Berryman Downing* (a clerk since 1848) became manager 1861; Thomas Bodilly d 1873, his eldest son Thomas Hacker Bodilly received his father's share in the business 1873; Charles Campbell Ross*, grandson of Joseph Carne and Nicholas Downing became partners 1872; Miss Carne d 1873 when her interest passed to Charles Ross; Nicholas Downing retired from the firm 1874.
* Branwell-Carne relations
References: Archives of Barclays Bank, Manchester; Raymond Forward of the Acorn Archive (on-line);

1799
[Abstract of 1799 Indenture] Made the twentieth day of May in the year of our Lord One thousand Seven hundred and Ninety nine **Between** Joseph Sleep of the Parish of Germoe in the County of Cornwall Yeoman of the one part and Francis Carter and Thomas Curtis both of the Parish of Breage in the said County Yeomen, Thomas Gundry of the Parish of St. Erth in the said County Yeoman, William Carne of the Parish of Penzance in the said County Merchant, John Boase of the same Town Joiner, John Fennel of the same Town Schoolmaster and John Thomas of the Parish of St. Just in the said County Shopkeeper of the other part. **Whereas** the said Joseph Sleep is now lawfully possessed of estated in and intitled unto among other things of **All** those Fields or closes of Land called or known

by the names of the higher or lower Heweis containing by estimation four acres of Land or thereabouts as part and parcel of the Tenement of Trethewey situated in the said Parish of Germoe parcel of the Manor of Godolphin for and during the remainder of a Term of Fourscore and Nineteen Years If the said Joseph Sleep, Catherine his daughter and George Bawden the Younger or either of them shall so live **Now this Indenture Witnesseth** that the said Joseph Sleep for and in Consideration that the said Francis Carter, Thomas Curtis, Thomas Gundry, **William Carne,** John Boase, **John Fennel** and John Thomas have undertaken and agreed to Erect and Build a Chapel or Meeting House on the plot of Ground herein fore mentioned and granted and also in Consideration of the yearly Rent Covenants and ….Providedalways that the said Person or Persons Preach no other Doctrine than is contained in the said John Wesley's notes on the New Testament and four Volumes of Sermons …..Joseph Sleep

1800

15 September, *Sherborne Mercury*. To be sold at auction, in lots, the fee simple of the following. Lot 5 – All those messuages, cellars and lofts situate near the Quay, in Penzance aforesaid, together with Ninnis Wharf, now in occupation of **Thomas Branwell** and others.

1807

NOTES ON THE TRIAL OF JOHN KINGSTON 1807

Fletcher/Tooth 4/9/8 reference: A letter from the preacher George Lowe at the Liverpool conference to Mary Fletcher (Fletcher-Tooth catalogue, vol. 5). In the letter it is said that **John Kingston** has taken upwards of £100 of book money with him, and also that he was suspected the previous year.
2. Minutes of several conversations, at a meeting of the Preachers in Birmingham District held July 1, 1807

Question I: What Preachers are present?
Richard Reece, in the Chair; Jonathan Edmondson, Secretary
William Horner, George Baldwin, George Lowe, John Furness, Henry Anderson, [written in over-line: **John Kingston**] John Nelson, Charles Gloyne, Joseph Brookhouse, Hump. Parsons, Joseph Fielding, William Harrison, James Blacket, John Lancaster, John Simpson, William Bird and James Heaton

Question II: Are there any objections against the moral character of the Preachers?
Answer: They were examined one by one, and no objections were proved but the following:
1. That Mr Kingston collected, in Shrewsbury Circuit, in the year 1806, the sum of £64.19.4 but that he paid no more into the Fund than 45.12.0 so that there was a deficiency of £19.7.4. Mr Kingston's defence was as follows: that he applied £5-5-0 of this sum to defray his own and Mr Chittle's expenses to the Conference: that there

was between twenty and thirty shillings in bad money; that he returned six shillings and sixpence to a person who had given him a seven shillings piece for a sixpence: and that he kept the remainder in his own hand to pay himself for a Horse, Saddle, and Bridle which he purchased in the Island of Barbadoes in the West Indies, in the year 1791.

2. That he had been guilty of improper behaviour towards two young men, the Circumstances of which must be explained to the Conference by our Chairman. The Meeting is unanimously of opinion that Mr Kingston's conduct in this matter has been very vile: that he shall be suspended till the Conference, and that the care of Shrewsbury Circuits shall be committed, till then, to Mr Lowe.

3. LIVERPOOL, JULY 27, 1807: No LXIV:

Q 6: Has any Preacher been expelled this year? A: John Kingston

1807

Reference Number: MAM/FL/2.16 Fletcher-Tooth Archive, University of Manchester.
Physical Description: 17 items
Letter (5 Aug 1807)
Reference Number: MAM/FL/2.16/1
Scope and Content

From **John Fennel** in Wellington to [Mary] Fletcher. He is taking the first opportunity of thanking Fletcher and their other friends in Madeley for their prayers on behalf of Shifnall, and to also to give some account of their visit there.

Having heard several accounts from there that the [Anglican] minister was determined to oppose [Methodist] preaching in the street, Fennel felt deeply torn between his affection for the people there and his unwillingness to place himself in the power of the magistrate. He set apart last Friday for fasting and prayer so that he might understand the will of God with regard to this matter; when he was fully satisfied which was to "fear not for I have many people in this city", he ventured forth and preached from John 11:25 to a congregation which was far more numerous and serious than formerly experienced. His listeners appeared to be much affected and many wept.

Fennel was asked when he would be coming again.

When he had stopped speaking, the [parish] constable approached and told him that the Vicar of Shifnall two weeks before, had left him with strict orders that if Fennel came again, he was to be prevented from preaching, and that if he refused and the people did not disperse, then the constable was to apply to the justices' clerk with whom the vicar had left instructions.

As the constable had not arrived until after Fennel had begun, he had thought it wrong to interrupt. In this, Fennel could see the hand of God. He believes that if the opportunity offered by preaching in the street is shut against them, then another way will be made open and a church raised in Shifnall against which earth and hell shall not prevail.

Fletcher's prayers are still most welcome both for Shifnall and for two other places which have similar circumstances and which he is also resolved to visit.

His wife and daughter send their regards

1808
Will of Thomas Branwell
Filed: CRO, and transcribed from handwritten document
IN THE NAME OF GOD AMEN

I Thomas Branwell of the town of Penzance in the County of Cornwall Merchant, being sick and weak in Body, but of sound and disposing mind memory and understanding (Thanks be to God) DO make and ordain this to be my last Will and Testament in a manner and form following, that is to say,

FIRST I give and bequeath unto my dearly beloved Wife Anne Branwell and her assigns for and during the term of her natural life one annuity yearly rent charge or sum of Fifty Pounds of lawful money of the United Kingdom of Great Britain and Ireland current in Great Britain free of taxes and all other Deductions, Parliamentary or otherwise, to be issuing and payable out of all and singular my Freehold and Leasehold messuages Lands Tenements and Hereditaments whatsoever and wheresoever lying and being and payable by equal quarterly payments, to wit at Lady day midsummer Michaelmas and Christmas the first payment to be made on such of the said Feasts as shall first happen after my death and I do hereby charge and subject all my said Freehold and Leasehold messuages Lands Tenements and Hereditaments with and to the payment of the said annuity or Yearly Rent Charge and it is my Will that my said Wife shall have and I do hereby give her full power and authority to enter upon and distrain all or any of my said freehold and Leasehold Messuages Lands Tenements and Hereditaments for the said annuity yearly Rent Charge or Sum of Fifty Pounds in case of non-payment thereof when and as the same shall become due and payable as aforesaid.

ALSO I give and bequeath unto my said Wife Anne Branwell all that my Leasehold Dwelling House with the garden and appurtenances to the same belonging lying and being at Causewayhead within the said Town of Penzance now in the Occupation of Michael Rowe, Butcher To hold the same unto my said Wife her Executors administrators and assigns from the day of my death for and during all the residue and Remainder of my Estate and Interest therein.

ALSO I give and bequeath unto my said Wife such parts and so much of my Household Goods and Furniture as she may chuse. [*sic*]

ALSO I give and bequeath unto John Batten the younger of Penzance, aforesaid Merchant, his Executors and Administrators for and during the term of the natural life of my daughter Jane Kingston, Wife of John

Kingston, now residing at Baltimore in North America, one annuity yearly Rent Charge on sum of Fifty Pounds of like lawful money free of Taxes and all other Deductions, Parliamentary or otherwise to be issuing and payable out of all those my several Fields or closes of Land, Dwelling House and Premises lying and being in and parts and parcels of Lescudjack and Leskinnick within the said town of Penzance and the Parish of Maddern, or one of them, which I hold by Lease or Leases under John Rogers Esquire and to be paid and payable by equal quarterly payments and on the several Feasts or Days of Payment in the Year herein beforementioned the first payment thereof to be made on such of the said Feasts as shall first happen after my death. In Trust nevertheless and to and for the only use and Benefit of my said Daughter Jane Kingston and to the intent that he the said John Batten the younger his Executors and Administrators shall and do pay the said annuity Yearly Rent Charge or sum of Fifty Pounds as the same shall from time to time, during the natural life of my said Daughter, grow due and be received into the Hands of my said Daughter Jane Kingston, or otherwise permit and suffer my said Daughter to receive the same to and for her own sole and separate use To the Intent that the same may not be at the disposal or subject or liable to the control or Engagements of her said Husband, but only at her own sole and separate disposal.

ALSO I give and bequeath unto my daughter Elizabeth Branwell and her assigns for and during the term of her natural life one annuity yearly Rent Charge or sum of Fifty Pounds of like lawful money [same wording as Jane above, without reference to JK]

ALSO I give and bequeath unto my Daughter Maria Branwell and her assigns for and during the term of her natural life One Annuity yearly rent charge a sum of Fifty Pounds of like lawful money

AND unto my Daughter Charlotte Branwell and her assigns for and during the term of her natural life One Annuity yearly rent charge a sum of Fifty Pounds of like lawful money, free of taxes and all other deductions, Parliamentary or otherwise and to be severally issuing and payable out of all and singular my freehold messuages or Dwelling House and Premises called or known by the Name of the Golden Lion Inn lying in or near the Market Place in Penzance aforesaid now in the Occupation of my brother Richard Branwell, my freehold Messuages or Dwelling House and Premises in the Chapel Street in Penzance aforesaid now in the occupation of Mrs Griffin and John Tremenheere, Gentleman; my freehold Dwelling House and Stable lying in the Lane, within the said Town which leads from the 'Chapel' Street to the New Road and now in the several Possessions of Jane Ball, Lemon Hart and others, my freehold cellars and Premises called the Content Cellar lying near the Quay within the said Town now in the several Occupations of me the said Thomas Branwell and John Badcock and my leasehold Dwelling House near Causewayhead aforesaid which I have let to William Carne Merchant, for the residence of the Methodist Preachers and my Leasehold Malthouse lying above and near the said Dwelling House and my Leasehold Dwelling House and Garden lying near the top of Causewayhead aforesaid now occupied by Thomas Colensoe; which said two several last mentioned annuities yearly rent charges or sums of Fifty Pounds each are also to be paid and payable unto my said Daughters Maria Branwell and Charlotte Branwell respectively and their respective assigns, by equal quarterly payments and on the several Feast Days of Payment in the year herein before mentioned. The first payment thereof respectively, to be made on such of the said Feasts or Days as shall first and next happen after my death and I do hereby charge and subject my said several Freehold and Leasehold messuages or Dwelling Houses, Cellars, Malthouse, Stable and premises, herein before particularly described, with their several and respective appurtenances, with and to the payment of the said two several last mentioned annuities or yearly rent charges and my Will is that my said Daughters Maria Branwell and Charlotte Branwell respectively and their respective assigns shall have, and I do hereby give unto them, full power and authority to enter upon and distrain the said several Freehold and Leasehold messuages or Dwelling Houses Cellars Malthouse Stable and Premises for payment of the said two several annuities yearly rent charges or sums of Fifty Pounds each, in case of non-payment of either of them, or of any part of either of them when and as the same shall respectively become due and payable as aforesaid.

LASTLY All those my aforesaid Freehold and Leasehold messuages cellars Malthouse stable and Premises (subject and liable as aforesaid to the payment of the said annuity yearly Rent Charge or sum of Fifty Pounds to the said John Batten the younger his Executors and Administrators during the natural life of my said Daughter Jane Kingston In trust for her sole use and benefit as aforesaid and also to the payment of the said three several annuities yearly Rent Charges or sums of Fifty Pounds each to my said daughters Elizabeth Branwell, Maria Branwell and Charlotte Branwell respectively and their respective assigns, during their respective natural lives/ And all other my freehold and Leasehold messuages Lands Tenements and Hereditaments whatsoever and wheresoever situate lying and being the whole of my Freehold and Leasehold messuages Lands Tenements Hereditaments and premises subject and liable to the payment of all my just Debts the said Annuity Yearly Rent Charge or sum of Fifty Pounds to my said wife Anne Branwell and her assigns for and during the term of her natural life/ AND also all the Rent Residue and Remainder of my Goods Chattles Personal and Testamentary Estate and Effects whatsoever and wheresoever of what Nature Kind or Quality soever the same may be I give devise and bequeath unto my Son Benjamin Carne Branwell, his Heirs, Executors and Administrators and assigns and I do hereby constitute and appoint my said Son Benjamin Carne Branwell sole Executor and Residuary Legatee of this my last Will and Testament hereby revoking all former and other wills by me at any time heretofore –

Made IN WITNESS whereof I have to this my last will and Testament, written on five sheets, set my Hand and Seal to each of the said sheets this twenty sixth day of March one thousand eight hundred and eight

SIGNED Sealed Published and Declared
By the said Testator Thomas Branwell as and   Signature Thos Branwell
For his last Will and Testament in the
Presence of us, who at his request and in
His presence and in the presence of each other
Have subscribed our names as Witnesses
Hereto_ _ _ _ _ _ _ _ _ _ _ _ _ _ _ _ _ _ _ _
Margaret Edmonds   [servant to Mr Branwell]
Jas Thomas Junior [plus one other, unreadable]

1811

Letters to Mary Fletcher from her 'precious young men'
Reference Number: MAM/FL/5.6/1
Dates of Creation: 1 Jul 1811
From William Morgan in Bradford to Mary Fletcher. Morgan is sending a few lines to inform her how he has been since leaving Shropshire. He has much to be thankful for. 'I have great cause to bless God for my leaving Wellington. The means which led to that circumstance though crooked led me I trust strait forward in the way I should go. I see more and more that men, both good and bad, are instruments in God's hands & that "He doth all things well"…'

He found that the Methodists at first were 'remarkably shy; but now we go on well. The different denominations in Bradford act towards each other in a manner highly consistent with those whose religion is - love.'

[John] Crosse left him soon after he arrived, intending to go to Bath and London for two months, but he went no further than Manchester where he stayed to assist Dr [Cornelius] Bayley who has been very unwell for a long time. Crosse has returned but is to leave again for three weeks to help Bayley.

Morgan finds that his health is very good. He likes the people here very much and the work load is not heavy. 'Religion is flourishing among us' - Morgan has heard some speak of Fletcher and there are some now in Bradford who were once her 'fellow pilgrims.'

Mr [Patrick] Bronte has got a living within seven miles of Bradford [Hartshead near Dewsbury, Yorkshire.] where he 'resides very comfortably and is very useful among his people. He desired me to present his Christian regards…He and I often meet…'

[John] Crosse sends his regards and was pleased to hear how she is doing. Crosse is very 'hearty' in all respects other than his near blindness. Morgan boards with him at the Vicarage and they enjoy much conversation together. 'He still retains all the

correctness of a gentleman with the graces of a Christian. He is universally respected by rich and poor. And I fear that they will not fully learn his value, but by his loss.'
Morgan would be pleased to receive a letter from Fletcher. He will also write to Mr Walters. [The Anglican curate at Madeley]
His regards should be passed to [Mary] Tooth.
Annotated by Fletcher - 'Letters to answer July 18 - [Anne] Tripp, [William] Morgan, [Eleanor] Dickinson'

1812

Memoirs of the Rev Joseph Entwisle (1812) by his son.
About John Fennell: "Mr. Fennel, the master, appears truly pious. Mr Fletcher, of Madeley, was his godfather, and often blessed him, and prayed for him. He partakes in some degree of Mr Fletcher's spirit. I felt much at parting with my dear boys: — grateful to God for a situation so favourable to learning and religion ; yet sorrowful at parting.
O my God, take them under thy special care. Bring them to an experimental knowledge of Christ, and early may they be devoted to thy service and glory. I leave my all in thy hands, O Lord." It was not long before a gracious answer to the above prayer was vouchsafed.
A few days after, my father received a most gratifying letter from Mr. Fennel, giving an account of a gracious work among the boys at Woodhouse Grove; twenty of whom were brought to a saving knowledge of God, among whom were his sons William and James. In the fullness of his heart he wrote to the Rev T Stanley, who, he knew, would rejoice with him in this gracious visitation. The following is an extract from the letter:

Liverpool, March, 24, 1812. A letter from Joseph Entwhistle:

My Dear Nephew,
I am almost too happy : the Lord deals so graciously and bountifully with me and mine, that 'the overwhelming power of divine grace,' nearly unnerves and unmans me. The accounts from Woodhouse-Grove are delightful. There is a glorious work at the school. The detailed account communicated to me by Mr Fennel and William, would fill sheets. I will give you a copy of Mr F's last letter.

'My Dear Sir, — Don't scold me for scribbling. I cannot help it. I am only doing for you what you would do for me on a change of circumstances. The wonder-working Lord is still going on with his blessed work here. I have had the pleasure of witnessing two or three blessed revivals of religion amongst the old and the young. I have seen one half and sometimes two-thirds of a congregation affected. I have heard children pray and speak of the work of God upon their hearts; but any thing to equal this, where there is scarcely one exception, I have never seen. The work in many of their souls is really deep. William, you know, is generally solid and steady; but James exhibits the most striking proofs of a

change; and a real, deep, rational work is on both their souls, as well as on twenty others. Yesterday was a glorious day among them. They spent the time from school-hours till supper in prayer to God in the school-room, where I had ordered them a fire. One of the servants put her ear to the key-hole of the door, and God smote her heart

Another of them stole unperceived into the school, and had not hearkened long before she began to cry for mercy. The third must needs see and hear for herself, and she also was deeply affected, and has set out, I hope, in good earnest. Thus, by the instrumentality of these dear boys, are three thoughtless girls brought to an acquaintance with themselves, and are determined for heaven. Surely the kind friends who have contributed to this institution, will rejoice to hear that they have been purchasing and furnishing a house for God; and that no sooner had they finished their work, than the Lord came down, took possession of the same, and began his. A blessed work it is. Lord, carry it on; and while we are preparing these children for this world, do thou prepare them for another. My dear Sir, by your advice and prayers, help me to nurse the lambs of this flock. They are brought forth, but they are in the wilderness, and the wolf of hell will be gaping. Yours, &c.

J. F.' [John Fennell]

1812 29 December: The triple wedding of Branwell brides
Jane Branwell Fennell to the Revd. William Morgan
Maria Branwell to the Revd. Patrick Brontë
Charlotte Branwell to Joseph Branwell, 1st cousin, in Madron Parish Church

1816 The death of the Revd. John Crosse, vicar of Bradford, friend and mentor to William Morgan and to John Fennell, friend to both the Revd. John Fletcher and his wife Mary Fletcher, the evangelist. This much venerated minister of the Gospel was blind in his later years of life but continued to perform his church duties and offices until a fortnight before his death. (See 1841 following for the record of his life.) **John Fennell** delivered his funeral oration at Bradford, having served as one of his perpetual curates for many years.

1817 in Penzance
Marriage of Keziah Green, mother of Chartist William Lovett, to William Carne of Newlyn. (A fisherman, later a miller and builder, and a son of Philip (Colensoe) Carne). A second cousin to Carnes.
17 Nov 1817 by Banns
　　William Carne, Sojourner
　　Keysiah Green [Mark]
　　Witnesses: George Green, Richard Pentreath

1818
Royal Cornwall Gazette Sat 25 July 1818: Announcement of 'the death of **Benjamin Carne Branwell, Esq.** of Penzance, one of the magistrates of that borough, after a lingering illness [probably consumption] leaving a wife and large family to deplore his loss.'

From John Fennel in Bradford to [Mary] Tooth in 1818

…They have just read the two- volume published life of Mary Fletcher - it is good and there was room for more. There need be no fear of printing anything that Mrs Fletcher wrote. If Tooth is still at Madeley, he trusts that she still watches over the precious souls which were so dear to 'our late mother' [Fletcher]. Madeley was highly exalted.

'When I look back from mine infancy upon the great kindness of God to Madeley, the incessant labours of much revered and truly valuable friend Mr [John] Fletcher and of those who have succeeded him, I cannot help saying to myself, surely Madeley should be [unreadable word] among the Churches'.

This area is increasingly wealthy, but he is afraid, not in holiness. The congregations are large - at the parish church they often have nearly three thousand. Fennel has been supplying Mr [William] Morgan's lack of service' for the last twelve months while he has been in London seeking to liquidate the debt on his church. Through the kindness of God, he has so far been able to reduce it from over £1,400 to less than £200 and has now returned to Bradford…

…Fennel and his family are well and he is busy, having recently performed three full services every Sunday, besides preaching on the week days in different parts of the parish, as well as speaking six hours every day at a large boarding school

1822 The Death of Anna (Cock) Carne, mother of Joseph Carne FRS

Wesleyan-Methodist Magazine, Vol 1 of 3rd series, Vol XLV from commencement, obituary printed in Chapter 4, And then came Wesley.

1827 Publication of The Canorum Conclave

Issued and passed around Penzance and West Cornwall, as from an anonymous source.
EXTRACT FROM THE MORRAB LIBRARY'S ARCHIVE CATALOGUE
Literature – MOR/LIT/7 [LIT pp. 1-2]; also available at the Courtney Library, RIC, Truro
HARVEY, John 1796-1844. Chemist and druggist, Penzance
The Canorum Conclave Copy, of satirical verses written in 1827-**28** "on the occasion of erecting an Organ in the Wesleyan Chapel, Penzance." "Canorum" is a derisive word of uncertain origin and meaning, formerly applied to Methodists. In the poem the leading Methodists of Penzance are lampooned as Cardinals in Conclave, under uncomplimentary names such as Sanctum, Barleycorn, Scratchback Calico etc., and an appendix gives their real identities and explains the allusions to them. The verses were written and circulated anonymously in two parts (the proposed third part was apparently never written), and there was intense speculation on the identity of the writer, which was not revealed until many years later. The verses have never been printed, and the only other copy known, in addition to the one owned by the Morrab Library, Penzance, is among the **Walter Eva** (Branwell kin) papers at Truro Museum. Unbound 22x14cm. 27pp. with Appendix.

1827

West Yorkshire, England, Births and Baptisms, 1813-1910: The birth of **William John Morgan**, son of the Revd. William Morgan, Incumbent of Christ Church, Bradford and his wife Jane Fennell Morgan. Baptized by the Revd. Joseph Cowell, Rector of Cross Stones, Todmorden, West Yorkshire. John Fennell, minister of the parish and grandfather of the child did not officiate at the baptism. Godparents are not listed. See Chapter 10: Travellers' Tales for detail.
Baptismal entry: No. 1175, Cross Stones in Halifax, 16 July, 1827.

Death of Jane Fennell Morgan, daughter of John Fennell and Jane Branwell Fennell and wife of the Rev William Morgan.
29 Sep, 1827— Age: 35
Bradford, Yorkshire, England
Buried at Cross Stone due to lack of burial ground at Christ Church, Bradford. The Fennells lived at Cross Stone in the Vicarage.
Presentation of her prayer-book: Presented to Patrick Bronte by William Morgan, BD in memory of his wife Jane Fennell Morgan on 2 October, at Haworth.

1829

The death of **Jane Branwell Fennell**, wife of the Revd. John Fennell, younger sister of Thomas Branwell, Merchant of Penzance, and Aunt of Maria and Elizabeth Branwell and their siblings.

Memento Mori.
Sacred to the memory of Jane, late wife of the Revd. John Fennell, Incumbent of Cross Stone, who departed this life May 26th, 1829 aged 76 years .
Farewell blest saint thou dear and faithful friend,
Beloved in life lamented in the end.
Instructed long in sharp afflictions school,
to make submission to the Lord,
thy rule to find when every hope of life was past.
Thy best, thy choicest comforts were thy last.
Thou now with him eternally shall dwell,
blest saint thou dear and faithful friend FAREWELL.

Also in memory of the Revd. John Fennell for 22 years the faithful, the diligent and the much respected incumbent of this chapelry whose sole aim was to testify to Christ as a Ransom for all. He died beloved and lamented Oct., 13th 1841 aged 79 years.

1833 Elizabeth Branwell made her will. It is printed here for 1842, when probate was granted.

1835

11/24 CASE for the Opinion of Edward Jacob of Lincolns Inn, London (with Answers)

re: **matters relating to the property of John Batten**
John Batten, late of Penzance, died 18/12/1834 intestate leaving a widow Mary Ann [Pidwell] and seven children (John, Benjamin, Henry, Ann, Josepha, Mary and Sarah).
John Batten married Mary Ann Pidwell in 1803.
12/5/1803 Marriage Settlement drawn up.
Batten lent **Benjamin Carne Branwell** (his brother-in-law) several thousand pounds: Branwell subsequently died. [1818, presumably this money was borrowed after his father and mother had died in 1808 and 1809 respectively]
18/10/1834 Mortgage by **Mary Branwell** of Penzance, widow, to [her brother] John Batten of Penzance. Children of Mary Branwell given as Benjamin, John, Mary Batten, Emma, Lydia and Amelia).
Mary Branwell agrees to lease John Batten the Golden Lion and the New Brewery and Malthouse at Causewayhead or North Street, Penzance and the reversionary interest in a shop and premises on the west adjoining the Inn (i.e. Francis Cock's premises, formerly part of the Branwell Grocery) also shops etc. on the east in the occupations of John Chester and Thomas R. H. Bodilly; a shop in Market Jew Street lately occupied by Bernard A Simmons and now leased to William Davy.
Also premises in Chapel Street occupied by John Lavin [now the iconic 'Egyptian House']; 4 messuages, dwelling-houses etc. at the Quay occupied by John Chapple and others; messuages and dwelling-houses and blacksmith's shop at Causewayhead occupied by Richard Rowe and others; fields at Lescudjack and "in the Coom" [Coombe] occupied by Elizabeth Bamfield, Richard Sampson, George Hosking junr and Joseph Thomas; two tenements near Gulval Churchtown (part of the manor of Lanisley) occupied by Ralph Corin and others, etc…
Queries: Nos 1-7 relate to the rights of the testator's heirs to the properties, interest arising therefrom and various shares in shipping and mining concerns.

1836

Deaths (via West Briton*) West Penwith Resources 1836*
'On Monday last, aged 82 years, **William Carne, Esq.** of Penzance. This venerable man, by the blessing of God upon his own industry and enterprise, rose from a condition of humble life to a station of high respectability, and has died trusted, honoured, and lamented. To great strength of character, he united an unusual measure of benevolence, and, to crown the whole, was remarkable for his fervid and consistent piety. The personal friend of the illustrious Wesley, the principal supporter of infant Wesleyanism in his own neighbourhood for sixty years in steady, active and beneficent communion with the society to which he thus originally attached himself, his name, throughout the world, is inseparably associated with Cornish Methodism. As he drew near his end, it was gratifying to remark the maturing of his spirit in humility, gentleness and love; and his last hours, undisturbed by doubts or apprehension, were joyous and even triumphant.'

1840

The Ladies' Magazine: or Entertaining Companion for the Fair Sex, Appropriated solely to their Use and Amusement [1770–1812]

> Charlotte Brontë read old numbers of the magazine as a young girl. See her letter to Hartley Coleridge, 10 Dec. 1840: [M. Smith (ed.) *Letters of Charlotte Brontë*, vol. I, p. 240.]

I am sorry Sir I did not exist forty or fifty years ago when the *Lady's Magazine* was flourishing like a green bay tree—In that case I make no doubt my aspirations after literary fame would have met with due encouragement … and I would have contested the palm with the Authors of Derwent Priory—of the *Abbey* and of *Ethelinda*.—You see Sir I have read the *Lady's Magazine* and know something of its contents—though I am not quite certain of the correctness of the titles I have quoted for it is long, very long since I perused the antiquated print in which those tales were given forth—I read them before I knew how to criticize or object—they were old books belonging to my mother or my Aunt; they had crossed the Sea, had suffered ship-wreck and were discoloured with brine—I read them as a treat on holiday afternoons or by stealth when I should have been minding my lessons—I shall never see anything which will interest me so much again—One black day my father burnt them because they contained foolish love-stories.

1841

The death of the Revd. John Fennell

His niece Elizabeth Branwell is known to have gone to Cross Stones to help with the nursing of her Uncle, and to assist his second wife with their young children.

1842

The death of Elizabeth Branwell (Aunt Branwell)
PUBLIC RECORD OFFICE: The National Archives
Catalogue Reference Prob 11/1971: Image reference 325
The Will of Elizabeth Branwell

Depending on the Father son and Holy Ghost for ?peace here and glory and bliss forever hereafter I leave this my last will and testament should I die at Haworth I request that my remains may be deposited in the Church in that place as near as is convenient to the remains of my dear sister I moreover will that all my just debts and funeral expenses be paid out of my property and that my funeral shall be conducted in a moderate and devout manner. My India workbox I leave to my niece Charlotte Brontë my workbox with a china top I leave to my niece Emily Jane Brontë together with my Ivory fan My Japan dressing box I leave to my nephew Patrick Branwell Brontë To my niece Anne Brontë I leave my watch with all that belongs to it as also my eye glass and its chain My rings silver spoons books clothes etc I leave to

be shared between my abovenamed three nieces CB EJB and AB allowing as their father shall think proper and I will that all the money that shall remain including twenty five pounds sterling being the part of the proceeds of the sale of my Goods which belong to me in consequence of my having advanced to my sister Kingston the sum of twenty five in lieu of her share of the proceeds of my Goos aforesaid and deposited in the Bank of Bolitho Sons and Co Esqs of Chyandour near Penzance after the aforesaid sums and articles shall have been paid and accounted shall be put into some safe Bank or lent on good landed security and there left to accumulate for the sole benefit of my four nieces CB EJB AB and Elizabeth Jane Kingston and this sum or sums and whatever other property I may have shall be equally divided between them when the youngest of them then living shall have arrived at the age of twenty one years and should any one or more of those my four nieces die her or their part or parts shall be equally divided amongst the survivors and if but one is left all shall go to that one and should they all die before the age of twenty one years all their parts shall be given to my niece Anne Kingston and should she die before that time specified I will that all that was to have been hers shall be equally divided between all the surviving children of my dear Brother and Sisters. I appoint my Brother in law the Revd. P Bronte now incumbent of Haworth Yorkshire the Revd. John Fennell now incumbent of Cross Stone near Halifax the Revd. Theodore Dury Rector of Keighley Yorkshire and Mr George Taylor of Hanbury in the chapelry of Haworth aforesaid my Executors Written by me Elizabeth Branwell and signed sealed and delivered on the 30th of April in the year of our Lord one thousand eight hundred and thirty three.
Witnesses: William Brown John Tootell William Brown Gent
Proved at London 12 December 1842 before the Judge
Note that this will was written nine years before the death of Elizabeth.

1848
An extract from the *Tenant of Wildfell Hall*, by Acton Bell (Anne Brontë): Gilbert Markham enters the sitting room of of Helen Graham at Wildfell Hall.

> Rachel admitted me into the Parlour and went to call her mistress....There was her desk left open....with a book laid upon it. Her limited but choice collection of books was almost as familiar to me as my own, but this volume I had not seen before....I took it up. It was **Sir Humphry Davy's** *Last Days of a Philosopher*. I closed the book but kept it in my hand and stood facing the door with my back to the fireplace calmly waiting her arrival.

1858
Cornish Telegraph 13 October 1858, p. 2/col. B 'Joseph Carne'

> At his residence, Chapel-street, in this town on Monday last, **Joseph Carne, Esq.,** banker, aged 77. Mr. Carne had for a great number of years occupied a prominent place in Penzance as a magistrate, a scientific

man, a member of the Town Council, and a Wesleyan. His services to the public while in the commission of the peace were most valuable, his knowledge of the law and of all local usages, his penetration, his firmness, and his integrity eminently qualifying him for the Bench. In earlier life Mr Carne was an ardent friend of Literature and Science. His fine library and mineralogical collection, as well as the interest he took in the Penzance Library and his valuable contributions to the first volumes of the *Transactions* of the Geological Society, prove this. Of late years, however, Mr Carne had very much withdrawn from public life. This scarcely lessened his influence, which though unseen, was widespread and powerful, and his advice was sought and acted on in the most important public movements, and in the most urgent and complicated private business. That influence extended to the Wesleyan body, of whose Missions he was a munificent patron. The result of his connection with Commerce is that he leaves immense wealth to his survivors – the result of long years of industry and thrift.

THE FUNERAL OF THE LATE JOSEPH CARNE, ESQ., took place on Saturday last, when the remains of that gentleman were deposited with those of his wife and children in the family vault at Phillack Church. The ceremony was strictly private. A bearer and six carriages left Penzance at eight in the morning. Mr. Carne's surviving children - four daughters - his son-in-law, Dr. Johnston, and his nephew, the Revd. Mr Carne were the chief mourners. His physician, Dr. Montgomery, his executors, T. S. Bolitho, Esq. of Penzance and G. Smith, Esq. L.L.D. of Trevu, Camborne, the Revd. Mr. Lord (Wesleyan Minister) the Mayor and some members of the Penzance Town Council, L. Vigurs, Esq., E. Bolitho, Esq., some of our tradesmen, J. Pool manager and cashier to Messrs. Sandys & Co., P. Marrack, Esq., manager of the Penzance Bank and the deceased gentleman's household formed the funeral cortege. The burial service was impressively read by the Revd. Mr. Haslam. The arrangements were entrusted to Mr. John Crocker, of Penzance.

1885 Extract from Introduction by Charles Campbell Ross,
In defence of genealogy: a collection of letters home by John Carne, author, 1813-1837

Though all enlightened people are agreed, more or less, as to the propriety of acquiring, at any rate, a general knowledge of the history of their own countries, very few are to be found who trouble themselves to acquire any knowledge whatever of the lives and actions of the members of their own families. There are not, of course, wanting [a lack of] those who are able to trace back their family names, link by link, through many centuries. But of those links themselves, they have little care, and perhaps little or no knowledge.

The fact that these connecting links were living men and women - that they were not only that, but that we, their descendants, are very bone of their bone, and flesh of their flesh – and that we, who are now living, are, in great part, but the sum of the sufferings, the sins and the heroisms of the generations that have gone before, - all this appears to be quite forgotten, or never even to have been at all realised, by most people. Genealogy is generally looked upon as a foolish fancy, unworthy [of] the notice [by the] wise man: and those who pursue its study are regarded either as vain persons, and endeavouring to aggrandise their own names; or, at best, as somewhat eccentric, but, on the whole, harmless drudges….

….We are all hurrying through time, ineffectually attempting to do this, or that, but with little leisure to do anything thoroughly….

Is it not then reasonable, that we should preserve, with almost sacred care, any family record of past scenes and years, by which we may gain some knowledge of what manner of men we derive our being from? Their faults and failings should especially impress us, so that we may learn to avoid, or at any rate walk with care over, those places where they fell.

Such is my apology, if any is needed, for the study of Genealogy – not a mere succession of dead names, but a panorama of living men and women.   JCR, June 1885

[Note: Extract from the 'Dedication' to Isobel Emily Ross by Joseph Carne Ross, June 1885 of the privately printed *John Carne, Letters 1813-1837* of which 100 copies were made.

Available online at https://archive.org/stream/cu31924104095504].

1898

The label at the Sedgwick Museum reads:

Joseph Carne (1782-1858) made a collection of Cornish minerals by visiting local copper mines. It was sold in 1899 as part of the liquidation of the assets of the Batten, Carne & Carne's Banking Company. William J Lewis (1847-1926) then Professor of Mineralogy at Cambridge successfully raised the £475 required to purchase the collection for the University. Some of these minerals are on display in the Whewell Gallery.

Reference: LEWS DDF 545

By Batten, Carne & Carne's Banking Company Limited
For Liquidators
CORNWALL
To Geologists, Mineralogists, Public Bodies, Trustees of Museums, Private Collectors of Minerals and others
Sale of a Large & Valuable Collection of Minerals
Mr George E Jenkin has received instructions from Mr H H Pezzack, the liquidators of Batten, Carne & Carne's Banking Company Ltd. To offer for sale by Public Auction in one lot, At the Liquidator's Office, Public Buildings, Penzance
On Tuesday the 13th day of December, 1898, at Three p.m
THE LARGE AND VALUABLE COLLECTION OF
≥*MINERALS*≤

comprising several thousand Specimens, at the Museum at Carne (now called Boskenwyn, one mile from Penzance), late the residence of Mr C C Ross

The above is recognised to be one of the finest private collections in England. It was founded by the late Joseph Carne, Esq. of Penzance, a gentleman well known as a Geologist and Mineralogist, and it has been added to by purchases of special minerals of Exceptional rarity by his Daughter, the late Miss Elizabeth C T Carne, and also by Mr C C Ross.

The Specimens (the larger portion of which being unique old Cornish Minerals from mines long since closed, now unobtainable, and unequalled in any public collections) are now in a Museum built for their reception and display. The smaller portion is fine illustrations of English and Foreign specimens. There is a descriptive catalogue of the collections which was carefully compiled by R H Solly, Esq. MA, FGS, Downing College, Cambridge and will be handed to the purchaser of the Minerals.

PART III

APPENDICES & INDEX

Detail from Plate 1 Penzance, by W Penaluna.

Appendix A

A Note on Names and Naming

As a general note to readers, there was no consistent stability in the spelling of forenames and surnames prior to approximately the mid-nineteenth century. By the time of Thomas Branwell's marriage to Anne Reynolds Carne in 1768, the Branwell spelling of their surname had stabilized. Nevertheless, other branches, having chosen other variants, still remained as recognized kin. Thomas's elder brother, Richard is most often found as 'Bramwell' as are his children. Mis-spellings occur not only in Cornish records, but in those of Yorkshire, and occasionally are not discovered by researchers, causing them to be overlooked and subsequently disregarded as part of the family register. Much of the mis-transcription is down to the illiteracy of the population, and what the recorder/scrivener hears when a name is given, because the registrants themselves did not know for certain how to spell their names.

Someone born as a Bremble or a Bromwell may be buried as a Bramwell or a Branwell and listed variously as Brannel, Brandwell or Bracewell. Ann in earliest documents may appear as Ane and Jane, sometimes as Anne and can be Hannah or Nan, and other variations on the same theme. Documents also vary and mis-transcriptions and mis-spellings are common.

Local historian and teacher Andrew Symons refers to Pool's study of *The Place-Names of West Penwith* where two examples of the element *bran*, meaning crow or raven, and as revealed in the name of the Celtic deity, 'Caer Bran' and 'Brane', both place-names found in Sancreed parish. Sancreed, Paul and St Buryan are all contiguous districts, in which the Carnes, the Branwells and the Battens are believed to have centred and worked the land. 'Bran-well could be a lost hybrid place name. It is curious that in a letter to William Smith Williams of 3 July 1849 that Charlotte Brontë writes, 'the raven, weary of surveying the deluge and without an ark to return to, would be my type'.[1]

In those families where sons are numerous and lives are long, the family researcher must resort to mentioning 'family' connections or kinship as opposed to connections with a specific individual, i.e. the 'banking Carnes' or the 'clock-making Carnes' or the 'mariner Carnes' though they are brothers, sisters or cousins, with the same chain of forenames. Indubitably, this is the reason that researchers dwell happily on one-name studies (patronymics) as much as possible and tend to go no further. Nevertheless, this habit drains the family of many relations (mainly the women and their offspring) which in 'real life' were critically important, and possibly of much greater influence on the children of the families than their male relations carrying the name. As with my own family the use of the terms 'big Vera' (my grandmother) and 'little Vera' (my mother) has meaning for contemporaries but loses its significance to outsiders and later research, especially when used through several generations. The quantity of William Carnes, John Carnes, John Battens and John Williams in the present study graphically illustrates this problem, at the same time as the familial use of a particular forename can also aid identification.

Social class terminology may also interfere with exact identification. The definition of 'Esq.' over time has changed considerably from men of higher social rank and is now generally used to apply to any professional or business man or male child. 'Gent.' implied, at the time, that the man considered himself an honourable, probably professional gentleman, and possibly of inherited wealth. Of these two distinctions Esq. took precedence and tended to indicate some relationship with the landowning aristocracy and royalty. But, all of these so-labelled people in common parlance, were considered 'gentry', or even 'small gentry' especially in Cornwall where social differences were often blurred. With frequency these social class appellations begin to appear in the 'parental' generations of Maria and Elizabeth of this study, suggesting an upper-class upbringing complete with a good training in housewifery skills and a solid education. From the correspondence of Maria with Patrick Brontë prior to their marriage, this assumption is confirmed in her case and probably for her sister Elizabeth as well, though we hear little about it.

The Madron Register, (1700-36)[2] states whether a person was 'of Madron' (which is a large farming district as well as a village of that name) or 'of Penzance' (which was at this date in the parish of Madron, but a constituted town on its own). It does not consistently state whether the baptism or burial took place in the parish church at Madron or in the Chapel of Ease, which was St Mary's Chapel, Penzance (in 'Our Lady' Street, now Chapel Street). All data refers to a precise location in 1720, and is maintained in subsequent registers. *All marriages before 1837 took place in Madron.* Charlotte Branwell's marriage to her cousin Joseph Branwell in 1812 to partner the Brontë and Morgan weddings in Yorkshire, took place in Madron on the day.

On 1 July 1837, **civil registration** was introduced. This had no effect on the keeping of baptism and burial registers but a standardized marriage register was adopted to satisfy both church and civil requirements. From this time the maiden surnames of women can be ascertained on marriage certificates. Much of the data found and studied for this project (Branwell/Carne & circle) was recorded prior to this date and therefore less standardized and less revealing.

R A Courtney (1909) states this problem thus:

> '…and I need hardly say this list seems to refer to sons alone, daughters being evidently of no account, as you would find if you examined the pages of Mr Millett's book,[3] where the women in the Marriage Register are as a rule entered with a Christian name only.'[4]

A peculiarity of the Madron Register, which is not helpful to family researchers, is that the father only is recognized on the baptismal record of a child. In other parishes in Cornwall the father's name is given in full and the mother's forename is also present. We can only speculate about the reason for this omission: The Vicar & his prejudices, or simply to ensure the social class of the family is realised.

The following are surnames (and variants) of the Carne group of families: Carne, Carn, Caine, Cairn(s), Cains and Carrens. Carne is an ancient name in both Cornwall and Wales, and the Carne family of West Cornwall had established connections and lines of descent in both 'countries'. It is of interest, for example, to find that one major figure in this study, William Carne, Merchant, Mining Agent, Ship-owner, and the reputed 'father of Cornish Methodism', married a Cornish 'cousin' of the Branwells (Anna Cock) from nearby Helston, prior to moving to Penzance where another cousin, Ann Carne Branwell with her husband Thomas, not only ran a grocery business in Market Jew Street, but also resided a few doors away on the same street, Chapel Street. Indeed, though it is not known for certain, the presence of the Branwells in Penzance, might have been a reason for the Carnes to settle there as well. This is, of course, a connection through marriages from differing directions, and there were several other religious and business connections in the same mix of relations.

The same tradition of naming eldest children with the same forenames as their parents and grandparents applies within the Carne family as with the Branwells and most other Cornish families. The custom enables more secure identification of family groups in areas where more branches reside – perhaps more distantly related. Though certainly not infallible, the repetition is indicative. The forenames chosen in all of these related families have both positive and negative features for research purposes. A positive is the reveal of the sequential nature employed in birth order of children and the parental connection in families with several branches living nearby. For example, the first son is frequently named for his father, or grandfather or both, and the first daughter is generally named for her mother and/or grandmother (forename) with the addition of the mother's maiden surname as a second name. This helps in the creation of family trees.

Negatively, this repetition of the same name throughout the family, by every childbearing male sibling of a nuclear family can also make identification difficult as many by the same name are alive simultaneously as discussed previously. Good examples of this are Richard Branwell, John Carne, John Batten and William Carne, of whom there are several of each name living concurrently. Sometimes these are identified as Sr. (senior) and Jr. (junior) in recordkeeping, or stated to be brothers, or father and son. Often there is no particular designation so one is left to guess by other associations if possible.

By looking at cohorts rather than individuals in a group of families who both knew and consorted with each other in various networks – social, political and religious – a firmer idea of the tenor of the times is raised to view. In earlier times the families remained and married largely where they were born. It is interesting to view how this changed over time, and the Cornish diaspora spread around the world.

As mentioned, in the Madron registers (local) used for checking dates of baptism, marriage and burial, the baptismal certificates often reveal a male name only; the marriage certificates do not list parents of the bride and groom unless they turn up as witnesses at the wedding. The burial registration reveals little but a name (which may be one of many of the same name). Hence, there can be a huge burden of detective work and speculation to be done on each individual, not all of which could be undertaken for this study, nor would be especially relevant. The exact blood relation of one member of the circle to another, is only of marginal interest, and can be used only as an indicator of possible closer connection and knowledge, though not confirmation of same. We are all familiar with the concept of 'broken' family ties and also plain ignorance and disinterest in family connections. The Cornish, however, are especially known for their clannish interests, and the Morrab Private Library holds a large number of genealogical pamphlets and histories.

Another habit, perhaps a peculiarity, but one which the Branwells observed with constancy, was to give a dead child's name to a subsequent newborn. This was considered to be honourable remembrance, and is common in Cornish naming patterns. To give the same name to a second child was commemorative, but if that child also died, the name would not be given a third time, as this would be considered 'bad luck'.

Relationships

First cousins share a grandparent, second cousins share a great-grandparent, third cousins share a great-great-grandparent, and so on. Therefore the degree of cousinhood ("first," "second," etc.) denotes the number of generations between two cousins and their nearest common ancestor.

The term "removed" refers to the number of generations separating the cousins themselves. So your first cousin once removed is the child (or parent) of your first cousin, i.e. one generation forward or backward. Your second cousin once removed is the child (or parent) of your second cousin. And your first cousin twice removed is the grandchild (or grandparent) of your first cousin.

As will be realized, in day to day contact with cousins and other relatives in the past as in the present, it is not always very important whether a distinction is made between kin – some will be friends and others will not. Some will be devoted and others disaffected or described as 'black sheep'. Though close connection is supposed when families grow up under the same roof, the families of those relatives that move away from the family home for any reason, inevitably risk lack of connection and knowledge of one another in any great detail.

A short list enumerating the incidence of the Brontë children's names within the Cornish-based relationship circle.

Maria Brontë(1814-1825) Named for her mother, Maria Branwell and her great-grandmother, Maria Bennetts. In the maternal family, there is also sometime connections to the ship/sloop *'Maria of Penzance'* belonging to relations (the Bennetts) of their great-grandmother.

Elizabeth Brontë (1818-1825) Named for her aunt, Elizabeth Branwell ('Aunt Branwell'), who had looked after Maria from infancy, and who had her own Aunt Elizabeth Branwell Keam, her father's sister, and many Elizabeths/Elizas in the family trees and branches. Cousin Joseph Carne's daughter born the previous year (1817) in Penzance, was Elizabeth Catherine Thomas Carne, who would also become a prolific writer (of non-fiction mineralogy papers and socio-religious philosophy).

Charlotte Brontë (1816-1855) Namesake for her mother's younger sister, Charlotte Branwell, who married her first cousin, Joseph Branwell in Penzance on the same day, at the same hour as Maria married Patrick, and her cousin Elizabeth Jane Fennell married the Revd. William Morgan, at Guiseley. **Charlotte** was also the name of James Carne's wife and the mother of Catherine and Edward Carne who lodged with the Joseph Carne family in Chapel Street, Penzance. (Census 1841) following the death of their parents.

Patrick Branwell Brontë (1817-1848) Given the family name as a middle name, and called 'Branwell' to distinguish between father and son.

Emily Jane Brontë (1818-1848) Local candidates for this name of Emily are the following:

Emily, Lady Delamont, Irish noblewoman who died in Penzance on 8 April 1818, a friend of the family. Emily was subsequently born on the 30th July, and it could be that Maria and Patrick were attracted to the name through letters (speculation only). She is buried in St Mary's Churchyard behind the Branwell home on Chapel Street, Penzance, her remains lodged in the family tomb of Sir Rose Price.

Emily Stackhouse (1811-1870), one of the illustrators of the works of Cornish naturalist Charles Alexander Johns (1811-1874), kin to the Branwells, was a prominent member of this family of Trehane, Probus, Cornwall, and of the RCPS of Falmouth begun by the Fox family.

Emily Johns (1814-1890) was the sister of Charles Alexander Johns who published poetry and married Henry Carrington, the son of the 'Poet of Dartmoor', Noel Carrington. Henry Carrington was the publisher and printing company owner of the *Bath Chronicle*.

The name of **Jane** is possibly in honour of Maria's eldest surviving sister, Mrs Jane Kingston, at home in Penzance since her return from America in 1809. She herself was named after Thomas's sister **Jane** who married John Fennell: these two produced **Jane** Branwell Fennell, the Brontë's cousin. Jane is represented in every generation of the family since Jane Tremearne, together with a great grandmother in the Carne line, being **Jane** Boase, and virtually may be seen as the iconic forename of the family. It is no surprise to find **Jane** as the forename of Charlotte's fictional heroine.

Anne Bronte (1820-1849) Namesake for Maria's mother, Ann(e) Carne (Branwell), and Maria's grandmother Ann Reynolds who married John (Calenso) Carne as well as Maria's own eldest sister Anne, who died soon after reaching her majority. Cousin Anne Batten and her daughter Anne Batten Cristall, the poet and friend of Mary Wollstonecraft, were additional contemporaries. William Carne's wife, Anna Cock, was also a close relation and honoured friend of the Branwell family.

Names of some interest

There are a number of names of both villages and people that pop up in Brontë literature, and have potential relevance to stories and lives lived in Cornwall.

Acton Castle: Acton Castle was constructed for the use of Admiral John Stackhouse as a laboratory for his studies of seaweed. It sits on the shores of Mount's Bay in the village of Perranuthnoe, and was given the surname of his wife Susanna's family (of London).

Ellis: The surname of Joseph Batten's wife, Elizabeth, and the second name of their son, the Revd. Samuel Ellis Batten (1792-1830), who was a cousin and friend from the Branwell childhood of Maria and Charlotte. After degree from Cambridge, he became the Headmaster of one of the Harrow School houses. He married Caroline Venn, and though not a scholar of note, attracted many pupils to Harrow-on-the-Hill.

Helstone: the town of Helston with which the Carnes had strong links, and from which Anna Cock, the wife of William Carne, came before settling with her husband in Penzance and bringing up her family there and in nearby Truro. There is also another village in Cornwall named Helstone.

Zenobia: From Latin *Zenobia*, from Ancient Greek *Ζηνοβία* (Zēnobía), name of a third century Queen of Palmyra. Ostensibly from *Ζήνων* (Zénōn), an ancient derivative of *Ζεύς* (Zeús), but also suggested to be a rendering of the Arabic زينب (*Zaynab*). It was first recorded as an English given name in Cornwall in 1586. Put the name Zenobia in to COPC on-line and you will be surprised at the large number of these ladies.

ENDNOTES

1 M. Smith (ed.) *The Letters of Charlotte Brontë*, vol. II, p. 227.
2 *Madron Register*, CRO, p. 133/1/3.
3 The first book of the *Madron Registers* was published by G. B. Millett in 1887 and is located at CRO.
4 R A Courtney (1909) *"A Passel of Ould Traade"* Being Sundry Papers read at meetings of the Penzance Natural History and Antiquarian Society, p. 22.

Appendix B

Bibliographies and further suggested reading

In the first instance, an invitation by the Cornwall County Women's Institute to hold a study day about the Brontë ties with Cornwall, led me to an edited volume of essays entitled *Reading the Family Dance, Family Systems Therapy and Literary Study* in which one chapter focused on 'The Enigmatic Jane Eyre'. The papers in this collection applied 'family systems theories' to the ways we look at literature. The basic argument is that we do not truly comprehend an individual person or character in a novel, unless we understand the author's family 'system', including the legacies of previous generations.

Where there was breakdown, illness and unhappiness, the keys to understanding lie in the secrets, blame and denial patterns built into that family system in the environment in which it [the family] lives. The article also shows how the individual and the family begin to break the habits and repetition of those problems by developing openness, intimacy, and emotional expressiveness – and in the case of the Brontë sisters through their literary expressions and their sometime explosiveness. The editors conclude their study with a call for more research "relating family systems ... to literary works from every time and culture". We might also say in response to such a strong challenge, that the potential for finding and understanding the family systems – in the present or the past – is highly unlikely, though inviting of much speculation.

Secondly, another textbook, raising relevant issues in the 'poetics of everyday life', spurred me on to apply to the Brontë Society for the Daphne Carrick scholarship in 2012. This book by William Lowell Randall opens many new fields for exploration of the Brontë novels, though none of the writers are mentioned as specific subjects. This book in turn treats of the subjects of aesthetics and creativity, life and literature, and the poetics of learning. He writes of 'the biographical imperative' in the production of literary work, which is the ground upon which social and personal life is led, and short and long term memories are processed and 're-storied'. Charlotte, Emily and Anne came to life as I read.

The third spur to this research, emerged from conference papers presented in 2009 at Telford (near Ironbridge and Madeley on the Severn) exploring the 18th and 19th century subjects of religion, gender and industry in that locale, and therefore in that specific context. This was inspirational to the formulation of the current review of the same period in West Cornwall, as it treats of the unavoidable kinds of 'luggage' of the mind which all of us, researchers, travellers and emigrants carry.

Cornwall and English Literature
The starting point for most studies of Cornish people:
The two standard Cornish bibliographies/biographical texts

a) *Bibliotheca Cornubiensis* 1874 Vol. 1 'A-O' and 1878 Vol. 2 'P-Z', with Vol. 3, a supplement issued in 1882 with updates and corrections to the original two volumes. The authors were George Clement Boase and William Prideaux Courtney. This bibliography purports to list in catalogue format 'The Writings, both Manuscript and printed of Cornishmen, and of works relating to the County of Cornwall, Biographical Memoranda and Copious Literary References.' This great work of reference is now on-line, digitized by the Google Corporation: though an outstanding collation of facts, genealogical connections should not be relied on, because there are too many inaccuracies or unknowns. Branwell-related family names can be followed – Batten, Boase, Carne, Cristall, Fennell, John, Johns, Vivian and Williams and more. The focus of this collection is 'literary Cornwall' rather than genealogy, much of which inevitably cannot be verified with additional documentation, and more often than not is patchy and inaccurate. It is, nevertheless, an amazing collection of data.

b) *Collectanea Cornubiensia* 1890, brought together by the indefatigable George Clement Boase (as above) containing a miscellany of civic documents and biographical family notes which are of some help to genealogists by indicating close connections between different branches of families sharing the same surnames. As of March 2014 this book has also been digitized. The same caveat applies however, though these massive volumes were written and collated without the modern technology of search engines. The Branwells feature as a merchant family in the biographical notes of this volume, but the generations are mixed together erroneously, and details are not accurate for the individuals named. Treat with caution. Though not complete in its coverage, all dates of birth, marriage and death should be confirmed with Cornwall On-line Parish Clerks (COPC) records, an excellent and carefully attended resource.

Archives and Institutional repositories consulted in Cornwall:
Cornwall Records Office, Truro
Cornish Studies Library, Redruth, Cornwall
Hypatia Trust Library (established 1996) Elizabeth Treffry Cornish Collection (now at Morrab Library from 2018).
Morrab Library, Penzance, Cornwall (established 1818), including Newspaper

Collections of *Cornishman* and *West Briton*, as referenced in footnotes.
Royal Geological Society of Cornwall (est 1814) Transactions
Royal Institution of Cornwall (established 1818) Courtney Library: Proceedings, journals and family papers, Methodist archives (CMHA Stock list)

Institutional resources in UK employed:
All Saints Parish Church, Wellington, Shropshire (Visited 2013 guided by Dr John Lenton and staff of the parish offices)
Barclays Group Archives, Wythenshaw, Manchester (Visited to view Batten, Carne & Carne bank records)
British Library (On-line registers)
Brontë Parsonage Museum & Brontë Society, Haworth, Yorkshire
Cartwright Museum & Gallery, Bradford, Yorkshire
Chapel Street Methodist Church
Charterhouse School Archives, Sussex (Carne records for London institution)
Holy Trinity Parish Church, Cambridge, Cambridgeshire (H Martyn & C Simeon)
London Library
Oxford Brookes University: Methodist Centre
Sedgwick Museum of Earth Sciences, Cambridge University, Cambridgeshire
Shropshire Records Office, Shrewsbury, Shropshire
Telford Public Library, Wellington, Shropshire
University of Manchester, Methodist Archives & Study Centre, Fletcher-Tooth Archive
Woodhouse Grove School & Archives, Apperley Bridge, Bradford, Yorkshire (Visited 2016)

Web resources
Acorn Archive of Penzance history, and Hearts of Oak (maritime site): R. Forward
Ancestry.com community
British Newspaper Archive [Online member] British Library [BL] *Sherborne Mercury*
Clergy Database, Church of England (CCED) www.theclergydatabase.org.uk
Cornwall On-line Parish Clerks (COPC): transcribed registers from all parishes of the county. Births, marriages, deaths and other legal records (tax, apprenticeships, some Wills and Probate information. This is an invaluable free resource which is kept up to date and corrected at all times. Simple and easy to use.)
Dictionary of National Biography (DNB)
Discovering Shropshire's History (Shropshire Records Office)
IGI – International Genealogical Index (family searches)
Nostalgic Cornwall on-line community
West Penwith Resources – Universal British Directory 1791
Wikipedia

Primary sources:
'An Account of the Families of Boase or Bowes, at Paul and Madron in Cornwall;

and of other families connected with them by marriage' by C.W., G.C., and F. Boase, Privately printed (75 copies only), Exeter: William Pollard, 1876. (now on-line)

Letters and Reminiscences of Emily Bolitho (1817-1886) Penzance: Beare & Son [containing transcriptions of two lengthy letters from her close friend Elizabeth Carne]

Branwell family of Penzance 1730-1940: deeds and family papers, CRO, Ref: AD 1803

'The Canorum Conclave' the unpublished comic poem of J Harvey (issued anonymously in 1824), handwritten. Transcribed and annotated by Susan Hoyle, St. Buryan, 2010 with identification of persons lampooned in Methodist circles, Penzance. An explanation of content and critique is published by the Penwith History Group (S. Hoyle) in its 2005 edition, *Treasures of the Morrab, A Penzance Library That Has More Than Books*, pp. 65-72.

Carne Ross, Joseph (1885) *John Carne, Letters 1813-1837*, Privately printed, Ltd. edition No 100 of 100 copies printed. Online at https://archive.org/stream/cu31924104095504 inclusive one handwritten letter from Joseph Carne Ross to his publishers 1886.

'Class list, The Methodist Society in Penzance' (Methodist Archives, RIC) 1 July 1767.

Cornish Methodist History Archive (CMHA): Library Stock List (C. Appleby, Hon. Librarian), Courtney Library, Royal Institution of Cornwall (RIC) Handlists, ephemera, diaries and preaching schedules, journals and biographies.

Dunkin: (Marion Smith) Privately published for family: 'Our Dunkin Ancestry', concerning the history of the famous sometime smuggling family. Communicated to author, 2019.

Eva Collection, Handwritten and typed transcriptions of original materials gathered by the Eva family (relations of the Branwell family) about personalities and businesses located in Penzance), RIC deposit, as above.

Journal/Register of the Ladies' Book Club of Penzance (est 1770), Penzance, Cornwall, Morrab Library, Penzance, information transcribed by Margaret Seccombe Brown.

Grylls, Richard G, *Branwell & Bramble, a brief history of a West Cornwall Clan*, (Tring, Herts: The author/researcher, 2006).

Hardie, Melissa (2000) *Penzance: The town and around*, Penzance: Penzance Town Council. Presented to all school pupils in the Penzance Education District for the new millennium. Illustrated by Jack Trowbridge and Alison Englefield. [Archive box: drafts, plates and original research material]

Horner, John *Even in this Place, 19th-century Nonconformists & Life in the Borough of Penzance*, (Newmill, Penzance: Patten Press & Jamieson Library 2010), illustrated. Publisher file: original manuscripts, edited Mss., related images. Hypatia Trust publications archive.

Hosking, James - Farmer (1813) *To America and Back with James Hosking 1811* Reprinted with additions of letters and historical background by James Martin Hosking 1970. Cornwall: Privately printed, St. Buryan.

'Journal of George John' 1779-1833, CRO AD72/12

John, George (fl 1793-1834) Attorney and Mayor, Penzance GB/NNAF/D95443 Former ISAAR ref: GB/NNAF/D1760) 1793-1834: journal includes details of family and town news, gardening and farming.

'Ministers Appointed to the Penzance Circuit (Methodist) from its formation in 1791' Shaw Collection, Royal Institution of Cornwall, Courtney Library, typescript of 2 pp. Covering the period from 1791-1867.

Minutes of the Governors, Wesleyan School at Woodhouse Grove, Rawdon, Bradford, Yorkshire in 6 vols. from 1812; vol. 1 consulted in transcription in school's archive. [Originals not accessible].

Oldham (Lilian) Archive, Morrab Library, Penzance, Cornwall.

Oldham, Lilian (nd) 'The Kingston Connection' unpublished manuscript (handwritten), Branwell Archive box 193, Morrab Library, Penzance, Cornwall.

Pool, P.A.S. 'The Branwell Connection', An address to the Brontë Society at the Union Hotel, Penzance, 21 May 1983, unpublished manuscript available at Morrab Library.

-------------(1990) 'The Branwells of Penzance' Lecture for Friends of Penlee House at Penzance Guildhall, 6 November 1989.

Rogers, Elizabeth, Unpublished family history papers: `Cornish Connections and the Battens of Penzance', based on research over many years. Communicated to the author, 2015-19.

Tremenheere, Seymour Greig *The Tremenheeres*, original research on family history, presented to the Morrab Library by the author, 1925, notes, illustrations. Bound and titled volume.

Directories and guides

Alexander, Christine and Smith, Margaret *The Oxford Companion to the Brontës*, (Oxford: Oxford University Press, 2006), paperback edition, with corrections.

Robert Barnard and Louise Barnard *A Brontë Encyclopaedia* (Malden, MA, Oxford, Carlton, Victoria, Australia: Blackwell Publishing, 2007).

Bird, Eric & Modlock, Lilian, *Writers on the South-West Coast, A Literary Journey from Dorset via Land's End to the Bristol Channel* (Wiltshire: Ex Libris Press, 1994).

Burke, Sir Bernard, *A Genealogical and Heraldic Dictionary of the Landed Gentry* (London: Harrison, Pall Mall, 1871) Fifth edition, vol. 1, p. 209 (Carne).

Concise Dictionary of British Literary Biography vol. 4 (of 8 vols.) 'Victorian Writers, 1832-1890' Detroit & London: Gale Research Inc.

Dawes, Margaret & Selwyn, Nesta, *Women who made money, Women Partners in British*

Private Banks 1752-1906, (North America & International: Trafford Publishers, 2010).

Domesday Book, A survey of the Counties of England, Compiled by direction of King William I, (1086) Winchester. Series ed: John Morris, No 10, Caroline and Frank Thorn (Eds.) from a draft translation prepared by Oliver Padel (Chichester: Phillimore, 1979).

Pigot's National Trade Directory, (1823, 1844).

Townsend, Sheila & Stephen, Transcribers (2000) *Nonconformist Registers for Cornwall held at the Public Records Office* (UK) (Cornwall: Shelkay, 2000) vols. 1-6.

The Universal Directory of Great Britain 1791 www.archivecdbooks.org, (Five vols.: Penzance, Cornwall, 1791 scan), vol. 4.

Wright, W. H. K. Ed. *West-Country Poets, Their Lives and Their Works* (London: Elliot Stock, 1896) Illus.

Contemporaneous history sources:

Carew, Richard *The Survey of Cornwall*, Written by Richard Carew of Antonie, Esq., introduced by Paul White. Redruth: Tamar Books, (2000 re-issue of 1602 text).

Carter, Captain Harry (1749-1809) *The Autobiography of A Cornish Smuggler*, with an introduction and notes by John B. Cornish, (London: Gibbings & Co, and Truro, Penzance & Falmouth: J. Pollard, 1900).

Cornwall Illustrated in a Series of Views, from original drawings by Thomas Allom (London: Fisher, Son & Co., 1831).

Courtney, Louise *Half a Century of Penzance 1825-1875*, (Penzance: Beare & Son, 1878; reprinted 1999 by Oakmagic Publications, Penzance).

Davy, Humphry *Four Hitherto Unpublished Geological Lectures Given by Sir Humphry Davy in 1805** (prior to Knighthood in 1812) with Introduction and Notes by Alexander M Ospovat. Reprint from *Transactions of the Royal Geological Society of Cornwall* (RGSC) Vol XXI, Pt. 1

Davy, John (1836), *Memoirs of the Life of Sir Humphry Davy* (accessed with nine volumes of the *Collected Works of Humphry Davy*, at the Morrab Library, Penzance. (London: Smith, Elder, & Co., 1839).

Dawson, James *The Autobiography of Mr James Dawson* Dedication: "Take my life and all"... I therefore venture, with the utmost deference, to dedicate my life to The Ladies of Cornwall, Actor and theatrical manager, recalling his theatrical tours through Cornwall, and playing at Georgian period stable theatre in Penzance. (Truro: J. R. Netherton, 1865).

Fox, Caroline of Penjerrick, Cornwall, *Memories of Old Friends, being extracts from the journals and letters of Caroline Fox from 1835-1871*, Horace N Pym, Editor, in 2 vols, 'To which are added fourteen original letters from J. S. Mill never before published.' (London, Smith, Elder, & Co., 15 Waterloo Place, 1882)

Samuel Kelly: *An Eighteenth Century Seaman* (autobiography) 'whose days have been few and evil, to which is added remarks etc. on places he visited during his pilgrimage in this wilderness', edited by Crosbie Garstin with Introduction (London: Jonathan Cape, 1925) Illustrated.

Davies Gilbert *Some ancient Christmas Carols, with the Tunes to which they were formerly sung in the West of England*, (London: J Nichols and Son, 1823)

Gilbert, Davies G. *The Parochial History of Cornwall* founded on the manuscript histories of Mr. Hals and Mr. Tonkin, with additions and various appendices. (London: J. B. Nichols and Son, 1838) 4 vols.

Gray, Todd *Cornwall: The Travellers' Tales*,(Exeter: Mint Press, 2000); includes 20 personal accounts of outside travellers to the area, from 16th to 20th centuries, incl an anonymous account of the funeral procession of William Carne (1754-1836) from Chapel Street, Penzance to the family tomb at Gulval.

Lovett, William *Life and Struggles of William Lovett*, preface by R H Tawney, London: MacGibbon & Kee. (lst 1876, Fitzroy Edition 1967, with new preface & additions) Original text of autobiography plus copies of Petition (1837), *The People's Charter* (1842) and the *National Petition*, pp. 331-4.

Martyn, The Revd. Henry B.D., Journals and Letters of edited by the Revd. S. Wilberforce, MA in Two Volumes, (London: R. B. Seeley and W Burnside, 1837) vol. 1 pp.143-63.

Polwhele, Richard (1803-1808) *The History of Cornwall*, introduced at reprint by A. L. Rowse, 7 vols. Repr. in 3 large vols.(Dorking: Kohler and Coombes Ltd. 1978).

Polwhele, Richard *Biographical Sketches in Cornwall*, 3 vols. (Truro: J. B. Nichols & Son, Longman & Co. 1831), vol. 1 'The Persons Eminent'.

Todd, A. C. *Beyond the Blaze, A Biography of Davies Gilbert,* (Truro: D Bradford Barton Ltd., 1967)

Wallis, John *The Cornwall Register* (Bodmin: Liddell & Son, 1847).

Wright, W. H. K. Editor, *West-Country Poets, Their Lives and Their Works*, (London: Elliot Stock, 1896).

Cornwall

Boase, G. C. *Reminiscences of Penzance*, 1883-84, edited by P. A. S. Pool, MA, FSA.

Brown, H. Miles *Cornish Clocks and Clockmakers,* 2nd ed of 1961 lst updated. (Newton Abbot: David & Charles, 1970).

Carter, David E. *Lydia Gwennap, A Cornish masterpiece uncovered…* (www.publishnation. co.uk: 2013).

Chesher, V. M. & F. J. *The Cornishman's House, An Introduction to Traditional Domestic Architecture in Cornwall* (Truro: Bradford Barton, 1968).

Courtney, M. A. *Cornish Feasts and Folk-Lore* Revised and reprinted from the Folk-Lore Society Journals, 1886-87, (Penzance: Beare and Son, 1890).

Courtney, R. A. *"A Passel of Ould Traade" being Sundry Papers read at Meetings of the Penzance Natural History and Antiquarian Society* (Penzance: Beare and Son, 1909), See

'Some Remarks on Mr G B Millett's Madron Registers', pp. 17-26.

Doe, Helen *Enterprising Women and Shipping in the Nineteenth Century,* (Woodbridge, Suffolk: Boydell Press, 2009).

Dundrow, Michael & Margaret, with the Revd. Tim Hawkins & Ann Jenkin, *Parish Church of St. Maddern, Madron.* (Madron History Project, 2007).

Eaton, Barbara *Letters to Lydia: 'beloved Persis',* (the story of Henry Martyn and his love for Lydia Grenfell), (Penzance: Hypatia Publications, 2005); Part 3: Fact turns to fiction, 'Reader, I married him' pp. 337-344.

Fletcher, J. R. and Dom John Stephan (Ed.) *Short History of St Michael's Mount Cornwall* (Marazion: St. Michael's Mount 1951).

Flynn, J. S. *Cornwall Forty Years After* (London: Truslove and Hanson Ltd. 1917), [This copy a presentation copy *This wonderfully sympathetic book is for The Lord Bishop of Truro from a Cornish Bradfordian. J Hambley Rowe M.B.C.M. F.S.G.*] Chapter XII: 'The Women of Cornwall'.

Green, Gillian 'The Boyhood of Humphry Davy in Penzance', *In and around Penzance during Napoleonic Times* (Penzance: Penwith Local History Group, c2000).

Halliday, F. E. *A History of Cornwall* (London: Gerald Duckworth & Co. Ltd. 1959), 249-80.

Halliwell-Phillipps, J. O. *Rambles in Western Cornwall by the Footsteps of the Giants,* with notes on the Celtic remains of the Land's End District and the Islands of Scilly, (General Books LLC, Memphis, TN, USA. 1861 reprinted 2012).

Hardie-Budden, Melissa 'Elizabeth Catherine Thomas Carne, A 19th century Hypatia and her circle', (*Transactions of the Royal Geological Society of Cornwall,* Vol. XXIII, Pt 1, April, 2014), pp. 16-39.

Hunt, Robert, FRS *Popular Romances of the West of England, or the Drolls, traditions & superstitions of Old Cornwall,* Illus. by G. Cruikshank, (London: Chatto & Windus, New Impr. 1923, 3rd edition after 1st, 1881).

Jenkin, A K Hamilton

The Cornish Miner and Cornish Seafarers (London: J M Dent & Sons, 1932).

Cornwall and the Cornish (London: J M Dent & Sons, 1933).

Cornish Homes and Customs (London: J M Dent & Sons, 1934).

Mines and Miners of Cornwall: 5. Hayle, Gwinear & Gwithian (Bracknell, Berkshire: Forge Books 1980).

Kent, Alan M. *The Literature of Cornwall, Continuity, Identity, Difference 1000-2000* (Bristol: Redcliffe Press, 2000).

Lamont-Brown, Raymond *Humphry Davy: Life Beyond the Lamp* (Gloucestershire: Sutton Publishing, 2004), Chap. 1-2.

Laws, Peter `Review of the Architecture of Penzance', Chap. VI pp. 182-202 [in] Pool, *A History of the Town and Borough of Penzance,* (The Corporation of Penzance, 1974).

---------------(1978) *The Industries of Penzance* Trevithick Society, 48 pp. illustrated.

Lyson's Cornwall (London: T Cadell, Strand, and G. and A. Greenland, Poultry, 1814) Four vols. Illustrated.

MacKenzie, Charlotte 'Merchants and smugglers in eighteenth-century Penzance: the brothers John and James Dunkin (Falmouth: TROZE, The Online Journal of the National Maritime Museum, Cornwall, Vol. 7, No. 2, December 2016).

_____ *Merchants and Smugglers in Eighteenth Century Cornwall* (Truro: Cornwall History, 2019).

Milton, Giles *White Gold, The Extraordinary Story of Thomas Pellow and North Africa's One Million European Slaves*, (London: John Murray, 2015 reprint of 2004 orig).

Pascoe, W H *CCC The History of the Cornish Copper Company* (Redruth: Dyllansow Truran, 1981).

Pawlyn, Tony *The Falmouth Packets 1689-1851* (Truro: Truran, 2003).

Pellow, Thomas and Dr Robert Brown, Ed. with introduction and notes (1890 photo reprint from original) the Adventures of *Thomas Pellow, of Penryn, Mariner, Three and Twenty Years in Captivity Among the Moors*, (Illustrated) London: T Fisher Unwin.

Penwith Local History Group (nd, c2000) *In and around Penzance during Napoleonic Times*, June Palmer, Ed., Penzance: Morrab Library. Illustrated.

-------(2014) *Eighteenth Century Life in West Cornwall*, Jenny Dearlove, Ed., Morrab Library. Illustrated.

Pool, P. A. S. with Peter Laws, *The History of the Town and Borough of Penzance* Penzance: The Corporation, 1974).

------------- *William Borlase*, (Truro: Royal Institution of Cornwall, 1986).

Procter, Ida 'The Brontës: Grand Daughters of Cornwall' *The Cornish Review*, 1973, No. 23, Spring issue, pp. 17-23.

Rees, Edgar A. *Old Penzance* (Penzance: The Author, 1956). Illustrated.

Russell, Sir Arthur, Bart. 'The Wherry mine, Penzance, its history and its mineral productions (With Plates XXVI-XXVIII), *The Mineralogical Magazine and Journal of the Mineralogical Society*, No. 205, Vol. XXVIII, June, 1949 (Read March 9, 1939), pp. 517-533.

Smelt, Maurice *101 Cornish Lives* (Penzance: Alison Hodge 2006).

Stoate, T. L. *The Cornwall Protestation Returns of 1641.* (Published by the author, 1974).

Treneer, Anne *The Mercurial Chemist, A Life of Sir Humphry Davy*, (London: Methuen, 1963).

Trevithick, Francis *Life of Richard Trevithick, with an account of his inventions*, (London/New York: Trevithick Society, 1872) two vols.

Val Baker, Denys *A View from Land's End, Writers against a Cornish background* (London: William Kimber, 1982) pp. 62-4.

Vale, Edmund *The Harveys of Hayle, Engine-Builders, Shipwrights and Merchants of Cornwall*

(Cornwall: Trevithick Society 1966, 2009)

Vivian, Lt. Col. J. L. Vivian *The Visitations of Cornwall*, comprising The Heralds' Visitations of 1530, 1573 and 1620, with additions by J.L.V., (Exeter: William Pollard & Co, 1887).

Walker, Dawn, Ed. *Homes & Households in West Cornwall 1550-1950*, (Penwith Local History Group. Cornwall: Morrab Library, 2010).

Whetter, Dr. James *Cornish People in the 18th Century* (Gorran: Lyfrow Trelyspen, The Roseland Institute, 2000).

Williams, Derek R., *A Strange and Unquenchable Race, Cornwall and the Cornish in quotations*, (Truro: Truran, 2007)

Brontëana

Alexander, Christine and Sellars, Jane *The Art of the Brontës* Cambridge: CUP, 1995.

Babcock, Rosemary D 'The Enigmatic Jane Eyre: A Differentiation Story without Family in Charlotte Bronte's *Jane Eyre*'. Knapp & Womack: *Reading the Family Dance* (Newark: University of Delaware Press, 2003).

Barker, Juliet *The Brontës*, (London: Phoenix Giant (paperback), 1997 impr. of 1994 copyright).

Baumber, Michael 'William Grimshaw, Patrick Brontë and the Evangelical Revival' [in] *History Today* Nov, 1992, 25-31 illustrated.

Braddon, Mary Elizabeth. 'At the Shrine of Jane Eyre'. *Pall Mall Gazette*, vol. XXXVII, 1906, 174-176, reprinted by J Carnell at the Sensation Press, Ltd edition (2001 reprint of 1906 article).

Brontë Society with contributions from A Dinsdale, B Heritage, E Butcher, S E Maier, A-M Richardson and C Brontë *Charlotte Brontë: The Lost Manuscripts*, (UK: Haworth, 2018)

Brontë Studies (formerly *Brontë Society* Transactions):

Alexander, Christine 'Early Ambitions: Charlotte Brontë, Henry Kirke White and Robert Southey' *BST*, Vol. 43: 1, January 2018, 14-31, 2018.

Edgerley, C Mabel. 'Elizabeth Branwell' *BST* Vol. 9: 2, Jan 1937, 103-14, 1937.

Edgerley, C.Mabel. 'Mrs. Brontë *BST* Vol 11: 1, Jan 1946, 29-32, 1946.

Emberson, Ian and Catherine 'Turns in the Circle of Friendship: "Uncle Fennell" 1762-1841' Vol. 30, July, 2005.

Flaherty, Clare 'A Recently Rediscovered Unpublished Manuscript: The Influence of Sir Humphry Davy on Anne Bronte' Vol. 38, No. 1 Jan: 32-41, 2013.

Gamble, Bob 'Robinson Reflections Part 2: Abolition and Evangelicalism' Vol. 38 No 1, Jan: 66-78, 2013.

Hall, Kate. 'Maternal Influence on Charlotte Bronte', Vol. 21, Pts. 1 & 2: 3-8, 1993.

Hardie-Budden, Melissa. 'Maternal Forebears of the Brontë Archive: 'Nothing comes from Nothing'; or Stories from another canon' Vol. 40, No. 4, November 2015, 271-277.

Hatfield, C. W., compiler. 'The Relatives of Maria Branwell' *BST* Vol 9: 4, Jan 1939, 245-252. Based on J. Hambley Rowe with additions.

Henck, Karen Cubie 'That Peculiar Voice': Jane Eyre and Mary Bosanquet Fletcher, an Early Wesleyan Female Preacher' *BST* Vol. 35 No. 1, March 2010, 7-22

Holgate, Ivy. 'The Branwells at Penzance' Vol. 13: 5, Jan 1960, 425-432

Lane, Margaret, MA. 'Maria Branwell', Pt. 93, Vol. 18, No 3: 208-216, 1983.

Newbold, Margaret. 'The Branwell Saga', Vol. 27: 1 March 2002, 15-26, 2002.

Oldfield, Jennifer. 'The Homely Web of Truth': Dress as the Mirror of Personality in *Jane Eyre* and *Villette*, Pt. 83, Vol. 16, No. 3: 177-184, 1973.

Oram, Eanne. 'Brief for Miss Branwell', Pt. 74, Vol. 14: No. 4: 28-38, 1964.

Pool, P.A.S. MA, FSA. 'The Branwell Connection' Pt. 93, Vol. 18, No. 3: 217-21, 1983.

Ratchford, Fannie E. 'The Loneliness of a Brontë Cousin' *BST* Vol. 13: 2, Jan. 1957, 100-110.

Rowe, J. Hambley. 'The Maternal Relatives of the Brontës' *BST* Vol. 6: 33, Jan. 1923, 135-146. First delivered to the Bradford Historical and Antiquarian Society in 1911.

Stonehouse, Sally. 'Cambridge Echoes of the Brontës' Vol. 19, Pt. 5: 211-214, 1988.

Walker, Michael. 'William Morgan, B.D. 1782-1858' Vol. 30, Nov. 2005.

Cannon, John. *The Brontës, A Family History*. Stroud: Sutton Publishing [formerly entitled *The Road to Haworth: The Story of the Brontës Irish Ancestry*], (London: Weidenfeld and Nicolson, 2007 issue of 1980 1st).

Chadwick, Mrs Ellis H. *In the Footsteps of the Brontës* (London: Sir Isaac Pitman & Sons, Ltd, 1914).

Chichester, Teddi L (1991) 'Evading "Earth's dungeon tomb": Emily Brontë, A.G.A., and the Fatally Feminine' University of West Virginia: *Victorian Poetry*, Vol. 29, No. 1, Spring, 1991.

Chitham, Edward and Winnifrith, Tom *Brontë Facts and Brontë Problems*, (London: Macmillan, 1983).

Chitham, Edward *Western Winds, The Brontes' Irish Heritage*, (Dublin: The History Press Ireland, 2015, after 1986).

Colloms, Brenda *Victorian Country Parsons*, (London: Constable & Co. 1977). See Chapter 4: 'The Rev Patrick Brontë, Parson with Literary Connections'.

Erskine, Ann 'Representations of Fear and the Construction of Text in Charlotte Brontë's *Jane Eyre*' Accepted for degree of Doctor of Philosophy, School of Humanities, Languages and Social Science, Griffith University, S. E. Queensland, Australia, April, 2018.

Erskine, Ann "Fevered with Delusive Bliss" Charlotte Brontë's Jane Eyre and the

Ambiguous Pleasures of The Turk, In press, at time of writing: *Australasian Journal of Victorian Studies* (AVSA) Vol. 22 (2018).

Gaskell, Mrs *Life and Works of Charlotte Brontë and Her Sisters,* An Illustrated Edition in Seven Volumes, Vol VII: *The Life of Charlotte Brontë* (London: Smith, Elder, and Co., 1878.)

Green, Dudley, ed. *The Letters of the Reverend Patrick Bronte* (Stroud, Gloucestershire: Nonsuch Publishing, 2005.) With an introduction by Asa Briggs.

Harman, Claire (2015) *Charlotte Brontë, A Life,* (Viking, Penguin Random UK, 2015).

Higuchi, Akiko *The Brontës' World of Music, Music in the Seven Novels by the Three Brontë Sisters* (Tokyo: Yushodo Press, 2005).

Hill, Kerrow *The Bronte Sisters & Sir Humphry Davy: A sharing of visions*, (Newmill: Jamieson Library, 1994).

Hill, Esther and Kerrow Hill *The Penzance Home of Maria Branwell, Mother of the Brontes* (Penzance: Self publication, 1996).

Holland, Nick *In Search of Anne Brontë*, Stroud, (Gloucs: The History Press, 2016, 2017).

Holland, Nick *Aunt Branwell and the Brontë Legacy*, (Barnsley, South Yorkshire: Pen & Sword History, 2018).

Holmes, Jonathan *A Short History of Penlee House & the Branwells*, (Penzance: Penlee House Gallery & Museum, 2007). Illustrated. 2007.

Howe, Bea *A Galaxy of Governesses* (London: Derek Verschoyle, 1954). Illustrated. Ch 5: 'Triumvirate of Governesses' [the Brontës] pp. 93-111.

Lock, John and Dixon, W. T. *A Man of Sorrow, The Life, Letters and Times of the Rev. Patrick Brontë 1777-1861* (London: Thos Nelson & Sons, 1965).

Ratchford, Fannie Elizabeth. *The Brontës Web of Childhood.*, (New York: Russell & Russell, Reissue 1964 of 1941 orig.).

Raymond, Ernest. *In the Steps of the Brontës.* (London: Rich & Cowan, 1949), Intro.

Rowse, A. L. *The Byrons and Trevanions.* (London: Weidenfeld & Nicholson, 1978).

Smith, Margaret *The Letters of Charlotte Bronte, with a selection of letters by family and friends*, Vol 1: 1829-1847 (1995); Vol II: 1848-1851 (2000); Vol III: 1852-1855 (2004); (Oxford: Clarendon Press).

Stoneman, Patsy *Brontë Transformations, The Cultural Dissemination of Jane Eyre and Wuthering Heights*, Second expanded edition (Brighton: Edward Everett Root EER, 2018 of 1996 first ed.).

Summers, Mary. *Anne Brontë, Educating Parents.* (Beverley: Highgate Publications, 2003).

Symons, Andrew C. 'The Branwells of Penzance', (Truro: *The Cornish Banner,* May 2000).

Bond, Chris, ed. *Charles Thomas Gathering the Fragments, The selected essays of a groundbreaking historian.* (Sheffield, The Cornovia Press. 2012) pp. 13-15. 'What Did They Do When It Rained in 1857?' Extracted from *The Scillonian*, (newspaper) issue no 223, Summer 1986, pp. 117-119.

Thormählen, Marianne *The Brontës and Religion* (Cambridge: Cambridge University Press, 1999, orig, 2004).

Wise, T J and Symington, J A, Editors *The Brontës, Their Lives, Friendships and Correspondence,* (Oxford: Basil Blackwell: The Shakespeare Head Brontë, 1932) 4 vols. Illustrated.

Woelfel, J. W. 'The Christian Humanism of Anne Bronte' in *Portraits in Victorian Religious Thought*, orig. published in *Texts and studies in religion*, vol, 77 (series) (Lampeter, Wales: Edwin Mellen Press, 1997).

Wright, Sharon *The Mother of the Brontës: When Maria Met Patrick*, (Barnsley: Pen & Sword 2019).

General

Agnew, R.A.L. *John Forbes FRS (1787-1861).* James Lind Library (JLI) (Bulletin: Commentaries on the history of treatment evaluation, 2008).

Briggs, Asa *The Age of Improvement 1783-1867*, (London: Longman, 1996, 12th impr. of 1959 orig.).

Brown, Ford K. *Fathers of the Victorians, The Age of Wilberforce*, (Cambridge: at the University Press 1961).

Madame de Chatelain (nd) edited by, *Forty Favourite Fairy Tales: Merry Tales for Little Folk* London: Crosby Lockwood and Co. This copy dedicated to 'Ralph Burland Bodily, from Mother' 1888 'Jack the Giant Killer' pp.129-143

Colloms, Brenda *Victorian Country Parsons* (London: Book Club Associates 1977), Ch. 4: 'The Rev Patrick Brontë, Parson with literary connections 1777-1861', pp. 79-97.

Cole, GDH (1941, 1965) *Chartist Portraits*, Revised with an Introduction by Asa Briggs (New York: Macmillan & Co Ltd. 1965 ed.) Ch. 1: 'William Lovett'

Crane, Harvey *Playbill, A history of the theatre in the West Country*, (Plymouth: Macdonald & Evans Ltd., 1980).

Diamond, Michael *Victorian Sensation, or the Spectacular, the Shocking and the Scandalous in Nineteenth-Century Britain*, (London: Anthem Press, 2003).

Griffin, Emma *Liberty's Dawn, A People's History of the Industrial Revolution* (New Haven & London: Yale University Press, 2013).

Hartley, Sir Harold *Humphry Davy,* with a new preface by the author, (EP Publishing: Open University Set Book, republished 1972, 1966 1st).

Hernon, Ian *Fortress Britain, All the Invasions and Incursions since 1066* (Stroud: The History Press, 2013).

Holmes, Richard *The Age of Wonder, How the Romantic Generation discovered the Beauty and Terror of Science* (London: Harper Press, an imprint of Harper Collins, 2008).

Kamm, Josephine *Hope Deferred, Girls' Education in English History*, (London: Methuen & Co., 1965).

Knapp, J V and Womack, K, Eds. *Reading the Family Dance, Family Systems Therapy and Literary Study* pp. 13-26 (Newark: University of Delaware Press, 2003).

Lewis, Roy and Maude, Angus *The English Middle Classes* (London: Phoenix House, 1949).

Malmgreen, Gail *Neither Bread nor Roses, Utopian Feminists and the English Working Class, 1800-1850*. (Brighton, Sussex: John L Noyce, publisher, 1978).

Maple, Eric *Supernatural England* (London: Guild Publishing, 1977, 1989) Ch. 7, pp. 180-98.

Matthews, C M *Haileybury since Roman Times, A study of a square mile of England* (Frome & London: Butler & Taylor, 1959, 1976 revised Guildford: Lutterworth Press).

Olivier, Christiane *Jocasta's Children, The imprint of the mother*, Tr from the French by George Craig, (London & New York: Routledge, 1989).

Pinchbeck, Ivy (1930) *Women Workers and the Industrial Revolution 1750-1850* (London: Virago, 1981 repr.).

Rogers, John Jope (1878) *Opie and his Works: Being a catalogue of 760 pictures by John Opie, R.A., preceded by a biographical sketch*, (London: Paul and Dominic Colnaghi, in Hardpress Classics Series (n.d.) reprint).

Tisdall, John *Joshua Cristall (1768-1847) In Search of Arcadia* (Hereford: Lapridge Publications, 1996) with a Foreword by Roy Strong.

Joshua Cristall 1768-1847 Exhibition guide by Basil Taylor for London: V & A (1975) with a Foreword by Roy Strong

Tomaselli, Sylvana, "Mary Wollstonecraft", *The Stanford Encyclopedia of Philosophy* (Winter 2012 Edition), Edward N. Zalta (ed.), URL <http://plato.stanford.edu/archives/win2012/entries/wollstonecraft/>.

Tomkins, Stephen *The Clapham Sect: How Wilberforce's circle changed Britain* Oxford: Lion, 2010).

Willson, Beckles *Lost England, The Story of our Submerged Coasts*, (London: George Newnes, Ltd., 1902).

Religion, faith and evangelism

Appleby, Cedric 'Anglican-Methodist Relations as revealed in pamphlets in the Morrab Library, Penzance 1833-1871 and beyond' (2013, unpublished study)

Arminian Magazine (1797) April issue p. 162: (from) 'The Experience of Mr Kirkpatrick', Shaw Collection, RIC (Truro)

Austin, Keith (On-line, first accessed 22/08/2010) 'A history of Methodism and Penzance Wesleyan Society' Accessed various times since 2000 AD – 2014 : http://www.chapelstreet.co.uk/methodist-history-1.html

Bunting, Theodore Percival *The Life of Jabez Bunting, DD with Notices of Contemporary*

Persons and Events (London: Longman, Brown, Green, Longmans, & Roberts, 1859).

Dray, Stephen *A Proper Old Confloption Down Penzance, An Account and Interpretation of the 'Tucknet' controversy of 1824 within the history of the Baptist movement in Cornwall* (Cornwall: Carn Brea Media, 2013).

Entwisle, Joseph (1848) *Memoir of the Rev. Joseph Entwisle, Fifty-four Years a Wesleyan Minister, by his son* London: Published for the author. On-line.

Forsaith, Peter S. *Unexampled Labours, Letters of the Revd. John Fletcher to leaders in the Evangelical Revival* (Peterborough: Epworth, 2008).

Forsaith, Peter S. (2011) *Wesleyan and Primitive Methodist periodicals: an introduction to the British Online Archives edition.* http://www.britishonlinearchives.co.uk/9781851172092.php. Last updated: January 2012.

Friedlander, Evelyn 'Lemon Hart' [in] *The Jews of Devon and Cornwall* (Bristol: Redcliffe Press, 2000).

Fyfe, Aileen *Science and Salvation, Evangelical Popular Science Publishing in Victorian Britain*, (Chicago and London: The University of Chicago Press, 2004).

Green, Richard *Bibliography of the Works of J. And C. Wesley*, 1896.

Hammond, Geordan and Forsaith, Peter S. Editors (2011) *Religion, Gender, and Industry, Exploring church and Methodism in a Local Setting* (Cambridge: James Clarke & Co., 2011) 13 papers on related subject related to Madeley, Shropshire and the Severn Gorge in place and time, 18th-19th century.

Hardie-Budden, Melissa 'Methodist Links with the Brontës: Places and faces on the Wesleyan trail' Unpublished p*aper* delivered at the Centre for Methodist Studies Spring Seminar, Oxford, 18th April, 2015. Archived on Academia.edu. on-line.

Harrison, G. Elsie *The Clue to the Brontës* (London: Methuen & Co. Ltd.,1948)

Hattersley, Roy *John Wesley, A Brand from the burning* (Boston: Little Brown, 2002).

Hempton, David *Methodism, Empire of the Spirit* (New Haven: Yale University Press, 2005).

Horner, John, *What Mean These Stones? 19th-century Nonconformists & Life in Rural West Penwith* (Published by author, 2015)

Iwig-O'Byrne, Liam *How Methodists were made: "The Arminian Magazine" and spiritual transformation in the transatlantic world, 1778-1803* PhD dissertation: University of Texas (Arlington, 2008), ProQuest Publishing document ID 304824700; http://search.proquest.com/docview/ (accessed 23/08/2013).

Lloyd, Gareth *The Papers of Dr. Thomas Coke: A Catalogue [1775-1814]* Index & Introduction by Dr John A Vickers, John Rylands Research Institute, University of Manchester, (online 2013)

Mack, Phyllis *Heart Religion in the British Enlightenment, Gender and Emotion in Early Methodism (*Cambridge: Cambridge University Press, 2008).

'Ministers appointed to the Penzance Circuit from its formation in 1791' Typescript 2 pp. 1791-1867, Shaw Collection: RIC (Truro)

Pearce, John *The Wesleys in Cornwall* (Truro: Bradford Barton, 1964).

Pearce, Keith *The Jews of Cornwall, A History, Tradition and Settlement to 1913* (Wellington, Somerset: Halsgrove, 2014).

Pearce, Keith and Helen Fry *The Lost Jews of Cornwall* (Bristol: Redcliffe Press, 2000).

Pritchard, F. C. (1978) *The Story of Woodhouse Grove School* Bradford: Woodhouse Grove School; visited June, 2013 with access to Archives.

Rosman, Doreen M *Evangelicals and Culture* (Cambridge: James Clarke & Co. 2011, 2nd edition).

Shaw, Thomas *A History of Cornish Methodism* (Truro: D Bradford Barton Ltd. 1967).

Slugg, J. T., *Woodhouse Grove School: Memorials and Reminiscences*, (London: T. Woolmer, 1885).

Southey, Robert *The Life of John Wesley* (London: Hutchinson & Co., 1820).

Terry, James Gordon *The Causes and Effects of the Divisions within Methodism in Bradford 1796-1857*, submitted for the degree of Doctor of Philosophy, University of Huddersfield, 1999, On-line.

Thomas, Sue 'Christianity and the State of Slavery in *Jane Eyre*' in *Victorian Literature and Culture*, 2007) pp. 35, 57-79

Townsend, W. J. D.D., Workman, H. B., D. Litt. and Eayrs, F. R., FRHS, Eds. *A New History of Methodism*, in two vols, illustrated.,(London: Hodder and Stoughton, 1909).

Trelease, G. M. *The History of the Church in Paul Parish* (Newlyn: Aurelian Publishing, 2006).

Warren, Max (nd) *Simeon, An essay on the Revd. Charles Simeon, M A (1759-1836)* Fellow of King's College and Vicar of Holy Trinity Church, Cambridge

Wesley, John J*ohn Wesley's Journal* Abridged edition, (London: Epworth Press, 1903).

Fictional sources:

Crow, Angela *Miss Branwell's Companion*. (Bradford: Alethia Publications, 2007)

De Leo, Maddalena *Removing the shroud of mystery, Maria Branwell's autobiographical novel*, Tr from Italian by author, (Lulu ed, 2012)

Eaton, Barbara *Letters to Lydia 'beloved Persis'* Part III: 'Fact turns to Fiction' (Penzance: Hypatia Publications, 2005)

Holme Lee (Harriet Parr) *Her Title of Honour* based on the letters of Henry Martyn to Lydia Grenfell & his journal (London, 1871)

Rhys, Jean *Wide Sargasso Sea* (London: Andre Deutsch, 1966)

Mrs Sherwood's *Little Henry and his Bearer* (1814, anon. 30 editions by 1840) based on the meeting of Henry Martyn in India, where he was a Chaplain to the East India Company

Urquhart, Jane *Changing Heaven* (London: Hodder & Stoughton, 1990).

Appendix B : Bibliographies and further suggested reading

The Carne-Branwell Kinship Bibliography

Bibliography of the Batten family

John Hallett Batten FRGS, MRAS (1811-1886)

(1838) 'Journal of a visit to the Niti Pass of the grand Himalayan chain' *Jnl. Asiat. Soc. of Bengal*, vii, 310-16. Reprinted *Bibl. Univ. Geneve*, xxii, 402-406, 1839.

(1842) 'Journal of a visit to Melum and the Odonta Dhoora Pass, in Juwahir' *Jnl. Asiat. Soc. of Bengal*, xi 1157-81.

(1844) 'Snow on the Himalayas' *Calcutta Jnl. Nat. Hist.*, iv 537-39.

(1845) 'Reply to Capt Hutton's Remarks on the line of Perpetual Snow' *Calcutta Jnl. Nat. Hist.*, iv, 537-39

(1851) *Official Report on the Province of Kumaon, with a Medical Report on the Mahamurree, in Gurhwal in 1849-50*. Agra: Secunda Orphan Press

The Revd. Joseph Hallett Batten DD, FRS (1778-1837) Father of JHB above.

Sermons and addresses: East India College, Haileybury

(1832) *Christian Courage*, London: Rivington, 28 pp. A sermon preached before the University of Cambridge, 4 March 1832, and in the Chapel of the East India College, Herts.

References:

C. M. Matthews, *Haileybury since Roman Times*, pp.150-53.

Family history papers of Pery Cristall (NZ), Elizabeth Rogers (UK) and Alan Cristall (UK); Archival research & papers of Imogen Thomas (daughter of C. M. Matthews).

Bibliography of Carne, Elizabeth Catherine Thomas (1817-1873)
(also wrote under the name of John Altrayd Wittitterly)

Subjects: Geology, landforms, travel, religion, economy, society, philanthropy, poetry (no fiction)

by Elizabeth Carne

Letters and Reminiscences of Emily Bolitho (1817-1886) Two long letters from ETC to EB, one from Penzance (1843), one from Switzerland (Penzance: Beare & Son, 1844)

Polwhele of St Clement papers, Cornwall Records Office: PW/126, 127, 128: 'Sketches in Europe and the Scillies' Three large sketchbooks filled with views of France, Switzerland, Italy, Madeira, Britain (Devon, Cornwall, Shropshire, Derbyshire), Scillies and Newlyn. (1830-1872). (Qty: approx 200)

Morrab Library Photographic Archives, Sketchbook of conchology from Scillies: *British Shells*, unpublished and annotated catalogue in her own hand.

Three Months' Rest at Pau, in the winter and spring of 1859, by J A W, Re-issued in British Library, Historical Print Editions, BiblioLife Network: History of Travel, (London: Bell & Daldy, 1860).

Country Towns, and the Place They Fill in Modern Civilization [by the author of 'Three Months Rest at Pau'] (London: Bell and Daldy, York Street, Covent Garden 1868). Available in Google books as a download.

England's Three Wants (London, Anonymous: William Macintosh, 1870-1) 23 pp, possibly a sermon

The Realm of Truth by Elizabeth C. T. Carne, Author of *Country Towns*, a major treatise in two parts on the nature and search for truth, in all respects and in all subjects, (London: Henry S King & Co.,1872) 255 pp. Henry S. King & Co, formed as a separate entity in 1868, from its parent partnership with Smith, Elder & Co, who were also the publishers of the novels of the Brontë daughters.

Scientific articles in the *Royal Geological Society Journal* (1860-75):

'On the evidence to be derived from Cliff Boulders with regard to a former condition of the land and seas in the Land's-end district' RGSC: LXXV p. 369

'On the age of that part of the district of the Maritime Alps which surrounds Mentone' RGSC: LXXX p. 433

'On the Transition and Metamorphosis of rocks' [published posthumously 1875]

'On the Nature of the Forces that have acted on the Formation of the Land's End Granite' [published posthumously 1875]

Carne, John 1789-1844

See The Online Books Page, for a large selection of his work and its reprints.

Carne Ross, Joseph (1885) *John Carne, Letters 1813-1837*, Privately printed, Ltd edition No 100 of 100 copies printed. Online at https://archive.org/stream/cu31924104095504 inclusive one handwritten letter from Joseph Carne Ross to his publishers 1886

He was also a steady writer in the *New Monthly Magazine* (1828-1830), the *Forget-me-not*, the *Gem*, the *Keepsake*, and other works. His work was regularly reviewed and advertised in *Blackwood's Edinburgh Journal* and in publishers' lists. About: *DNB*: John Carne

Poems (containing 'the Indian' and 'Lazarus' Anon, (London: Baldwin, 1820)

Letters from the East (London: Henry Colburn, 1826)

Tales of the West, 2 vols, (London: Henry Colborn, 1828)

Stratton Hill, a Tale of the Civil War, 3 vols, (London: Henry Colborn, 1829)

Recollections of Travels in the East (London: H. Colborn and R. Bentley,1830)

The Exiles of Palestine, a Tale of the Holy Land, 3 vols. (London: Saunders and Otley, 1831)

Lives of Eminent Missionaries, 3 vols. (London: Fisher, Son, & Jackson, 1832-5)

Letters from Switzerland and Italy (London: H. Colburn by R. Bentley,1834)

Syria, the Holy Land, Asia Minor, &c, 3 vols. Illus. by W. H. Bartlett (London, Paris & America: Fisher, Son & Co. 1836 lst., further reprints)

https://archive. See also http://onlinebooks.library.upenn.edu/webbin/book/lookupname?key=Carne

Carne, Joseph, FRS, FGS, 1782-1858 [Abbreviation to JC in this section only]

President, Penzance Natural History & Antiquarian Society,

Cambridge Philosophical Society (Hon)

On Elvan Courses, **I:** 97-106, 1818.

On the Discovery of Silver in the Mines of Cornwall, **I:** 118-126, 1818.

Notice relative to the Formation of Swimming Stone, **I:** 239-240, 1818.

Notice on Elvan Courses, **I:** 241, 1818.

On the Relative Age of the Veins of Cornwall, **II:** 49-128, 1822.

On the Mineral Productions, and the Geology of the parish of St Just, **II:** 290-358, 1822.

On the Period of Commencement of Copper Mining in Cornwall; and, on the Improvements which have been made in Mining, **III:** 35-85, 1828.

On the Singular State of some Ancient Coins lately found in the Sands of Hayle; and, on the evidence deducible from them relative to the period *of* the Earliest Deposition of Sand on the Northern coast of Cornwall. **III:** 136-149, 1828.

On the Granite of the Western part of Cornwall, **III:** 208-246, 1828.

Notice on the Work Performed by the Steam-engines in the Mines of Cornwall, **III:** 335-337, 1828.

A description of the Stream-work at Drift Moor, near Penzance, **IV:** 47-56, 1832.

An account of the Discovery of some Varieties of Tin-ore in a Vein, which have been considered Peculiar to Streams; with remarks on Diluvial Tin in general, **IV:** 95-112, 1832.

On the Pseudomorphous Minerals found in Cornwall Illustrative of a Replacement of One Material Substance by Another, **VI:** 24-31, 1841.

Additional contributions to the Mineralogy of the parish of St Just, **VI:** 47-49, 1841.

Notice of the Remains of a Submarine Forest in the North-eastern part of Mount's Bay, **VI:** 230-235, 1845.

On the Geology of the Islands of Scilly, **VII**: 140-154, 1850.

Notice of a Raised Beach lately discovered at Zennor, **VII**: 176-178, 1851.

About:

'Canorum Conclave' [satirised as Bishop Bankum's son].

Bibliotheca Cornubiensis: Carne, Joseph, vol. 1.

Collectania Cornubiensia: Carne, p. 131.

Dictionary of National Biography (DNB) and online (ODNB).

Hamilton Jenkin, A K (1980) *Mines and Miners of Cornwall* 5. Hayle, Gwinear & Gwithian.

Royal Cornwall Polytechnic Society (RCPS) Annual Transactions, series 1833-58.

Royal Geological Society of Cornwall (RGSC).

Royal Society of GB (Archive).

Cornish Telegraph 13 October 1858, 2: Col B 'Joseph Carne'.

Pascoe, W H (nd c1982) *CCC The History of the Cornish Copper Company* [valuable lists of partners, tradesmen and labourers of West Cornwall] Partners over the life of the company equalled 47, five of whom were women who inherited their shares from husbands and fathers.

Vale, Edmund (1966, 2009 rev) *The Harveys of Hayle, Engine-Builders, Shipwrights and Merchants of Cornwall* Published by the Trevithick Society 2009.

By:

J C Letter to Davies Giddy [Gilbert], 22 April 1807. *Philosophical Transactions of the Royal Society*, Vol 97, pp. 293-5

J C, 'On the discovery of Silver in the Mines of Cornwall', *Transactions of the RGSC*, Vol 1

JC, 'Design for working bellows by means of the mine engine, as a ventilator' Reported to the RCPS. 1855, p. xxxvii

Bibliography for Cristall: Ann Batten Cristall

(1795) *Poetical Sketches* London: J Johnson

Subscribed to in Penzance by: Revd. J. Batten 4 copies (grandfather); Mr Hallet Batten (cousin of Penzance, and Trinity College, Cambridge); Mr Nichols, Junior; W Usticke, Esq. (of Penzance and London), Mary Wolstonecraft, George Dyer, and numerous others with literary connection.

Refs:

Bibliography: *DNB* (Ann Batten Cristall, Joshua Cristall)

Tisdall, John *Joshua Cristall (1768-1847) In Search of Arcadia* (Hereford: Lapridge Publications, 1996).

Wu, Duncan, ed. *Romantic Women Poets, an Anthology* (Oxford & Malden, MA: Blackwell Publishers Ltd., 1997) pp. 270-345.

Dennis, Thomasine

Poems (not published) MSS lodged with Cornwall Records Office.

Sophia St Clare (1806) in two vols., St Paul's Churchyard, London: Joseph Johnson

About: Obituary of cousin Alexander Dennis, includes summary of Thomasine Dennis writings, extracted to *Cornishman*, Dec 6, 1894 review, p. 2.

CRO: Cat. Archive 87: Correspondence, Thomasine Dennis and Davies Gilbert (DG) (DG/87, DG88;

DG/160 R S Woof: Coleridge and Thomasine Dennis

DG/180 *Sophia St Claire* (sic) in 2 vol.

John Fennell

Fennell, John (1808) 'A serious address to youth: being, the substance of a sermon, preached at the Methodist chapel in Wellington, on the 17th of April, 1808, being Easter Day' Book format, Shropshire Archives, ID class: L92, Ref. XLS1254

Fennell, John (1816) 'A Sermon, Preached at the Funeral of the Revd. John Crosse, Late Vicar of Bradford, on Sunday, the 23d of June, 1816', T. Inkersler, Printer, 28 pp.

'Fletcher-Tooth Archive' John Rylands University of Manchester, Letters to Mary Fletcher.

The Ladies' Diary, London (1796) Dec: In this & following vols JF replies to mathematical questions.

Methodist Magazine (1801) 'Letter from Rev John Fletcher to John Fennell in 1784' Vol XXIV 91-93, rendered by John Fennell

Methodist Magazine (1799) 'An Account of the death of Mrs H Barnicoat of Falmouth' Vol XXIII 304-7, rendered by John Fennell

Methodist Magazine (1801) 'An Account of the death of Susanna Taylor of Penzance' Vol XXIV 531-33, rendered by John Fennell

Methodist Magazine (May 1812) Article appears by Joseph Entwisle about Woodhouse Grove School and the good treatment received by his sons.

Pritchard, F C (1978) *The Story of Woodhouse Grove School*, Chapters 1 & 2, Letter from JF to Joseph Entwisle about his sons, p. 15. Reprinted in Chap 12, Document Register.

Slugg, J T (1885) *Woodhouse Grove School, Memorials and Reminiscences* (London: T Woolmer, published for the author, 1885).

About: Emberson, Ian and Catherine (2005) 'Turns in the Circle of Friendship: "Uncle Fennell" 1762-1841' *Brontë Studies*: vol. 30, July.

Bibliography for Charles Alexander Johns

Son of Henry Incledon John/Johns, Professor of drawing, poet

Cousin of Margaret 'Margery' John, mother of Thomas Branwell, grandmother of Maria Branwell Brontë

Dare, Deirdre, Hardie, Melissa and Evans, Clifford *A Passion for Nature, 19th-Century Naturalism in the Circle of Charles Alexander Johns* (Penzance: Patten Press, an imprint of Hypatia Publications, 2008). Appendix III: Publications by Charles Alexander Johns, pp. 214-222, with illustrations, poetry and reference to Emily Johns Carrington (1814-1890); Emily Stackhouse (1811-1870), Ann Catherine Johns (1847-1903) and Maria Johns Jacob (1806-1884), Editor and author.

Academia.edu

Available for download and free access: 'Annotated Bibliography of Publications by Charles Alexander Johns (1811-1874) [to include Emily Stackhouse, and the Carrington family], 16 pp.

Bibliography for John (Osborne) Kingston

John Kingston, husband of Jane (Carne) Branwell

Brother-in-law to Maria and Elizabeth Branwell

Methodist Magazine 1799

1809 Publishes: *The Reader's Cabinet*, consisting of More than a hundred papers, original and extract, in Prose and Verse, calculated to instruct the Mind, Reform the Morals, and Amend the Heart, Baltimore: published by John Kingston, Bookseller, No. 164, Market-Street. Samuel Magill, Printer 1809. Copyright page, Recommendations page (Ministers of various Protestant institutions, and Presidents of Colleges) and in the back a catalogue of the books he has for sale, which include both Wesley's Life and Fletcher's life, in addition to Bibles, sermons, school books, and the advanced notice of a Dictionary: *The New American Biographical Dictionary*, which he plans to issue, printed on good paper and substantially bound. Price to Subscribers, One dollar.

He also presents intentions to publish by subscription, in six parts *A Dictionary of the Holy Bible*, one part to be delivered every 3 months. One dollar per part.

1810 Publishes: *The New American Biographic Dictionary*, or Memoirs of many of the most eminent persons that have ever lived in this or any other nation Baltimore: J Kingston. 303 pages Author: John Kingston. Publisher: Printed for John Kingston and sold at his book and stationary store; Warner and Hanna, printers. Biography.

Advertises for sale with Edw. I. Coale: *The Refusal*, by Mr. West. Price two dollars. Who have likewise for sale, a valuable collection of BOOKS and STATIONARY – SCHOOL BOOKS and every article suitable for country merchants, Sept 25. [Federal Republican 26/9/1810]

26 September 1810 in Federal Republican:

1810-1811 Publishes: *The New Pocket Biographical Dictionary* containing memoirs of the most eminent persons both ancient and modern, who have ever adorned this or any other country, embellished with Portraits, Second edition, improved. Off-print in Hypatia files. This appears to be the 2nd edition of the book first published in 1810 of the same length. R. W. Sower & Co., printers.

2 April 1811 *The New Pocket Biographical Dictionary*, 2nd edition, improved, by John Kingston, published by J. Kingston, Bookseller, 164, Market-Street, Baltimore, B. W. Sower & Co., Printers

Publishes: *The New American Hymn Book*: for the use of all people, at home and in the church. 239 pages. (Published by J. Kingston, bookseller, 164 Market-Street. B. W. Sower & Co., printers, 1811).

1813 Author of: *The Life of General George Washington*, Baltimore: Published by J Kingston; and sold by all the principal Booksellers throughout the United States., A Miltenberger, printer. In preface: *'In his Religious principles, Washington was, (I believe) a moderate Episcopalian….I well remember being one Sunday afternoon, in the month of October, 1795, at Christ Church in Philadelphia; Bishop White read prayers, and Doctor Magaw preached. General Washington and his lady were there, and none in the congregation seemed more impressed with the sacred service than they. I was particularly struck with the manner in which himself and his wife walked from the pew to their carriage, at the church door, without stopping to bow or to speak to any one. General Washington (I presume) considered Religion what in reality it is, the soul devoutly adoring its maker, a personal transaction between a man's conscience and his God.'*

[Preface dated Baltimore, January 1, 1813 J.K.]

America [cross ref. from 1795 In the introductory chapter of his *Life of George Washington* (Baltimore, 1813, published by J Kingston) he reports seeing the great man and his wife Martha at church in Philadelphia, Pennsylvania. He landed in Massachusetts (Kennebunkport), and stayed in Boston, Baltimore and Philadelphia, and visited also in New York during periods of plague and fever.

1814 Document, confirming USA Naturalization for John Kingston, Baltimore, Maryland

Publishes: *Fletcher's Appeal to matter of fact and common sense, or, A rational demonstration of man's corrupt and lost estate: with the address to earnest seekers of salvation and an appendix: to which is now added, the life of the venerable author.* Authors: John Fletcher, John Kingston, printed for and sold by J. Kingston, 460 pages. Subjects: Sin, Original.

Advertisement 13/Feb/1815: Just published, by the Subscriber, and for sale at the Bookstores of Neale, Wills and Cole, John Kingston, John J Harrod, William Warner and John Hagerty, the work heretofore advertised by the subscriber, entitled A SELECTION OF ALL THE LAWS OF THE UNITED STATES on commercial subjects, To the close of the Second Session of the Thirteenth Congress. The customary discount will be made to those who may purchase for sale, J Brice, Jr.

13 February 1815 in *Baltimore Patriot*:

Just Published, By the Subscriber, and for sale at the Bookstores of Neal, Wills and Cole, John Kingston, John J Harrod, William Warner and John Hagerty, the work heretofore advertised by ay the subscriber entitled: *A Selection of all the Laws of the United States, on commercial subjects*. To the close of the Second Session of the

Thirteenth Congress. The customary discount will be made to those who may purchase for sale, J. Brice, Jr. [Feb 3]

1822 Author of: *The songs of Zion, or, The Christian's New Hymn Book for the Use of the Methodists*, 240 pages, published by Cushing & Jewett, 1822 (2nd edition).

Bibliography: William Lovett, step-son of William (Colenso) Carne, miner and builder

J. J. Beckerlegge, *William Lovett, of Newlyn* (Mousehole, 1948) Quoted from W Lovett in his autobiography and available at the Cornish Studies Library.

G.D.H. Cole (1965) *Chartist Portraits* New York-St Martin's Press with an Introduction by Asa Briggs.

Conway, Moncure D. 'William Lovett, Working Man, Chartist, Prisoner and Author' in Biographic Sketches, (*Harper's New Monthly Magazine*, vol. LIV, 1877).

[Lovett, W] *Life and struggles of William Lovett* (1876, repr. 1967 by London: MacGibbon & Kee, the Fitzroy Edition) Preface by R H Tawney. The subtitle of this autobiography: "In his Pursuit of Bread, Knowledge & Freedom, with some short Account of the different Associations he belonged to & of the Opinions he entertained."

The above edition contains three appendices, containing the writings of William Lovett, on behalf of the Chartists and their goals: A. Petition Agreed to at the 'Crown and Anchor' Meeting, February 28th, 1837. B. 'The People's Charter' and C. National Petition.

Margaret Perry, 'William Lovett, Social reformer' (Cornwall Association of Local Historians, Autumn 2001 issue, pp. 32-7). Typescript given to M. Hardie, 2002.

Bibliography: William Morgan

Morgan, William (1782–1858). *Christian Instructions consisting of Sermons, Essays, Addresses, Reflections, Tales, Anecdotes, and Hymns, on various subjects for the use of Families, Schools and Readers in General.* 2 vols. London: J. Dennett, 1824/25

'Fletcher-Tooth Archive', University of Manchester, Brief biography (incomplete data) and copies of Letters from William Morgan.

Morgan, William (1841) *The Parish Priest, a life of John Crosse* (the blind priest of Bradford) Published by the author. (Not found)

Morgan, William (c.1851) 'Simplicity and Godly Sincerity exemplified in the Life and Death of Mrs Morgan of Hulcott, Buckinghamshire and late of Bradford, Yorkshire.' (Not found)

Known street addresses of Branwell families in West Cornwall:

1, New Street (location of Branwell [Margery John & Richard Branwell] family home, house at the rear of Star Inn, re-constructed to allow for Jewish synagogue)

25 Chapel Street, Penzance (from construction 1780s) by the Thomas Branwell

family until c1810 -1811.

17 St Clare Street (possibly from 1811, house left to Anne Branwell by Thomas in his Will, later inhabited by Branwell sisters who became schoolmistresses)

St Clare Street (Lydia Branwell, annuitant, 1861 Census, lodger with Mary Clarke, with Bottrell family to left and Carne family to right of their home)

46 St Clare Street (Lydia Branwell, annuitant, 1871 Census, lodger with James & Mary Matthews – kinsmen & dairyman)

1 Windsor Terrace *(1841 Census)* Jane Kingston & EJK

3 Morrab Terrace, the Misses Branwells' Private Lodging House (1862) *Gazette*

10 Morrab Place (Mary Batten Branwell, Lydia and Benjamin B Branwell until Mary's death, later a home for Elizabeth Jane Kingston)

Penlee House Gallery & Museum

This Branwell 'mansion' spoken of by some authors as evidence of family wealth was not constructed until 1864, and would not even have been a 'twinkle' in the family eyes of earlier times. The story of that house – now the Penlee House Gallery & Museum in Penzance – can be found in a small, illustrated monograph, published in 2007 to mark the Tenth Anniversary of the reopening of the museum, after a period of extensive renovations and improvements. (See J. Holmes in 'Bronteana' list above)

Known addresses of the Carne families:

Chapel Street, Large end house, No. 29 (now hotel) home of Joseph Carne, FRS and his wife Mary Thomas, and family.

Chapel Street, Penzance (Now, No 15, the Bank House of Batten, Carne & Oxenham from 1795.

Riviere House, Phillack, Hayle (Joseph Carne & family 1807-1818)

The Abbey, Abbey Street, Penzance (John Carne, author, until 1844)

6 Coulson Terrace, Penzance (Elizabeth Carne died in this house, 1873)

Index

n= note relating to subject

Act of March 1751 (calendar change to Gregorian) 87
Acton Castle 71, 105, 225, 236
Agnew, Dr. Robin A. L., biographer xi, 20, 251
America xv, 4-5, 13-15, 40, 61, 64, 72, 89, 92, 94, 97, 169, 176-8, 199, 200, 204, 216, 243, 260-1
American War of Independence (American Revolution) xviii, 16-17, 183-4
Andrew, Richard, Wesleyan of Helston 54
Appleby, Cedric, Methodist historian xii, 53, 252
Apreece, Mrs. Jane (Lady Jane Davy) 37, 98, 192
Arminian 35, 64, 252-3
    Magazine, see Methodism, J Wesley, editor
Arundel family (kin) 86, 117, 130, 199
Arthur, King (of Legend) 30, 32
Australia xii, 13, 130, 185, 194, 210
Authorship, impetus to write xvii, 25, 28-9, 40, 139

Banks & bankers, Penzance xi, 13, 18, 43, 93, 138, 190-1, 212.
    Location 56, 59, 212
    Bankers 80, 93, 103-4, 129, 130-1, 137, 155, 212
    Bank failure 157, 205, 227-8
Barbary coast & trade (See smuggling, white slave trade) xviii, 3-4, 182-5
Barron, Keith, actor 5
Barwis family (kin) 79, 119
Bassett, Sir Francis (of Tehidy), Lord de Dunstanville 12 notes 7,8
Batten family (kin)
vii-viii, 16, 41-4, 59, 63, 85, 88-9, 111, 116, 128, 134-8, 161, 189-191, 200, 211-15, 223, 233.
    (Ann) Elizabeth Batten, Mrs Cristall (See Cristall);
    John Batten I-VI
    Joseph Hallett Batten 180-2
    John Hallett Batten 182
    Mary (Bodinnar) Batten, Mrs Benjamin Carne Branwell 16-17, 43, 55, 78, 94, 113, 128, 134, 137-8, 181, 190 263
    Samuel Ellis Batten, 2nd marriage C Venn, Clapham sect 182, 190-1, 236
Beddoes, Dr. Thomas of Bristol 28, 37-8, 47 n53 & n54, 93, 198
Bennetts family (kin) 7, 64, 117, 125-6, 151, 235
Bethlehem Hospital, London 20
Boase family (kin) 83 n 20, 129
    Henry Boase M.D. 18, 33, 38, 99, 101, 129, 191, 212
    Jane Boase, g-grandmother (John family) 86, 191
Bolitho Bank 138, 225
Bolitho family 77, 115 226
    Emily Bolitho, friend of Elizabeth Carne 59, 66 n23, 242, 255

Bonaparte, Napoleon 17, 19, 29, 48 n 65, 83 n4
Borlase family 41, 100, 147
    Revd. John Bingham Borlase 37, 195
    Borlase, the Revd. Walter, Vicar of Madron, anti-Wesley 32, 53, 66 n 15, 107 n9
    Borlase, the Revd. William, FRS, Rector of Ludgvan, Vicar of St. Just 32, 46 n34, 65 n7, 247
Bosanquet, Mary, preacher (see Mary B Fletcher, wife of Revd. John)
Bottrell, William (kin) folklorist 29, 46 n18 & n19, 118, 263
Boulton, Matthew, steam engineer, inventor & partner to Watt 39
Branwell family of Penzance vii, xvii
    Individuals see Chapters 7, 8 and 9
    Timeline for Branwells & Carnes & some of their links, see Chapter 6
    Elizabeth Branwell, Aunt Branwell (1776-1842) vii-viii, xvii, xx, 4, 14, 33, 45, 76, 81, 99, 101, 104, 127, 134 (Table), 138, 139, 149 (Table), 168, 179, 170, 216-7, 222, 224, 235; Marriage witness 94, 98, Will (full extract) 89, 104, 225
    Maria Branwell, mother of the Brontë children (1783-1821) vii-viii, xv, xviii, 9, 15, 34-5, 40, 43, 60, 63, 76, 92, 96, 98, death 101, 125 (Table), 134-5 (Table), 140, 142 (likeness), 149, 152, 156, 170, 172, 190, 196 leaving Cornwall, 216-7, 220, 235, 259
    Thomas Branwell, patriarch of Maria's family, (c1745-1808) Will (full extract) 215-218
Briggs, Asa, historian 2, 47 n 55, 250, 251, 262
Broadley Wilson, John, See Wilson
Brock, Elizabeth, Jewish historian 21 n8, 73, 83 n12
Bromwell, Martyn, gg-grandfather, butcher, 57, 59, 73, 83 n20, 125, 126-7, 209
Bronte family, fame of vii-viii, 8;
Brontë, Anne[Acton Bell] xv, 20, 47 n50, 62, 64 66 n28, 100, 105 (death), 178-9, 224-5, 236, 248, 250, 251;
Brontë, Charlotte [Currer Bell] xvi, 8, 15, 20, 21 n16, 27, 28, 34, 65, 99, 104-5 (death), 120 n4, 136, 138, 160, 168-9 174-5, 184-5 186 n34, 204, 224, 231, 235, 248-9, 250;
Brontë, Emily Jane [Ellis Bell] xv, 20, 100, 105, 171, 172, 178, 199, 224, 235 240, 249;
Brontë, The Revd. Patrick, (father of Brontës) 29, 35-6, 55-6, 60, 63, 95-6, 104, 105, 112, 125 (Table), 134 (Table), 139, 149 (Table), 169, 172, 222. Move to Wellington 97, 172, 177, Marriage 98, 166, 170, 220
Bunting, The Revd. Jabez 27, 45 n8, 47 n39, 98, 152, 162 n1, 191 206 n2, 252
Byron, Lord George Gordon, friend of H. Davy 36-7, 47 n49, 96-7, 99, 100, 101, 102, 111, 143 n3, 192, 250 Grandparents: Trevanions of Cornwall 111, 250

Cambridge University 19, 60, 63, 93, 99, 181, 190-1, 205, 227, 249, 254, 257 Cambridge Union 103, St. John's College 56, 96, 204
    Sedgwick Museum 157, 228, 241
    Trinity College 17, 47 n62, 61, 96, 103, 157, 182, 191, 201, 205, 258
Canorum Conclave (see Harvey family) 103, 221, 242, 258
Carew, Richard of Antony, *Survey of Cornwall 1602* initiates literary tradition 31-2, 244
Carne family xi, xiii, 13 ff, 91 (Wesley visit) , 255-8 (Bibl)
    Individuals see Chapters 7-9, 146-163 (Tables)
    Carne of Tresillian + Keigwin 85, 147
    Anne Reynolds Carne, mother of Maria + 11 siblings Branwell xvii, 73, 88, 92, 97, 111 (marriage), 150-1, 194
    Elizabeth Catherine Thomas Carne, cousin of Brontës vii, 13, 39, 146 (plate), 156 (Table),

157, 158, 161-2, 197, 206 n6, 212, 246, 255-6
  John (Calenso) Carne, grandfather, silversmith, 13, 86, 117, 149 (Table), 151 (Table), 162 n5
  John (Cock) Carne, cousin of Anne, journalist, author, storyteller 26, 30, 99, 158-160, 256-7
  Joseph (Cock) Carne (of Penzance) FRS, mineralogist, banker 13, 15-16, 19-20 ff, 146 (plate), 152, 154-8 (Tables), 257-8, 258 (satirised in *Canorum Conclave*),
  William (John/s) Carne Sr., Merchant, banker, 'father of Cornish Methodism' 13ff, 34, 54, 62, 152-6 (Tables), 158
Carter family of Prussia Cove 71-2, 93, 127, 212
Celts, celtic xx, 1, 51, 196, 231, 246
Chapel Street Methodist Chapel 56, 99, 103, 112, 199, 241
Chapel Street, Penzance, 'Court end of town' 4, 6-7, 11, 16, 20, 57, 73, 75-7, 94, 112, 114, 138, 161, 199, 216, 223, pack train of mules 7
Chartism, (see William Lovett)
Church Missionary Society (CMS) 58, 96
Clapham Sect/Set, evangelical reformers 60, 63, 96, 182, 191, 252
Class systems, social x1, 5 28 31, 35, 52-3, 58-9, 65 n9, 69, 74, 80, 83 n23, 94, 99, 112, 114, 155, 198, 232-3, 252
coinage, coigned 7, 11-12, 21 nn4-6
Cock family (kin) 93, 154, 193-4
  Anna (Cock) Carne 101, 131, 150, 152 (table), 154 (table), 156, 194, 233, 236
  Solomon Cock, builder, kin 17, 88, 90-1, 93, 98, 131, 194
Coke, The Revd. Dr. Coke, Wesleyan, 34 n40, 66 n27, 91-2, 95, 118, 176, 194, 253
Colenso, Calensow family (kin) 58, 66 n20, 95, 149-51 (table), 194-5, 203, 206 n9
Colenso, the Revd. William FRS 1811-1899, botanist, Bible translator into Maori 58, 130, 194-5, 206 n9
Coleridge family (West country heritage)
  Derwent Coleridge, Headmaster, Helston, son of S. T. 22 n29, 26-8, 165, 197
  Hartley Coleridge, Brother of Derwent, son of S. T. 28, 197, 224
  Samuel Taylor Coleridge, friend of H Davy & CV Le Grice 26-8, 38 41, 201, 205, 259
Colman the Younger, playwright 69-70
Congregationalists, non-conformist religious group 55-60, 62, 64, 89, 181-2, 211
Corin/Coren, Joseph (kin) 83 n13, 100, 118, 126
  Father of Corin, Joseph Jr (1773-1832), cousin, scrivener
Cornish Copper Company 13, 37, 56, 95, 97, 193, 247
Cornish language, literature, Cornish identity xv, xx n2, 46 n32, 128
Cornish character of
  'island mentality' 1 'land of Saints' 51
  landscape (geographical, geological) 1 n2, 6 19, 46 n14; (spiritual) 30, 52
  Penwith Hundred, administration 1-9
  occupations, crafts xvii, 6, 73, 75, 113, 115, 120 n3, 132 (Table)
  transport, maritime & land 2-3, 6-7 16, 55, 127
Courtney, J. S., diarist & antiquarian 6, 9 n18
Craik, Mrs. Dinah Maria Muloch, novelist and poet 30
Cristall, Alexander family (also Chrystal) viii, 83 n22, 88, 118, 180-1, 186 n22 & n23, 190 (Table), 196
  Ann Batten Cristall, poet, xiii, 41-4, 113, 180 n1, 236
  Joshua (Batten) Cristall, water colourist xiii, 43, 83 n22, 88, 107 n5, 180 (birth), 186 n22

& n23, 190
(Table), 252, 258
Curtis, Thomas Sr. (of Breage) & Jr. (Wherry Mine adventurer) 15, 212-3

Davy, Professor Edmund Davy, local cousin of H. Davy 19, 195
Davy, Sir Humphry (Millett) FRS, chemist and kin 2, 13, 18, 22 n30, 26, 28, 33, 36-9, 41, 47 n52, 66 n19, in Timeline: 85-107, 103 (death), 118, 159, 161, 181, 192-3, 195-7, 199, 206 n5, 225, 244, 246-8, 250-1.
    Grace (Millett) Davy, kin, mother & milliner 75, 89, 113, 195
    nitrous oxide (laughing gas, with Coleridge & Southey) 205
    Davy, Lady Jane (Apreece) Davy, wife of H. Davy 37, 47 n50, 98, 100, 192
    Davy, Dr. John, brother of H. Davy 13, 38, 195, 244
Dennis, Thomasine, kin, novelist, poet, governess 45, 113, 118, 196, 259 (Coleridge link)
Diodorus Siculus, Historian c44 BC 11, 21 n3
disease, pulmonary tuberculosis 20 (see Dr John Forbes)
Dolcoath Mine, Camborne xiii, 10 (Plate), 39, 40, 101
Donne, Benjamin, Bristol Mathematical Academy 78
Druids, druidic 29, 51 203 (Masonic lodge)
Dunkin family (smuggling) 71-2, 127, 242, 247
Dyer, George, poet, friend of A. B. Cristall & circle 43, 186 n23, 196, 258

Economies (see Chapter 2) 1-3, 113
Edgeworth family of Bristol 38, 47 n54 (Beddoes link), 81
Edinburgh City & university 19, 156, 256
Edwards, John, Cornish Copper Company 37

Fables, folklore & fairytales 25-6, 30, 46 n20, 81, 251
    Aesop's Fables 29
    Arabian Nights 195
    Jack the Giantkiller 30
    Travels of Baron Munchausen (Erich Rudolph Raspe) 40, 47 n58
    See Bottrell, William; Carne, John; Hunt, Robert in bibliographies, chapter 12
Fennell family viii, xvi-ii, 7, 56, 75, 97-9, 100, 125 (Table), 150, 166-71, 173, 175 (Table), 177-9, 184 (Lister link), 236
    Jane Branwell, Mrs. Fennell, Aunt of Maria, sister of Thomas 36, 54, 66 n13, 77, 87 (birth), 91, 102-3 (death), 135-6, 172-3, 222
    Jane Fennell Morgan, daughter of J & J Fennell, mother of William John Morgan, 97, 102, 139, 166 (marriage), 167, 173 (birth of son), 222
    The Revd. John Hodgkiss Fennell, Uncle of Maria 34, 56-7, 61, 63, 75-7, 81, 87 (birth), 90-2, 94, 96-7, 103-4, 107 n7, 118, 136, 158, 166-171, 185 n4 & n6, 191, 196 (Davy link), 199 (Johns link), 206 n14, 210, 219-20, 248, 259
Fenwick, Eliza, author of *Secresy or the ruin on the rock 44, 48 n73*
Fisher, Charles, Gent, brother in law 80, 93, 134 (Table), 135, 175-6, 213
Fletcher, The Revd. John of Madeley, Shropshire 88, 90, 167-8, 172, 185 n5, 210, 220, 253, 259, 261
Fletcher, Mary Bosanquet 97, 98-9, 169, 172, 185 n5, 186, 213, 220-1, 249, 259

Index

Forbes, Dr. John (later Sir) 19-20, 22 n33, 97, 100, 251
Fox family of Falmouth 13, 18, 27-8, 41, 130, 197-8, 235
    Caroline Fox, diarist, friend of Elizabeth C.T. Carne 27-8, 197, 244
French Revolution & Napoleonic era xviii, 16, 91, 100, 152, 246-7

Garstin, Crosbie, novelist, *Penhale Trilogy* 41, 245
Gaskell, Mrs., biographer of Charlotte Brontë 5-6, 16, 191
Geological Society of London 38, 47 n62
Giants of Cornwall (mythical & thematic)
    Bolster (Plate) xiii, 24; Corineus, Gogmagog 31; Jack, the Giant-Killer 30, 251
Giddy family of St. Erth 17, 78 (pupil of Hannah More), 198-9
Gilbert, Davies Giddy, MP, PRS, author, mining engineer & inventor 8, 17, 28, 33, 37, 38-9,
    44-5 n51, 47 n57, 147, 155, 159, 196, 198, 199 (death), 206 n13, 259
Gentlemen's News Room, Penzance 20, 43, 100
German, Germany 12, 19, 39, 73, 161
Germoe parish, Wesleyan preaching house, Carne, Fennell & Carter trustees 56, 66 n17, 94
    212-3
Gilbert, W. S.*HMS Pinafore* 7
Graham, Winston, novelist, *Poldark* 32, 41
Gilpin, Joshua (Vicar of Wrockwardine) 168, 172
Green, Keziah, Mrs. Carne, and mother of William Lovett 73, 94, 100, 113, 202, 220
Grenfell, Lydia (Tremenheere) 94-6, 98, 107 n9, 199, 200, 204, 207 n20, 246, 254
Guiccioli, Teresa, mistress of Byron 37, 100, 192
Gwennap, Lydia Bunster, See Broadley Wilson 60, 65 n25, 245
Gwennap (place) 66, 92, 107 n7, 147, 148, 151, 162, 183, 204, 206 n3

Halifax, John, Gentleman, fictional Cornishman by Dinah Maria Mulock 30, 46 n29
Halliday, F. E., Historian 11, 21 n2, 246
Hals, William, Historian 32-3
Harrison, Elsie Grace, Brontë & Methodist author 63-4 66 n 30, 253
Hart family, Jewish merchants 21 n 10, 73, 216 Mary, 'The white rose' 73
    Lemael, Lemon Hart rum 73
Harvey family 13, 118, 247
    Author of *Canorum Conclave* 103, 221, 242
Hawkins, Sir Christopher, mine & landowner, patron of steam 14, 21 n3, 38, 47 n62
Hawkins, John, writer, geologist14, 40, 47 n42 & n62
Hays, Mary, novelist & essayist 44, 48 n73
health, hygiene, sanitation 73-5, 83 n16
Henderson, Charles, historian & antiquarian 52, 65 n5
Heritage, Barbara, author 36, 48 n66, 96
Herland Mine , Gwinear 13, 152, 162 n5
Hewitt, Rachel, social historian 40, 48 n64
Hitchens, the Revd. Malachy, cousin of Henry Martyn, astronomer, Vicar of St. Hilary 95,
    ?117, 198-9
Holmes, Jonathan (Penlee House curator) author 250, 263
Holmes, Richard, biographer and historian xviii, 30, 38, 46 n31, 251
Horner, the Revd. John, Methodist historian & author 54, 107 n6, 162 n10, 242, 253

Hucarius, the Levite of St. Germans 31
Hughes, Molly Vivian, (author, *The Vivians, A Family in Victorian Cornwall; A London Child* (series) 132
Hughes, Richard, 'father of provincial drama' 7, 70
Hunt, Robert, Folklorist & storyteller 24, 29, 30, 46 n19 & n25, 47 n58 (exposes Raspe), 246

Industrial revolution xviii, xix, 18, 112, 116, 147, 251, 252
Imitation of Christ, The, by Thomas à Kempis 60, 63
Ireland 15, 21 n16, 51-2, 63, 83 n3, 89, 102, 126, 130, 195, 249
Island mentality, isolation 1-3
Italy, Genoa 16, 72, 101, 184, 190

Jaco/Jacka, Peter, Methodist preacher 44, ?162 n9
Jamieson, Prof. Robert, Edinburgh University 19
Jerdan, William (describes John C Carne) 158-9
Jewish, Jews 12-13, 21 n8, 60, 73, 83 n12, 262
John Bull, play 69, 83 n2
John of Cornwall, Latinist & traveller. 12th century 31
John/s families (kin) viii, 26 John: 130-1 (Table), 143 n16, 153 Johns: 80, 185 n2
    Charles Alexander Johns, natural history, botanist, author 26-7, 259-60
    George John, (kin) Mayor, solicitor 86, 107n1, 130, 137, 153, 199, 206 n14, 211, 243
    Henry Incledon Johns, Artist, poet, father of C A Johns 26, 130 (Table), 259
    Margery/Margaret (Boase) John, g-grandmother, wife of Richard Sr. 12, 92, 129-30 143 n16, 191, 199, 259, 262
    Mary (Ferris) John/s, mother of William Carne Sr. of Penzance, banker 153-4
    Samuel John, solicitor, brother of George, thief 86, 94, 129, 153, 199-200, 211
    Thomas John, g-g-grandfather 86, 116-7, 129, 162 n8, 191, 199, 210-11
Johnson, Joseph, London radical publisher 43-4, 48 n71, 196, 259

Keam, John, bro-in-law of Thomas Branwell 87, 95, 125-6 (Table), 136, 210, 212
Keigwin family of Mousehole 44, 57, 85, 116, 143 n12, 147
Kingsley, The Revd. Charles Kingsley 26-7, 130, 165, 197
Kingston family
Kingston, Mr. John, Methodist preacher, bro-in-law to Maria 61, 66n, 91, 94-6, 102, 134 (Table), 163 n15, 169, 176-80 (Table), 186 n10, n11 & n21, 194, 260-2
    Ann Branwell Kingston, daughter of Jane & John 89, 134, 179 (Table)
    Eliza Jane Kingston, daughter of Jane & John, 134, 179 (Table), 200, 206 n7, 213-14
    Jane Branwell Kingston, wife of John, mother of 5, xv, 61 (marriage), 89, 97 105, 142 (plate), 143 n17, 179-80

Ladies Book Club, Penzance 42, 44 48 n68, 80-1, 88
Lady's Magazine, The 35, 41 81, 167, 254
Lamb, Charles, essayist & poet 26, 201
Le Grice, The Revd. Charles Valentine, priest and poet, 26, 41, 45 n5, 55, 66 n16, 69-70, 94, 98 201-2, 207 n18, n19
Libraries xi ff See Ladies Book Club and Gentlemen's Newspaper Reading Room
 1750: 20 (first), 42, 48 (n 69) Napoleonic Collection, 80, 83 n23, 87, 100, 157, 165,176, 226,

240, 242 Reading habits, See chapter 3
Love, Thomas, merchant 72
Lovett, William, Chartist, a Carne stepson, 100, 113, 202-3, 220, 245, 262
Lyonesse, legendary kingdom under the sea 30, 46 n26

Macaulay, Thomas Babington, historian 53, 65 n9
Mack, Phyllis, Methodist historian, 'heart religion' 64
MacKenzie, Charlotte, historian 21 n17, 44, 48 n73, 72, 127, 247
'Madeley circle' 168-9, 172, 221, 259
Malthus, Thomas Robert (1766-1834) political economist, friend of J Hallett Batten, 181, 186 n24, 191, 196
Maternal influences vii, xv; family influence (Rowse extract) 111, 245, 250, 206 n3
    John Martyn, Methodist father of Henry, friend of William Carne 56, 66 n18, 191
    Henry Martyn, Cornish missionary to Persia 93, 95, 96 246, 254
Mayflower pilgrims 5, 9 n14
Methodism, 'methodies' 34-6, Chap. 4 50-67, Jane B. Kingston 61-2
Methodist Magazines 34-6, 41, 64, 66 n27, 176 (Kingston link)
mining industry, See Chapter 2: 10-22
military history, family involvement xix, 3, 6, 17, 41, 92-3, 95, 97-8, 136, 183, Battery Rocks, 4, 17, 86
moors, moorlands (Penwith) 5, 158
More, Hannah, author and teacher, bluestocking 44, 78, 81
Morgan, The Revd. William, husband of Jane B. Fennell, cousin-in-law, xvii ff, 171-5 (Tables), 262
Morrab House Library & Gardens, see Libraries (first)
Mulock, Dinah Maria, novelist & poet 30, 46 n29, n30
Munchausen, Baron (fictional author), 40, 47 n58, see Raspé, R. E.

Names, naming traditions 31-2, Appendix A
Napoleon, See Bonaparte
Napoleonic Collection, Morrab Library, 48 (n 69)
Nelson, Admiral Horatio, Viscount, death at Trafalgar xix, xx n8, 96
New Zealand 58, 130, see Revd. William Colenso FRS (kin)
Nunn, The Revd. John (Shrewsbury curate) 168, 172, 177, 178

Oldham, Lilian, local historian of Penzance 54, 66 n21, 120 n6, 123, 143 n1, n18, 243
Olivers, Thomas, Cornishman, editor, Wesleyan preacher 35
Oral traditions xx, 29-30

Paris, Dr. John Ayrton, medical practitioner, Founder RGSC, 18-20, 38
Pearce, John, medievalist & early belief systems 52, 65 n3, n6, 254
Pearce, Keith, Historian, 12, 21 n9, 53, 83 n15, 117, 254
Pellew, Admiral Sir Edward, (kin) naval officer, Vice Admiral of Mediterranean Fleet
    Viscount Exmouth, friend of Wellington 4, 41, 87, 92, 117, 182-5, 186 n26
Pellew, Admiral Sir Israel Isaac, naval officer (kin) 4, 92, 183, 186 n26
Penlee House, museum, art gallery xi, xv, xx n3, 45 n3, 243, 250, 263
Penzance

Penzance Bank (Carne, Batten & Oxnam) 13,80, 93 129, 137, 157, 190-1, 212, 226
Penzance, sloop, see ships
Population & statistics 5, 7-8, 11, 12 32, 94, 181
Polwhele, the Revd. Richard, (kin, Carne) historian and poet 33, 41 44, 47 n37, 78, 119, 156, 201, 245, 255,
Pool, Peter A (aka PAS Pool), historian of Penzance, 51, 111, 112, 119 n1, 152
Pope, Alexander, poet 33, 165, 185 n1
Printing press (first, c1750) 87

Quaker influences, Quakers (See Foxes of Falmouth) 18, 41, 45 n9, 55, 59, 60, 63, 95, 166, 197-8

Raspé, Rudolph Erich, 'Baron Munchausen' author, Dolcoath mine 39-40, 47 n58
Ratchford, Fannie, Brontë scholar xv, 29, 46 n17, 105, 163 n15, 206 n7, 250
Raymond, Ernest, Brontë historian 25, 45 n1, 250
Religious Census of 1851 54
Rigg, The Revd James Harrison, non-conformist 27, 45 n8
Romanticism, literary movement xviii, 28, 40-5, 48 n63
Rowe, J Hambley, Brontë chairman & scholar xv, xvii, xx n1 & n2, 143 n5, 171, 246, 249
Rowse, A L 111, 245, 250
Royal Cornwall Gazette News 69, 79-80, 94, 220
Royal Cornwall Polytechnic Society (RCPS), Falmouth xiii, 18, 45 n9, 157, 206 n12, 258
Royal Geological Society of Cornwall (RGSC), Penzance viii n1, xi, xiii, 13, 18, 20, 21 n3 & n21 (bibl), 33, 39 42, 46 n16, 47 n62, 71, 99, 136, 191, 192 (first female member), 198, 241, 244, 246, 256, 258
Royal Society (RS) xiii ff Presidents (PRS): Sir Humphry Davy, Davies Giddy Gilbert 39

Schools, education
    Branwell's Classical, Mathematical & Commercial Academy, Penzance (Queen St. Academy) 79-80
    Misses Branwell School 78
    Charterhouse, London x1, 57, 205, 241
    Christ's Hospital (The Blue Coat) x1, 26, 201
    Helston Grammar 26-7, 130-1
    Keynsham School, nr Bristol 57, 158
    Kingswood School, Bristol 34, 54, 170
    Woodhouse Grove School for Methodist sons 56, 98, 107 n10, 137, 139, 166, 169-71, 206, 219, 241, 243, 254, 259
    Writing School (Fennells), Penzance 167, 168, 196, 199
Science, scientists, literature of science Chp 3: 36-40
Scotland 19, 40, 51, 101
Secresy, or the ruin on the rock, see Eliza Fenwick 44
Sedgwick Museum, Cambridge See Cambridge University
Shaw Collection (Royal Institution of Cornwall, Courtney Library) 16 n18, 21, 243, 252
Shelley, Percy B. Poet (death with C Vivian) 101
Shipping, ships
    Aran, troop ship (1779) 17

Friendship, brigantine 16, 72, 127
HMS *Indefatigable* (Pellew) 184
Liberty, sloop (Dunkin) 72, 127
Maria of Penzance 235
Penzance, sloop 16
HMS *Pickle* xx
HMS *Pinafore* 7
HMS *St. George* (Jutland 1811) 97-8
HMS *Venerable* 22 n32
Swallow 127
Simeon, the Revd. Charles 56, 60, 63, 66 n31, 95, 96, 104, 107 n9, 182, 204, see Clapham Sect
    Links with Henry Martyn 56, 204, 241, 254
Smith, George, publisher, Smith Elder 20, 22 n34
St. Mary's Chapel of Ease(C of E) 55, 77, 144 n21, 201, 232
St. Michael's Mount 17, 29-30, 46 n24, 143 n3, 246
Stackhouse family & Acton Castle 71, 117, 130, 235, 236, 260
Smith, Marion (Dunkin family) xii, 71, 242
Smuggling 6, 16, 71-2, 127, 183, 242
Solomon, Mary ('the white rose') See Hart family
Sophia St. Clare, see Thomasine Dennis
Southey, Robert, poet laureate & biographer,Ed., *Remains of Henry Kirke White*, Author, *Life of Wesley*, godfather of Derwent Coleridge: xv-xvi, 27-8, 36, 38, 47 n43, 66 n29, 101, 205
Spanish, Spain 8 n6, 12, 16-17, 57, 127, St. James of Campostella 51

Taylor, Jeremy, editor, *The Golden Grove* 60
Thackeray, W M 46 n12, 157, 182, 205
Thomas, Professor Charles xiii, 8 n2, 17, 46 n30, 50 (plate as Wesley), 250-1
Tonkin families 32-3, 41, 89, 116-7, 119, 126, 128, 195-6, 200,
    Tonkin, James, portrait artist 206 n10.
    Tonkin, Thomas of St. Agnes historian, antiquarian 32
Treffry, Richard Sr & Jr 55-6, 92-3, 95 155, 162 n10 & n11, 202, 205-6
Tremearne family (of St. Buryan) Branwell & Batten ancestry 43, 57, 73, 85, 86, 92, 117, 125 (Table), 127-9, 136, 189, 209, 236, Dorcas Keigwin, Jane Bromwell, and Susan Batten, 3 Tremearn/es: 128
Tremenheere family 17, 41 94, 107 n9, 137, 216, 243
Trevithick, Richard, Sr., mining engineer, Methodist 13, 40
Trevithick, Richard, engineer-inventor, 'Captain. Dick' 2-3, 8 n4, 14, 37 94-5, 247-8
Trevithick Society 247, 258
Turks (Algerines, Moslems, Islamists, pirates 3, 8 n6, 184
Turk's Head (inn), Penzance Chapel Street 4, 8 n11
Tyack, Anna, Mary, Philippa, Branwell cousins 34, 58, 66 n21, 79, 115, 117-9, 132 (Table)

Union Hotel, formerly 'Ship & Castle' xx n8, 7, 18, 70, 91, 94, 126, 131, 243

Veale family 66, 86, 131-2, 168, 195
Venn family
    Intermarriage with Batten family 63, 182, 191, 236

Intermarriage with Leslie Stephen family 182
Virgil, *Aeneid* 29
Vivian family 13, 111, 118, 119, 130, 132, 143 n3, 152-3, 193, 248
    Andrew Vivian of Dolcoath 10, 101
    Charles Vivian, son who died in Italy with Shelley 101
    Mary Carne Vivian (sister of William Carne Sr., banker) of Reskadinnick, Camborne 101, 152
Volunteers, See military

Wales, Welsh 2, 13, 54, 61, 85, 97, 112, 116, 147, 153, 156, 162 n6 171, 194
Water supply 5, 9 n14, 74-5
Watt, James & son Gregory, steam engine developer 14, 37, 47 n52
Wedgwood, Josiah 14, 37
Wellington, Duke of, Arthur (Wesley) 'Wellesley' 29, 184 (support to Wellington)
Wesley, John and Charles, 27, 32, 34-6 See Chapter 4: 50-67
West Indies 16, 61, 72, 91, 93, 94, 176, 180, 194, 214
Wherry Mine, Penzance 14-15 (plate), 21 n12 & n16, 93, 247
Whitefield, George, English evangelist & cleric, Calvinist 58, 191 206 n4
White, Henry Kirke, poet xv, 35-6, 41, 47 n46, 96, 248
'white slave trade' Also see smuggling xviii, 4, 40, 182-5
Williams, John Branwell, son of J P Williams (below) Visitor in Yorkshire to Fennells and Brontes
87, 136
Williams, John (Pellew), Gent, husband of Alice Branwell, father of John B Williams 87, 92, 107 n 7, 125 (Table), 126, 136
Wilberforce, William, social and political reformer, anti-slavery campaigner 60, 65, 66 n25, 91, 96, 182, 204, 245, 251-2
Wilson, John Broadley, Clapham set, evangelical 60, 66 n25, Wilson, Francis, father of John 60
Wittitterly, John Altrayd (J.A.W) See Elizabeth C. T. Carne, viii n1, 255
Woelfel, James W., theologian & philosopher 62, 66 n28, 251
Wollstonecraft, Mary & Everina 43-4, 48 n71, 78, 180, 186 n23, 196, 236, 252, 258
Women 1ff-
    Documentation, lack of xvi- xviii, 13, 112, 116, 119 n2, 232-3
    Education 18, 22 n29, 31, 44, 53, 78, 83 n23, 161, Chartism: 100, 202-3;
    Employment 72 (fish jowsters), 75, 83 (bal maidens)n17, 113, 243-4, 252
    Literary & reading life 28, 42-3, 48 n68, n69, n71; 196
    Mothercraft xvi, 64, 75, 113, 203
    Religion 169, 207 n17, See Mary B Fletcher
Woolcock, Richard, Branwell cousin, mariner & shoemaker 54, 71 (privateer), 72, 116, 127, 129, 145 n9
Woolf, Virginia xvi, xx n5, 182
Zenobia 236
Zinzendorf, Count Nicolaus, Moravian Bishop of Saxony 64

www.ingramcontent.com/pod-product-compliance
Lightning Source LLC
Chambersburg PA
CBHW061126010526
44116CB00022B/2986